AUTHORS IMPRINT

Dedicated to discovering and sharing knowledge
and creative vision, authors and scholars have endowed
this imprint to perpetuate scholarship of the highest caliber.

Scholarship is to be created ... by awakening a pure interest in knowledge.

—Ralph Waldo Emerson

D0879165

The publisher gratefully acknowledges the generous support of the Authors Imprint Endowment Fund of the University of California Press Foundation, which was established to support exceptional scholarship by first-time authors.

THE LAND OF OPEN GRAVES

CALIFORNIA SERIES IN PUBLIC ANTHROPOLOGY

The California Series in Public Anthropology emphasizes the anthropologist's role as an engaged intellectual. It continues anthropology's commitment to being an ethnographic witness, to describing, in human terms, how life is lived beyond the borders of many readers' experiences. But it also adds a commitment, through ethnography, to reframing the terms of public debate—transforming received, accepted understandings of social issues with new insights, new framings.

Series Editor: Robert Borofsky (Hawaii Pacific University)

Contributing Editors: Philippe Bourgois (University of Pennsylvania), Paul Farmer (Partners In Health), Alex Hinton (Rutgers University), Carolyn Nordstrom (University of Notre Dame), and Nancy Scheper-Hughes (UC Berkeley)

University of California Press Editor: Naomi Schneider

THE LAND OF OPEN

GRAVES

LIVING AND DYING ON THE MIGRANT TRAIL

Jason De León

With photographs by Michael Wells

 UNIVERSITY OF CALIFORNIA PRESS

University of California Press, one of the most distinguished
university presses in the United States, enriches lives around the
world by advancing scholarship in the humanities, social sciences,
and natural sciences. Its activities are supported by the UC Press
Foundation and by philanthropic contributions from individuals
and institutions. For more information, visit www.ucpress.edu.

University of California Press
Oakland, California

Library of Congress Cataloging-in-Publication Data

De León, Jason, 1977– author.
    The land of open graves : living and dying on the migrant trail
/ Jason De León ; with photographs by Michael Wells.
        pages   cm.— (California series in public
anthropology ; 36)
    Includes bibliographical references and index.
    ISBN 978-0-520-28274-2 (cloth : alk. paper) —
    ISBN 978-0-520-28275-9 (pbk. : alk. paper) —
    ISBN 978-0-520-95868-5 (ebook)
    1. Immigration enforcement—Social aspects—Arizona.
2. Immigration enforcement—Social aspects—Mexican-
American Border Region.   3. Border security—Social
aspects—Arizona.   4. Border security—Social aspects—
Mexican-American Border Region.   5. Mexico—Emigration
and immigration.   6. United States—Emigration and
immigration—Government policy.   I. Title.
    JV6475.D4 2015
    325.73—dc23
                                    2015016328

Manufactured in the United States of America

24   23   22   21   20
10   9   8

The paper used in this publication meets the minimum
requirements of ANSI/NISO Z39.48-1992 (R 2002) (*Permanence
of Paper*).

For Ignacio Cruz,
María José,
A., N., y W.

But home was a dream, one I'd never seen . . .

—Jason Isbell

US-Mexico border near Sasabe, Arizona. Photo by Michael Wells.

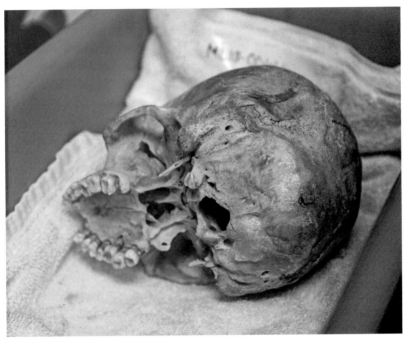

Unidentified human remains from the Pima County Office of the Medical Examiner. Photo by Michael Wells.

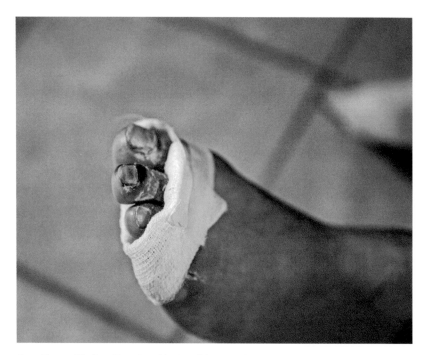

Juan Bosco Shelter, Nogales, Mexico. Photo by Michael Wells.

Migrant campsite near Green Valley, Arizona. Photo by Michael Wells.

Storytelling, 2014. Photo by Michael Wells.

José Tacuri with his sister and niece, Cuenca, Ecuador. Photo by Michael Wells.

CONTENTS

Introduction

Flies.

I mostly remember the goddamn flies.

It's funny how memory works. I made a thousand mental notes of the scene—and wrote a good many of them down soon after the event—but only a couple of years later they now seem to be forgotten, buried, reduced to background noise. After spending just a few weeks on the US-Mexico border hanging out with the desperate people looking to breach America's immigration defenses, I quickly learned that death, violence, and suffering are par for the course. It all started to blur together. Disturbing images lost their edge. As an observer, you grow accustomed to seeing strangers cry at the drop of a hat. Tears no longer had the impact they once did. Tragic stories repeatedly told under the strain of a cracking voice transformed into well-worn hymns that lost their provenience and became difficult to seriate. I fought sensory overload so as to not lose sight of the big picture or the brutal details. I tried to write it all down so that I could later connect the observed realities to larger structural forces. This, at least, is what I kept telling myself I needed to do during my five years of fieldwork on the Arizona-Mexico border and later as I wrote this book. It's what I told myself in this first encounter with death. It's easier said than done. It didn't matter, though, because on this day in July 2009 none of it could be comprehended, much less theorized. All I could do was stare at the flies and wonder how the hell they had gotten there so quickly.

It happened on my first day conducting ethnographic research in the border town of Nogales, Mexico. I had spent the sweltering morning sitting in the shade talking with recently deported migrants. These were women and men who had just attempted and failed to walk across the Sonoran Desert of Arizona to illegally enter the United States. A few of them had been deported from elsewhere by the Department of Homeland Security (DHS)[1] in hopes that being placed in geographic proximity to the desert, where hundreds die each year while migrating, would be enough to deter them from attempting a crossing. I didn't know his name, but I had seen him earlier in the day. Among the tired masses of deportees, he didn't stand out. Recently repatriated people are easy to spot in Nogales because of the uniformity of their appearance: dark T-shirts with powdery salt rings under the armpits and circling the neck; sneakers that look like they have been through a meat grinder; dusty black backpacks stuffed with extra socks, a few cans of food, and whatever meager personal possessions they have managed to hold on to. Their brown bodies broadcast exhaustion and vulnerability like a scarlet letter. Faces show a mix of sorrow, weariness, fear, and optimism. They may have walked for three days lost, quenched a paralyzing thirst at a cattle trough where the water was mostly algae and swimming insects, been robbed at gunpoint by bandits, and raped by a Border Patrol agent before being deported.[2] Still, the next time is going to be different. There is a husband waiting in Carrboro, North Carolina. A guaranteed job painting houses in Phoenix. A little girl with an empty belly back in the tiny village of El Manchon, Guerrero. *Si Dios quiere, voy a pasar.* The next time is going to be different.

I don't remember what he looked like when he was alive. In fact, I didn't really notice him at all until I was making my way toward the convenience store a block from where I had been conducting interviews down on *la linea*[3] in front of the Grupo Beta Office.[4] Like many who get caught in the cycle of repeated crossing attempts, he decided to spend the morning drinking a *caguama* (quart-sized bottle of beer) while planning what to do next. I passed him a few hours prior as he headed to an abandoned field across from the store. I took more notice of the early happy hour he was having than of his actual facial features. All I remember is that he was tall and skinny and had a shaved head. The next time I saw him was when I spotted a crowd gathering near the abandoned field. I walked up to investigate and found myself standing behind a chain-link fence with several migrants, including a short bald man I would soon come to know as Chucho.[5] For ten minutes Chucho and I stared in silent awe at the limp body flopped on the dirt. This dude had been dead for less than an hour and yet the flies were already there in full force.

They were landing on his milky eyeballs and crawling in and out of his open mouth. His head was turned and facing the crowd of migrants. He seemed to be staring right through everyone. We watched flies lay eggs on this man's face for what seemed an eternity.

Finally some Good Samaritan showed up with a Dallas Cowboys bedsheet and covered him up. A paramedic and a few of the neighbors milled around the corpse chatting, but no one seemed to be fazed. Death lay there like a casual summer breeze. I thought to myself that maybe this guy was headed to Dallas to wash dishes at an Applebee's. Maybe he hated the *pinches* Cowboys[6] after spending too many years in Philly doing landscaping jobs and rooting for the Eagles. No one seemed to know him. They just knew that he needed to be covered up to keep the flies away. I turned to Chucho for some insight into this spectacle. He shrugged and said, "This happens all the time. Some people get tired of trying to cross the border after many failed attempts. Some turn to drugs and alcohol to kill time. Who knows what killed him?" Reading the worry on my face, Chucho continued, "You watch. No one will remember this tomorrow. It's like it didn't even happen."

He was right. I would ask migrants the following day about the dead body in the field three hundred feet from the Grupo Beta Office, and no one would know what I was talking about. It was almost as if it didn't happen.

—————

This book is about the violence and death that border crossers face on a daily basis as they attempt to enter the United States without authorization by walking across the vast Sonoran Desert of Arizona. If you live in the United States, you already know about many of the people you will meet in these pages. They pick your fruit, detail your cars, and process your meat. They toil in occupations that US citizens can't or won't do.[7] Keep in mind, though, that not everyone who crosses the desert is a first-timer. In the Obama era of mass deportations, close to 2 million people were removed from the country through fiscal year 2013.[8] Many of these deportees are now running scared across Arizona's Mars-like landscape to reunite with family members or simply return to the only place they have ever called home. My argument is quite simple. The terrible things that this mass of migrating people experience en route are neither random nor senseless, but rather part of a strategic federal plan that has rarely been publicly illuminated and exposed for what it is: a killing machine that simultaneously uses and hides behind the viciousness of the Sonoran

Dallas Cowboys death shroud, Nogales, Mexico, 2009. Photo by author.

Desert. The Border Patrol disguises the impact of its current enforcement policy by mobilizing a combination of sterilized discourse, redirected blame, and "natural" environmental processes that erase evidence of what happens in the most remote parts of southern Arizona. The goal is to render invisible the innumerable consequences this sociopolitical phenomenon has for the lives and bodies of undocumented people.

Those who live and die in the desert have names, faces, and families. They also have complicated life histories that reflect an intimate relationship with transnational migration and global economic inequality. We just rarely ever get to see them up close as they make these terrifying journeys or hear them describe this process in their own words. In what follows, I bring into focus the logic and human cost of the US border enforcement monster known as "Prevention Through Deterrence," a strategy that largely relies on rugged and desolate terrain to impede the flow of people from the south. I also present stories of survival, failure, and heartbreak that happen on *la linea* and beyond from the perspective of those who directly experience this unique security apparatus. Documenting these largely undocumented stories and giving the reader an up-close look at faces and bodies can perhaps help us remember tomorrow that people lived and died in this desert today.

BORDER STORIES

Keeping track of the sheer number of publications that focus in some way on the US-Mexico divide is an impossible task. It seems as though every month a new exposé hits the shelves and tantalizes the public with the trials and tribulations of the troubled geopolitical margin where the phrase "the Third World meets the First World" is still thrown around as if it means something. We don't like to admit it, but the United States is simultaneously afraid of and intrigued by its southern border. The general public can't shake its love of the movies, news programs, reality television shows, and tell-all books that reassure us that this is in fact a zone that is "out of control." If you're a writer, toss in words like *danger* and *violent* and come up with some creative (or not so creative) uses of war metaphors, and you've got yourself a best-selling piece of immigration pornography.

Don't get me wrong, there are many excellent books written about the border. It is a place full of captivating tales and complex histories, but also a well-worn path that many others have mapped out better than I ever could. Rather than giving you a history lesson that you could learn elsewhere, this book abruptly starts in 1993, the year that the policy later coined "Prevention Through Deterrence" (PTD) was first deployed in El Paso, Texas. At the time, PTD was just an off-the-cuff homegrown preventive measure against the unsightliness of brown-skinned illegal fence jumpers and the subsequent chaos the Border Patrol caused by chasing them through poor Latino neighborhoods where it was impossible to figure out who belonged and who didn't.[9] By placing a gaggle (or is it a "murder"?) of crew-cut Border Patrol agents in combat boots and crisp green uniforms in and around downtown El Paso, the immediate goal of discouraging boundary offenders from attempting to hop the fence in these populated areas was achieved. Frustrated, but undeterred, these scrappy individuals, many of whom were locals from Ciudad Juárez simply commuting to work in Texas, went to the edge of town where the fence magically disappeared and agents were few and far between. Business quickly got back to normal.

Everything changed, though, after the passage of the North American Free Trade Agreement (NAFTA) in 1994. The United States promised economic prosperity for its southern neighbor if it would only open up its ports of entry and take shipment of cheap goodies. Soon after Mexico signed on the dotted line, it found itself drowning in a *pinche montón*[10] of subsidized *gringo* corn that crashed their economy and put millions of peasant farmers out of work. As they had done in previous generations when things were bad in Mexico or when *los Yanquis* needed cheap labor,[11] this impoverished population started making their way north by the hundreds of thousands. Optimistic *campesinos* lined up in Tijuana, Juárez, and Reynosa and waited their turn to try and get past *la migra* so that they could join the US undocumented labor force.[12]

This NAFTA-induced human flood now meant there were hordes of fence hoppers in San Ysidro, California, and McAllen, Texas. Once again, the Border Patrol needed a way to reduce the bad press that comes with an avalanche of poor people spilling onto the streets of border towns daily. That little experiment in El Paso to push the Spanish-speaking invaders to the edge of town soon became a nationwide security paradigm that is still in place today. The basic premise was, and continues to be, that if they can't stop the huddled masses, at least they can funnel them into remote areas where the punishment handed out by difficult terrain will save money (or so some foolishly thought) and get this unsightly mess out of public view, which it did.

Between 2000 and 2013, approximately 11.7 million people were apprehended while trying to make the illegal pilgrimage to the United States via Mexico. During this same period, 4,584,022 of these arrests occurred in the Border Patrol jurisdiction known as the Tucson Sector, a craggy, depopulated, and mountainous patch of land that stretches westward from New Mexico to the Yuma County line in Arizona.[13] If you include the neighboring Yuma Sector during this same period, the number of arrests in this state climbs to

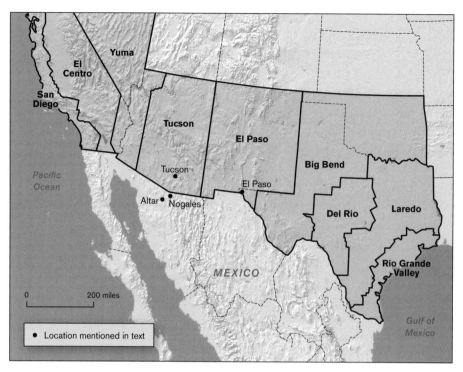

Border Patrol sectors and locales mentioned in the text.

5,304,345 people. This is equivalent to the population of Houston, Texas. It's no wonder Arizona hates immigrants;[14] for close to two decades the federal government has been using that state's backyard as a gauntlet to test the endurance of millions of border crossers and has often left local communities holding the medical bill.[15] Still, everyone knows that if you survive this death race, the backdoors of US stockyards, carpet factories, meat rendering plants, and sushi restaurants are wide open.

Much of what is described in this book took place in the strip of desert just south of Tucson between the Baboquivari and Tumacácori mountain ranges. This beautiful and challenging landscape has been home to the indigenous Tohono O'odham[16] ("Desert People") and their ancestors for millennia. Long before the arrival of colonial-era Spaniards seeking gold and Christian converts, nineteenth-century American geological surveyors itching to draw new maps, and twentieth-century Border Patrol agents,[17] the O'odham people were cultivating a set of cultural traditions and practices that has allowed them to thrive in an environment that to most outsiders appears too barren to sustain agriculture or human life.[18] As ethnobotanist Gary Nabhan writes: "The perspiring and panting in the middle of the saguaro forests—they are part of the raw intimacy the [O'odham] maintain with the desert. Somewhat ugly to the outside eye, this routine is an honest indicator of the strong bonds between the Desert People and their surroundings. Instead of running away from the desert during its driest, hottest time, some still run to the heart of it."[19] O'odham poet Jeanette Chico sums up this intimacy: "When I walk in the desert the animals stop and look at me as if they were saying 'Welcome to our home.'"[20]

Unlike the Desert People, the border crossers who pass through this region do not share in the cultural acumen that conceptualizes this landscape as inviting. Try to envision what it is like going from the lush tropical lowlands of Veracruz or the cool mountains of Oaxaca to the sparse and smoldering desert. Migrants will tell you, "I never imagined it would be like this." How could they? They are fugitives traversing a deadly alien planet. The Border Patrol counts on this. This terrain is that federal agency's not-so-secret weapon, and the migrant injuries and death toll provide evidence that it is a painfully effective one. What's agonizing for the O'odham is that the American federal government has turned their sacred landscape into a killing field, a massive open grave.

The line in the sand that currently exists between Arizona and Mexico was first drawn after the Gadsden Purchase of 1854. This geopolitical space has since had a troubling history marked by colonial and postcolonial subjugation and violence, much of which I skip so that I can draw a tighter focus on the lives of those who have passed through this political geoscape between 2009 and 2013. There are, however, several excellent publications that influenced my thinking about boundary enforcement and its evolution over the past hundred years. For those looking for a deeper, diachronic view of the geopolitics of this region, I recommend Patrick Ettinger's *Invisible Lines* and Rachel St. John's *Line in the Sand*;[21] both of these superb books provide up-to-date syntheses of archival material and previous historical research. Despite the amount of ink I dedicate to Border Patrol policies, this book lacks anything resembling a "History of Boundary Enforcement" section. Instead, I lean heavily on Kelly Lytle Hernández's thorough, eye-opening analysis of the US Border Patrol, Joseph Nevins's seminal book *Operation Gatekeeper*, and Peter Andreas's *Border*

Games to provide the reader brief glimpses into the history of immigration policing and the political chicanery that often (mis)guides how the United States negotiates the property line between its backyard and that of its Mexican neighbors.[22] Finally, Timothy Dunn's books *The Militarization of the U.S.-Mexico Border, 1978–1992* and *Blockading the Border and Human Rights* helped me appreciate the crucial backstory to our modern border industrial complex and describe the seeds that sprouted the current enforcement paradigm that I take to task in this book.[23] Obviously, many others have written about the US-Mexico border, and I cite them throughout this work, but the aforementioned authors proved especially useful for understanding how and why things have gotten so bad in southern Arizona and northern Mexico in the past two decades.

Having briefly lamented the quality of many recent books on the current border situation, I now find myself in the awkward predicament of needing to justify writing yet another book about this exhausted subject. I didn't start this project out of some misguided hubris that I was somehow going to get the story right. I'm the first person to tell you that no matter what you do, you can never get full comprehension of what is *actually* happening on our southern frontier. The system in place has too many moving parts traveling at sometimes blinding speed. Your view of any single part is blurry at best. But it doesn't matter what you can actually see, because there are always things going on out of sight. I'm not just talking about some gold-toothed *coyote*[24] speeding away in a primered minivan full of migrants or glue-sniffing cholos hiding in the bushes waiting for the next pack of border crossers to rob. I mean the closed door strategy meetings at Border Patrol headquarters in Tucson where new forms of "deterrence" are plotted and schemed using euphemistic defense jargon and slick corporate promotional videos touting next season's line of unmanned aerial drones. Sometimes it's those secretive moments when two nervous agents sit in their truck on a dusty road and try to get their story straight about why they shot some unarmed Mexican kid while he was hopping the border fence to run back into Mexico.[25] Don't forget the off-the-record dinner conversations when politicians and their federal contractor friends eat Delmonico steaks and drink single malt while laughing about how they are going to fill newly constructed private detention facilities and charge the government a pretty penny.[26] You are never going to capture all of the things that make the border system (dys)functional, and that is not my intention here.

CROSSING OVER

It started as nothing more than dinner conversation sometime in the fall of 2008. Fresh out of graduate school, I found myself teaching at the University of Washington and struggling to find a post-dissertation project. I had just spent a couple of years scrutinizing thousands of tiny pieces of obsidian in an attempt to reconstruct the political economy of the ancient Olmec,[27] those precocious indigenous people who built Mesoamerica's first great civilization. During the course of my doctoral fieldwork, I had become increasingly fascinated by the lives of the local Mexican women and men I had worked with on various excavations. These individuals, many of whom I became close with over the years, had a significant amount of experience migrating to the United States, including firsthand knowledge of what Prevention Through Deterrence felt like in the Arizona desert.

As soon as I finished my thesis, I said good-bye to ancient stone tools and made the first in a series of questionable career choices when I decided to change subdisciplines and reinvent myself as an ethnographer. As an undergraduate at UCLA and later a graduate student at Penn State, I had bought into the idea that anthropology's major contribution to knowledge production was its comprehensive approach to the human condition: past, present, and future. The discipline's holistic combination of archaeology, biology, language, and culture provides a vast set of tools and approaches to understand the things that make us human. By logical extension, all archaeologists, ethnographers, osteologists, and linguists are anthropologists at the end of the day. This is what we tell our students and that's what I believed when I made this career shift. I was simply following my anthropological interests.

Over dinner one night with an archaeologist friend, I began talking about Luis Alberto Urrea's moving book *The Devil's Highway*.[28] This tragic tale of fourteen border crossers who lost their lives in the Yuma Sector in 2001 was on the reading list I was using that semester to develop what was then a vaguely defined project about immigration. This friend said to me, "You know, when I was conducting archaeological surveys in the Arizona desert, we would often come across the things that migrants left behind. Once we found a backpack that contained a love letter in Spanish. It was really sad." She then joked, "I bet someone could do some sort of weird archaeological project on that stuff." A month later I was standing in the wilderness south of Tucson staring at an overwhelming pile of empty water bottles and abandoned clothes.

When I started the Undocumented Migration Project (UMP) in 2009, my goal was modest. I wanted to test the idea that archaeology could be a useful tool for understanding the evolution of border crosser technology and the economic system that undergirds clandestine migration. I quickly realized that I should also be asking other types of questions about this phenomenon and that archaeology was only one of the many tools I could use to get answers. One of the first conclusions I came to during the planning stages of this work was that, despite the intense public and academic interest in the subject, few scholars or journalists had attempted to write carefully about the physical movement involved in unauthorized migration. The firsthand accounts of border crossings in recent times largely came from the musings of gonzo journalists who headed down to the border and teamed up with some overly trusting Mexicans who let these people shadow them as they headed for El Norte. Privileged journalists running across the desert with their passports in their back pockets while chasing migrants produce little beyond what I consider problematic "Choose Your Own Adventure" books for American consumption.[29] One of the goals of the UMP was to collect robust data on the migration process that could provide a counternarrative to this literature.

DOCUMENTING THE UNDOCUMENTED

Given the furtive and illegal nature of undocumented migration, it is no surprise that academics have looked at it largely from a distance. Two outstanding books, for example—Leo Chavez's *Shadowed Lives* and David Spener's *Clandestine Crossings*—provide nuanced insight into the act of border crossing. The one limitation of both studies, from my perspective, though, is the fact that much of their data are collected after crossing events happened,[30] or their descriptions are almost exclusively based on interviews, a problem that Spener himself points out.[31] That being said, I am also not convinced that participant observation, the methodological cornerstone of ethnographic research, is an appropriate tool for understanding this type of migration.

Medical anthropologist Seth Holmes begins his recent book *Fresh Fruit, Broken Bodies* with a description of a clandestine border crossing through the Sonoran Desert that he undertook with indigenous Triqui migrants whom he first met while conducting research on a farm in northwestern Washington State.[32] Holmes writes that he decided to cross the border with his interlocutors because, "early in my fieldwork, I realized that an ethnography of suffering and violence and migration would be incomplete without witnessing firsthand such an important site of suffering for Latin American migrants."[33] Although I understand his desire for an up-close view of a key aspect of the lives of the undocumented farmworkers he studies, I have never been comfortable with this type of ethnography.

Over the course of five years of research, many people I met in Nogales invited me to accompany them into the desert. For a number of reasons, I declined every offer. First, I have always believed that my participation in a border crossing would be an unnecessary risk for my informants to take and something that would have reinforced, if not exacerbated, the hierarchy between me (a college professor) and the working-class migrants who trust me with their stories. Putting myself into a research scenario where my interlocutors are highly vulnerable while I am protected by my citizenship status is at odds with the type of anthropology that I want to practice. A second, albeit from my perspective less important, issue is that "entry without inspection," which is what US citizens are charged with when they cross the border through a nonofficial port of entry, is a crime (a mere civil offense) and something that could potentially jeopardize my employment and federal grant funding. If I had undertaken such a problematic endeavor, the headline in the right-leaning media outlets that occasionally throw stones at this research would no doubt read: "Mexican Professor Helps Illegals Cross the Desert and Uses National Science Foundation Money to Pay for It."[34]

An unspoken issue that I think undermines Holmes's attempt to "witness" this process is the fact that his participation in a crossing is highly disruptive and guarantees that the event is anything but "normal."[35] By his own account, Holmes's presence in a group of migrants made various smugglers nervous, led to him being singled out by Grupo Beta, and resulted in his companions asking him if he could drive them to Phoenix to get past a Border Patrol checkpoint.[36] Moreover, his Triqui companions were no doubt well aware of the shit storm that would ensue if something happened to a *gringo* in their care.[37] It is easy to imagine how the media would spin a story about an American graduate student who died while crossing the desert with a bunch of undocumented migrants. Essentially, whether he liked it or not, Holmes became a concern and burden for the group as he attempted to observe this process. This phenomenon is something that journalist John Annerino experienced firsthand when he became sick while traveling through the Yuma Sector and ended up having to be cared for by the Mexican border crossers he was photographing.[38]

Although rattlesnakes and heat stroke can kill you regardless of citizenship, these "documented" observers don't have to worry about being abandoned by their *coyote* in the desert or getting brained by a Border Patrol Maglite.

Despite the good intentions behind accompanying migrants, these anthropologists and journalists have authorization to be in the United States, and after getting caught, they are inevitably set free. Holmes's description of his crossing routinely highlights that he had a lawyer whom he could call on for help and that his credentials as a student studying migration were a get-out-of-jail-free card. Although he was not allowed to use the phone or given toilet paper while in detention, Holmes was put into his own cell and received special treatment by law enforcement, which highlights just how abnormal his presence was for all parties involved. The Border Patrol threatened to charge him with illegal entry, but this turned out to be part of the normal scare tactics that agents use against citizens and noncitizens alike. In the end, the anthropologist was let go with a warning, while his nameless companions were processed and deported.[39]

Finally, this type of participant observation has always struck me as problematic because it tends to focus on the experiences of the writer[40] and doesn't necessarily give us insight into the terror and violence suffered by Latino border crossers. Holmes's descriptions emphasize his feeling "like a rabbit, vulnerable and hunted," while the voices of his traveling companions are noticeably mute or altogether absent.[41] To compound this issue, two of the three photographs of this event position Holmes as the center of attention and are labeled with captions such as "The author and Triqui men in the border desert." We get to see the grinning anthropologist's face and hear about his suffering, while these men are relegated to the status of anonymous undocumented border crossers. While I greatly value the work that Holmes has done to reveal the brutality and racism that indigenous farmworkers experience, I think that we as ethnographers need to be more critical regarding the contexts where participant observation is deployed and more reflective about how we write about the act of witnessing other people's trauma. In my approach to clandestine migration, I have sought to paint crossers not as anonymous shadows scrambling through the desert, but as real people who routinely live and die in this environment and whose voices and experiences we should be privileging.

I am inspired by Audrey Singer and Douglas Massey's recognition that undocumented migration is not the chaotic event often depicted in popular media but rather a "well-defined social process whereby migrants draw upon various sources of human and social capital to overcome barriers erected by US authorities."[42] The Undocumented Migration Project has long been concerned with improving the resolution of the ethnographic data we have on this social process while also avoiding the problematics of directly observing a clandestine and illegal act. Accordingly, over the years I have freely borrowed various methods and theories from the anthropological toolbox. As you will see, this book draws on a four-field anthropology—that is ethnography, archaeology, forensic science, and linguistics—in the name of enhancing our understanding of the process of undocumented desert migration. In many ways, this project is intended to challenge preconceived notions about what a holistic anthropology can look like and how it can be deployed in politically hostile terrain.

If my writing is at times acerbic or in nonstandard academic English (or untranslated Mexican slang), it is because I am trying to match the frankness, sarcasm, and humor of my interlocutors, as well as the grittiness of the difficult worlds they inhabit. It is also because I see little public or personal benefit to "toning down" what I have seen, heard, and experienced while trying to get an anthropological handle on the routinely chaotic, violent, and sometimes tragicomic process of clandestine migration. Like many scholars before me, I aim to sully the often sterile anthropological discussion about undocumented Latino migration and its associated geographic, cultural, political, and economic boundaries.[43] By doing so, I want to show how productive it can be to sneak back and forth across the border between "accepted discourse and excluded discourse" in the name of generating new knowledge and new forms of cultural understanding.[44]

As I began working with a population in transit, it soon became obvious that a multisited ethnographic approach was needed to capture various elements of the migration process.[45] Over the years, I followed people across multiple states, countries, and continents. Although I conducted several dozen interviews during a ten-day trip to Ecuador in 2013, numerous short trips to New York in 2013 and 2014, and some two dozen domestic and international phone calls and Skype interviews, most of the ethnographic, forensic (chapter 3), and archaeological data (chapter 7) were collected in the border town of Nogales, Mexico, the northern Mexican town of Altar, and the deserts of the Tucson Sector between Nogales and Sasabe (see map of Tucson Sector, opposite).[46]

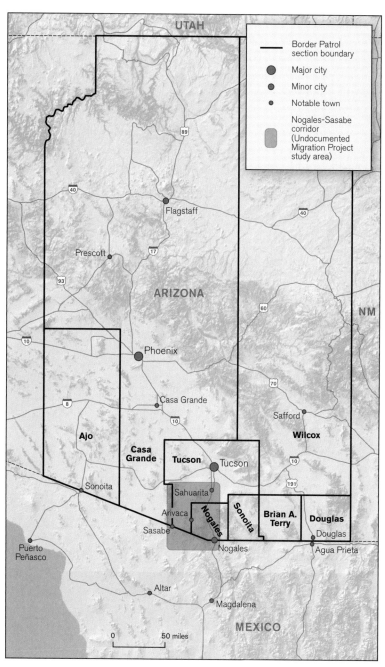

Undocumented Migration Project study areas and corresponding Border Patrol substations in the Tucson Sector. Based on map by Cameron Gokee.

From 2009 to 2013, I interviewed hundreds of men and women between the ages of eighteen and seventy-five who were in the middle of the migration process.[47] These conversations took place at bus stations, on street corners, in restaurants, bars, humanitarian shelters, cemeteries, and any other place I encountered border crossers. The majority of people were Mexican nationals, though some Central Americans were also interviewed. Our interactions tended to be unstructured, and depending on the situation, I either took written notes, used a digital voice recorder, or both.[48] On several occasions, people were shown photographs of the desert and other migration-related settings and asked to comment on them.[49] In addition, I spent countless hours observing deportation proceedings in Tucson, touring government facilities with Border Patrol agents, and walking on the trails that migrants use to cross the desert.[50]

The interviews I conducted were almost exclusively in Spanish and are presented here in their translated English form, with some phrases and words left in their original language for effect. Because people often ramble, repeat themselves, or tell complicated stories out of order, at times I have edited material to preserve the narrative flow and reduce redundancy.[51] I made these edits carefully and sparingly, striving as much as possible to preserve the speaker's original meaning and tone. In all except a few cases, I used pseudonyms and changed some personal details to protect identities.[52] The names of the dead and missing have not been changed. Their families wanted their "real" stories told. They wanted to guarantee that the lost were not forgotten.

DEPICTING VIOLENCE

The primary theme of this book is violence: how it is constructed in the desert, its productive nature from the perspective of those benefiting from it, and how its victims come to know its destructiveness. The things that happen to the undocumented migrants who experience the strong pull of the US economy and the simultaneous blunt force trauma of its immigration enforcement practices can be generally characterized as a form of *structural violence*.[53] It is violence that is indirect (i.e., the result of federal policy). No one individual is responsible for it. Moreover, it often occurs out of site, many portray it as "natural," and it can easily be denied by state actors and erased by the desert environment.[54] Throughout this book the scale of analysis and perspective on this form of structural violence change depending on the context, moment, and analytical goal. In some instances, the discussion focuses on federal enforcement discourse and large-scale infrastructure. At other times I give the viewer a full-frontal view of how those on the ground experience this policy.

The intent is to show what the violence looks like up close, and thus avoid sanitizing it, but also to offer what Žižek terms "sideways glances" that may help foster new ways of thinking about border crossings and the routinized pain and suffering that accompany them.[55] Theoretically, these efforts are aided by two key ideas. First is the proposition that nonhumans (e.g., the desert) play a major role in this process (see chapter 2) and should be considered crucial elements of the Border Patrol's enforcement strategy. The second argument is that the types of death people experience in the desert reflect their precarious political position and that the postmortem biographies of their corpses provide insight into the production of trauma that has a hemispheric reach.

There is no easy way to represent violence, a fact that I was acutely aware of throughout the course of writing this book. I spent many nights worrying whether the descriptions contained here are too graphic or insensitive. Admittedly, much of this endeavor is written from a male perspective. As a Latino researcher, I had significantly more access to men than women, at least during the phases of ethnographic work that took place on the northern Mexican border. For various reasons described throughout the text, men were more readily available for interviews, and it was their perspective on border-crossing violence that I became most familiar with. This means that I came to know about much of the sexual violence that women experience en route through the eyes of men who bore witness.[56] One researcher estimates that as many as 90 percent of women who attempt to cross undocumented into the United States through northern Mexico suffer sexual assault,[57] which indicates that there are many untold stories of trauma.[58] In fleeting moments the physical traces of the sexual assault that women experienced were visible to me. This sometimes manifested itself as blackened eyes or bruised wrists on the bodies of recent deportees. On a handful of occasions, I encountered deported women who were in catatonic states or were so visibly shaken that they couldn't be consoled. These are just the rare instances in which assault left visible marks. Whatever events caused these bruises or moments of trauma, they were largely inaccessible to me because of a combination of ethical, methodological, and gender issues.[59] That being said, I have tried to include as much as I can in this book about the gender-based violence women experience.

Although they are present throughout this text, at certain moments women are visible only through male eyes.[60] This is especially true in part 2, "El Camino." It is not my intention, however, to make "woman an icon, displayed for the gaze and enjoyment of men,"[61] but rather to emphasize that males primarily between the ages of eighteen and forty make up the bulk of apprehended border crossers (86.5 percent in 2012)[62] and were the population whose perspective I became most familiar with. I acknowledge the male perspective as a recurring framework in parts of this book largely for the purpose of illustrating that in this research context that perspective shouldn't be written off as simply patriarchal or pornographic. Instead, the viewpoint of men can highlight the power and experiences of female border crossers and illustrate the extent to which the narratives included here signal male "identification with, sympathy for, or vulnerability to the feminine."[63] In the end, I hope that my prose and the various perspectives I seek to represent strike a balance between reflecting violent realities and maintaining all people's dignity.

Finally, to complicate my written descriptions of violence, I have risked including photographs of vulnerable people in all types of precarious positions. This was a decision influenced by the new wave of photoethnographies published in the past ten years.[64] I was particularly inspired by Bourgois and Schonberg's *Righteous Dopefiend* and Danny Hoffman's *The War Machines*, both of which sensitively pair difficult-to-view images with insightful analyses of violence.[65] From the start of this project I knew that words alone could never capture the complexity, emotion, or realities of the violence, suffering, and victories that people experience during the migration process. You have to hear their voices *and* see their faces to appreciate them as human beings. Over the past several years many undocumented people in the United States have bravely come out of the shadows to tell their stories.[66] The people you will meet in this book wanted to do the same thing. They wanted to be heard and seen. For this reason, I have included pictures taken by border crossers while en route, troubling photos of physical injuries, and graphic images of death. Perhaps by humanizing that nebulous mass of humanity that we call the undocumented, we can begin to have a serious conversation about how to fix America's broken immigration system.

Although some of these pictures were taken by me or migrants themselves, the bulk were shot by my friend and longtime collaborator Michael Wells. Present from the beginning of this project, Mike Wells (everyone calls him by his full name) spent countless days with me hiking in the desert, hanging out in shelters in Mexico, interviewing people in New York, and visiting with families of migrants in Ecuador. He is not an anthropologist by training, but for me his photos reflect a keen ethnographic sensitivity attuned to both the subtle reflections of humanity that happen in the blink of an eye and the minute details of the multiple worlds that migrants pass through. I have paired Mike's and the other images used here with various anthropological lenses (e.g., migrant narratives, archaeological typologies, and forensic descriptions) with the firm belief that long-term anthropological work that fuses text and photographs is "more than the sum of its parts analytically, politically, and aesthetically."[67]

The decision to include people's faces in a large number of the images in this book was largely informed by those whose stories are included here. The undocumented wanted you to see them as people. They wanted you to see what they go through and how the process of migration impacts their lives. I once asked Christian (whom you will meet in chapter 10) whether he wanted me to obscure his face or include photos of his sister-in-law in this book. He responded: "I want you to put photos that show our reality. That is better. That way people can see what happens. The realness. That way people will believe what is happening. That they will know that this is the truth. A lot of people think it's all a lie. That this stuff doesn't happen." Maybe the photos and stories revealed in the following pages will somehow help those of us who will never know the desperation required to head into the desert or the sorrow that accompanies losing someone to this process get a little closer to "the realness."

PART ONE

This Hard Land

Looking west toward the Baboquivari Mountains. Photo by Michael Wells.

CHAPTER 1

Prevention Through Deterrence

NOTES FROM A CRIME SCENE

Drive out in the late afternoon to one of the many hills on the outskirts of the tiny Arizona town of Arivaca and look west. You will see the golden sun creep behind the Baboquivari Mountains. The vanishing orb makes it look as if the distant peaks and valleys have been cut out of thick black construction paper. It's the stenciled silhouette you see in old western films. For an hour or so, the backlit barren landscape glows as though it's slowly being covered in liquid amber. The beauty of this Sonoran Desert sunset is overwhelming. It can convince you that there is goodness in nature. It will make you briefly forget how cruel and unforgiving this terrain can be for those caught in it during the height of summer. Right now I'm dreaming about that sunset; visualizing my hand plunging into a watery ice chest full of cold beers. I can feel the touch of the evening breeze on my skin. These are the tricks you play in your head during the dog days of July in the desert.

The Norwegian explorer Carl Lumholtz once wrote that the summer heat in the Sonoran Desert felt like "walking between great fires."[1] That's putting it nicely. Right now it feels more like walking directly through flames. Despite the protection of my wide-brimmed cowboy hat, the sides of my face are sunburned after only a few minutes of exposure. Tiny water-filled blisters are starting to form on my temples, cheeks, and other places that get exposed to the sun when I lift my head or stare up at the empty blue sky. I try not to look up unless I have to duck under a mesquite tree or the trail makes a hard break left or right. Better to keep your gaze downward to watch for sun-bathing rattlesnakes and ankle-twisting cobbles.

Sweat beads up and rolls off my chin, leaving behind a trail of droplets on the ground as I walk. It takes only a few seconds for these splashes to evaporate. My clothes, on the other hand, are soaking wet. I find myself periodically shivering and getting dizzy; my body is working hard to make sense of this inferno. The overpriced backpack I am wearing has started to heat up along with the water bottles it contains. This means that from here on out, every time I try to quench my thirst, it's like drinking soup. It is easily over a 100 degrees and it is only 10 A.M. My sunset and cold beer fantasies are starting to lose their efficacy. Mike Wells and I are climbing through the Tumacácori Mountains with my longtime friend Bob Kee,[2] a member of the southern Arizona humanitarian group the Tucson Samaritans. Bob has been haunting these trails for years, leaving food and water for unseen migrants and occasionally giving first aid to abandoned souls he comes across.

It's a rough path full of sharp-angled rocks and angry mesquites whose branches all seem to be aiming for your eyes. We are moving at a fast clip, which is typical for any outing led by Bob. He is almost thirty years our senior, but is running us ragged as we struggle to keep up. Mike and I are being led by a wilderness Zen master who never seems to sweat, complain, or slow down. Every turn he makes seems to lead to another steep climb. I am convinced he seeks out the most arduous routes just to make sure that those he takes into the desert get a sense of how punishing this environment can be for migrants and anyone else who dares to hike this terrain in the middle of a summer day. "We're almost there. I promise," Bob says. I force a smile because in the past when he has told me this, it was a white lie to make me feel better. "Almost there" is one of Bob's euphemisms for "four more miles to go." On this day, however, the tone in his voice is different. He is not his normal jovial self. He hasn't been joking around, which usually includes offering to carry me on his back. It is clear that he is on a mission. We round a bend and stop. Bob calmly says: "This is the spot where I found the person. The sheriff's department came out and took away what we could find, but it was getting dark and we didn't have a lot of time to go over the entire area. It was mostly arm and leg bones and some pieces of clothing. I want to see if we can find the head. That would make it easier to identify the body. I'm sure there are still bones out here."

Just a few weeks earlier Bob had encountered the fragmented and skeletonized remains of a border crosser in this area. It was the second person he had found in under a month. He called the police, who sent two detectives out to remove what bones they could find. Bob says they spent five minutes poking around before they called it quits. It was too damn hot and the cops were unprepared and unmotivated to do a large-scale survey. Besides, searching for the bones of dead "illegals" has never been a top priority for any law enforcement agency out here. The three of us have returned and are now looking for the rest of what was once a living, breathing person.

Bob is right. There are bones that the detectives overlooked, but we have to cover a lot of ground before we find any of them. There are pieces strewn everywhere. We walk downslope and see part of an articulated arm wedged between two rocks. Aside from sinew still holding the bones together, it has been picked clean of skin and muscle by an unknown creature. Further up the trail I notice several white flecks that stand out against the red mountain soil. It looks as if someone dropped a box of blackboard chalk on the ground. I get closer and realize they are splinters of human bone, mostly sun-bleached rib fragments that have been cracked and gnawed by some long-gone animal. Just off the trail I spot a complete tooth lying on top of a rock. This dental find gives us hope that the skull is nearby.

We start a desperate search for this person's head. Rocks are overturned. Subterranean nests are probed. Bleeding hands blindly grope under thick brush in hopes of finding bones that may have been squirreled away by scavengers or deposited by monsoon flood waters. Everyone is moving with great urgency despite the debilitating heat. After forty-five minutes of intensive survey, we give up. There is no skull. There are no other teeth. We do, however, come across a pair of worn-out hiking boots in close proximity to some of the bones. Where the hell is the skull? I start imagining what has happened to it. A montage of laughing vultures rips this person's eyeballs out of the sockets. I hallucinate two coyotes batting the head around like a soccer ball so that they can access brain matter through the foramen magnum. It's a moment when you despise the capacity of the human imagination. People whose loved ones have disappeared in this desert will tell you that it's the not knowing what happened to them coupled with the flashes of grotesque possibility that drive you insane.

Mike starts snapping photographs while Bob collects bones. The gnarled arm fragment goes into a black trash bag. The ribs and tooth fall into a Ziploc. Bob scribbles down the GPS coordinates and will later deliver the remains to the sheriff's office, where he will be scolded for "disturbing a crime scene." The irony of the statement is that the police were already out here once and Bob is

Human tooth, Tumacácori Mountains, 2011. Photo by Michael Wells.

simply collecting what they overlooked during their hasty survey. The fact of the matter is that although this is a crime scene, few people actually care or want to know what has happened here. For many Americans, this person—whose remains are so ravaged that his or her sex is unknown—is (was) an "illegal," a noncitizen who broke US law and faced the consequences. Many of these same people tell themselves that if they can keep calling them "illegals," they can avoid speaking their names or imagining their faces. The United States might be a nation founded by immigrants, but that was a long time ago. Countless citizens today suffer historical amnesia and draw stark divisions between the "noble" European immigrants of the past and Latino border cross-ers of today. How quickly they forget about the violent welcome receptions that America threw for the Irish, Chinese, and many other newly arrived immigrant groups. The benefit of the chronological distance from the pain and suffering of past migrations is that many Americans today have no problem putting nationality before humanity. A cursory glance at the online comment section of a recent article titled "Border Crossing Deaths More Common as Illegal Immigration Declines"[3] provides insight into some of the more extreme anti-immigrant perspectives on migrant death:

I'm not condoning deaths or anything, and I do think it's cruel to let a human being die in pain, but in a way isn't it better? I mean after all some of these people are risking their lives because there are nothing better [sic] back home, and if they die on the way, at least they end their sufferings [sic].[4]

Since it is a common practice to print indications on everything in the US, and since just printed indications will not . . . [deter] people from entering the US illegally [sic], why not . . . take some of those dried out corpses, hang them at the places where they [migrants] are known to cross with a legend, "This may be you in a couple of days."[5]

When you see such comments, which accompany practically every article about migrant death on the Internet, you think you're mistakenly reading the American Voices column from the satirical newspaper *The Onion*. It should be easy to dismiss responses like these as extreme forms of Internet hate speech, but this disregard for the lives of undocumented people and the idea that dead bodies should act as a form of deterrence to future migrants are fundamental components of the US federal government's current border security strategy.

But that fact doesn't really matter as we survey the ground for more human remains. The desert has already started to erase this person, along with whatever violence and horror she or he experienced. This event will soon be forgotten before it was ever known.

BONE DUST: RENDERING BARE LIFE

Many border researchers turn to Giorgio Agamben's influential work on sovereignty, law, and individual rights to understand the role that the physical space between adjoining nations plays in the construction of citizens, noncitizens, and state power.[6] Agamben's *state of exception*—the process whereby sovereign authorities declare emergencies in order to suspend the legal protections afforded to individuals while simultaneously unleashing the power of the state upon them—is a particularly salient concept for those working on the margins of nation-states. It is here that the tensions of sovereignty and national security are both geolocated and visibly acted out on a daily basis.[7] Like Agamben's characterization of the concentration camp, the spatial arrangement of borders often allows a space to exist outside the bounds of normal state or moral law. Border zones become *spaces of exception*—physical and political locations where an individual's rights and protections under law can be stripped away upon entrance. Having your body consumed by wild animals is but one of many "exceptional" things that happen in the Sonoran Desert as a result of federal immigration policies.[8]

Roxanne Doty has pointed out that the US-Mexico border forms an exemplary space of exception where those seeking to enter the country without permission are often reduced to *bare life*—individuals whose deaths are of little consequence—by border policies that do not recognize the rights of unauthorized migrants.[9] At the same time, these policies expose noncitizens to a state-crafted geopolitical terrain designed to deter their movement through suffering and death.[10] The perception that the lives of border crossers are insignificant is reflected in both their treatment by federal immigration enforcement agencies and in the pervasive anti-immigrant discourse, including the online comments cited above. Contributing to this dehumanization is the fact that the Sonoran Desert is remote, sparsely populated, and largely out of the American public's view. This space can be policed in ways that would be deemed violent, cruel, or irrational in most other contexts. Just imagine how people would react if the corpses of undocumented Latinos were left to rot on the ninth hole of the local golf course or if their sun-bleached skulls were piled up in the parking lot of the neighborhood McDonald's.

The isolation of the desert combined with the public perception of the border as a zone ruled by chaos allows the state to justify using extraordinary measures to control and exclude "uncivilized" noncitizens. It is a location "where the controls and guarantees of judicial order can be suspended—the zone where the violence of the state of exception is deemed to operate in the service of 'civilization.'"[11] Sovereign power produces migrants as excluded subjects to be dealt with violently while simultaneously neutralizing their ability to resist or protest. The environment becomes a form of deterrence so that "the raw physicality" of the desert "can be exploited and can function to mask the workings of social and political power."[12] If we dare to approach this frightening geopolitical space, we can see how America's internal surveillant gaze functions,[13] and understand why maps of this region should be labeled "Here be monsters."

As we start to walk away from this death site, I notice something on the ground. Crouching down, I pick up a piece of bone smaller than my fingernail. It immediately crumbles to dust. I try to hand it to Bob, and an unexpected breeze passes through and blows many of the particles off my hand. I scrape what I can from my finger and sprinkle it into the bag. It's a futile gesture. There is little that forensic scientists can do with bone dust. This person will likely become a line in the Pima County Office of the Medical Examiner's database of migrant fatalities reading: "Name: Unknown. Age: Unknown. Country of Origin: Unknown. Cause of Death: Undetermined (partial skeletal remains)." The identity of this individual and much of his or her body has been swallowed up by the desert, and there were no witnesses. Bare life has been reduced to shoes, shards of bone, and the "Unknown."

I often think about this particular day, for two reasons. First, we know this death and its physical erasure are by no means a unique event. Between October 2000 and September 2014, the bodies of 2,721 border crossers were recovered in southern Arizona alone.[14] Approximately 800 of these individuals are still unidentified.[15] Second, this particular moment in the desert perfectly illustrates the structure, logic, and corporeal impact of current US border enforcement policy. This point was driven home in the spring of 2012 when I visited the Juan Bosco migrant shelter in Nogales (see chapter 5). The stucco walls of this nonprofit organization are always decorated with glossy Mexican government fliers that warn about the conditions in the desert, oversized maps produced by the group Humane Borders showing locations of border crosser deaths, and photocopied posters put up by family members of missing migrants. It wasn't until 2012, though, that I noticed for the first time a tiny sign on the wall of the men's bathroom that had been produced by the US Department of Homeland Security. In Spanish the flier warned, "The next time you try to cross the border without documents you could end up a victim of the desert." This line was accompanied by a pathetic cartoon drawing of a saguaro cactus.

I laughed at this crude representation of the desert, but also started thinking about how this was one of the few times I had seen a warning sign produced by the US government in a Mexican shelter. More interesting, however, was that the wording of the pamphlet personified the desert as a perpetrator of violence targeting migrants.[16] Conveniently, this flier contains no mention of the tactical relationship between federal border enforcement policy and this harsh landscape. When put in historical context, however, this public service announcement offers insight into the structure of the Prevention Through Deterrence (PTD) strategy that since the 1990s has deliberately funneled people into the desert. It also illustrates the cunning way that nature has been conscripted by the Border Patrol to act as an enforcer while simultaneously providing this federal agency with plausible deniability regarding blame for any victims the desert may claim. In what follows, I outline the history and logic of PTD and begin to draw the connections between border enforcement policies and the migrant suffering and death that I explore in detail in the rest of the book.

OUT OF SIGHT

In July 1993, the Immigration and Naturalization Service (INS)[17] promoted Mexican American Border Patrol agent Silvestre Reyes to chief of the El Paso Sector. Reyes was brought in during a moment of crisis when a series of lawsuits and claims of human rights violations had been brought against the Border Patrol in the region. Two of the major grievances lodged against the agency were that legal Latino residents were subjected to unfair racial profiling and harassment, and that the consistent pursuit of undocumented border crossers through neighborhoods was a dangerous and abusive practice.[18] The majority of El Paso residents who lived along the border were Latino, which made it difficult for *la migra* to figure out who was "illegal" without directly interrogating people. Locals were tired of law enforcement questioning them about their citizenship while they were going about their daily business. In response to these complaints, Reyes came up with a radical new enforcement strategy that would fundamentally change how the border was policed. Timothy Dunn describes what happened on September 19, 1993, when Reyes launched "Operation Blockade":

> The emphasis of the operation was to deter unauthorized border crossings in the core urban area between Ciudad Juárez and El Paso by making a bristling show of force. . . . This took the form of posting 400 Border Patrol agents (out of 650 total in the sector) on the banks of the Rio Grande and adjacent levees in stationary, ubiquitous green and green-and-white patrol vehicles around the clock, at short-distance intervals (from fifty yards to one-half mile) along a twenty-mile stretch between El Paso and Ciudad Juárez. . . . This mass posting of agents created an imposing line, if not [a] virtual wall, of agents along the river, which was supplemented by low-flying and frequently deployed surveillance helicopters.[19]

Prior to this strategy, the standard operating procedure had been to try to apprehend border crossers *after* they had crossed the boundary line. The circuslike atmosphere created when dozens of people at a time jumped the border fence while agents in green uniforms chased after them like Keystone Cops was ludicrous. Comedian Cheech Marin even built his film *Born in East L.A.* around this borderwide phenomenon. These daily scenes exemplified the difficulties of trying to seal the border. Reyes's mass deployment of agents in and around the El Paso port of entry was an effective public relations move that seemed to satisfy local residents. This "show of force", however, didn't stop illegal immigration. It mostly frustrated migrants accustomed to crossing in urban zones and forced them to move toward the edge of town where they could easily hop the fence in depopulated areas.[20]

In addition to funneling traffic away from downtown, this strategy also made migration less visible and created a scenario in which the policing of undocumented people occurred in areas with few witnesses. Out of sight, out of mind. Despite the fact that this "deterrence-displacement" strategy only made border crossers harder to see,[21] some politicians soon touted it as a success.[22] The operation's effects were felt along much of the US-Mexico border during the 1990s when it was adopted in Southern California ("Operation Gatekeeper" in 1994), Arizona ("Operation Safeguard" in 1994 and 1999), and South Texas ("Operation Rio Grande" in 1997). When Reyes set Operation Blockade in motion, he intended to shift traffic away from the city and "put [migrants] out in areas where they're on [Border Patrol's] turf."[23] Little did he know that this approach would soon evolve into a large-scale policy that would strategically use the natural environment and subsequently become the foundation for border security in a post-9/11 world.

HOSTILE TERRAIN

The logic behind Operation Blockade was straightforward. Placing heightened security in and around the downtown urban port of entry in El Paso would force undocumented migrants to attempt crossings in more rural areas that were easier for law enforcement to monitor. Although this initial strategy in El Paso had neither been officially sanctioned nor fully evaluated by INS, it immediately garnered media and political attention and was soon adopted as a part of a new federal project. Less than a year after Operation Blockade, INS published its Strategic Plan,[24] which essentially repackaged what Reyes had done informally into a national program: "The Border Patrol will improve control of the border by implementing a strategy of 'prevention through deterrence.' The Border Patrol will achieve the goals of its strategy by bringing a decisive number of enforcement resources to bear in each major entry corridor. The Border Patrol will increase the number of agents on the line and make effective use of technology, raising the risk of apprehension high enough to be an effective deterrent."[25] One of the primary components that structured the new PTD strategy was the recognition that remote areas along the border (e.g., the Sonoran Desert) are difficult to traverse on foot and hence can be effectively used by law enforcement. This, however, was by no means a recent epiphany, as noted by historian Patrick Ettinger: "From their earliest work enforcing the Chinese Exclusion Acts [enacted in 1882], immigration authorities had discovered that the desert and mountain wilderness could be made effective allies in the fight against undocumented entry. Desolate routes deprive migrants of access to food and water. Only along well-defined roads or on railroads could immigrants obtain the necessary resources for travel, and it was along those routes that immigration patrols might be best stationed to capture undocumented immigrants."[26] As one federal agent testified in 1926, the goal of border enforcement was to "at least make attempts to cross the border dangerous and hold illegal entry down to small proportions."[27]

The acknowledgment that the desert, as well as the other extreme environments cross-cut by the border, could strategically be used to deter migrants from illegal entry on a large scale was not, however, formally laid out in policy documents until the start of the official PTD era, after 1993. The initial Strategic Plan memorandum was among the first to refer to environmental conditions as a potential resource for securing the geopolitical boundary: "The border environment is diverse. Mountains, deserts, lakes, rivers and valleys form natural barriers to passage. Temperatures ranging from sub-zero along the northern border to the searing heat of the southern border effect [sic] illegal entry traffic as well as enforcement efforts. *Illegal entrants crossing through remote, uninhabited expanses of land and sea along the border can find themselves in mortal danger*" (emphasis added).[28]

Although policy makers have written extensively about PTD for decades,[29] only the earliest documents associated with this strategy articulate a clear vision of the role that officials imagined the environment playing in enforcement: "The prediction is that with traditional entry and smuggling routes disrupted, illegal traffic will be deterred, or forced over more *hostile* terrain, less suited for crossing and more suited for enforcement" (emphasis added).[30] Prior to PTD, the dominant enforcement practice emphasized catching people after an illegal entry had been achieved and then processing them through the *voluntary-departure complex*, whereby apprehended migrants were permitted to waive their rights to a deportation hearing and returned to Mexico without lengthy detention.[31] Many have described this as a relatively useless process that individuals become familiar with, and less afraid of, after repeated apprehensions.[32] PTD was a direct reaction to the ineffectiveness of this previous disciplinary practice.

In the 1994 Strategic Plan, the use of the word *hostile* suggests that this new form of boundary enforcement was intended to be more aggressive and violent (and thus more effective) than previous programs. The word choice is also interesting given that the architects of the Strategic Plan did not involve only the Border Patrol, but also included "planning experts from the Department of Defense Center for Low Intensity Conflict,"[33] experts who had previously been charged with developing strategies for quelling insurgencies in the developing world.[34] The great irony is that some of the migrants whose movement these defense experts were working to stop were fleeing violence in Central America that US interventionist policies had sanctioned and supported.[35]

After this initial report was issued, the words used to characterize the desert environment would be gradually changed from "hostile" to "harsh," "inhospitable," and the like.[36] This shift in tone reflects but one of many bureaucratic attempts to sanitize the human costs of this policy. For example, although actual desert conditions are a linchpin of this enforcement strategy, relatively few public documents focused on PTD describe them or comment on the correlation between the strategy and migrant fatalities.[37] In addition, despite showing numerous photographs of agents both on patrol and "rescuing" people in the Sonoran Desert, the 2012–2016 Border Patrol Strategic Plan makes no mention of this landscape or its key role in deterring migration. This hostile terrain is now camouflaged in policy memorandums.

———

In 1994, it was predicted that PTD would push the migrant experience beyond simple apprehension and deportation. The architects of the Strategic Plan relied on a number of key assumptions, including the fact that "violence will increase as effects of strategy are felt."[38] *Violence*, however, was poorly defined in this document and probably too blunt for some people's liking. Later policy briefs substitute this word for euphemisms such as "costly." A congressional report written just three years after the Strategic Plan stated: "The southwest border strategy [previously known as the Strategic Plan] is ultimately designed to deter illegal entry into the United States. It states that 'The overarching goal of the strategy is to make it so difficult and so costly to enter this country illegally that fewer individuals even try.'"[39]

Although no public record explicitly states that a goal of PTD is to kill border crossers in an attempt to deter other would-be migrants, the connection between death and this policy has been highlighted by both academics and various federal agencies charged with evaluating Border Patrol programs.[40] An excerpt from a 2010 report to Congress reads: "'Prevention Through Deterrence' ... has pushed unauthorized migration away from population centers and funneled it into more remote and hazardous border regions. This policy has had the *unintended consequence* of increasing the number of fatalities along the border, as unauthorized migrants attempt to cross over the inhospitable Arizona desert without adequate supplies of water" (emphasis added).[41]

This comment that the increasing number of migrant fatalities is an "unintended consequence" of PTD is misleading and ignores previous evidence suggesting that policy makers were well aware of the role that death would play in this enforcement strategy. For example, a 1997 report by the Government Accountability Office (GAO) identifies as one of the "Indicators for Measuring the Effectiveness of the Strategy to Deter Illegal Entry Along the Southwest Border" the "deaths of aliens attempting entry." Concerning the "predicated outcome if AG's [the attorney general's] strategy is successful," the same report claims that it "depends on how enforcement resources are allocated. In some cases, deaths may be reduced or prevented (by fencing along the highways, for example). In other cases, deaths may increase (as enforcement in urban areas forces aliens to attempt mountain or desert crossings)."[42] I had to read the foregoing quote several times before I fully grasped its message. It clearly and publicly states that one way for the government to measure the efficacy of PTD is via a migrant body count. In some ways this is merely a sanitized version of the many anti-immigrant comments that accompany online articles about border crosser deaths; for example: "As long as the immigration numbers are declining ... I can live with the border death numbers."[43] The sector of the American public that attributes a low value to the lives of migrants seems to mirror the federal government's perspective.

The statement from this official document suggests both that early on in the planning of this policy the migrant death rate was considered a useful metric to gauge the program's effectiveness (i.e., "violence will increase as effects of strategy are felt") and that the Border Patrol clearly understood that fatalities would rise as "enforcement in urban areas forces aliens to attempt mountain or desert crossings." This report was published prior to the spike in deaths that occurred in the Arizona desert starting in the early 2000s.[44] As early as 1997, however, evidence clearly showed that the body count associated with PTD was primarily caused by "environmental exposure (falls, hyperthermia, dehydration)."[45] Rather than shooting people as they jumped the fence, Prevention Through Deterrence set the stage for the desert to become the new "victimizer" of border transgressors.

CONNECTING THE DOTS

Since the beginning of PTD, both the number of people who have been apprehended in the remote regions of Arizona and the annual rate of migrant fatalities have risen steeply. In 1993, 92,639 people were caught by Border Patrol in the Tucson Sector. By 2000, this number had grown to 616,346, an almost sevenfold increase (see appendix A). Although overall apprehension rates across the southern border did not rise significantly during this seven-year period, the funnel effect of PTD became visible as crossing attempts in the Tucson Sector skyrocketed. In 1993 this sector accounted for 8 percent of total southern border apprehensions. By 2000, 37 percent of all immigration arrests happened in this region. For almost two decades, until recently, the Tucson Sector was the primary crossing corridor for undocumented migrants.[46]

Although Prevention Through Deterrence redirected people toward more "hostile" ground, it has not significantly dissuaded would-be crossers, a point recognized as early as 2001 by the GAO: "Although INS has realized its goal of shifting illegal alien traffic away from urban areas, this has been achieved at a cost to ... illegal aliens.... In particular, rather than being deterred from attempting illegal entry, many aliens have instead risked injury and death by trying to cross mountains, deserts, and rivers."[47] Many have died since the implementation of this policy, and the correlation between the funneling of people toward desolate regions of the border and an upsurge in fatalities is strong.[48] Still, even when the connection between PTD and migrant death is recognized by the federal government, there is generally a refusal to causally link the two phenomena. As a 2012 GAO report notes:

> Known migrant deaths fell from a high of 344 in 1988 to a low of 171 in 1994 before climbing back to 286 in 1998. According to DHS data, known migrant deaths climbed from 250 in 1999 to 492 in 2005, and averaged 431 deaths per

year in 2005–2009 before falling to an average of 360 per year in 2010–2011. . . . The apparent increase in migrant deaths is particularly noteworthy in light of the declining number of alien apprehensions (i.e., estimated unauthorized entries) during the same period. . . . *Overall, these data offer evidence that border crossings have become more hazardous since the "prevention through deterrence" policy went into effect in the 1990s, though once again the precise impact of enforcement on migrant deaths is unknown.* [emphasis added][49]

There is also significant disagreement among the federal government, social scientists, and human rights groups regarding how to count dead border crossers. Compared to other organizations, the Department of Homeland Security routinely publishes the lowest number of recorded migrant deaths.[50] Given the unpopular and controversial nature of such statistics, it is not surprising that the government lowballs these body counts. A conservative estimate is that 5,596 people died while attempting to migrate between 1998 and 2012;[51] and between 2000 and September 2014, the bodies of 2,771 people were found in southern Arizona,[52] enough corpses to fill the seats on fifty-four Greyhound buses. These grim figures represent only *known* migrant fatalities. Many people may die in remote areas and their bodies are never recovered. The actual number of people who lose their lives while migrating will forever remain unknown (see chapter 3).

Silvestre Reyes's Operation Blockade in El Paso in 1993 may be separated by 350 miles and almost two decades from the ravaged skeleton described at the start of this chapter, but the two phenomena are unequivocally linked. Operation Blockade became the cornerstone of a nationwide border policy that used, and continues to use, the desert as a weapon. Prevention Through Deterrence has evolved from an explicit program that once acknowledged that the dangers posed by the desert could be strategically exploited as a weapon in the war on immigration to a sterilized description of an enforcement paradigm that has unfortunately (and "unexpectedly") resulted in migrants "risking their lives."

In 1994, the federal government clearly appreciated that people could be funneled over "hostile terrain" where law enforcement had "tactical advantage." Twenty years later, the common Border Patrol discourse focuses on blaming the smugglers who "endanger migrants in the desert." This shift in federal tone that now deflects culpability away from policy and toward the environment and *coyotes* is summed up well in an article in the *Arizona Daily Star* in which a Border Patrol agent reflects on the discovery of several migrant bodies: "The Sonoran Desert is extremely vast and remote with very few water sources. . . . [I]t is important to realize illegal immigrants are being victimized and lied to by smugglers who lead them through treacherous terrain and expose them to extreme conditions."[53] Joseph Nevins has wisely pointed out that the federal government's refusal to acknowledge any responsibility for this death toll, coupled with the blaming of *coyotes* for taking people through high-risk areas, overlooks the fact that the "significant growth in use of *coyotes* has been the predictable, direct result of the enhanced border-enforcement strategy."[54]

The increase in migrant traffic through Arizona and the rise in crossing fatalities indicate that security practices have effectively and systematically funneled people toward violent terrain and made the process more deadly. In no uncertain terms, Prevention Through Deterrence relies on the desert to "deter" people from attempting to cross. But what does this "hostile" landscape look like? What are the environmental factors that are meant to stop people? In the following chapter I address these questions and offer a theoretical framework to help understand the complex relationship between border crossers and the many humans and nonhumans who act as agents of deterrence.

CHAPTER 2

Dangerous Ground

HYBRID COLLECTIF

It's been twenty years since Border Patrol sector chief Silvestre Reyes lined up hundreds of green-uniformed agents along the banks of the Rio Grande to stop border crossers from scaling the fence and running into downtown El Paso. It's been twenty years since Reyes's plan set off a chain reaction that fundamentally transformed how the federal government polices the border from Brownsville to San Ysidro. He didn't know it at the time, but Reyes planted the seed that would soon give rise to the phrase "Prevention Through Deterrence."

Prevention Through Deterrence. It has a nice ring to it. It looks good in big bold letters splashed on the front of federal documents. It stands proudly at the top of PowerPoint slides that the Border Patrol shows to visiting politicians who want to know how the agency is fighting the War on Terror and the War on Illegal Immigration. Prevention Through Deterrence. It sounds powerful, but not vicious. It wants to convince you that it's a humane policy designed simply to prevent crime, to discourage it before it happens.

Prevention Through Deterrence. It's an ambiguous and sterile phrase. Much like the insipid language that defense intellectuals use to sanitize discussions of weapons of mass destruction and their human costs,[1] the Border Patrol has adopted a lexicon that's full of euphemisms and abstractions (e.g., "Aliens," "Other Than Mexicans," "Tactical Advantage"). Like other federal government security jargon, "Prevention Through Deterrence" has "no graphic reality behind the words."[2] It's a semantic cloak that hides all of the blood, sweat, and tears from public view. As I said, it looks good on a PowerPoint slide.

Two decades after El Paso, what has *deterrence* come to mean in the context of border crossings? What hides in the shadows of "hostile" terrain? Flesh-roasting temperatures? Steel walls and remote ground sensors? Thousands of heavily armed agents on the ground? What about venomous snakebites or bandits with a propensity for gang rape? Shoes that break apart after stagger-ing in them for miles over lonely mountains? An undiagnosed heart condition exacerbated by days in the desert? Although all of these things (and countless others) have become incorporated into the Border Patrol's system of enforce-ment, none of these realities are captured by policy rhetoric. But the deploy-ment of the word *deterrence* is not just a political magic trick used to mask the human impact of this strategy.

Even if policy planners changed the phrase to "Prevention Through Death" or "Prevention Through Suffering," it still wouldn't come close to capturing the complexity or brutal violence of this system of enforcement. The variables, processes, and actors that structure PTD defy simple linguistic description. There are too many parts, too many unknowns, too much randomness. In essence, the things that "deter" people can never be fully known. How, then, can we begin to understand this intricate system that is sometimes random and always beyond complete human comprehension? How do we level the analytical playing field to simultaneously account for bored agents sitting in their air-conditioned SUVs watching green video surveillance screens along with flash floods, scorpion bites, dislocated knees, 100-degree weather, drone planes scouring the desert for heat signatures, and carrion eaters who tear human flesh from the bone? How can we begin to understand the structure of a wall of deterrence that is equal parts human, animal, plant, object, geography, temperature, and unknown?

My attempt to illuminate the complexity and ambiguity of Prevention Through Deterrence draws inspiration from Callon and Law's theory of the *hybrid collectif*,[3] which posits that agency is an emergent property created by the interaction of many heterogeneous components known as *actants*, sources of action that may be human or nonhuman.[4] In simple and less French terms, people or objects don't act in isolation, but instead have complex relationships at different moments across time and space that sometimes create things or make things happen. It is these relationships that "perform agency," not isolated humans or solitary objects. Agency cannot exist (or come to be) in a vacuum, or as Jane Bennett puts it, "An actant never really acts alone. Its efficacy or agency always depends on the collaboration, cooperation, or interactive interference of many bodies and forces."[5]

To comprehend the intricacies of how agency is constructed, our gaze must widen to include all of the components—human, animal, mineral, weather pattern, and so forth—that make up a hybrid system. We also need to move beyond the simplistic binaries that draw stark divisions between humans and nonhumans, a philosophical framework that scholars from diverse backgrounds have long scrutinized.[6] This problematic dualism is part of the futile quest to ascribe to humans credit for all action while assigning randomness or inanimate status to all matter outside our species, a phenomenon largely attributed to Western elites.[7] For those willing and open to rethinking the relationship between humans and nonhumans,[8] which partly means moving beyond this particular typology, the concept of the collectif reveals itself as the "emergent effect created by the interaction of the heterogeneous parts that make it up."[9]

To identify the significance of, or contribution by, nonhumans to forms of action, we need to first do a few things. People have to be decentered in the agency equation, the hierarchy that places us above all others needs to be destroyed, and we must recognize that *Homo sapiens* are not always at the center of (or present in) a particular universe of action. As Stanescu points out, we've been fooling ourselves for a long time about just how special we are: "To believe in human exceptionalism requires a certain level of transcendental faith; it requires one to believe that we were set apart from the rest of the world rather than being subjected to the same evolutionary forces as all other living beings."[10] This is not to say that we are not important or that it is not often our fault that things in the world are the way they are. People are frequently the prime movers in major systems that extend beyond our species (e.g., global warming). But we couldn't destroy our planet without factories, automobiles, greenhouse gases, fossil fuels, the sun, and other nonhumans. All of us—humans, objects, minerals, environmental conditions, nonhuman animals—are inextricably and simultaneously connected in myriad ways. The architecture that these heterogeneous pieces produce when they are connected, and the subsequent agency performed by these structures, varies across time and space and comes in different shapes and sizes.[11]

Because humans are forced to describe and conceptualize the hybrid collectif through the filter of language and our species-specific form of cognition, we admittedly miss out on a lot. There are many moments in our daily lives whose complexity we can neither fully comprehend nor describe linguistically.[12] Try charting out the actants and experiences of those responsible for the hamburger you ordered for lunch yesterday. Does your chart include the perspective of the cow? What did the view from the cattle pen look, feel, and smell like? Did you imagine the person charged with delivering the captive bolt shot to the cow's head? Was the shot "successful," or did the animal writhe in pain high above the kill floor until someone wrangled her still and shot her again?[13] What about the person responsible for the bolt gun's maintenance, or the woman who drove the truck that delivered the hamburger bun to the restaurant? Does your chart account for the chemical reaction occurring between the delivery vehicle's engine and the refined oil that was brought in from the Middle East? What about the food that the cow was fed prior to her death or the temperature in the room of the factory where her body was rendered? Did you visualize the undocumented Guatemalan teenager who grilled the patty in the kitchen, or the *E. coli* that, you hope, was destroyed by cooking the meat at the proper temperature? You get my drift.

Depending on the scale and analytical lens, the hybrid collectif may expand into infinity and drive a human mind insane. Let's not forget all the systems our brains can't even begin to comprehend (like the human brain), much less describe in words. The point is that there is a lot of action that happens in our daily lives that we have either little control over or little understanding of. Hybrid collectifs are complex.

A final point needed to understand the efficacy of Callon and Law's theory as an explanatory framework has to do with the concept of intention. The human tendency is to ascribe agency strictly to those entities able to make choices, attribute significance to their choices, and then evaluate those choices. The latter two actions are usually achieved through the lens of language.[14] Framing agency in this way once again reproduces the human-nonhuman binary. This might make us humans feel that we are masters of our own universe, but it is nonetheless problematic for at least two reasons. First, this thinking suggests that only *Homo sapiens* can be agents and thus completely ignores, or at least downplays, the role of others that might be more responsible for the production of agency. This is what Callon and Law call *attributions:* "Agents are effects generated in configurations of different materials. Which also, however, take the form of *attributions.* Attributions which localize agency as singularity—usually singularity in the form of human bodies. Attributions which endow one part of a configuration with the status of prime mover. Attributions which efface the other entities and relations in the *collectif,* or consign these to a supporting and infrastructural role."[15] In other words, many parts are responsible for the production of agency, but the human inclination is to reduce the "effects generated in configurations of different materials" to people, even when they may have played a minimal role. This human need to isolate (or appropriate) agency and claim sole responsibility for action typically occurs when it suits our purposes.[16] In this process, other parts of the collectif are relegated to supporting roles. This assumes that nonhumans are passive until humans mobilize them for some purpose.[17] In other moments, we may employ nonhumans as scapegoats when unwanted forms of agency are created (e.g., "machine malfunction" or "act of nature").[18]

By erroneously positioning humans as the sole agents responsible for action, we end up reducing all others to background noise, uncontrollable variables, or randomness. This results in the characterization of all agency as intentional and motivated by people—a line of thinking that fails to acknowledge that a hybrid collectif is sometimes strategic from a human perspective and other times not. This way of thinking also reduces agency to forms that only humans can recognize, which, as my crude hamburger example shows, means we miss out on quite a bit. Callon and Law make the compelling argument that agency comes in all forms, many of which humans can't even begin to imagine. Much of this agency is "nonstrategic, distributed, and decentered" and hence difficult, if not impossible, for us to understand.[19] I would add that although we can attempt for analytical purposes to isolate the relationships that perform action at any one moment, agency needs to be conceptualized as a dynamic and ongoing process.

As I argue below, twenty years after it was first implemented, Prevention Through Deterrence is still evolving. New forms of agency emerge every day as a result of the infinite number of interactions that occur among the many actants in the desert. The Border Patrol may have officially (and intentionally) started the PTD hybrid collectif in 1994, but many others, human and nonhuman, have since become implicated in the process over time and space.

As the desert and all the actants it contains have become incorporated into the Prevention Through Deterrence hybrid collectif, the Border Patrol has attempted to separate its policy from the subsequent trauma that migrants experience as a result of being funneled toward this "hostile" environment. Rather than being viewed as a key partner in the border enforcement strategy, the desert is framed as a ruthless beast that law enforcement cannot be responsible for. Nature, in the Border Patrol's disinfected public discourse, is a runaway train that has no conductor. When asked in June 2013 about three decomposing bodies found in the wilderness over a two-day period, Tucson Sector chief Manuel Padilla Jr. simply replied, "The desert does not discriminate."[20] Padilla failed to mention that dying in the Arizona desert is largely a problem faced by undocumented Latinos.

The two key points I make in this chapter are as follows: First, the Prevention Through Deterrence strategy has created a setting in which the Border Patrol can draw on the agency of animals and other nonhumans to do its dirty work while simultaneously absolving itself of any blame connected to migrant injuries or loss of life. This is what Doty calls the federal government's "moral alibi."[21] Second, describing the desert as a "deterrent" to migration both flattens the three-dimensionality of what Sarah Whatmore terms the "hybrid geography" that border crossers face and renders the various human and nonhuman political subjects who influence the movement of people across this landscape largely invisible.[22] By focusing the ethnographic lens on the migrant experience, we can start to add a graphic reality to federal policy discourse.

Because of the scale, complexity, and randomness of the crossing milieu, it is impossible to account for or describe every single element or actant involved in this process. This is a difficulty characteristic of all hybrid collectifs. They can never be fully illuminated and it is impossible to identity all parts of the system from one spot.[23] The best one can hope for is to "create appropriately monstrous ways of re-presenting [hybrid collectifs] on those rare occasions when our paths happen to cross and we find, for a moment, that we need to interact with them."[24] In the following account I attempt to "re-present" some of the heterogeneous actors who commonly make up the Sonoran hybrid collectif by describing a typical crossing experience, including various geographic, environmental, and social obstacles that act as deterrents to the movement of people through the Nogales-Sasabe corridor.[25]

The story I present is a composite drawn from hundreds of interviews and conversations with migrants, field observations made in Nogales and the desert, and formal and informal interactions with Border Patrol agents.[26] Humphreys and Watson call this type of account *semifictionalized ethnography*, or a "restructuring of events occurring within one or more ethnographic investigations into a single narrative."[27] This pastiche of perspectives, gazes, and variables reflects in many ways the overall approach of the Undocumented Migration Project, which seeks to combine various, sometimes seemingly disparate data sets to paint a more nuanced picture of the crossing process. By drawing on specific details told to me by migrants and filtering these descriptions for readability and flow, I elucidate how the parts of the collectif work together to perform agency that seeks to deter; in this way I attempt to bring the reader phenomenologically closer to the everyday terror of the desert.

DAY I (JUNE)

"Wake up! Time to go!" screams El Gordo as he pounds his fat knuckles on the hotel room's plywood door. Javier cracks his eyes and stares at the yellow stain on the stucco ceiling directly above him.

"Wake up? Who can sleep in this shit hole?"

The room is thick with sweat, a pungent mix of salt and body grease. Javier has a good excuse for smelling so awful. He's been sleeping in a cemetery for five days and washing his face, armpits, and undercarriage at a rusty spigot behind the nearby bus station. He hasn't changed his socks or underwear since he crawled out of the desert over a week ago. He turns his head and stares at the other dark-skinned strangers in the room.

Two black-haired women are sharing the lone single bed. Both slept all night with their shoes on. The rest are splayed out on the floor in various uncomfortable poses. Some huddle in corners; a few lie on their backs on impromptu mattresses of clothes. Javier rests his head on the cheap nylon backpack that contains his only possessions: an extra shirt, an oversized green plastic comb, and a religious pamphlet he got from the cristianos *who hand out food down on la linea. The pamphlet is missing several key pages about the Rapture. God almighty himself saved the day when Javier needed shit tickets while squatting in a crypt that the cemetery locals converted into a polished marble outhouse.*

In total, there are nine of them in the room. Three women and five other men. Everybody smells as if they have just come from the desert or the cemetery. Javier tried to crack the door the previous night to get some much-needed ventilation, but the noise from the neighbor's room was deafening and unsettling. It was either smell the stench of his fellow compañeros *or listen to the prostitute next door go back and forth between fighting with her pimp and playing porn videos at full volume in hopes of coaxing an erection from one of her drunken johns. Javier opted for the solitude of this sweat lodge.*

These nine strangers have been holed up in a hotel in Nogales, Mexico, for two days. El Gordo, the coyote Javier recently met, promised to get him a nice room so he could rest before they tried to cross the desert. That son of a bitch never mentioned that he would lock him in a windowless room in a cut-rate bordello. Javier's cousin Western Union'd him $500 a few days before, and he gave the smuggler $400 as down payment.

El Gordo pulls hard on a Marlboro Red. "Your family can pay me the other $3,100 once we get to Phoenix."

"I'm not giving you their phone number, so don't even ask. They know not to send any lana *unless they speak to me directly."*

Contracting a coyote on the street is risky. Javier has to take as many precautions as possible.

El Gordo sucks on his crooked front teeth and feigns astonishment. "Don't worry, brother. Yo soy una persona de confianza." He then tells Javier it's gonna cost $40 for a two-night stay at the Hotel Jodido.

Despite spending almost forty-eight hours together, they have made little small talk. Everyone has been quiet as he or she struggles to catch a few hours of troubled sleep before they have to leave. Javier has learned only a few people's names. There is Lupe, a twenty-seven-year-old mother of two from Oaxaca (¡No mames, güey! ¡Todos son de Oaxaca!) who has spent the past fourteen years living in the United States. She worked the cash register at a Dollar Store in upstate New York where she struggled to put food on the table for her two children, who are US citizens. She has already failed once trying to get through the desert and will not give up until she reunites with her kids. She tells Javier that the fat lady she lived next door to called immigration on her because she wants to steal her children. It's a crazy-sounding story, but it's probably true. Everyone on la linea *has an unbelievable story. Surreality is the new normal.*

Pushing tears out of her eyes with the palm of her hand, she says, "The only thing I want is to get my kids back. I don't need to go back and stay on American soil. I just want my children. I love my children." Her red-rimmed eyes are wet and dull. She has obviously told this story before, because she no longer has the energy to say it with passion. Traumatized is the new normal.

There's a young vato *in the corner named Carlos who can't seem to sit still. Javier could hear him fidgeting all night as he hammered out text messages to some* morena *in a faraway* rancho. *The kid woke up this morning somehow more hyperactive than he was the night before. Carlos asks questions to anyone who makes eye contact with him: "When are we leaving? Which route are we taking? What's it like in the desert? How far is it to Hollywood?" No one knows the answers, so they ignore him. Carlos doesn't seem to care. He is just excited to be finally making the trip to El Norte. He has a cousin who is gonna hook him up with a job at a car wash. They are gonna sit in the bed of his primo's shiny red F150 and get fucked up on Tecates after work. His cousin knows a club where they can pick up some morras. ¡Bien buenas carnal! En serio. Carlos has it all planned out.*

Javier likes him because the kid is goofy and innocent. He can't be older than eighteen and has a dumb smile that suggests the world has not yet been cruel to him. Sure, he comes from a poor family, but his parents love him. His dad even slipped him $50 Americano the day he left Guerrero. "I'm gonna send money back as soon as I can," he told them. His papá waited until Carlos was gone before he went out behind the house, sat down on a plastic bucket, and cried.

The kid reminds Javier of his little brother Andrés, who is impatiently waiting back in Veracruz for something exciting to happen in his life. Their small hometown is killing him. He wants to join Javier in Bremerton, Washington. He wants to get a job doing construction. He wants to finally meet his little gringa niece Yennifer (Jennifer), who was born four years ago when Javier was shacking up with a white girl he met while working at Wendy's. Andrés doesn't know that Javier was recently deported for driving with a busted taillight and Budweiser on his breath. He doesn't know that Javier has already failed once trying to cross the border and has spent a week restlessly sleeping under bridges and in a mausoleum. Andrés doesn't know that three nights ago in the cemetery Javier watched a migrant from El Salvador get his brains kicked in by demon-eyed glue sniffers over a $3 bottle of Tonayán, everyone's favorite hangover in a plastic jug. Javier doesn't want to worry his family with such details.

Carlos keeps chattering away and asking questions. Lupe nods and pretends to be interested. She is busy grinding her teeth and wondering if someone is feeding her kids breakfast at this very moment. Javier thinks about his bed in Washington State and the smell of little Jennifer's hair. They are warm and comforting images. Carlos is a first-timer. Nothing anyone tells him will approach the reality he is about to experience, so why bother trying? He doesn't know what the desert has in store for him. He doesn't know that in a few days he will vomit blood and then look forever into a sea of cobalt and fractured shadows.

A man in his early thirties stands up and starts getting his effects together. El Gordo dropped him off late last night, and he introduced himself as "Marcos from Puebla." Everyone just nodded. No one pointed out that he was obviously not from

Puebla. *Probably* salvadoreño *or* guatemalteco. *You can just tell.* "Ni modo. *That's his fucking problem," Javier muttered to himself at the time. Javier doesn't know the rest of the people's names and doesn't bother to ask. In a few cycles of the sun he won't be sure if there were seven, nine, or fifteen people in the group. The desert does something to your brain. The sun's rays overexpose your memory. Details are lost. Names and faces wash out. Insanity becomes reality and no one can tell the difference: "We must have walked over 200 miles. . . . We came across nineteen dead bodies huddled under a tree. . . . We were attacked by monkeys. . . . La* migra *saw us because they had birds with little cameras on their backs."*[28] *Homeric desert tales are told with enough conviction and impossibility that it all becomes believable.*

They grab their stuff and assemble in the hotel lobby. Conspicuously, they are all head-to-toe in black cloth and sneakers. They look like a group of misfit jewel thieves preparing for a heist. El Gordo shuffles his pollitos[29] *outside where a rickety pickup truck waits. Everyone piles in the back. El Gordo squeezes up front next to a dark-skinned female driver with bottle-blond hair named La Güera. El Gordo yells, "Just act normal, goddammit!" as the truck rattles away from the hotel. Nobody understands what the hell he means.*

They drive east on International Boulevard running parallel with the border fence. Javier can see Nogales, Arizona, through the spaces in the rusty metal poles that make up the new wall. Migra *says the new fence is to protect* agentes *from people hurling rocks.*[30] *Locals say they changed the fence so that the* gabachos *could draw a better bead on the Mexicans. They zoom past a white office building whose wall is checkered with bullet holes. A small iron cross and a few sad-looking candles congregate on the ground out front.*

"That's where la migra *killed a kid," someone whispers. They are correct. That is where sixteen-year-old José Antonio Elena Rodriguez was killed by Border Patrol on October 12, 2012. Law enforcement contends he was throwing rocks at them. Witnesses on the Mexican side say José Antonio was an innocent bystander walking on the sidewalk when a group of people jumped the fence into Mexico to get away from Border Patrol. An autopsy conducted by Mexican officials reports that José Antonio was "shot about eight times: twice to the head, once on his arm and five times on his back. At least five bullet wounds clustered on his upper back had to have struck him after he was down."*[31] *Despite having multiple high-tech video cameras mounted in the area where he was killed, the US federal government has yet to release any footage of the event. The investigation is still pending.*

The truck stops in front of a small grocery store. Everyone hops outs and walks in. La Güera sits in the cab and listens to norteña *music on her cell phone. She* takes a head count as people enter and converts each of them into dollars and pesos. She fantasizes about breaking a beer bottle on El Gordo's head and stubbing a cigarette out in his eye if he tries to pull that shit again about "I've had some extra expenses on this run."

El Gordo does an overly complicated handshake with the store owner.

"Buy whatever you think you're gonna need for the trip," he says to people as they enter.

Javier grabs three gallons of water, a loaf of white bread, some limes, a clove of garlic, and eight cans of tuna. The cashier starts ringing him up. Javier realizes he is being charged almost triple the normal price.

Twenty minutes later the truck is once again sputtering down International Boulevard. They pass the Grupo Beta office, where dozens of recently deported migrants are lingering outside and jockeying for spots in the shade.[32] A few wave at the truck, well aware of what the ragtag group of passengers are about to do. The vehicle makes a right turn, passing the cemetery that Javier has recently been calling home. He catches a glimpse of a frail old man crouching behind a giant tombstone wiping himself with a sock, an ashen gargoyle hiding from the light.

They climb a small hill and curve left. To the north is the government port of entry known as La Mariposa. The Butterfly. It is a metal and cement archway into the Sonoran Desert. Everyone avoids looking out into the unknown.

La Güera picks up speed. Carlos plays it cool and pretends he isn't worried about being ejected from the vehicle. Lupe has her head buried in her arms. Marcos from Puebla stares intensely at the driver and El Gordo through the truck's cracked back window. Javier can't tell if Marcos is really chingón or just acting.

They turn right at the first dirt road and La Güera punches the gas. The truck is chased by a ball of crimson dust. Nogales quickly disappears behind them. After fifteen minutes of shaking and bouncing through a field of dirt and gravel, the vehicle comes to an abrupt halt.

"Everyone out!"

El Gordo turns to La Güera and passes her a folded wad of maroon and green pesos. She looks at it and doesn't move her open hand. After a few seconds of awkward silence, he grudgingly pulls a few more sweaty bills from his shirt pocket and hands them over without saying a word.

As La Güera pulls away, she sticks her head out the window and yells, "Good luck!" She always yells it. Every single time. She thinks it's funnier than shit.

El Gordo starts walking into the wilderness without saying a word. The pollitos trail behind him in a twisting single file line that from the sky looks like a row of black ants. *The sun is starting to bloody the sharp mountain silhouettes in the distance. It's five o'clock in the afternoon. The temperature has cooled down to 90 degrees Fahrenheit.*

The great expanse before them is the western Sonoran Desert, one of the most arid regions in North America. In June and July the average daily temperature often exceeds 100 degrees, with some bleak corners of this expanse of rock and sand hitting highs of 120.[33] This scratch of earth is the hottest desert in Arizona. It is also the part of the Sonoran region (referred to as the Altar Desert) where average annual rainfall is barely measurable. In a good year it gets 250 millimeters of rain, the bulk of which happens in late summer during the monsoon season or as light winter rains. This lunar landscape is a place where you can die of thirst in June, drown in a flash flood in August, or freeze to death in January.[34] Most are killed by the sun.

The band of black-robed travelers marches. Javier feels the muscles in his thighs tighten and burn. It's been eight days since he was last here. His fatigued body has not yet fully recuperated. He hasn't been drinking enough liquids while waiting in Nogales. Surprisingly, there's no water fountain in the cemetery. It has been weeks since he got more than four hours of sleep at any one time. He has a low-grade headache and, ironically, his mouth tastes like sand. He is just entering the desert and already suffering from the early stages of dehydration.

The group silently walks west for hours. Some occupy themselves by memorizing what the backside of the person they are trailing looks like. Lupe keeps herself entertained by fantasizing about her homecoming. She knocks on the front door of her small apartment, and little Lucia sticks her head out from behind the living room blinds. "It's Mamá! Let me in! I lost my keys in the desert." Lucia and her baby brother, Herman, come running out to hug her. Angela, her evil neighbor, barrels out of the next-door apartment screaming she is going to call immigration police again. Lupe grabs a dented shovel from her neighbor's porch and throws it wildly at Angela's head. It smacks the side of her skull and makes a dull metal clank. Lupe especially likes that part of the story, so she replays it over and over again.

Javier is sweating and has already started taking big chugs from his first gallon of water. They climb a large hill and then fall down into a steep canyon. If they had a map, they could see that they just passed through the Pajarito Mountains and have to scale at least three more mountain ranges before getting to a point where they can be safely picked up. No one except El Gordo knows this unfortunate fact, and he has no interest in sharing this information. It's easier to keep the pollos in line if they have no clue where they are, where they are headed, or how far they have to walk.

The trail they take down into the canyon is a twisting dirt maze of cracked rock and loose gravel. It's like trying to walk down a hill covered in billiard balls. At any moment you can turn an ankle or slip and fall on your ass. One of the nameless men in the group trips and stumbles. The gallon of water he is holding goes rolling down the canyon. It splashes its metallic-colored contents as it bounces off the rocks below. Someone helps him up by the elbow. No one says a word. They get to the bottom of the canyon and start lumbering across a bed of sandy gravel. All you can hear is the sound of hurried feet in Converse fighting to keep moving across the sinking hot sand. The canyon veers left and right like a weekend drunk behind the wheel. The turns are disorienting. Are we headed west? Are we still in Mexico? The pale sky completely disappears behind the steep cliffs above their heads. The canyon walls threaten to swallow them up.

After hours of walking, they turn a corner and the smell of marijuana hits them in the face. El Gordo freezes in his tracks and mumbles, "Puta madre." Footsteps come running toward them.

"Don't you fucking move!"

They stare at an emaciated cholo wearing baggy jeans and a black Brujería T-shirt. A poorly rolled joint dangles from the side of his cracked mouth. There is a matte-black 9-millimeter in one of his claws. The gun is pointed sideways as in los videos de hip-hop.

"¡Ya pagamos! ¡Ya pagamos! We're with Grillo," cries El Gordo. It is the first time anyone has seen him show any vulnerability. It scares them.

The cholo pulls El Gordo aside. They smoke cigarettes and whisper out of ear-shot. Fifteen minutes later their guide tells them to sit down and get comfortable. "We can't cross tonight. They are running a load through here so we'll have to wait until tomorrow."

A few quietly groan, but nobody dares make a scene.

"I'm starving. What do you fuckers have to eat?" the cholo asks. They start handing over some of their food and water. Rough calculations are made in people's heads. The unspoken group consensus is that they don't have enough supplies to survive an extra day of waiting and still walk several days through the desert. It's too late to turn back.

DAY 2

At 10 A.M. the cholo tells them they can leave, but not before bullying people into giving up more of their food and water. No one really slept the night before, which means they are exhausted before they even cross the border.

Out of the corner of his eye, Javier sees Lupe quickly kiss a tattered photograph of her kids and stuff it into her red bra. "Hey, nena, give me your number so I can call you!" the cholo barks. Lupe mumbles "Fuck you" under her breath.

The ants start marching behind El Gordo otra vez. After less than two minutes, they make a sharp right, and the canyon breaks open to reveal a barbed-wire fence with a small gate. Their fearless leader unwraps a piece of wire and opens it. "¡Bienvenidos a Gringolandia!" he says. The door on the fence is a joke, but no one is laughing. They hurry through and El Gordo closes the gate behind him. They have just crossed into the United States through Walker Canyon and now have to navigate the Atascosa Mountains.

More winding through steep canyons. More hot sand and loose gravel. El Gordo points to the top of a ridge and says, "We need to go up that way." The group clumsily bushwhacks up the steep hill. Everyone gropes at rocks and branches, anything to pull them up the canyon wall. Carlos squeezes a tree branch and screams as a two inch thorn pierces his fleshy pad. "Watch the plants," El Gordo says as he continues to guide them up the hill and through a nasty patch of jumping cholla and barrel cacti.

Every native organism in this environment has adapted to deal with extreme temperature fluctuations, fight off dehydration, and survive excessive heat. Many are heavily armored with all forms of spikes, spines, lances, and other natural weaponry to help them battle predators and guarantee seed dispersal off the fur, skin, and clothing of all passersby. Red devil's claw, whitethorn acacia, pincushion cacti, crucifixion thorn: Unpleasant creatures pepper a landscape that botanists refer to as an "arboreal forest."[35] This is a world ruled by mountain lions, ocelots, black bears, javelinas, giant centipedes, bark scorpions, coral snakes, and black widows. More species of rattlesnakes (eleven) dwell in the Sonoran Desert than any other place in the world. In this hard land the power of nature is on full display.

They approach the hilltop. Everyone's pant legs are decorated with yellowed cholla spines. When Carlos reaches down to remove some of them, they immediately stick to his fingertips. The jumping cactus is as alive as any animal out here. Lupe has tried to crawl under a giant mesquite tree to avoid the minefield of cacti. Her tanned arms are a mess of red swollen scratches. No one thought to wear a long-sleeve shirt in this natural laboratory where lessons in the evolutionary biology of extreme environments are learned firsthand. The temperature approaches 100 degrees. Javier has already drained one of his three bottles of water. Some in the group have only one gallon left.

At the top of the ridge El Gordo tells them, "Wait here. I need to go make a call." He scurries off with his cell phone while the haggard group looks for any kind of shade. People assemble underneath the few scattered mesquite trees, but they offer little respite from the sun. The powerful noontime rays easily penetrate the tree's minimal foliage, baking the ground beneath them. Javier and Carlos huddle near a small stand of bushes. Carlos pulls a yellow bandanna out of his back pocket and starts wiping the sweat off his brow. He forgot to bring a hat. His face is bright red from the sun.

"My cousin says there are gringo *cazamigrantes* out here who shoot Mexicans like deer," he tells Javier.

"I think those are just stories people tell to fuck with you."

Separating fact from fiction in this desert is difficult. Red-necked neo-Nazis playing shoot-the-wetbacks, though, are not just migrant campfire stories. In recent years numerous border crossers have reported being fired at in the Sonoran Desert by white men decked out in camouflage. The murders of several people remain unsolved.[36] "Try not to think about that stuff and just stay positive. You have to have faith," Javier says. It's unclear if he himself believes this.

The group hears footsteps coming from the bushes and think it's El Gordo returning.

Two lanky figures appear like specters materialized out of the red dust. They are shadows of men in the bright sun. One is cradling a rifle, an American-made AR-15 bought at a gun show in Phoenix and smuggled into Mexico. For a moment they stand silently looking at the group; their dark eyes and raw mouths are overly accentuated by the black ski masks both are wearing. "Nobody move!" the guy with the assault rifle shrieks.

Bajadores. The Spanish verb *bajar* means "to bring down, to lower, to drop." That is exactly what happens in a matter of minutes. They line the group up and proceed to make everyone toss their wallets and money into a dirty burlap sack. Nobody has much to offer.

"Where's the fucking money?"

Crickets.

"Fine, take off all of your clothes."

A gentle breeze passes.

Three shots are fired into the air in quick succession. Gold shell casings ring like tiny bells as they hit the desert floor.

Belts unbuckle. Pants wiggle past knees.

"Take off everything!"

They are all standing naked doing their best to modestly cover up their genitals and breasts. One of the women is crying. Carlos fights back tears. While the gun is aimed at them, the other bajador starts walking down the line excavating pockets and feeling clothes for squirreled-away treasures. He runs a finger along the inner waist seam on Carlos's blue jeans and finds a homemade patch where he has tried to conceal the $50 his dad gave him.

"You think we're stupid, asshole?"

Before he can answer, Carlos feels a fist to the stomach that makes him almost vomit. He falls over.

"Stand up, jotito, and stop crying or we'll give you something to really cry about."

He gets upright and tries to pull himself together. All he can do is look away from the group and wipe the tears from his eyes with his shoulder. He is a virgin and doesn't want the women to see him naked.

"Who in the group is Centro Americano?"

Dead air.

Lupe can hear her heartbeat in her right eardrum.

The guy with the greasy bag walks over to Javier and Marcos. They are standing naked side by side cupping their vergas.

"Where are you from, puto?"

"Puebla."

"¿Y tu, moreno?"

"Veracruz."

"No mames. Show me some fucking ID."

Javier bends down and pulls his Mexican voter card from his sock.

The bajador twists the credencial in the sunlight like a TSA agent checking for the background hologram. He throws it on the ground.

"OK, paisa, give me your fucking watch."

He makes his way down the line and finally gets to Lupe. She is the youngest of the three women by almost twenty years.

He grins and shows a broken set of muddy teeth through the hole in his mask.

"What do we have here?"

Lupe shivers in the blinding sun, her hands vainly trying to cover her chest and crotch.

He squeezes one of her brown breasts like he is testing the ripeness of some fruit.

She slaps his hand away with the arm that was covering her pubic area.

Quickly, a closed fist brings a bright flash to her eyes. She stumbles backwards. An unexpectedly strong hand grabs her by the throat and straightens her posture.

"We're not fucking around, bitch!"

Her eyeballs bulge as she gasps for air. It feels as though he's going to break her windpipe.

Lupe stares straight back at the two red eyes poking through the mask. She tells herself not to fight back even though there are only two of them this time. Maybe it will be over quicker. The pulsing in her eardrum is deafening. It gives her something to focus on.

A dirty hand awkwardly walks down her chest and stomach. It passes over a black patch of wiry hair and suddenly two fingers are in her. She winces and squirms. The grip on her neck tightens. A rough fingernail scratches her insides.

She chokes on his hot stale breath.

Carlos whimpers.

Javier starts thinking about the last time he saw Jennifer.

Marcos makes a gesture as if to do something. The gun is turned on him.

"Stop fucking around, Abel. Let's go!" the gunman yells.

Five minutes later they are picking up off the ground what's left of their things. Lupe is quietly getting dressed. She wipes the dust off the photo of her kids and sticks it back into her bra.

They wait all afternoon for El Gordo to return. By nightfall, they know he is gone and that this was part of his plan. "I'm gonna kill that son of a bitch if I ever see him again," Javier says to no one in particular. It's a goddamn lie and he knows it. Still, the hollow declaration makes him feel a little better after not doing anything to stop the assault. When he tells the story later at the basketball court in Nogales, he will say that it was him who threatened to kill the bajadores and that's why no one was raped.

DAY 3

Javier, Marcos, Lupe, and Carlos decide to keep moving. The rest of the group wants to stay behind and turn themselves into the Border Patrol. They've had enough. The men shake hands. A few hug. Javier thinks he knows the way. "We just have to stay in the mountains and off the trails. The harder it is for us, the harder it is for la migra," *he says.*

They set off a few hours before daylight and follow a trail on a high ridge for several miles. The sun starts to show itself on the distant horizon, and they drop down into a canyon where there is more cover from Border Patrol and the heat. Carlos offers some unsolicited advice: "If a helicopter comes, we should all lie on the ground and close our eyes. My cousin says they can detect you by the whites of your eyes."

"Your cousin sounds like a genius," Javier scoffs. It sounds ridiculous, but everyone in the group has heard this line enough times to believe that it might be true.

Around 10 A.M. they limp out of the canyon and approach a dirt road. They hide in the brush like animals and debate what to do next. "We need to cover our tracks," Marcos says. Everyone is startled by this utterance. He has been so quiet for the last three days that people were starting to wonder if he knew how to talk at all. "One person go in the lead and the rest of us will walk in their footsteps. I'll sweep the tracks away."

Marcos commandeers a branch from a nearby tree. The group slinks across the road while he follows behind and does his best to erase their steps. They have just passed Ruby Road, which as the crow flies is less than eight miles from the border. It has taken them almost seventy-two hours to reach this point.

Javier leads them toward the Tumacácori mountain range, which they can see in the distance. The angular red peaks cut an intimidating profile against the empty Sonoran sky. It's like a demon waiting patiently for them. They work their way into another steep canyon.

For hours they crawl through a graveyard of boulders decorated with upturned trees, sand, and discarded migrant clothes deposited by seasonal floodwaters. They pass a rusted-out Volkswagen flipped over like a helpless insect. It's obvious you don't want to be down here when a monsoon starts unless you're looking to get washed back to Nogales. Where the canyon dead-ends, they start working their way up the side of a mountain. Javier leads the group toward a high trail that he can see in the distance. It's risky to take a route like this in midday, but they don't want to stop moving or double back. They cut through more fields of dense mesquite and cholla. "Where are we headed, El Gordo?" Lupe asks. Javier laughs for the first time in weeks.

They reach the high trail and Javier collapses under a tree. Lupe is right behind him. They both look downhill and see that Marcos is carrying Carlos's backpack. The skinny kid is struggling to get one foot in front of the other. It's like he's wearing ankle weights. "We should rest a little until the sun goes down. It is too hot to keep doing this," she says. For several hours they rest under the tree and share what food they have left. In total, they have less than three gallons of water.

The sun is sitting directly above them when Marcos gets up and walks down the trail. "Voy al baño," he says. A few short minutes later they hear yelling. In a panic Lupe and Javier stand up and grab their bags. They are unsure whether to run or try to help. Marcos comes barreling around the corner with his pants halfway down screaming, "Run! Run!" Before anyone can react, they see a bristly haired javelina galloping behind him. Lupe finds a rock and hurls it with full force. It makes a dull thud when it smacks the animal's meaty gut. He stops his chase and starts grunting and whining. It's a bold taunt. Lupe grenades another rock and this time hits the beast square in the head. It barks disapproval and scampers away. Marcos quickly buckles his pants. He gives the audience his trademark serious look. Within seconds, they are all laughing hysterically. "Man," Marcos says, "they warned me about rattlesnakes, but not about horny javelinas!" This keeps them entertained for several hours as they simmer in the shade.

At nightfall they begin again. The temperature is in the upper 80s and the water is going quickly. The group takes periodic rests, but the rocks and ground around them are emitting heat after a long day spent absorbing sunlight. Resting seems as painful as walking. "We need to keep moving before the sun comes up," Lupe says. The pace is considerably slower than the previous day, but Carlos is still barely able to keep up. At 3 A.M. they stop. Everyone is exhausted and needs a break. It is obvious that the kid can't go much farther. Carlos closes his eyes and quickly falls asleep. They settle in under black skies and the disfigured silhouettes of tree branches. Coyotes whine in the distance.

They stir at dawn and take stock of their supplies. A gallon of water is spread across three scratched-up bottles. After days in the sun, their life-sustaining supply of liquid is now the temperature of warm piss. Carlos complains of thirst. His pink skin is clammy to the touch.

"He needs water. We need to keep going until we find a cattle tank."

Again, feet drag across the desert floor. It is slow going and they stop every twenty minutes to wet their lips with what is left at the bottom of their bottles. This crawling goes on for hours until the only one with any water left in their bottle is Lupe. They pass her jug around and force Carlos to take a little extra. They are beyond the point of return, buried alive in the Tumacácori Mountains. Everyone is looking up at the sky, hoping that a helicopter will fly by. They keep walking and walking.

The day is bright and sunny and warm when Carlos collapses on the trail. Blood quietly drips from his nose as he shivers. A string holds a tiny wooden cross around his neck. One of his shoes has come untied. His burned skin is ice cold. Javier and Marcos drag his thin frame under a mesquite tree. The ground is hot to the touch, so they take their shirts off and make a comfortable bed for him. Lupe kneels and slowly pours what is left of their water into his mouth. "Graciela, hand me that Coca Cola, please," he says. Lupe shoots Javier a quick look that reads, "This is bad."

Migrant campsite, Tumacácori Mountains. Photo by Michael Wells.

It is decided that Lupe will stay behind while Marcos and Javier go for help. "I'm fine," she says. "You go find water or Border Patrol and come back for us. My feet are bad anyways." She takes off one of her silver running shoes to reveal three raw patches of skin where her toenails once resided. They give her what is left of their food, and the two men start down the trail with empty white jugs tied to their backpacks like boat buoys.

"Don't worry, Carlos, we will be back in a few hours."

The kid waves a limp hand and smiles softly.

Lupe waits with him for two days. At the end of the first day, she urinates in her hands and drinks it. At the end of the second day Carlos starts babbling something about a gray horse. Lupe pisses again into her hands what little liquid her body has left to give. She slurps some of it out of her palm and then trickles the remaining brown fluid into Carlos's mouth. He gags and spits up a little blood and pink foam. She massages his frail arms and legs until he falls asleep. Two hours later he starts shaking and babbling about the horse again. Lupe grasps his flailing arms. After a few fitful minutes he gets quiet. When the Border Patrol finally shows up, she is too dehydrated to cry. Carlos is quietly staring at the open sky.

DAY 4

"Look, you can see the lights of Tucson."

"¡No mames, cabron! ¡Estás alucinando!"

It is broad daylight. Tucson is 35 miles away.

They are lost, but no one wants to talk about it. The trail they were on ended abruptly, forcing them to climb a hill to find a new route. By the time they decided to turn back after seven hours of walking, it was too late. They couldn't remember which direction they had come from. The only option now is to find water or help.

After a restless night lying in the dirt dreaming about pools of shimmering silver water, they start again in the morning. They are filthy skeletons staggering through the brush. Heads hang heavy, oblivious as to what is ahead on the trail. Marcos bulldozes a branch and almost knocks himself out.

They sit under a tree and wait for the sun to go away. Javier spots a nopal cactus nearby with red tunas perched on top. He grabs a cluster of fruit and starts sucking on it. It's nothing more than a mouthful of bone and spines that shreds his gums. He is oblivious to the pain and can't tell if he is swallowing juice or his own blood. He doesn't care. Marcos takes a piece of fruit but is too exhausted to eat it. Javier spits the bloody pulp onto the cracked red earth. Ants crawl all over it.

In silence they wait for hours, periodically nodding off. By midafternoon, they both feel a little better. Javier turns to Marcos and says, "Oye, cabron, remember when we caught you trying to screw that javelina?"

Into the mountains they continue as the sun fades into the glowing horizon. Two hours later they stumble upon a dried-up lagoon used to water cattle. A shallow puddle of green liquid sits at the center. It is no bigger than a coffee table. With what little energy they have left, they run toward it. Marcos falls down before he can get there and crawls the last fifteen feet. Javier starts filling his bottle with the sludge. It is more algae and mud than water, but it is the best thing he has ever tasted. "Little sips. You have to take little sips or you will get sick," he tells Marcos. Marcos pays him no mind. He grabs the filthy bottle and squeezes the contents into his mouth.

DAY 5

They sleep next to the lagoon, despite worries that animals might be attracted to the water. That night, Javier dreams he is drowning in a pool of red black mud. The viscous liquid covers his body and he struggles to free his arms. Something pulls him down into the deep and his open mouth takes in mud. He wants to swallow but his throat closes up. Arms flail. He gags and chokes as he disappears into the murk. A shortness of breath startles him awake. He becomes aware of a low grumbling sound. "Marcos, can you hear that?" Marcos is gone.

He hears the noise again. It is muffled and coming from somewhere through a patch of trees whose branches are backlit by the moon like a giant spider web. Javier walks toward the sound.

It is the bellowing of a man in violent pain. In the pale gray of the night stars he can see Marcos on the ground holding his guts as though they're spilling out of some invisible war wound. Green foam rings his mouth and pools on the ground next to him. Watery shit drips out of the bottom of one of his pant legs. Javier pulls him up and they walk arm-in-arm back to the tree where they slept. It is an act of kindness only strangers who meet in moments of great shared trauma can comprehend.

Javier waits until the horizon line is outlined in orange. He stands and says, "I will be back with help. I promise." His last line of defense is a white jug full of cloudy green paste.

He is walking away when Marcos whispers, "My name is Manuel Saucedo Gutierrez. I am from San Marcos, El Salvador. Please tell them my name."

"Don't worry, mano, *you can tell them yourself when I come back."*

Through half-closed eyelids, Marcos watches him disappear over a hill and then stares off into the distance. For the first time he notices the three oblong shapes perched in a nearby tree quietly eyeing him.

By noon, Javier has swallowed all of the cattle tank water he brought with him. He tries to follow the trail, but each time it makes a sharp turn, he rambles through fields of nopal cacti and acacia. His ankles are bleeding; his lips are cracked open and black; blisters cover his face. Like a Depression-era hobo, his toes stick out from the front of one of his floppy shoes. Somewhere the water bottle went missing, but he doesn't remember when. The sun laughs from high over his head while slow-roasting his brain. He tries to imagine what saliva tastes like. He tries to remember how many days he has been walking. When the Border Patrol find him on the side of the road, he will be weeping and mumbling, "You have to help Marcos." A crew-cut EMT will give Javier an IV drip before he is driven to a detention center in Tucson. Two days later he will be deported to Nogales in the middle of the night.

UNMASKING DETERRENCE

Although Lupe, Carlos, Marcos, and Javier are fictionalized characters whom I use to illustrate the phenomenology of a border crossing, their experiences and dialogue are quite real and drawn from hundreds of interviews I have conducted with migrants over the years.[37] As fantastic as these tales may seem, they are by no means unique, a point driven home by the dramatic nonfictionalized stories that make up the rest of this book. People like Lupe and Carlos are living and dying in the desert at this very moment.

In this chapter I have contaminated the phrase "Prevention Through Deterrence" by providing graphic details regarding how this policy is experienced on the ground. I have also sought to illuminate the strategic role that nonhumans play in federal border enforcement by using the hybrid collectif as an explanatory framework. This second point is critical given that many conceptualize the injuries and deaths that result from border crosser engagements with animals, terrain, and temperature as "natural outcomes," or outcomes with no causal link to federal policies. Migrants have been purposefully funneled into the desert through various enforcement practices, a tactic that has enabled Border Patrol to outsource the work of punishment to actants such as mountains and extreme temperatures. Labeling migrant deaths an "act of nature" is a convenient way to ignore the hybrid collectif of deterrence that was intentionally set in motion by policy strategists twenty years ago and that continues to function today. There is also strong evidence that Border Patrol agents remotely monitor migrants and let them continue walking in the desert for prolonged periods before attempting to apprehend them.[38] Using the Sonoran Desert to grind people down makes apprehension significantly easier and follow-up crossing attempts more difficult. As I have shown, a lot can happen in a few days of walking.

Knowing the inner workings of this system is crucial both for understanding the border-crossing stories told in the following sections of this book and for connecting the dots between singular events that happen in the desert and the macroscale political and social processes that shape undocumented migration as a whole. By shining a light on the many parts that structure federal enforcement and the forms of agency that emerge from the collaborative efforts of a host of actants working to deter border crossers, I intend to demonstrate that while certain events in the desert may be random, the entire system has an unpleasant and systematic logic. In no uncertain terms, Prevention Through Deterrence is designed to hurt people.

In her book *Vibrant Matter*, Jane Bennett writes that demystifying sociopolitical relations is a key element of democracy that allows us not only to hold those in power accountable to the law but also to keep a close watch on discriminatory systems.[39] Bennett warns, however, that the process of demystification may lead us back to the troubling human-nonhuman binaries that often undermine our attempts to truly understand how agency works: "What demystification uncovers is always something human, for example, the hidden quest for domination on the part of some humans over others, a human desire to deflect responsibility for harms done, or an unjust distribution of (human) power. Demystification tends to screen from view the vitality of matter and to reduce political agency to human agency."[40]

It is not my intent to downplay the agency of nonhumans in PTD (a point that I expand upon in chapter 3), but quite the opposite. In the Arizona desert nonhumans are major players without which this system of boundary enforcement could not exist. My point is rather that the Border Patrol has intentionally set the stage so that other actants can do most of the brutal work. Despite the claim by some that the desert has become uncontrollable, even from the perspective of federal law enforcement officers who find themselves at risk while patrolling this great expanse,[41] I see this environment as the perfect silent partner in boundary control. Although I am sympathetic to the ontological turn toward nonhumans as key political actors, I am not ready to decenter or disconnect human agency from the brutal boundary enforcement strategies currently in place. In this context, agency is relational and produced as part of a human-induced chain reaction. Once set in motion, humans and nonhumans as political actors cannot be separated, even if the former have more obvious intentions.[42]

PTD should thus be thought of as a perpetual motion machine started by the Border Patrol and powered by other politically implicated actants. The diversity of the forms of deterrence that have emerged from the actions of environmental conditions, terrain, and animals in fact testifies to the agency of these nonhumans and the uniqueness of this hybrid collectif. Although it is impossible to know how entities will react until they are brought together,[43] it is obvious that Border Patrol expected the desert to inflict harm on migrants. This was a point clearly spelled out in the initial 1994 Border Patrol policy plan with a bulleted point that simply reads: "Violence will increase as effects of [Prevention Through Deterrence] are felt."[44] The actants that have been drawn into federal border enforcement have clearly gone above and beyond the call of duty in helping to escalate border violence. Subsequently, each day offers the hybrid collectif an opportunity to create new forms of unimaginable agency.

CHAPTER 3

Necroviolence

EXPERIMENTING WITH DEATH

Everyone knows that something really awful is about to happen, especially the pig. As soon as Freddy gets close, the animal starts jumping back and forth in his tiny metal cage, slamming his head into the sides and grunting loudly. Somehow this pig recognizes the gun and wants nothing to do with it. He is afraid.[1] The desert is quiet this morning; no wind, no birds chirping. All you can hear is grunting and the sound of the cage shaking. Freddy coolly places the .22-caliber pistol a few inches from the pig's head and squeezes the trigger.[2] The gun makes a pathetic pop that is immediately followed by squealing and the cage rattling as it gets kicked by muscular hind legs. A calloused brown hand reaches down and flicks the door open. The 150-pound animal comes staggering out: a punch-drunk boxer at the end of the twelfth round. He loosely steps left and then right before stumbling and falling flat onto the ground. High-pitched squealing. Floating dust. The pig forces himself back up and begins the death dance again. It's a pitiful sight and several bystanders look away. Blood mixed with foamy white cerebrospinal fluid drips out of the quarter-inch hole at the top of his skull. He is screaming in pain.

I have read that this is the most humane way to kill a pig in the field.[3] It sure as hell doesn't feel humane. It's also not instantaneous. The animal keeps falling down and getting back up. He walks in half-circles and defiantly refuses to die. "I gotta do it again," the gunman tells us. "His skull is too thick." Freddy grabs a piece of dirty rope from the back of his truck. I walk over and take hold of the pig's stomach and hind legs. I am trying to be gentle, which is ironic given that I purchased this animal from a university meat vendor for a dollar a pound and paid for someone to come out and kill him on site.

I pull the pig to the ground and Freddy grabs his legs. He literally hog-ties him. The animal is now whipping his head and splashing blood everywhere. It's on the dirt, our boots, our shirts. We try to hold him still, but he starts flopping against the ground. The weight of his body makes a deep dull sound every time it hits the dirt. Thud. Thud. Thud. Puffs of dust rise into the air with each spasm. Deep crimson mixes with the brown soil. "OK, step back." I let go and the pig tries to stand up. In an instant, another shot rings out, and he falls to the ground heavy like a sack of dry cement. This time he can't get up. I drop to my knees and put my hand on his warm body. Blood is dripping from his mouth and forming a shallow pool. I start patting the coarse white hairs on his stomach and whispering, "It's OK. It's OK." A hind leg twitches. One of his large eyes is wide open and seemingly staring at nothing. Dirt and grass are stuck to his cornea. For a few seconds his breathing is rapid and shallow and then it stops. I keep quietly saying, "It's OK," even after he is dead. I keep saying it even though I don't believe it.

Because of their fat distribution, degree of hair, torso size, and internal anatomy, pigs have long been the preferred proxy for a human body in forensic experiments.[4] Scientists shoot them with bullets to measure gunshot residue on their tissue; they kill, bury, and try to find them with ground-penetrating radar; they rub lubricants on their skin in hopes of better understanding trace evidence associated with sexual assault.[5] *Sus scrofa domesticus* is the unsung hero of forensic science experimental research. On this day in the summer of 2013, we are in the midst of conducting a second season of experiments on body decomposition in the desert, and this pig is one of our case studies. After years of listening to migrants, colleagues, Border Patrol, and the media speculate about what happens to corpses left exposed to this environment, I decided to see for myself.

In 2012, three juvenile female pigs were killed, dressed in clothes similar to what migrants wear, and placed in different environmental contexts (e.g., direct sunlight and shade). We monitored the decomposition process via daily field observations and motion sensor cameras that recorded still images and videos of any movement near the animals.[6] In 2013, two adult male pigs (including the one described above) were killed. One was placed in the shade of a large tree, and the other was covered with a pile of rocks and brush mimicking an ad hoc burial. The goals of this research are to observe how fast decomposition happens in the desert and to document the impact that scavenging animals have on bodies.[7] I also want to provide an up-close view of what it looks like when carrion eaters descend on a corpse. This latter aim is connected to my desire to show how the hybrid collectif of border enforcement has set the stage for scavenging animals to come into close and (from a human perspective) violent contact with the bodies of hundreds of fallen border crossers a year. To understand this postmortem violence, I have had to commission several brutal acts against the pigs used in this research.

There is no other way to say it. Killing these animals was violent despite all the precautions we took. They all writhed in pain for upwards of three minutes before succumbing to the gunshots. None of them went peacefully. These acts were justified, I argue, because other than obtaining human bodies that have been donated to science for forensic experiments,[8] I found no feasible alternative to using pigs for this research. I, along with others, have argued that the federal government holds the problematic view that migrants are *bare life*, or individuals whose deaths are of little consequence.[9] My killing of these animals in the name of science thus reeks of hypocrisy.[10] How can someone hope to critique violence against one group while simultaneously carrying it out against another?

I convinced myself that the death of these animals was a means of generating knowledge about a hidden sociopolitical process that affects hundreds of dead bodies a year. Still, this was no easy decision. By highlighting the gruesomeness of these pigs' deaths, something completely avoided in forensic science publications, and providing an up-close perspective of how other animals engage with both human and Suidae bodies in the desert, I strive for what Kirksey and Helmreich call a *multispecies ethnography*; that is, an ethnography that focuses on how the lives and deaths of humans and nonhumans are closely intertwined and jointly shaped by cultural, economic, and political forces.[11] As others have recently done,[12] I too seek to complicate the concept of biopolitics by drawing animals into the equation.

My expansion of the ethnographic lens to encompass more than humans doesn't excuse the fact that I paid to have five sentient beings shot in the head, proceeded to dress them up like Latino border crossers (admittedly another questionable endeavor), and then fed them to nature.[13] The animals described here are agentive creatures that were sacrificed so that I could better document the demise of people the federal government has constructed as nonsubjects; people whose lives have no political or social value. The desert, like the beef slaughterhouse studied by Timothy Pachirat, is a "zone of confinement," a place no upstanding citizen is supposed to see.[14] However, ethnography in this instance is used not just to bear witness to animal suffering but also to demon-

Deceased male pig dressed and placed in shade. Photo by author.

strate how pigs can do the social work of providing humans with access to the largely invisible suffering and violence associated with the postmortem lives of migrants.[15] This is a strange role reversal given that these pigs are beings that many "manage to ignore, to unsee, and unhear as if the only traces of [their] lives are the parts of their bodies rendered into food."[16] These animals are now tasked with humanizing death. My hope is that their demise gets us closer to understanding the intimate connection among animals, insects, the environment, and humans in the Sonoran Desert hybrid collectif.

—————

As soon as the pig is dead, everyone gets to work. We untie his legs, and a graduate student and I drag his lifeless body over to the shade of a large mesquite tree. He is quickly dressed in a bra and underwear, blue jeans, a gray T-shirt, and tennis shoes. These are the same clothing items we would expect a female border crosser to wear. Someone puts a wallet in one of his pockets along with other personal effects, including several coins and a slip of paper with a phone number written on it. A black backpack and bottle of water are placed next to his body. Final checks are made on the angles of the cameras mounted nearby. Batteries are at full power and memory cards are empty and ready to record video data. We turn the machines on and walk back to the field house. In a few days birds will rip this pig to shreds.

NECROPOLITICS

Contrary to the Border Patrol's sterile language ("Prevention Through Deterrence"), feigned naiveté ("this policy has had the *unintended* consequence of increasing the number of fatalities along the border"[17]), and deflection of blame ("Not a day goes by when we don't find immigrants who say they were abandoned by their smuggler"[18]), it is the federal agency that has created an infrastructural funnel along the US-Mexico border that intentionally directs people toward the desert. This arid landscape is the federal government's savvy political-ecological response to Middle America's periodic calls for more border security. It is also a money-generating landscape where overpriced technologies of exclusion underperform (see chapter 6) as they simultaneously fill the coffers of government contractors and the Washington lobbyists whom they have in their back pockets. But what of the human costs of this politicized terrain? How do the lives of those lost to the most extreme forms of "deterrence" articulate with notions of American sovereignty?

Achille Mbembe has critiqued the tendency of Foucault's concept of *biopower* to conflate politics, war, racism, and homicide to the point that they become difficult to disentangle and interrogate individually.[19] This consolidation, he argues, does not adequately account for the specific ways that death and the right to kill (or let live) are exercised in contemporary forms of political power.[20] More generally, rather than seeing politics as simply "a project of autonomy and the achieving of agreement among a collectivity through communication and recognition," Mbembe calls for the pessimistic acknowledgement that, increasingly, the political is masked as war, resistance, security, or the battle against terror. Each one of these endeavors "makes the murder of the enemy its primary and absolute objective."[21] *Necropolitics*, or killing in the name of sovereignty, is not about abstract notions of reason, truth, or freedom. It's about the tangibles of life and death: a suspected terrorist disappears forever into the bowels of Guantanamo Bay;[22] a drone strike in Yemen intended to kill Al Qaeda fighters ends up vaporizing members of a wedding procession;[23] a fifteen-year-old kid walking down a Nogales, Mexico, street is shot in the back eight times by Border Patrol standing on the US side because they thought he was throwing rocks at them.[24] Mbembe may very well have been thinking about the United States when he wrote, "The ultimate expression of sovereignty resides, to a large degree, in the power and the capacity to dictate who may live and who must die."[25]

Even a cursory glance at the technology (e.g., drones and night-vision goggles), discourse ("bodies," "aliens," "Homeland Security"), and casualties associated with southern boundary enforcement (more than 2,600 bodies recovered in Arizona alone since 2000[26]) suggests that a war on noncitizens is in fact taking place on US soil. The geopolitical boundary with Mexico is ground zero where federal law enforcement battle both armed drug smugglers moving loads of *mota* on their backs and Oaxacan peasants running across the boiling sand in *huaraches*. This conflict even makes great television. Just ask the producers of the National Geographic show *Border Wars*, who proudly proclaim they aren't "afraid to show the heartbreaking, jaw-dropping, and action-packed side of issues like illegal immigration and smuggling."[27] American television audiences cheer on their favorite Border Patrol agents as they chase Mexicans through the desert. Stephen King's dystopian boob-tube nightmare *The Running Man* is now reality.

While many people, both citizen and noncitizen, have been shot and killed by Border Patrol in recent years (42 since 2005[28]), of the 2,238 dead migrants examined by the Pima County Office of the Medical Examiner between 1990 and 2012, 1,813 either had a cause of death linked to "exposure or probable exposure" (45% of the 2,238) or had remains too fragmented or decomposed for the cause of death to definitively be determined (36%).[29] Given the location where they were recovered, the people represented by this latter statistic (i.e., rotting bodies and animal-gnawed bone fragments) were likely also killed by "exposure."[30] These numbers represent only bodies that were found.

As the policy documents highlighted in chapter 1 attest, the desert is a tool of boundary enforcement *and* a strategic slayer of border crossers. The federal government doesn't call the policy killing; they call it deterring, and justify it as the cost of guarding the homeland. The fact that this violence has been outsourced to mountains, extreme temperatures, and thousands of square miles of uninhabited terrain does not mean these fatalities should be characterized as "unintended consequences" or natural events. It's not that simple. These deaths are the fruits of an innovation in murder technology, like the guillotine, gas chamber, or the General Atomics MQ-9 Reaper drone—more refined forms of homicide. Nature "civilizes" the way the government deals with migrants; it does the dirty work. As the architects and supporters of PTD are well aware, this policy also cleverly increases the degrees of separation between victim and perpetrator.[31]

The US government has little regard for the rights or lives of border crossers, a point exemplified by a security apparatus that transparently seeks to deter them through pain, suffering, and death. Migrants exist in what Agamben terms a *state of exception*: the process whereby sovereign authorities declare emergencies in order to suspend the legal protections afforded to individuals while simultaneously unleashing the power of the state upon them. The US-Mexico border has long existed as an unspoken *space of exception* where human and constitutional rights are suspended in the name of security.[32] Border crosser deaths are justified by a person's lack of citizenship (i.e., exceptional status), his or her commission of a civil offense, and the hypocritical desire to protect the United States from the very people we rely on to pick our strawberries, pluck our chickens, and valet-park our cars. Lacking rights and protections when they illegally cross into sovereign territory, undocumented people are killable in the eyes of the state. Prevention Through Deterrence is necropower operationalized.

NECROVIOLENCE

As the state's power to kill people in the name of political projects has attracted the attention of social scientists, a growing number of researchers have focused on the postmortem biographies of the dead, including the sociopolitical contexts of burial, the agency of corpses, and the political afterlives of bodies.[33] Many of these studies of death emphasize corpses as actants and focus on how a multitude of cultural, economic, and political factors shape the dead's interactions with the living.[34] Some argue that the reach of modern necropolitics now extends beyond the moment of death: "If the exercise of sovereignty is tantamount to the prerogative of pursuing war on life, then it is equally pertinent to consider its war on the corpse."[35] Although they are unarmed civilians, the bodies of border crossers are not immune to this war.

Hostility directed at the dead is by no means a new cultural phenomenon. Humans have been doing it for millennia and with fervor: Achilles dragging the lifeless body of Hector around the city of Troy; enraged Aztecs mounting the heads of conquistadors and their horses on a *tzompantli* (skull rack) as a not-so-subtle message to Cortez and his men that it is time to evacuate Tenochtitlán;[36] Catholics during the French Wars of Religion feeding the bodies of Protestants to crows and dogs in hopes they would carry their souls to hell.[37] As Foucault notes, excesses of violence are what make these deeds "glorious" to the perpetrators and allow torture to extend beyond the moment a person stops breathing: "Corpses burnt, ashes thrown to the winds, bodies dragged on hurdles and exhibited at roadside. Justice pursues the body beyond all possible pain."[38]

Attention may have shifted during the Enlightenment away from the body as a site of punishment, but waging war on the dead has never stopped being an important cross-cultural practice.[39] The United States is not immune to this impulse, a point driven home recently when four Marine Corps snipers were reprimanded in 2012 after a video was posted on the Internet showing them urinating on the dead bodies of alleged Taliban soldiers. When asked about it later, Sgt. Joseph Chamblin bluntly responded:

> These were the same guys that were killing our family; killing our brothers. . . . We're human. Who wouldn't [want to get revenge] if you lost your brother or mother? Wouldn't you want revenge? . . . If anything it was more of a psychological effect on the enemy because of their cultural belief. If an infidel touches the bodies they're not going to Mecca or to paradise. So now these insurgents see what happens when you mess with us. . . . I didn't do it to be appreciated. I did it because I love my country and love what America stands for. I don't regret my service.[40]

Such forms of humiliation have long functioned as a tool to alienate the victims from their entire social context so that spectators to this violence can be united in feeling morally superior while ridiculing them.[41] In moments of war, the desecration of the enemy's body is practically a cultural universal.[42]

These different engagements with dead bodies are forms of what I term *necroviolence*: violence performed and produced through the specific treatment of corpses that is perceived to be offensive, sacrilegious, or inhumane by the perpetrator, the victim (and her or his cultural group), or both. Unlike Mbembe's necropolitics, which centers on the capacity to "kill or let live" associated with modernity and the exercise of sovereignty, necroviolence is specifically about corporeal mistreatment and its generative capacity for violence. These macabre social processes are ancient and transcend cultural, geographic, and political boundaries. By labeling this phenomenon, I seek both to connect it to modern forms of political power and to provide a framework for facilitating a conversation about this postmortem violence across subdisciplines of anthropology. Much can be learned about ideologies of conflict and social inequality by interrogating necroviolence across time, space, and fields of study.

Corporeal mistreatment has a diverse range of forms and functions. In some cases, postmortem violence is aimed at the victim's spirit, soul, or afterlife, and historical and contemporary examples of this abound. In the *Iliad*, Diomedes tells Paris that "he who faces my spear shall redden the earth with his blood, and there shall be more vultures about his body than women (mourners)."[43] The implication is that Paris's body will be desecrated and his soul robbed of funeral rites. The vultures represent a "threatening and horrifying image of the future," making for a "brutal, degrading, and solitary" death.[44]

A manipulated dead body can also be a vector for violent messages directed at the living.[45] Putumayo Indians were dismembered and decapitated for failing to collect sufficient amounts of rubber for their British overlords.[46] Their body parts became rotting trophies that simultaneously illustrated colonial power over native life and what happens to those who don't work hard enough. Racist mobs in the American Deep South lynched and burned black men, women, and children accused of various indiscretions against whites. These gruesome spectacles were followed by the crowd digging through the ashes for souvenirs while the victim's family waited their turn to collect whatever was left for burial. For the angry mob this dismemberment transformed the corpse into "lynching souvenirs," which erased both the "whole" body and the person who inhabited it, while simultaneously constructing objects that embodied a brutal ritual and represented the "determination to prevent the social ascendancy of African Americans."[47] Mexican drug cartels hung the corpses of their rivals from bridges, skewered their heads on fence posts, and dressed bodies in costumes for media photo ops. You don't have to speak Spanish to understand the message intended when someone rolls a bag of severed heads onto the dance floor in a Michoacán nightclub: "Do not test us, because our violence knows no bounds." Rather than viewing these types of performances as senseless or random, anthropologist Rocío Magaña pointedly demonstrates in her discussion of narcoviolence in Mexico that as a "technique of terror," body mistreatment is a recurrent theme in the construction of state authority and sovereignty, a point long recognized by archaeologists.[48]

Finally, the complete destruction of a corpse constitutes the most complex and durable form of necroviolence humans have yet invented. The lack of a body prevents a "proper" burial for the dead, but also allows the perpetrators of violence plausible deniability.[49] As many recent historical events highlight, corporeal destruction is often a deeply political act. Dissidents during Argentina's Dirty War were naked and sedated when navy officers dropped them from airplanes into the ocean, forever exiling them to oblivion and the status of "disappeared."[50] Forty-three troublemaking students from a teacher's training college in Ayotzinapa, Guerrero, vanished without a trace. Rumors abounded that corrupt local officials and narcotraffickers burned them alive and then disposed of the bodies through various insidious means. The Mexican government says that the investigation is still pending. Although such practices are relatively "subtle" compared to grotesque displays of severed heads and limbs, having no corpse is arguably more sinister in that it robs an enemy of voice and agency and "confines the traces of . . . repression purely to the discursive domain." Eradicating flesh and bone is now part of the postmodern "politics of disappearance."[51]

The erasure of a body also prevents the necessary funeral rites associated with mourning from taking place. It stunts the development of the social relationships that the living need in order to "make sense of the life and death of the deceased" and negotiate (and renegotiate) the positions of the dead inside the living community.[52] What is more troubling about this form of necroviolence is that it places mourners in a permanent state of what clinical psychologist Pauline Boss calls *ambiguous loss*, a loss that remains unclear.[53] Not knowing where your loved one is, if she is dead or alive, is traumatizing and long lasting. This ambiguity "freezes the grief process" and renders closure impossible.[54] It is the form of necroviolence that is seemingly without end.

A brief stroll through the annals of war, conflict, and aggression suggests that necroviolence is a cultural practice whose genealogical tree has deep roots and many branches. It is also a type of violence that can be easily outsourced to animals, nature, or technology. Feeding someone to the dogs, leaving a person to rot on the battlefield, incinerating bodies in an oven: these forms of corpse (mis)treatment all have an intermediary between the human perpetrator and the victim, but nevertheless achieve their primary goal of producing different forms of violence against the dead and the living.

It is the postmortem lives of those who succumb to the Sonoran Desert hybrid collectif that I am most interested in. How does the desert operationalize necroviolence? How can forensic science and a multispecies ethnographic approach make visible a violence intended to be inaccessible to the human eye? What physically happens to the bodies of the people killed by nature and left to decompose in its embrace? What can animals scavenging a corpse tell us about the political nature of migrant fatalities? In what follows, I argue that the unique deaths that border crossers experience and the ways nature affects their bodies are a form of postmortem violence that developed out of the underlying logic of Prevention Through Deterrence. When examined as part of the hybrid collectif of desert deterrence, the seemingly "natural" physical, chemical, and biological processes of decomposition show themselves to be political facts representative of the value placed on the lives and deaths of undocumented people. These facts become inscribed upon the bones of the dead.[55]

TAPHONOMIES OF VIOLENCE

How we have physically handled corpses through all time periods of protohuman and human existence has been of major interest to anthropologists.[56] The depth of the grave, the position of the body, the items commingled with the skeleton: the postmortem treatment of the dead tells much about the cultural perspective of the living. It is not, however, just the actions of the deceased's loved ones that impact their physical remains. Depending on the scenario and timing, wind, rain, groundwater, insects, chemicals in the soil, grave robbers, floods, gravity, and animals are but a few of the multiple factors that can transform bodies.[57] Soviet paleontologist Ivan Efremov coined the phrase *taphonomy* in the 1940s to refer to the analysis of the combination of human and nonhuman elements that impact biological remains.[58] In its modern usage, taphonomy is typically considered "the science of postmortem processes,"[59] or the "study of the phenomena that affect the remains of biological organisms at the time of and after death."[60] It is also a crucial element of many forms of necroviolence.

Interest in taphonomy gained traction in the 1970s, especially among archaeologists focused on the biasing effect that postmortem events have on the material record (e.g., how erosion impacts burials). Their goal was usually to find ways to strip these effects away under the assumption that the only thing nonhumans did was destroy important "cultural" information.[61] By the 1980s people began to recognize that some of these nonhuman processes were in and of themselves quite interesting.[62] For example, rather than seeing scavenging animals as only negatively impacting archaeological data, paleoanthropologist Pat Shipman argued that identifying their presence taphonomically could be used to test theories of early hominid hunting and scavenging.[63] Still, despite some groundbreaking work on postdepositional patterns, taphonomy continues to be a source of confusion for some researchers, particularly archaeologists who have erroneously tried to exclude cultural processes or human behaviors from the definition.[64]

Whether it is pounding on a corpse with a wooden mallet to render it useless to grave-robbing witches or interring bodies in soils that quickly lead to mummification,[65] all processes that impact dead organisms are "taphonomic." Recognition of this fact has been an important step toward overcoming the nature-culture dichotomy that has often stunted our analytical ability to understand the complex intermingling of animals, insects, humans, and environmental processes that occurs once a body stops pumping blood. By far the most important contribution to this more nuanced anthropological understanding of depositional and postdepositional patterns comes from anthropologist Shannon Dawdy: "Taphonomy describes the complexity, the mix of accident and manipulation, the silences and erasures, the constraining structures, and the sudden ruptures that all go into the creation of history and into the formation of the 'ethnographic present.' . . . [Taphonomic] processes are not simply an archaeological mirror of social processes—they are social processes."[66] Building on this idea that taphonomy is a social process constructed of equal parts human and nonhuman, animal and mineral, living and dead, I argue that the postmortem events that affect the bodies of migrants in the desert are a form of necroviolence largely outsourced to nature and the environment but intimately tied to Prevention Through Deterrence, territorial sovereignty, and the exceptional (i.e., killable and disposable) status the US government ascribes to undocumented border crossers. Rather than stripping away the net effect of processes that erase biological information, in the following discussion I illustrate the destructive and inhumane elements of taphonomy in the Arizona desert and how they produce violence.

DESERT TAPHONOMY

Before the Undocumented Migration Project began experiments in 2012, only two academic publications had focused on human body decomposition in the Sonoran Desert.[67] These studies were based exclusively on retrospective analyses of coroner reports from the 1970s and 1980s when most of the deaths in this region were murder victims, individuals who died of natural causes in their homes, or US citizens who went missing in the desert.[68] This forensic research predated the era of Prevention Through Deterrence and thus did not address the skyrocketing number of border crosser fatalities in the early 2000s associated with this policy or the unique demographic and depositional profiles of this particular population.[69]

These two published reports improved our understanding of some of the unique taphonomic conditions found in the Arizona desert, but the data they presented have been relatively difficult to correlate with migrant death. This is because border crossers die in depositional contexts different from those of murder victims buried in shallow graves or people who expire in their houses and are shielded from the outside environment and wild animals. Moreover, while both of the previous studies briefly mention scavengers, primarily coyotes and dogs,[70] their presence is inferred from skeletal analyses, and there are no data from direct observations of animals interacting with bodies. Surprisingly, neither study mentions vultures, a long-recognized member of the Sonoran scavenging guild.[71] Because migrants often die in remote areas and lie undiscovered for months or years (or are never recovered), it has been difficult to document what decomposition looks like over time or how animals engage with corpses. The following descriptions attempt to make these hidden postmortem processes visible via experimental research.

"Fresh"

When death approaches in the Sonoran Desert, there are few places to hide. The region has no giant oaks or cool elms to seek refuge under; just spindly cacti and bony paloverdes. If you can find shade, it is a luxury that often lasts only as long as the sun sits still. Anyone dying of dehydration or hyperthermia may or may not have their wits about them, but they may be aware enough to crawl under the nearest tree to temporarily get away from the light.[72] Unfortunately, the shelter found in the early-morning shade of a scraggly mesquite may not last long. By noon the sun is staring directly down at you, its rays easily cutting between the narrow green leaves (if you can call them leaves) and baking the ground underneath you. To protect yourself, you end up having to chase the *sombra*, jumping from shadow to shadow like a dog on a hot summer afternoon. Border crossers on the verge of death often huddle under trees, only to be found later dead after being rotisserie-cooked by the rotating sun.[73]

The pig described at the start of this chapter was dressed and placed upright in the shade, leaning against the trunk of a large mesquite tree. The animal sat for four days relatively undisturbed.[74] In the mornings his body was shaded and in the afternoons it was exposed to direct sunlight. During the course of an average day the air temperature around him fluctuated between 50 and 120 degrees Fahrenheit.

If you have ever come across a carcass left out in the open that is in the early stages of rot, you know such bodies are miniature biological laboratories. Flies buzz around. Ants crawl on skin. Maggots shuffle inside of mouths and nostrils. Gases build up and are then expelled. Over the course of just a few days this is what happened to the pig's body as it passed through the "fresh" and "early" stages of decomposition.[75] His skin became discolored and began to slip; his stomach ballooned; maggot activity became intensive. Swelling in the legs and abdomen caused one of his shoes to fall off and his shirt to ride up, exposing his fleshy white belly. Fluids dripped from the anus and the umbilical area, staining both his pants and the surrounding ground. As his body slowly mutated and expanded, scavenging birds patiently sat in nearby trees waiting for their moment. It took five days before turkey vultures (*Cathartes aura*), the most widely distributed carrion bird in the New World,[76] descended upon him.

Meet Cathartes aura

Get up early enough in the Sonoran Desert to watch the sunrise and you may catch a glimpse of a turkey vulture perched high in a tree. She sits motionless with her large black wings spread open to the sun. Her red fleshy head is turned to the side. For those unfamiliar with this bird, the first view of this posture can be frightening. The large wings and hooked beak cast a long shadow across the desert floor. It looks like the ending of most vampire movies, when the cloaked protagonist raises his gangly arms in terror as he meets the punishing rays of the sun. For turkey vultures, this posture is less about drama and more about thermoregulation and feather drying. This stance, however, illustrates that despite having a mass of only about 2 kilograms, these birds are large (average length, 64–81 centimeters) with an impressive wing span. It can be even more intimidating to see these animals out on the migrant trail when their silhouette moves rapidly back and forth across your path. Unlike the Old World griffon vultures (*Gyps fulvus*) in Spain and southern France, which have reportedly started to kill and eat cattle,[77] *Cathartes aura* (roughly translated as "purifying breeze") is almost exclusively an opportunistic feeder of wild and domestic carrion.[78] Since the late 1990s this carrion has included the flesh of dead migrants.

Turkey vultures rely on a highly developed olfactory sense to find carcasses in the optimal state of decay. In other words, these creatures specialize in eating the rotting dead, those left unburied. But even when a carcass is located, these birds may observe from a distance for days before approaching. Researchers posit that the dead flesh of large mammals has to reach a particular level of putrefaction (with its associated aroma) before these animals will commence feeding. As Eduardo Kohn's Runa informants in the Upper Amazon of Ecuador say, "What we humans perceive as the stench of rotting carrion, a vulture experiences as the sweet-smelling vapor emanating from a boiling pot of manioc tubers."[79] It took 120 hours before the vapors emanating from this pig's body were sweet-smelling enough to convince *Cathartes aura* that it was time to eat.

The three birds to approach at daybreak are timid. Unsure if the pig is dead, they pace around the body and avoid close contact. A motion sensor camera mounted on the ground catches several close-up shots of their blood-red heads and black eyes. Their ivory beaks, like tiny meat hooks evolved to flesh-tearing perfection, cut a sharp profile across the picture frame. It's 5:30 A.M. and a cool 52 degrees outside, but the temperature is quickly rising. More pacing and circling; it goes on for hours. Finally, at 8:37 A.M. one of the vultures makes a bold move and darts in to rip a piece of tongue away. The pig doesn't move, so the bird goes in again. A few more nervous pecks. Small hesitant chunks are ripped from the mouth and neck. It flinches with each bite, expecting the pig to yelp or squirm. No movement, so it tugs on a leg. Nothing. Within seconds a beak is ripping at the urogenital opening on the pig's stomach.

The feeding builds slowly, a grotesque crescendo. Talons claw at pink flesh as one of the brave pioneers climbs on top of him. Another bird continues to rip at the hole in the stomach, the pig's stiff body reluctantly rocking with each bite. Others continue to pace as if planning an attack strategy in their bird brains. Flies loudly buzz in and out of the camera view. At 10:33 A.M. the stomach starts to bleed and ooze through various puncture wounds. These holes have caused the abdominal cavity to deflate, and pungent gases are slowly expelled into the air. Shadows pass overhead from all directions. A bird flies across the camera frame and shows off its silvery gray ventral feathers. It is 90 degrees and someone has rung the communal dinner bell.

The bird picking at the stomach makes a breakthrough and draws out a two-foot piece of intestine. The body teeters as it is opened up. The chunk of diges-

26.13 inHg - 111°F 06/26/2013 05:56PM SHADE

Vulture scavenging activity recorded by motion-sensor camera.

tive tract is inhaled in just a few seconds. Immediately two more vultures swoop down and start jockeying for position. Black wings with silver undersides are spread in hopes of intimidating a rival. According to ornithological field reports, "Feeding vultures rarely tolerate conspecifics at carcass; usually only 1 bird feeds, sometimes 2, although others may wait nearby."[80] By 11 A.M., six birds are simultaneously feeding on him. On the camera audio you can hear flesh ripping and feathers ruffling. More entrails have been exposed. Claws crunch down on dried grass as creatures play tug of war with a long piece of pink meat. It is now 100 degrees. The pace of the feeding continues to build.

Eight are eating. Then it's nine. Others gather around and watch from the trees. More approach the body. Heads boldly dive into flesh. It soon becomes difficult to count them. There are black wings everywhere. Three vultures stand on the body picking at the stomach, while others go for any other open skin. Flesh rips; wings extend. Newcomers swoop in. At one point as many as twenty-two birds will be near the body to feed, with another eight monitoring from a close distance. He is completely surrounded. The piles of defleshed bones and ripped migrant clothes found over the past fifteen years make it clear that this scene has happened, and continues to happen, to the bodies of mothers, fathers, daughters, and husbands who have died while crossing the desert. The feeding rages on.

A black vulture (*Coragyps atratus*) shows up and is swiftly pushed out of the way. The fighting has started: low guttural hissing, biting, more intimidating wing displays. You can't see the body anymore. There is just a giant black ball of moving feathers. Every orifice and piece of exposed skin has small white beaks nimbly picking at it. More entrails shoot out of the stomach like a magician's handkerchief; it looks as if it will go on forever. Two red faces step back to fight over the stomach contents. Another set of birds aggressively flare their wings and crash into each other as they tussle for a feeding position. The loser is pinned to the ground by his rival's more powerful claws. During these brief bouts a leg or the head is momentarily exposed to the camera only to be quickly obscured by a new set of feathers. The T-shirt is ripped to expose untouched skin. A barrage of ivory beaks snap at meat, snap at one another. Birds continue to swoop in and out. Dust and feathers are everywhere. The body lies helpless as talons and beaks manipulate and destroy it. It is 11:17 A.M. It is 108 degrees.

This scene goes on all day and varies in intensity between daybreak and sunset. When the number of vultures eating decreases, it becomes possible to observe individual animals meticulously working the body over. Claws keep digging into flesh as they try to steady themselves for better tearing. By noon, the other shoe and both socks have been removed. As the sun starts heading west, beaks dig deeper into open holes. Sporadic fighting continues. The birds tear more clothes, exposing every last bit of precious organ meat and muscle. The temperature gets as high as 122 degrees. As the sun goes down, a few stragglers keep working. The shoes and socks have been moved several feet away from the now deflated body.

The sun rises the following day and casts a soft orange light on the now ravaged figure. The shirt is torn to pieces and covered in blood, other bodily fluids, and vulture shit. Black feathers decorate the ground around the body. Early-morning camera footage shows some birds patiently waiting in trees, while from high above shadows zigzag. Once there is enough light, they descend again. More hissing, more ripped flesh. By 12:30 P.M. an enterprising vulture has managed to remove the blue jeans and the underwear. While one bird digs at the flesh stuck to the denim pant legs, another crams its head deep into the anus, demonstrating the selective pressure to evolve featherless heads. This is the hybrid collectif at work, and it will once again continue unabated until nightfall.

Pig head and femur after several days of vulture scavenging. Photo by Michael Wells.

Just like the previous two days of feeding, the third starts at daybreak. The difference is that by now the body is a pathetic shell of what it used to be. Even though the bulk of the viscera and muscle were consumed within the first forty-eight hours, the birds keep working. One of them finally manages to rip the shirt off and expose the red bra underneath. The shoes and pants are nowhere to be seen. Hooked bills continue to pick at the remaining meat, though there is not much left beyond skin and bone. Ribs and femurs are defleshed and exposed. Maggots work on what little tissue remains between the vertebrae. By the end of the day he is reduced to a mummified skin suit with the red bra still attached. The body is now light enough for birds to pick up and move around to access any remaining meat. Later, some skeletal elements and personal effects will be recovered over 50 meters from their original location. *Cathartes aura* will continue to scavenge at the remaining spine and skull for fourteen more days until we stop the experiment and collect what bones we can find.

Replication

This experiment was repeated several times with similar results.[81] Every animal that we dressed in clothes and left exposed to the elements was eventually picked clean by scavengers. The pig we placed in direct sunlight at the top of a small hill in 2012 rotted for seventeen days before vultures became interested, a delay likely caused by early rains that came that summer. During this time, however, coyotes (*Canis latrans*) and domestic dogs (*Canis lupus familiaris*) from a neighboring residence were spotted ripping chunks of back meat and chewing pieces of ruptured intestines. A map of migrant deaths that have occurred in southern Arizona in the past two decades reveals that many people die near rural residences while seeking help.[82] A number of canine companions in this region likely have dined on human flesh and then trotted home to lick their owner's face.

When vultures did finally approach this particular animal, it took eight of them only twenty-four hours to completely skeletonize the body. For two days they scattered bones and personal effects as far as 27 meters away from the original site of death. In the end, our survey recovered 66 percent of this animal's bones. The great distances from the skeleton that many of the clothes she was wearing were carried would, in a human death scenario, make it difficult to connect personal effects to a corpse. Even though the body was placed in a semi-enclosed area and an extensive surface survey was conducted, the card with a phone number that we placed inside her pants pocket was never found.

In 2012, we also laid a female pig under a mesquite tree several hundred meters from the one left in direct sunlight. She was visited on numerous occasions by two local dogs that sniffed her, moved the body with their paws, and urinated on her. The intense scavenging of this animal's body by vultures did not occur until twenty-two days after death. Over the course of five days, between two and eight birds were recorded intermittently feeding and attempting to remove her clothing. It took approximately twenty-five days for her to be completely skeletonized, and afterward vultures were spotted circling the area and sporadically moving bones and clothes across the landscape. Parts of her were carried as far as 20 meters from the original death site. In addition, the slip of paper with a phone number written on it that was inserted into her pocket was found 20 meters from where the body was originally placed and not directly associated with any clothes or bones. After only five weeks of exposure to the elements, we recovered just 62 percent of her skeleton. Had we not collected the remaining bones, scavenging would have continued. This constant physical movement and destruction of body parts and personal effects suggests that with enough time, a person left to rot on the ground can disappear completely.

Burying the Dead

The old man is lying on a bunk in the Juan Bosco shelter, blankly staring up at the ceiling. He is wearing a white button-down shirt, brown polyester slacks, and dusty black dress shoes. I notice him because it is 6 P.M. and no one is supposed to be in the men's dormitory for at least another two hours. I say hello as I pass him on the way to the kitchen, but he either ignores me or doesn't hear. I ask Samuel, one of the shelter workers, who he is. He tells me, "They just brought him in. His wife died out in the desert and they had to leave her body behind. Can you imagine that? They just covered her up and left her." He is in shock. That's why he gets to lie down early. Even in this space, where everyone is in dire straits, there is a clear hierarchy of suffering.[83] The old man will remain mute for the entire evening. At one point two shelter workers will take him by the arms and escort him to the kitchen. His feet barely leave the ground as he shuffles down the hall. He sits quietly and stares at an untouched bowl of beans for twenty minutes before being escorted back to his bed. There is nothing left to say.

Later I am sitting with another shelter volunteer named Patricio, and we talk about death in the desert. He tells me:

> Sometimes on the trail you will see pieces of skin or pieces of human bone. I think it's people who stayed behind. It's coyotes or I don't know what kind of animal [eats them]. People get left behind. People who get cramps get left behind and then they get eaten. All that's left is bone.

Jason: Have you seen this on the trail?

Patricio: Yes, I don't think they are animal or deer bones because they are normal looking. They look like leg and knee bones, ankles, an arm with finger bones.

I show him a photograph of a pile of rocks I encountered while hiking.

Jason: Have you ever seen something like this in the desert?

Patricio: Yeah. Sometimes when people die, they cover them with rocks. It's like when they can't dig a hole they will cover the bodies with rocks so that desert animals can't get to them. That's why they do it. A lot of times it's when a family member or someone from your group dies. They will organize the group to do this.

Three months after this conversation I am piling brush and rocks on top of a dead pig. I tell two other students working on the experiment that we have fifteen minutes to cover the body and we can only use our hands to break branches and carry stones. This is what I imagine a hasty burial would be like if someone in my group died en route. Rocks from a 20-meter radius are collected and carried over to the body. Bare hands bleed as we rip dried mesquite branches off trees and pile them up. We finish covering the body and turn the cameras on.

Placing material on top of a dead body to protect it from the elements and animals seems logical, which is why migrants often do it. In preparing our experiment, we too anticipated that this activity would slow the rate of scavenging. What we failed to remember is that rocks are excellent for conducting and retaining heat. That's why you find them in ancient hearths and modern saunas. Encasing this body in stones in the middle of the summer when midday temperatures were in the low 100s had the opposite effect of what we expected. The rocks quickly absorbed the sun's radiation and ended up cooking the body. Of all our experiments, the rate of scavenging by vultures was fastest when we built this ad hoc cairn. Winged shadows circled the body within forty-eight hours and feeding began on the third day. The birds easily picked between the brush and cobblestones. Some bones and clothing were immediately carried as far as 20 meters away from the original death site. The pig was skeletonized in less than a day. In the end, all that was left under the rocks and brush were two polished leg bones and a moist pair of blue jeans.

DESERT NECROVIOLENCE

Differential treatment or deposition of remains reflects the beliefs
and attitudes of the agents involved.
—Komar 2008:123

Unless you are a Tibetan Buddhist making a final offering of generosity via a *sky burial* or you knowingly donate your body for a forensic science experiment involving raptors,[84] having your corpse ripped apart and devoured by vultures and your remains scattered to the wind is what many would call a "bad death"—a death that occurs in the wrong place and at the wrong time. It's a demise that signals a loss of control and inhibits the performance of culturally appropriate burial procedures and rites.[85]

For the predominantly Roman Catholic people who migrate from Latin America, this destruction of the corpse is threatening for at least two religious reasons. An absent body makes it virtually impossible to have a wake for the deceased and prevents the family from constructing a grave where they may visit the dead and pray for his or her soul. On an ideological level, a destroyed or incomplete corpse is seen as a threat to the afterlife in that it may stop people from rising from the dead to be judged at the end of time.[86] This breach of Catholic burial norms in the desert is "symbolically potent, as an exceptional and avowedly demeaning act."[87] Close examination also reveals it to be an inhumane handling of remains even for secular people or some enemies.[88] This necroviolence reflects the physical and symbolic disregard that border enforcement policies like Prevention Through Deterrence have perpetuated against migrants. Such taphonomic events have systematically occurred for more than a decade, and we can now add it to the tail end of the social process of undocumented migration.[89] Dying in the desert has become routinized enough to now warrant labeling it.

This (mis)treatment of bodies is an ethical concern, but the physical destruction by the environment has other implications. The remote locations where people die, the rapid scavenging of corpses, and the destruction of clothes, personal effects, and bones by various processes mean that the current death tally for the desert undercounts the actual number of people who die out there. The hybrid collectif destroys evidence and there are few witnesses to this act. Flesh is shredded by beaks, bone is cracked by mammalian canines, and ants carry off what is left.[90] Nature sanitizes the killing floor. Given what we now know about desert taphonomy, it is clear that there will never be an accurate death count, a point echoed in a 2006 Government Accountability Office report titled *Border Crossing Deaths Have Doubled Since 1995*: "The fact that a number of bodies may remain undiscovered in the desert also raises doubts about the accuracy of counts of migrant deaths. . . . [T]he total number of bodies that have not been found is ultimately unknown."[91]

This destruction of corpses erases evidence of the human costs of federal policy and simultaneously sends shock waves of grief back to the families of missing migrants, whose members are left wondering whether their wife or son, husband or daughter is dead or alive. Drawing parallels with those in Latin America whose loved ones disappeared during moments of political conflict, many have adopted and repurposed the term *desaparecidos* to refer to those swallowed up by the desert and never heard from again.[92] My graphic descriptions of what happens to bodies are not meant just to shock. The broader goal of this chapter is to contextualize the bones of border crossers in the desert geopolitical landscape, make manifest the hidden deaths and post-mortem lives of migrants, and show that these violent taphonomies are logical extensions of a political process. As this book progresses, I add names, faces, and life histories to ravaged human remains in the desert.

––––––––––

The federal government has knowingly created a border security infrastructure that puts people in harm's way. The "natural" processes that impact or destroy bodies may be carried out by animals, insects, and various chemical and environmental actants, but they are nevertheless part of a larger enforcement paradigm designed by the Border Patrol. The vultures eating flesh and ripping clothes represent the final stage of "deterrence" that emerges from this hybrid collectif. While at various moments the US government has expressed sympathy for migrant deaths, this usually occurs only when considered a politically savvy move.[93] However, officials have never accepted direct responsibility for setting the death machine in motion. Describing necroviolence in the desert operationalizes less obvious elements of deterrence and illustrates how this theory can help us better understand the context, form, function, and effect of postmortem violence that largely happens out of sight. Like Agamben's camp, the desert is a remote *deathscape* where American necropolitics are pecked onto the bones of those we deem excludable.[94] This desert ossuary is eerily similar to archaeological descriptions of medieval and early modern times in places like Ireland: "There is . . . a patterning to the location of remains within the centers of power: the heads and body parts tend to occur at the boundaries of the medieval sites. Placing the remains in liminal locations would have amplified the visual messages sent to those both inside and outside the settlement while also reinforcing the symbolic exclusion of those whose body parts were treated in this manner."[95] Looking at the bodies left in the desert reveals what the physical boundary of sovereignty and the symbolic edge of humanity look like.

Postscript

Vicente is sitting under a mesquite tree on the side of a dirt road when Bob Kee and I encounter him one afternoon while leaving the Coronado National

Forest. From a seated position he waves a weary hand to attract our attention. Had we been driving fast, we would have missed him. Vicente is a short portly man in his late forties. His clothes are sweat-stained and tattered and he is carrying a jug half-filled with opaque water. He can barely stand up to greet us. "I was with a group but they left us behind. A lady and I couldn't keep up with the guide. I left her on the trail by a big tree and went to get help," he tells us. This was hours ago. Vicente is in bad shape and obviously needs to go to the hospital. His story unravels as he gingerly drinks the water we have given him:

> I live in Idaho and was deported a week ago for driving without a license. I need to get back because I was supposed to have internal surgery next week. I just need to get back to my family. They need me. Can you tell me how far it is to Idaho? I have to keep going.

Every aspect of him radiates desperation: his voice, his eyes, his physical movements. What can you possibly say to someone in this condition? Bob and I walk a few feet away to discuss the situation. We decide that to let him continue walking would likely be a death sentence. There is no way he will make it another day by himself. We talk to Vicente about his physical state and his family.

> *Bob:* Vicente, you can die out there alone. You are in no condition to keep walking. Tucson is over forty miles away and Idaho is even farther.[96]
>
> *Vicente:* I have to keep going. I need to get back to my family.
>
> *Bob:* We know you don't want to go to the hospital or back to Mexico, but we think your family would want you to be alive. Will you please let us call an ambulance?

He nods his head and looks down at the ground. It's too much for him to handle—the physical strain of walking so far, the mental anguish of being removed from his family, the desperation to keep going at any costs. He starts weeping. Someone puts an arm around him. We dial 911. An hour later we watch paramedics load Vicente into the back of an ambulance. We then get into our vehicle and start driving around the desert aimlessly until the sun sets. We are looking for a lady who was left on the trail near a big tree.

Memo y Lucho en el camino, Desierto de Sonora, Agosto 2009. Photo by Ángel.

CHAPTER 4

Memo and Lucho

I lend myself to the social game, I pose, I know I am posing, I want you to know that I am posing, but . . . this additional message must in no way alter the precious essence of my individuality: what I am apart from any effigy.

—Roland Barthes, *Camera Lucida*

¡VACAS MEXICANAS!

I am laughing uncontrollably and can't help it. The more I laugh, the more animated Memo gets. He has a captive audience and he knows it. If Cantinflas, the iconic Mexican comedic actor known for his humorous and satirical portrayals of peasants, had a chubby brother who actually did real manual labor, it would be Memo. They both have round faces, dark mustaches, and contagious smiles. They both have sarcasm down to a science. The difference is that Memo doesn't have the Hollywood look, unless your image of Hollywood involves the men who landscape the lawns of movie stars' homes on Sunset Boulevard. His scarred arms, fractured teeth, and weatherworn face reflect a life of economic hardship and rough living, much of which has taken place for the past two decades in the fruit fields of Fresno, California. He embodies the *habitus*[1] of the Mexican working class, which also includes being able to turn a tragic tale into a funny and ironic story.

Memo reminds me of my now dead Tío Cruz, which is probably why I instantly liked him. Tío Cruz was born in the Mexican state of Zacatecas and spent most of his life living, working, and drinking hard in the Rio Grande Valley of Texas. He loved to tell dirty jokes and is the person who taught me how to appreciate the important cultural role of Mexican *chingaderas*, the working-class verbal "play routines" that are laden with humor, sexually charged double entendres, and expletives.[2] This included referring to me only as *pinche cabron* for many years, until I turned nine and looked the words up in the dictionary. I bawled my eyes out when I read one of the literal translations and thought that my uncle had been calling me a "goddamn bastard" for close to a decade. I still remember the smell of cigarette smoke and his cheap cologne when Cruz sat me on his bony knee and said, "Don't be sad, Yason![3] It just means that I love you, you little bastard!"

At almost forty years old, he might not have movie-star good looks, but Memo has the cadence, mannerisms, and timing of a seasoned joke teller. This includes knowing when and how to appropriately call someone a *cabron* for comedic effect. Memo's partner in crime is Lucho, who is seven years older, a foot taller, and twenty pounds lighter.[4] Lucho is dark-skinned with an unbelievably mellow disposition. He always seems to have a slight grin on his face. It's as if he is in on some secret that he wishes he could tell you but can't. Lucho has also lived and worked undocumented for more than thirty years in various manual labor jobs in California and Arizona, but has managed to keep a perfect set of teeth and doesn't show the physical wear and tear that Memo does. From first appearances, he also seems the more serious of the two. However, as soon as Memo starts in on his story, Lucho adopts the role of comedic foil, interjecting colorful details and infectious cackles. Their tandem storytelling is effective: I am laughing hard, even though it feels inappropriate to be carrying on like this in a shelter for recently deported migrants.

> *Memo:* Supposedly he knew the route.[5]
>
> *Lucho:* He didn't know nothing! [laughs]
>
> *Memo:* He had passed two or three times, right?
>
> *Lucho:* No way, he'd never been.
>
> *Memo:* That's what he said.
>
> *Lucho:* Then why did he get lost?
>
> *Jason:* This is the person you crossed the desert with the first time?
>
> *Memo:* Yeah, García. He was an older man in his sixties that we met in detention. We went with him because he said he knew the way. He said he had crossed there three years before.
>
> *Lucho:* We climbed this hill and then crossed a fence. It was getting dark and there were trucks driving by.
>
> *Memo:* It was near the Mariposa [border port of entry]. We crossed this fence and kept walking and walking. We walked a long ways and then finally sat down to rest. Then García says, "OK, we crossed over. We are here in the

United States." It was dark and hard to see. I said, "Are you sure?" He says, "Yeah, we are here. We made it. I crossed through here three years ago." We saw cars going by and thought they were Border Patrol so we hid under a tree.

Lucho: We sat there for a long time and waited. Then we saw this couple walking by way off in the distance. We got really worried that they were lost.

Memo: I started yelling at them, "Hey! Are you OK? Do you need some water?" I wanted to try and give them some water because those poor things didn't have anything with them. No backpack or anything. They stopped for a second and waved at us. I kept yelling at them to give them water but they just waved. I started getting really scared for them because they could get robbed by *bajadores*. They didn't seem worried, though, and just kept walking. We got up and kept going. A little while later we came across a bunch of trash piles. I said, "García, are you sure we are in the US? This place is filthy! I don't think gringos are this dirty." He kept reassuring me that we had crossed.

Lucho: [snickering] Then we walked pass this corral full of cows.

Memo: When I saw the cows, I started getting really suspicious [laughing]. I said, "Hey García, these fucking cows are skinny, man! Look how ugly these cows are! Gringos have fat cows! Gringos have good-looking cows! You bastard! These goddamn cows are Mexican! [¡*Oye cabron! ¡Estos pinches vacas son mexicanas!*] What the fuck! We are still in Mexico!" [all of us laughing]

Lucho: That's why that couple didn't stop to talk to us. We were on the Mexican side and they thought we were crazy. They were on a date and he was walking her home or something!

Memo: What a fucking adventure! We were lost all night on the Mexican side trying to hide from trucks crossing *into* Mexico [laughs]. We finally figured out where the fence was and crossed over. We eventually ran out of water and a few days later García got sick from drinking from a cattle tank. He was vomiting and had bad diarrhea.

Lucho: They caught us in Agua Linda [Arizona]. We spent like five nights in the desert. García couldn't walk anymore, so we turned ourselves in. We weren't going to leave him behind. We left Nogales together. We had a pact. If someone can't go on, we would turn ourselves in. No one would get left behind. For example, if one of us gets sick, we turn ourselves in, or I would run to the store to find a pay phone to call 911 to say that my friend was dying or that he was left behind. This is what happened with García. He got really sick. His stomach was bad. [Tone changes to serious.] We came back and took him to the hospital in Nogales. He went back to Mexico City after that.

When I first heard this story, it had happened only a few weeks before. Memo and Lucho had returned to Mexico with García, and the two of them had then attempted a second desert crossing and once again failed. Both of these events were recounted to me with a great deal of laughter. These humorous reframings of a tragic story, however, were not unique instances. Over many years of interviewing hundreds of people, joking was commonly used to describe difficult or painful border-crossing experiences. For many of my male interlocutors, humor played a complex role in storytelling and remembering, which some outsiders might erroneously reduce to stereotypical *macho* behavior or refusals to appear vulnerable to the researcher.

As Latino studies scholar José Limón points out, these linguistically spirited moments are "dynamic forums that interactionally produce meaning, mastering anxiety by inverting passive destiny through active play."[6] The humor, expletives, subtle forms of irony, and self-deprecation that color many people's stories, which are often referred to as *chingaderas*[7] or *pendejadas*, are key elements of Mexican working-class subjectivity, as well as important forms of resistance and migrant identity construction.[8]

The seemingly light moments that characterize some of the tales that Memo, Lucho, and others tell in this book should be taken seriously. This humor reflects an understanding of people's own precarious social positions and at times functions as a "weapon of the weak" as migrants discursively resist the power of the US federal government to deter them from crossing.[9] Border crossers may not always have a deep understanding of the complexities of state power or immigration enforcement strategies, but as individuals they experience both on a daily basis, either when attempting to cross the border illegally or while living undocumented in the United States. The joking that occurs on many occasions described in this book happens within, and is shaped by, not just "Mexican working-class culture" but also the systems of federal immigration policy and capitalism. Migrant humor can highlight the tensions experienced during various parts of the crossing process, soften the blows of border enforcement and social marginalization in Mexico and the United States, and help people stay positive and focused. As one of Manuel Peña's informants in his study of Mexican fruit pickers in Central California remarked, "We carry on like this—taunting and joking—to make light of things for a moment, to forget the problems of life for a moment—the toil, the struggle."[10]

I realized early on that being a male researcher from a working-class Latino background often influenced the ways people interacted with me and how they recounted their crossing stories. Many of the men I spoke to told their hard-luck tales through the lens of *chingaderas* because they knew that I would understand the nuances of this linguistic frame.[11] This included peppering their narratives with expletives, sexual innuendos, and jokes at my expense. However, these *chingaderas* were not intended to insult me, but rather functioned as a form of speech play that signaled the *confianza* and *respeto* that the men I interviewed accorded me.[12] In this *contexto*, to be the butt of your male interlocutors' sexual jokes signals trust and also softens the division between worlds.

It is not surprising that graphic and sexually charged Mexican humor in the context of often traumatic border crossings has been largely ignored by social scientists. This is likely the result of the cultural and class differences between researchers (who are predominantly middle-class, white non-native-Spanish speakers or educated middle-class Mexicans) and their informants.[13] Either border crossers have been speaking to researchers and journalists using relatively formal language, or the jokes have been going right over people's heads. My sense is that a combination of both of these factors has tended to paint crossing stories as completely serious endeavors devoid of humor or irony. This effect could also be complicated by the tendency of some researchers to paint their subjects as noble creatures who don't swear or crack anal-sex jokes at the drop of a hat. Moreover, many of those who have written about *chingaderas,* at least in the classic literature on border culture, have tried to delegitimize its cultural importance and reduce it to simple linguistic manifestations of sexual anxiety, humiliation, and macho aggression.[14]

I do not mean to say that being a Latino gives me privileged insight into the plight of border crossers, but only that many of the people I interviewed felt comfortable enough to dispense with linguistic formalities and knew that I had the cultural competency to understand their use of *pendejadas* in various contexts. The tension between my roles as an insider (Latino male) and as an outsider (a university professor) allowed me to share in the "thickness" of border-crossing culture without foolishly thinking that my ethnicity alone would somehow give me an emic perspective into the desperation required to enter the desert.[15]

When I asked Memo once about his joking and his attempts to stay positive, his response included a mix of humor and sorrow:

> *Memo:* Imagine that we are walking on a giant mountain. You can't start thinking this mountain is going to be too difficult. I tell people you have to be

positive; be energized to keep moving forward. You have to pretend that you are on a picnic. I just say, "Let's go climb this little hill!" You have to have jokes while you're doing it, to keep going, to persevere, to stay energized. I just say, "We are going to keep going" and stay happy and positive. Some people will ask me, "Hey, aren't you exhausted?" I tell them of course I am exhausted but we need to stay positive. . . . Imagine how good tortillas taste when you have walked that far. They are cold, hard, but so tasty [laughing] when you are starving. People will complain and say, "I want warm tortillas." I just say, "They may be hard, but they are still delicious!" . . . I mean it's something so ugly and so sad. I don't know. I remember sometimes walking with incredible hunger and thirst. My hands and my feet [were in pain]. . . . I have faith in God. I've met a lot of people in the shelter: kids, women. Poor things. Even pregnant women. I always ask God to protect the people who cross walking; the families, the kids.

HISTORIAS

I met Memo and Lucho in July 2009 at a migrant shelter in Nogales, Mexico, called Albergue Juan Bosco (discussed in more detail in chapter 5). This shelter houses recent deportees for a maximum of three days, but these two men had convinced the owners to let them prolong their stay in exchange for helping with cooking, cleaning, and supervising the large numbers of migrants (anywhere between twenty and two hundred people) whom this nonprofit organization assists daily. I didn't know it at the time, but these two who had me laughing about *pinches vacas mexicanas* would soon become key informants.

My first impression was that they were lifelong friends who were trying to cross the border together. They had such an easy rapport with one another, I was shocked to learn that they had met only a few weeks before I showed up at the shelter. They were *amigos del camino* whose friendship blossomed one night as they sat in federal detention and were then sent to Nogales the following day. These men quickly bonded over their need to survive deportation to an unfamiliar border town and their shared desire to cross back into the United States. They also had similar life histories.[16] Both came from working-class families and had migrated to the United States in the 1980s with little difficulty.

> *Memo:* I was born in 1969 in a small town on the border of Jalisco and Michoacán. I moved to Veracruz when I was little and basically grew up there. Life was very beautiful in Veracruz but the thing is that they paid very little. The salaries were low. The economy was in a crisis,[17] like it is now in the

US.[18] There was only money to eat and barely dress yourself. If you had the chance to go to school, you did. If you didn't have much money, you studied in the morning and then worked half a day. If you had no money, then you just went to work. What happened to me was that I was already working in the afternoons and just ended up leaving school in the fifth grade with about a month to go until graduation. After that, I just kept working and working.

When I was in my twenties, I met a guy who invited me to cross the border with him. I didn't know anyone who had crossed and didn't really have any family over there in the US. My friend really wanted to cross, but he was afraid. He had a brother-in-law in California who he said we could stay with and who could help us get jobs. I said, "Let me think about it." Four months went by and he still wanted to go. This was like 1988. I had two young kids at that time, but I had already broken up with their mother, so I was single. My friend was really pressuring me to go. He was saying, "Come on, come on. I spoke to my brother-in-law. He is waiting for us." So I got together what little money I could and we left. We crossed through Agua Prieta [the Sonoran border town just south of Douglas, Arizona] and just walked a little bit up the freeway. It was only like three or five hours of walking. I don't really remember, but it wasn't much. We crossed the freeway and a car came for us and took us to Phoenix. From Phoenix, my friend's brother-in-law sent someone to come get us. That's how I got to California. That was the first time I crossed. I was about nineteen years old at the time.

Lucho left Mexico almost a decade before Memo, and his recollection of the trip was vague, despite my pressing.

> *Lucho:* I left Jalisco in 1980, when I was eighteen years old. I took a bus to Tijuana and then crossed in San Diego. It was really easy at the time. We crossed the fence and our *coyote* took me to Los Angeles, where my grand-mother and aunt were living.

In subsequent years, both men would end up crossing the border multiple times, though in different ways and for different reasons. In general, Lucho benefited by leaving Mexico earlier than Memo and by already having a strong family support network in California. In 1986, the US Congress passed the Immigration Reform and Control Act (IRCA), which provided approximately 2 million undocumented people with Permanent Resident Status (i.e., "green cards").[19] Under this program, Lucho qualified for amnesty, which allowed him to travel back to Mexico to visit his ailing mother. Much to the chagrin of politicians hoping to stop the flow of undocumented migration by provid-ing amnesty to those already in the country, Lucho (like many others during that era) used his status to illegally bring his remaining family to the United States.

> *Lucho:* In 1987 I went back to see my mom in Mexico when she was dying. By that time I had my amnesty papers [Permanent Resident Status]. I brought my dad, two sisters, and my two little brothers back with me. I was with my brother-in-law, who was also a resident. He helped us get them across through Tijuana. We crossed through La Libertad.[20] We crossed there and got to San Ysidro [California]. From there we piled everyone into a van and I drove us to Los Angeles. We were all afraid, but I said that I would drive because I had my papers. We got around the Border Patrol checkpoint and made it to Los Angeles. I had a good job in California at that time and was able to take care of my siblings and my dad.

In 1994, Lucho moved with his US-citizen wife to Tucson, where she had grown up. She helped him petition to get his residency renewed, but he had failed to file the proper paperwork on time and lost his legal status. This forced him to keep a relatively low profile and avoid immigration officials. A few years after arriving in Tucson, Lucho was picked up by Border Patrol and deported. He then ended up crossing the border illegally through Nogales with relative ease.

> *Lucho:* They caught me when I was working one day. They kicked me out because I didn't have papers on me. They caught me on a Friday afternoon and sent me to Mexico that night. My wife went to Nogales to find me. I was going to try to cross by myself that Friday night, but it was really dark. It was like 10 at night when I got to the border, and I said to myself, "No way!" Can you imagine trying to cross through Río Rico [a mountainous part of southern Arizona] alone? I was afraid. [laughs] I told my wife that I couldn't cross that night but that I would try on Sunday. I told her to meet me at the *entrada* [Nogales-Grand port of entry] where they check passports and where cars pass through. I was in the line to walk across and I tried to sneak past the agent. I started walking past him, and he yelled, "Hey! Get back in line!" I tried to keep walking and they grabbed me and sent me to the end of the line. I said, "OK," and just when he turned his back again, I snuck right passed him. [laughs] I just walked by really quick when he wasn't looking. I got through and started running. I ran over to the little stores [wholesale stores in Nogales, Arizona] on the US side. You know the ones owned by Asian people? I got to the traffic light and ran into a store. The Border Patrol were driving by slowly looking for me, and I was looking at them through the glass from inside the store. I waited and then my wife drove by. I ran out of the store quickly while she was at the traffic light. I

jumped into the car and she started screaming, "What did you do?" I told her to just start driving.

We went about three blocks and then we got pulled over by a cop. He asked where we were coming from, and I said Nogales [Mexico], because my wife has her citizenship. I told him we were headed to Tucson. He asked whose car we were driving, and I told him it was mine because my name was on the registration. He asked for my license and my wife took it out of her purse. I showed it to him and then he wanted to check the trunk. That's when my wife started getting scared. She was really nervous. I opened the trunk and they checked it and said, "OK. We just stopped you because the car was giving off a little bit of smoke. Just be careful and have a good day." I was laughing and my wife was shaking! She was yelling, "What the hell are you doing? I'll leave you here in Nogales!" I said, "No way! If anyone stays behind, it's you because the car is in my name!" [laughs] I drove us back to Tucson. It was pretty easy because there was no checkpoint in those days on the freeway. I was back at work that following Monday. It was a quick crossing then, like it was nothing.

After this event, Lucho was able to avoid apprehension by immigration authorities for more than a decade. In 2009, he was arrested for driving under the influence of alcohol and sent to federal detention in Eloy, Arizona.

Lucho: I got in trouble with the law in 2009. I was trying to get my citizenship papers fixed and I got arrested for a DUI.... That was when they sent me to Eloy. I spent three months there. I got a lawyer and I was able to get out on bail. I was fighting the case with my lawyer. We went to court three times. Finally the judge said that we were going to lose the case and that they were going to deport me. They gave me a card that was from ICE [Immigration Customs Enforcement] that said that I needed to present myself with all of my possesions because they were going to deport me. But I didn't go. I was like, "I ain't going. They can come looking for me." This resulted in ... Well, I worked really close to the ICE office. Like five blocks from there [laughs]. Yeah, I'm telling you it was like three months later when I saw a car driving slowly past my work with someone looking around [mimics driving and peeking his head out of the window]. Later when I was working, there was a car parked out front with tinted windows. I kept asking about the car, but no one knew whose it was or who they were. Three days later, six officers arrived and grabbed me. A fuckload of them came out of nowhere. They threw my lunch down and everything and handcuffed me. They took me to the immigration office [detention center], and then they threw me out of the country. They tossed me into Mexico. That was when I met Memo. We spent one night together in detention and became friends.

Jason: How did that happen?

Lucho: You know, you start talking to people while you're in there like, "Hey, where are you from? Where did you try and cross?" We just started talking and then became friends. The three of us [including García] hung out together when we got sent back to Nogales.

Memo's border-crossing experiences and run-ins with the law were far more harrowing and frequent than Lucho's. Between the late 1980s and 2009, he lived in Fresno, California, where he periodically got in trouble with the police and was deported on numerous occasions. Unlike Lucho's family, the bulk of Memo's stayed in Mexico.

Memo: After that first crossing in 1988, I went back to Mexico a few times. I made some mistakes. I got deported a few times in Fresno, usually for driving without a license or with no insurance. The first time I got deported, in the 1990s, I went back to Mexico for three months to see my family, and then I returned to the US and went back to work picking grapes in Fresno. In those days we crossed the border pretty easily. There weren't a lot of problems. Before, when I would get caught and sent me back, I'd be like, "Ni modo" [Whatever]. I'm going to try again." However, after that second deportation, I didn't want to go back home to my house in Mexico. I just called home from Tijuana and spoke to my neighbor and said, "Tell my family that I'm fine." I never told my family that I had been caught. I didn't want them to feel bad. It was like that for a while. I would get across, go back to work, and send money home when I could. I had a good job and nice salary in Fresno. Years ago, there weren't a lot of problems with immigration. Crossing the border was easier.

Following the escalation in security after the terrorist attacks on September 11, 2001, Memo found it harder to migrate. After one deportation in early 2009, he made several failed attempts, each more dangerous than the previous.

Memo: The problems really started after 9/11. When the towers fell, that is when things really got complicated and it was harder to cross. After that there were more checkpoints and everything. Now it is always a fight to cross. . . . I had a good job in Fresno, but I was drinking too much. That was my problem. I was picking grapes, working in the fields. I really liked my job. I got promoted to driving the tractor and it was a great job. The problem was I got drunk once in the afternoon and thought it was a good idea to drive the tractor to the store to get more beer. I was going slowly down the street on that tractor drinking a beer and waving at my friends. I was having a great time! I was getting crazy in those days! I got arrested that time and deported to Tijuana for drunk driving.[21]

Jason: How many times have you tried to cross the border?

Memo: Like fifteen times.[22] I have crossed by myself, sometimes with others. I have always told myself that I am going to keep trying until I get through. I crossed through Tijuana like five times. They were getting pissed. They said, "You've been caught here too many times. You know what? We are gonna send you someplace else." Then they sent me someplace else. One time they sent me to Ciudad Juárez.[23] When they caught me the last time in Tijuana, they separated me from my group and sent me to Sonoyta [Mexico].

In Sonoyta, I met a guy from Puebla who was with his wife. From there we tried to cross in a group of about ten people with a guide. We walked a long ways that time and got really close to the pickup spot. It was a . . . I don't know how to tell you, we were so close and it was terrible when they caught us. We were inconsolable because we had gone so far and were beat up. It was just all blood. People's feet were bad, and the group wanted to leave some behind, like my friend from Puebla and his wife. I told the group, "No way! I will stay with them and we will keep going slowly." Anyway, they caught us that time and sent us back to Sonoyta. We tried right away to cross again and we immediately started struggling. I knew that my friend's wife couldn't do it, and I wasn't really able to either. It felt as if we were going to get lost, but I kept saying to the group, "We are not going to die. We are not going to die." God gave us the strength to keep going and not die. I just kept saying that we needed to keep going. We found some water, but my friend's wife's feet were really bad because we had walked for eleven days. We spent eleven days and nights in that desert with the guide, and they just kept taking us all over the place until we finally got caught.

Jason: How did you feel after eleven days?

Memo: Relieved to be caught because who knows if we would have even made it. We were close to dying. Border Patrol gave us *suero* [electrolytes] and water. We kept drinking water and I had cramps from trying to drink. After that, they took our fingerprints and stuff and then they separated us. One of the Border Patrol agents said to me, "You know what? You have crossed a lot of times. Why don't you rest for a bit, because you can die out there. Look, don't try again right now. Take a little break."

Jason: *La migra* said this to you?

Memo: Yeah, he said, "Take a break. Like a year, because we have your record here and you have tried to cross a lot of times recently." I said, "No way, I am going to try again."

He told me, "Not here you're not. We are going to send you to Nogales." I said, "Fine, but I am going to try again."

The agent said, "OK, I think it is easier to cross in Nogales than here in Sonoyta."

I said, "Well, if that is your recommendation. Fine."

They sent me to Nogales. He was being honest with me, and I figured I would talk to him truthfully as well.

He said, "You know what? Try again, but take a break first and next time bring a lot of *suero*. Bring a gallon of water or three. And bring a lot of *suero*."

Jason: The agent said all of this?

Memo: Yeah.

Jason: Was the agent white or Mexican?

Memo: I think his parents were Mexican. He was like a Latino. He told me that if I was going to try again, that I should rest for a bit and take a lot of vitamins. He also told me to take vitamins with me in the desert.

He said, "I understand your case because I saw your entire record. All the places you have been struggling to cross the border. Why are you trying so hard to get to the US?" I said, "Well, I am trying to support myself. I want to do something. I'm working because I want to buy a little piece of land in Mexico. I want to build some small rooms that I can rent out and with that I'll ask God to help me get ahead." I told the agent not to hunt me down because I didn't want my family to suffer, my wife and my kids. I'm suffering by myself. It's no problem to do it alone. But I can't sit waiting in Mexico with my wife and my kids, watching them suffer and me struggling to make money.

He said, "You know what? We are going to send you to Nogales. It is much closer to cross than Sonoyta, but it is dangerous. There is danger everywhere there. You have to be careful of rattlesnakes and who you cross with." At that time, I guess there were a lot of *bajadores*.

He told me, "If you have money, it's better to give it to the *bajadores*. That way they won't kidnap or kill you. Just give them your money. That's what I can tell you to help you get across."

I said, "Instead of advice, if you want to help me, why don't you just give me a ride? Instead of locking me up, drop me off down the street." [laughing]

Jason: What did he say? [laughing]

Memo: He said, "¡No, cabron! What do you want me to do? Drive you around and help you find a job too?" [laughing] Man, what adventures I've had. After that, they deported me to Nogales. Well, first they sent me to detention in Tucson. That is where I met Lucho. That was the first time I came through Tucson. When they deported us to Nogales, we had already started hanging out together in detention.

It was clear after my first conversation with Memo and Lucho that both were determined to get across the border at any cost. Neither of them considered staying in Mexico to be a viable option. Despite having different life experiences and social networks in the United States, both were habitual border crossers who had significant knowledge regarding how to overcome border security and live under the radar of immigration enforcement.

BORDER MYTHS

One of the major misconceptions about immigration control is that if the government spends enough money on fences, drone planes, motion sensors, and Border Patrol agents and makes the crossing process treacherous enough, people will eventually stop coming. Close to two decades of research has shown that boundary enforcement efforts play only a minimal role in discouraging people from attempting to cross the border and that social and economic factors are the key determinants of trends in migration rates.[24] During his State of the Union address on February 12, 2013, President Barack Obama perpetuated this misconception when he argued for heightened security as a way to slow undocumented migration flows: "Real reform means strong border security, and we can build on the progress my administration has already made— putting more boots on the southern border than at any time in our history and reducing illegal crossings to their lowest levels in 40 years."[25] Rather than linking the slowing of migration to "putting more boots on the southern border," President Obama would have been more correct had he connected the decrease in unauthorized crossing rates to the effects of the economic crisis that began in 2008, which included a reduction in available jobs for undocumented people and rising anti-immigrant sentiment. Such reasoning would of course have been an unpopular framing of the side-effects of US economic trends and would have contradicted the problematic perception held by many Americans that if the border can be secured, immigration can be stopped.

The year before I met Memo and Lucho, the Center for Comparative Immigration Studies at the University of California, San Diego, published findings on how views of the perils associated with border crossing influenced people's decisions to migrate from three Mexican states:

> A multivariate regression analysis [of data from Oaxaca] . . . reveals that perceptions of border-crossing difficulty and dangers have no statistically significant effect on the intent to migrate in 2008, when we control for the effects of age, sex, marriage, educational level, previous migration experience, and the number of family members currently living in the United States. We have performed the same analysis of responses to the same survey questions in three previous studies (done in different migrant-sending communities in the states of Jalisco and Yucatán), getting the same results. In sum, seeing the fortified border as a formidable and dangerous obstacle course does not deter would-be migrants.[26]

These data suggest that people know that the geopolitical boundary is more dangerous than ever before, but that this knowledge has relatively little impact on their decision to undertake a crossing. The authors of this report also note that the success rate of people was astonishingly high: "In four . . . studies, we found that fewer than half of migrants who come to the border are apprehended, even once, by the Border Patrol. . . . [T]he apprehension rate found in these studies varied from 24% to 47%. And of those who are caught, all but a tiny minority eventually get through—between 92 and 98 percent, depending on the community of origin. If migrants do not succeed on the first try, they almost certainly will succeed on the second or third try."[27]

These findings support Peter Andreas's argument that the security in place between the United States and Mexico has always been relatively ineffective at keeping people out.[28] Regrettably, such statistics are generally ignored by politicians and federal agencies invested in using the fear of foreign invaders and the image of a porous border as both a political smokescreen to distract the American public from other economic and foreign policy issues and an easy way to systematically generate funds for their war chests.

"NOTHING TO GO BACK TO"

Lucho and Memo bonded over their shared desire to reenter the United States, but their motivations for crossing and their recent migration histories were quite different. When he met Lucho, Memo was in the midst of a long cycle of repeatedly trying and failing to get across the border using multiple routes that included California, Arizona, and Texas crossing points. Memo has a cousin in Fresno, but his primary reason for crossing is economic. After two decades, he has become fully integrated into the undocumented labor force in the United States and sees returning penniless to his family in Mexico after years of being away a failure. Because of his limited education and the lack of economic opportunities in his country of birth, Memo chose for years to continue working undocumented and crossing the border illegally whenever he was deported. His desire to stay in the United States so that he could send money home to his children came at a high cost. He hasn't seen his kids in more than ten years, and it is clear that his status as a serial border crosser is a source of shame and embarrassment for him.

Jason: What did your family think about your crossing?

Memo: They thought that I passed fine with documents. But later I told them the truth, that I had crossed walking. My kids were worried. They said, "No Dad! That is very far to walk. Something could happen to you!" I said, "No, don't worry. Everything is fine." I called them when I got there. After I was there for a little time in California, they wanted me to go back to visit. They would call me to ask when I was coming back. I would always say, "I'm not sure, maybe tomorrow." But I never said I was leaving that day to go visit them. Never. I didn't want to lie. Sometimes I would just get deported to the border and go right back to the US. I don't want to go back there to Veracruz unless I have some money.

Jason: Do you think it is hard to live in the United States by yourself and without papers?

Memo: No. Well, it's hard because you don't have family, but not really difficult because you find ways to get work and keep moving forward. But I think it is a lot harder to live in Mexico than the US. For ten dollars you can eat for three days in the US. You can't do that with 100 pesos in Mexico. That is like food for one day and very little food at that. Then if you have a family it doesn't last for nothing. In the US there are more possiblities to do things. You can survive.

Unlike some migrants who are able to accumulate capital and return to Mexico to start small businesses or buy pieces of land to farm, Memo has never accrued any substantial savings. Moreover, he has no identification card and thus can't open a bank account. He has lived hand to mouth for most of his time in the United States and has long been subject to the fluctuating demand for undocumented labor. When work was plentiful, he could send some money home. When work was hard to come by, he scraped by on odd jobs and with the help of friends and neighbors. He wants to visit his family but not until he has money saved up. The experience of being caught between the pull of a semi–living wage working in the often exploitative US undocumented labor force and the shame of returning to Mexico penniless is common for many male Mexican migrants.[29]

Lucho, on the other hand, has significant family roots in the United States and, prior to meeting Memo, had not attempted a border crossing since before 9/11. Right after I first heard the cow story, he and I were sitting outside the Juan Bosco shelter talking about why he was trying to get through the desert.

Lucho: I've lived in Arizona for a long time and have spent almost a month now trying to get back across. I have a house. Well, it's a trailer, but I have lived there for a long time. I have two cars and all my stuff is there. My girlfriend and family are also there waiting for me. Almost all of my family is over there now in the United States. I have nothing really to go back to in Jalisco.

Me and Memo have been trying to get across for almost a month and have been caught twice. I thought they were going to throw me in jail because I had already been deported. I have a friend whose son works for immigration. She said, "I talked to my son about your case and he says be careful because if they catch you they may throw you in jail for two or three months. I have some brothers there [in Nogales] who can help you. You can rent a room and they can help you with the rent. You can sleep there. If nothing else, it's a job."

Jason: But really, it sounds as though you don't have a lot of options: stay here in Nogales, or try and cross again.

Lucho: I have no one here. It's all over there in Arizona. Crossing is my last option. My only chance.

JUAN BOSCO

My relationship with Memo and Lucho developed over the next several weeks. During the day I would hang out on *la linea* conducting interviews with recent deportees, usually in front of the Grupo Beta Office or in the nearby cemetery. In the evenings I would walk the three miles back to Juan Bosco and often arrive just in time to help with dinner preparation and last-minute cleaning duties.

For several weeks, I spend every night with Memo, Lucho, and the other shelter workers and do what I can to help out. This usually includes handing out soap and toilet paper, explaining the shelter rules to recent arrivals (e.g., no smoking, no loitering outside because the neighborhood gang likes to rob migrants), and serving meals. I make a lot of small talk with migrants but don't do any formal interviews in the shelter itself. When people arrive there, they are often tired, starving, and in desperate need of a shower and clean clothes. The last thing they need is someone shoving a voice recorder in their face.

I have always imagined the shelter as one of the few places where migrants are relatively safe and not in danger of being exploited or mistreated. Over many years, though, I have observed other researchers bullying exhausted people into participating in their study and journalists aggressively trolling the mass of deportees for "good" stories. I vividly remember overhearing a famous television journalist telling his camera man, "We need to find a mother that has been deported and lost her kids. We need to find someone with a really fucked-up story. That's pure gold."

Rather than using the shelter as a site to conduct interviews or troll for "fucked-up" stories, I spend the majority of my time trying to be helpful to the staff and explaining to guests that I am an anthropologist writing a book about migration. The shelter becomes a place where I make my face familiar to people who will likely see me the following day on *la línea*. Over five years of research, the bulk of my interviews are conducted on the streets the day after I first meet someone in the shelter.[30] That being said, Juan Bosco does become an important place for me to meet potential interview subjects; observe how deportees are treated by the Red Cross, various humanitarian groups, and other agencies; and learn about migration from the shelter workers, all of whom have border-crossing experience.

Guests at Juan Bosco generally shower and eat between 7 and 11 P.M. Once the first group of women, men, and children have been fed and assigned beds, there is usually a lull in activity. This is the time when all of the workers retreat to the kitchen area to hang out, watch television, and play cards. I soon found that the period between 11 P.M. and 2 A.M. was an important time for talking to the staff, including Memo and Lucho, about their lives and experiences migrating. These men also proved crucial in helping me understand the interview data and field observations I was collecting during the day. Although alcohol was forbidden, Memo was adept at sneaking beers into the kitchen to lubricate our late-night games of *baraja* (Mexican poker). These moments are some of my fondest memories from that first season of fieldwork. I learned about the lives of the shelter workers, and their friendship helped me fight some of the loneliness of research. They were happy to have a new target for their *chingaderas*.

I focus on the crossing stories of Memo and Lucho for a few reasons that warrant brief explanation. Out of the hundreds of migrants I have known over the years, they were the two with whom I spent the most amount of time on the Mexican side of the border. When I first met them, they were at Juan Bosco for weeks, and their role as temporary staff meant that I had a significant amount of access to them at night and could follow them closely as they prepared to cross. Other migrants that I subsequently watched prepare and enter the desert were people whom I knew for only a few days at the most and with whom I rarely had the opportunity to socialize. Because Lucho and Memo were able to stay at the shelter for weeks as they prepared to cross for the third time, the two of them had their days relatively free for hanging out. We often ate lunch together, went to baseball games, and did other normal activities. The other migrants I knew from *la línea* were typically rushing to undertake another crossing. If they stayed in the shelter, they were forced to go to sleep at 11 P.M. and were not able to fraternize with me or other staff. If a person had exhausted their three-day stay at Juan Bosco, they were likely hiding out in the Nogales cemetery or someplace else where they wouldn't be robbed at night.

I want to point out that Memo and Lucho are not unique examples of migrants, outside of the fact that they put up with me. They are in most ways fairly typical examples of undocumented border crossers. They are male, lack formal education, have crossed the border multiple times, and have been fully incorporated into the US undocumented labor force for years. Both have spent most of their lives living in the United States, and neither sees returning to Mexico as an option. In addition, by the time I met them, they were intimately familiar with the dangers of the Sonoran Desert hybrid collectif and determined to be part of the "92% to 98%" of those who eventually get past the many barriers along the US-Mexico border.[31] By providing insight into their lives, I seek to put faces to immigration statistics and show that their crossing stories are just two of the hundreds that occur each day in southern Arizona alone. The events described here are just a few of the millions of crossing attempts that have happened in the region since 2000.[32]

CHAPTER 5

Deported

A nondescript metal door opens and an armed guard enters the nearly empty courtroom. He catches the attention of the Border Patrol agent sitting nearby, who looks up from his Smartphone and gives a quiet nod. A stocky man in his thirties with charcoal-colored hair slinks through the open doorway. His arms and legs are shackled and his head hangs low. Heavy manacles dangle from his body. The Mexican prisoner is wearing a New York Yankees T-shirt with giant salt stains around the armpits. The dirty blue jeans and frayed sneakers he has on, with the laces removed so that he doesn't hang himself in captivity, show the characteristic wear that accompanies several days of dancing through the desert. As he shuffles toward his seat, the rattling chains attached to his wrists, ankles, and waist break the room's silence with every tired movement. It sounds like the shaking of a bag of nails.

The next prisoner to enter is a lanky teenager with spiky hair and a baby-blue knock-off Abercrombie & Fitch polo shirt. He looks at the dozen or so courtroom spectators to his left, a mix of college student activists and local humanitarian observers, and raises his shackled hands to wave hello. He smiles at the two young blonde women present and tries to look cool. Waddling behind him is an older *señor*, barely five feet tall, who looks as though he just stepped out of a Zapotec village in the Valley of Oaxaca (he probably just did). The oversized chains on his tiny frame exaggerate his small stature and make everyone around him look like giants. He struggles to keep up with the kid in front of him and winces with every step he takes. It's as if he's walking on broken bottles. More prisoners follow, each one slightly increasing the volume of the jangling metal. This limping chain gang is a mix of baby-faced eighteen-year-olds, bleary-eyed middle-aged men and women, and a few exhausted-looking elderly people. The aroma of cheap industrial cleaning products used to sanitize the courtroom is soon overpowered by the collective smell of sweat that these bodies have accumulated while hiking in the desert and later sitting in overcrowded detention cells waiting to see *el juez*.

In less than fifteen minutes, fifty-five men and fifteen women have taken their seats at the front of the courtroom. Bound hands awkwardly put on wireless headphones so that people can listen to the court-appointed Spanish translator explain the judicial process that is unfolding. While waiting for the proceedings to begin, the defendants stare at the court officers, the audience, and their surreal surroundings. Some eyes dart around the room. Others smile nervously and finger their plastic headsets. A few people are softly crying. Most are squirming in their seats as they try to get comfortable with their hand and ankle cuffs, which results in a steady shaking of chains. The rattling fills the room like a white-noise machine. Welcome to Operation Streamline.

In recent years, nations around the globe have increasingly militarized their borders in response to the influx of economic migrants and displaced people fleeing the effects of globalization, global warming, and armed conflict.[1] This worldwide ramping up of boundary security has led many to draw on the US-Mexico border as both a global metaphor for tensions between nation-states whose economic and political power are vastly unequal,[2] and a model response to unwanted (or seemingly unwanted) immigration. More walls, more surveillance cameras, more barbed wire: as immigration control has ratcheted up internationally, so too has the use of deportation[3] as a routinized disciplinary method crucial to the maintenance of state sovereignty around the world.[4] This formalized practice of removal, however, is rarely recognized as a unique policy strategy with its own "sociopolitical logic" and ramifications that extend far beyond the borders of any particular nation.[5]

Although deportation is an essential element of the social process of undocumented migration into the United States, little ethnographic work has focused on what it looks like, how it is experienced, and its relationship to other aspects of border crossing.[6] In this chapter I provide snapshots of the steps, settings, and actors involved in the deportation process in southern Arizona and northern Mexico to demonstrate how this phenomenon is both a bureaucratic and a physical component of the hybrid collectif that is largely understudied. An analysis of this process can reveal much about the impact of forcible removal on people's lives as they attempt to survive and regroup on the Mexican side of the border.

ENFORCEMENT WITH CONSEQUENCES

In the decades leading up to immigration reforms enacted in the mid-2000s, those apprehended entering the country illegally from Mexico were typically returned with minimal processing in a procedure known as voluntary departure.[7] Unlike formal deportation, which involves an administrative hearing, voluntary departure is a quick process whereby migrants waive their rights to see a judge and are returned to Mexico without a trial or prolonged time spent in detention.[8] For decades, captured *alambristas* (fence jumpers) simply answered a few Border Patrol questions, sat in detention for a short time, and were then quickly dropped off at the nearest port of entry. Within a matter of hours they could be back down at the fence trying their luck again. It was not uncommon during most of the twentieth century for an agent to apprehend the same person more than once in a twenty-four-hour period,[9] creating a game of catch-and-release that frustrated Border Patrol and did little to discourage someone from trying again.[10]

If you were a novice border crosser, the first time you came face to face with *la migra* was no doubt a bit frightening. Would the officers beat you up? Shoot you in the back? Throw you in prison? Once people realized that Border Patrol were not likely to harm them (for the most part) or throw them in jail, being caught grew less intimidating. Over time, repeat offenders became socialized to the routine process of deportation.[11] Catch and release. Catch and release. One cynical agent interviewed by Josiah Heyman in the early 1990s summed up the cyclical nature of this ineffective policy: "They know the game, they're docile if caught. They're delayed eight hours and then they do it over again. That's all we basically do, delay them."[12] This sociojuridical process has long been comedic fodder for popular cultural critiques of US immigration policy.[13] During this same era, non-Mexican nationals, known in Border Patrol parlance as "other than Mexicans" or "OTMs," who were caught transgressing the geopolitical boundary fared even better, as they were usually released on bail and told to appear in court for a formal deportation or removal hearing at a later date. Unsurprisingly, this practice yielded a low courtroom appearance rate.

In 2005, the Department of Homeland Security (DHS) began experimenting with new types of deportation proceedings as part of its strategy to develop more punitive forms of removal, or as policy writers call it, "enforcement with consequences."[14] One of the more controversial systems that the DHS put into place was Operation Streamline, a southern-border program that, instead of allowing someone to voluntarily return to their country of origin, routes nonviolent immigration law breakers through the federal criminal justice system. Under this program first-time offenders are convicted of a misdemeanor and can serve up to six months in jail. A repeat visitor to Streamline can find herself charged with felony reentry, which generally carries a two-year maximum penalty or up to twenty years in prison if the defendant has a criminal record.[15] In theory, this "zero tolerance" initiative seems a more effective strategy compared to previous, expedited removal processes. Unfortunately for DHS, the logistics of trying to prosecute in federal court the hundreds of thousands of people who get caught crossing the border each year are overwhelming and make this an impossibility.

While Operation Streamline happens five days a week in Arizona, California, and Texas, federal courthouses, such as the one in Tucson, can handle a maximum of about seventy people a day. This means that in a Border Patrol sector where several hundred migrants may be apprehended in a twenty-four-hour period, only a portion of those detainees will be marched in front of a judge. The majority of those caught still find themselves voluntarily returned to Mexico with little fanfare. Catch and release. Catch and Release. Like the random events that migrants encounter in the desert that may impede their journey or assist in their success, the criteria Border Patrol used to select the seventy people I am watching being federally prosecuted on this day in Tucson in 2013 are arbitrary.[16] Having your day in court is often just a matter of dumb luck.

Kangaroo Court

Fourteen lawyers are sitting at the front of the gallery waiting for their clients to be called up to the judge, who is running late. A few busy themselves by rifling through their case files. A disheveled-looking man in a cheap suit plays a word game on his cell phone, while the person next to him yawns and reads the *New York Times*. Two attorneys are laughing and joking with one of the federal marshals seated at the front of the room. On a typical day these lawyers arrive at 9 A.M. and have three hours to see four or five of their clients. This amounts to about half an hour to both read the case file and interview an individual before appearing with him or her in front of the judge to make a plea and receive a sentence.[17] For their time, these lawyers earn $125 an hour. Each of them can easily make an estimated $125,000 annually on Operation Streamline cases alone. No wonder they're laughing.

The judge finally arrives, twenty minutes late, to this 1 P.M. session, and the proceedings get under way. Instructions and orders are read in English and then translated by a court interpreter sitting next to the bench. Five people at a time are called up to the front of the room and prosecuted simultaneously.

> "When your name is called, please come forward with your attorney. 12–31324MP.[18] USA versus . . ."
>
> "Jonathan Rivas Saucedo"
>
> *"Presente"*
>
> "12–31325MP"
>
> "Vicente Badillo Rivas"
>
> *"Presente"*
>
> "Ricardo Díaz Ordóñez"
>
> *"Presente"*
>
> "David Ruiz González"
>
> *"Presente"*
>
> "Rufino Juárez García"
>
> *"Presente."*

Once all five defendants are accounted for, each person is then asked the same basic set of questions.

> "Mr. Rivas Saucedo, did you enter the United States illegally near the town of Sasabe on or about March 13, 2013?"
>
> *"Sí."*
>
> "Mr. Díaz Ordóñez, did you enter the United States illegally near the town of Nogales on or about March 12, 2013?"
>
> *"Sí."*

Not everyone will fully understand what is going on, including the tiny man with bad feet who was one of the first defendants to enter the room.

> "Mr. Juárez García, did you enter the United States illegally near the town of Sasabe on or about March 13, 2013?"

Silence.

"Mr. Juárez García, did you enter the United States illegally near the town of Sasabe on or about March 13, 2013?"

Silence.

"Can you please explain to your client that he needs to verbally respond to my question?"

Mr. Juárez García looks confused. His lawyer whispers something in his ear, and he suddenly kneels down on the ground in front of the judge as if praying for mercy.

"Please tell your client to stand up. Mr. Juárez García do you understand what is happening here today, sir?"

"Your honor, my client doesn't speak a lot of Spanish. He is not a native Spanish speaker. He speaks a native dialect."[19]

"Do you think he speaks enough Spanish to enter a plea?"

"I think so, your honor."

"Mr. Juárez García, do you understand what is happening, sir?"

"*Culpable.*"

"Sir, I am not asking for a plea yet. I am asking if you understand what is happening today."

"*Sí.*"

"OK, very well. Let's continue. Mr. Juárez García, did you enter the United States illegally near the town of Sasabe on or about March 13, 2013?"

"*Sí.*"

Eventually all five will have the charges against them read out loud, and each will be asked to submit a plea. The word *culpable* (guilty) is uttered five times. An estimated 99 percent of Streamline defendants plead guilty.[20] Charges are then read to each person.

"Mr. Rivas Saucedo is sentenced to seventy-five days. Mr. Baldillo Rivas is sentenced to thirty days. Mr. Díaz Ordóñez sentenced to thirty days. Mr. Ruiz González sentenced to thirty days. Mr. Juárez García is awarded time served."

The process starts again.

"When your name is called please come forward with your attorney. 12–31329MP. USA versus . . ."

At the end of one hour, seventy men and women will have had their initial court appearance, arraignment, plea, and sentencing condensed into one expedited hearing. Most who pass through this courtroom will receive a sentence of time served, though some may have to go to jail for as many as 180 days. The average detention period is approximately thirty days.[21] Because these defendants are non–US citizens, this dog-and-pony show's obvious lack of due process or adequate legal counsel is generally overlooked by the federal government and the program's supporters. It is a judicial charade that makes the government look "tough on immigration" by subjecting non–US citizens to the heavy hand of the law while simultaneously robbing them of the normal rights, privileges, and procedures accorded to citizens who face federal prosecution. This "judicial" process makes Agamben's call for the recognition of new locales where states of exception are created especially poignant: "If the essence of the camp consists in the materialization of the state of exception and in the subsequent creation of a space in which bare life and the juridical rule enter into a threshold of indistinction, then we must admit that we find ourselves virtually in the presence of a camp every time such a structure is created, independent of the kind of crimes that are committed there and whatever its denomination and specific topography."[22]

Although Operation Streamline is touted by DHS as an effective deterrent against unauthorized migration, no strong supporting data back this claim. Many analysts have argued that a downward-spiraling US economy and a rise in smuggling costs are the most likely causes of the slowed migration rates that appeared around the time the program began.[23] As Lydgate and others point out, though, there is substantial evidence that this legally questionable procedural process is highly effective at generating large amounts of federal spending.[24] Together the lawyers in this Arizona courtroom, for example, make about $2.3 million annually, while the $100 a day it costs to house a detainee in Tucson results in a price tag of about $52.5 million dollars a year in this sector alone.[25]

The escalating war on immigration has become a profitable business over the past decade. Private corporations that specialize in detaining nonviolent immigration offenders at high costs to American tax payers now report annual revenues in the billions. This rise in profits is partly thanks to the unethical business relationships that these corporations have with anti-immigrant legislators across the country.[26] Both parties seem to have agreed that if one builds more detention centers the other will find ways to fill them.

As the last person in the courtroom is sentenced and then shooed back to a holding cell, another seventy people sitting in detention in Tucson are being randomly selected to see the judge the following day. The chains of justice will once again rattle at 1 P.M. A few hours later Mr. Juárez García and dozens of others find themselves on a bus headed to Mexico.

BIENVENIDOS A NOGALES

It is 11 P.M. on a Tuesday at the DeConcini port of entry. Traffic going into Nogales, Mexico, is relatively light compared to the dozens of vehicles impatiently inching forward in line as they wait their turn to enter the United States. A red pickup truck with Arizona plates headed south is being inspected for money, assault rifles, and other contraband by two Immigration and Customs Enforcement agents in dark-blue uniforms. One of them is using a mirror attached to a metal rod to check under the engine. The other walks a panting German shepherd in circles around the vehicle. A white bus with barred windows and tinted glass idles loudly on the US side fifty feet from the pedestrian entrance to Mexico. The logo on the side of the bus that used to say "Wackenhut Transportation Division" has been covered up with white vinyl. Following a buyout by G4 Security Solutions, this controversial private security corporation has tried to maintain a lower profile in the wake of allegations that it and other such firms have been abusing the hundreds of thousands of migrants that they are contracted annually by the federal government to temporarily house and later transport back to Mexico.[27]

The bus door opens and an out-of-shape, armed private security guard steps down to meet two Border Patrol agents waiting on the sidewalk. "*Adelante*," says one of the agents. A group of disheveled and exhausted-looking men slowly file out. Some are carrying black and camouflage backpacks with tags attached that read "Department of Homeland Security Baggage Check." A few have their personal items in clear plastic bags that read "Property" and have the Department of Homeland Security logo stamped all over them. Several individuals have no possessions at all, the result of losing their stuff in the desert after having been forced by Border Patrol to throw backpacks away, or of having personal items permanently confiscated by one of the many custodial agencies that they have interacted with since being apprehended days prior. Food, water, extra clothes, diabetes medication, voter ID cards, and wrinkled photos of giggling toddlers lie piled up in trash cans in detention centers. Some of these same items sit on the desert surface, forming the archaeological record of this clandestine social process.

The darkly clad passengers are visibly spooked by the prospect of being dropped off at the border at night, which is understandable. Their tired faces, camouflage clothes, dirty sneakers, and black backpacks with government tags mark them as vulnerable deportees. Wearing what some migrants refer to as the "uniform of the defeated," they stick out like sore thumbs. I once asked a Border Patrol public information officer about who gets deported after dark. "It's really dangerous at night," he told me, "so we only drop off men. We don't deport women and children at night." Based on reports by the humanitarian group No More Deaths and my own observations, this protocol is not always followed.[28]

On this and most evenings, those who seem especially scared are the people who have been laterally deported to Nogales from a different border area as part of the Alien Transfer and Exit Program (ATEP), another of DHS's "enforcement with consequences" projects. The Border Patrol contends that by busing deportees to ports of entry distant from where they were apprehended, they can achieve two goals. First, such transfers "disrupt the ability of alien smuggling organizations to operate by deterring aliens from repeatedly crossing the border illegally and from seeking the assistance of smuggling organizations."[29] Second, the practice "safely [removes] aliens from the waiting hands of the smugglers who would certainly force them to endure several days in the harsh environment in another attempt to illegally cross the border."[30] These are dubious claims, given that smuggling organizations exist in every Mexican border town and connecting up with a new *coyote* is easier than checking your email. Moreover, many people deported from urban areas such as San Ysidro, California, to places like Nogales find themselves deposited in a region where the path of least resistance is to try and cross the desert.

As I have argued elsewhere, this practice is less about disrupting smuggling rings or protecting people than about disorienting deportees and literally placing them in harm's way.[31] David Spener has shown that the safest strategy for contracting a *coyote* is to find one from your home community, which greatly reduces the likelihood of being swindled, assaulted, or left behind in the wilderness.[32] By sending people to a foreign border town and disconnecting them from a smuggler with whom they may have had some social tie, the Border Patrol simultaneously places people in a geographically hostile environment and encourages them to contract an unfamiliar smuggler who is more likely to rob them than help them cross over. Although ATEP officially began only in 2008, the practice of shipping deportees to exotic towns to spatially and socially dislocate them dates back to at least the 1950s and has long been recognized as having violent consequences.[33]

I'm on the Mexican side of the border near a taxi stand directly in front of the pedestrian entrance to the country. Several slick-haired men are sitting on nearby benches and leaning against a wall, smoking cheap cigarettes and waiting for deportees to come through the gate. One of them is Gallardo, a chubby, one-legged *coyote* who has worked this corner for years. He acts as a middle-man who connects newly arrived migrants with *guías* who can lead them through the desert.[34] Evidently he is relatively trustworthy: he has a small home range, is easy to find, and can't really run away from unsatisfied customers who might return to Nogales after being robbed or abandoned by their guide. Like Old Faithful, Gallardo can be spotted sitting in front of the Hotel Regis bar off International Avenue or parked in front of the cemetery near the Mariposa port of entry, shooting the breeze with recent deportees. He travels back and forth between his posts in a beat-up maroon Pontiac using his wooden crutch to operate the gas pedal and remaining leg to step on the brake. Tonight, he and others are eyeballing the group of migrants standing in front of the idling bus, trying to identify their next client or victim. Armed with promises of a warm bed followed by a cheap and quick passage across the border, many of these men, and occasional woman, are as likely to kidnap and hold someone for ransom as they are to lead them through the desert.

Unfortunately for Gallardo and his *compañeros* (and luckily for the migrants), a shiny orange government truck pulls up to the port of entry and two Grupo Beta officers step out. Grupo Beta, a wing of Mexico's Instituto Nacional de Migración, is charged with offering medical assistance, information, and general help to migrants, including non-Mexicans, en route to the United States.[35] Part of the group's work involves protecting deportees from the abuses of smugglers, gangs, and organized criminal networks. The two clean-shaven male agents are here to give the dozen or so people *un raite* to Juan Bosco, the largest Nogales migrant shelter, which is located several miles from the port of entry. Had they not shown up, the new arrivals would have had to try their luck on the streets or wait until the sun came up before attempting to find the Grupo Beta Office.

The last time Memo and Lucho were deported at 2 A.M., they slept on benches near the port of entry for fear that the men waiting just outside at the taxi stand would assault them. The misinformed who try to walk to the shelter at night often find themselves being chased by the neighborhood cholos who specialize in migrant beat downs. As the truck pulls away from the port of entry with its bed full of human cargo, Gallardo hobbles back across the street and resumes his perch in front of the bar. He will be back in a few hours.

GIMME SHELTER

It is a typical summer night at Juan Bosco. After a long day with temperatures hovering in the low 100s for most of the afternoon, the sun has finally set, and the oppressive night air now sits on everyone's skin like a moist blanket. About sixty men, twelve women, and three children all under the age of ten are crammed into the shelter's chapel. The room is set up to hold religious events, but it functions mostly as a waiting area for arriving migrants or as an ad hoc dormitory when all the beds fill up. A wobbly fan slowly rotates in the corner, pushing hot air from one side of the room to the other. The local news blares at an ear-shattering volume from a nearby television. For some reason the sound is always turned up. It doesn't matter, though, because it is virtually impossible to hear the newscaster over the dozens of conversations taking place.

> "*No mames cabron.* We crossed in Sasabe and our *pinche coyote* abandoned us. We got robbed twice by *bajadores.* I'm pretty sure the *coyote* was working with them."
>
> "Do you know where there is a Banco Azteca? My brother is going to wire us some money to try again. He doesn't understand why we haven't gotten across yet."
>
> "*Oye,* what's the name of this place we are in? Zonora?"

Memo pops his head into the room and says loudly, "*Caballeros,* line up out here as fast as possible because there are a lot of people here tonight." He sounds serious because he wants to convince everyone that he has some authority despite the fact that he has only been here a few weeks and is a deportee himself. Grumbling, the men rise from their seats and start filing out of the room. On the way to the door they pass by a small altar to the Virgin of Guadalupe and a wooden sculpture of crucified Jesus. There is a pile of prayer cards, coins, and photographs at the base of the Virgin's altar, items left by pilgrims passing through. Jesus's neck hangs heavy with donated rosaries and scapulars, offerings that may help someone avoid *la migra* on the next trip or guarantee that she doesn't run out of water. Dripping blood is painted on Christ's head, hands, and feet. One of the men who walk past the statue has

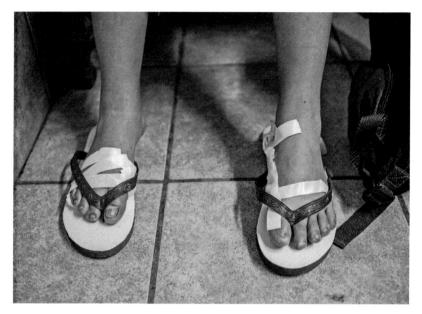

Juan Bosco shelter, 2013. Photo by Michael Wells.

bandages on both feet. There are dark ink blots of blood pushing through the gauze. Several people cross themselves and whisper quiet prayers as they greet two of Mexico's religious heavy hitters.

Samuel sits behind a chipped wooden desk, scratching today's date on several intake sheets. He is not tall, but looms large from his seated position. His jet-black hair is perfectly parted and held in place by a generous handful of aromatic styling gel. It looks as if he is about to grill some nervous job candidate about their qualifications for being here. Out of all the shelter workers, he is by far the most stoic and the only one who commands any real respect. He tends to speak at a low volume with little affect in his voice. Each word out of his mouth is pronounced hard as if carved on blocks of wood. The tone gives you the impression that he is perpetually pissed off, which directly contradicts his propensity for delivering deadpan *chingaderas*. It is impossible to know if he is messing with you when he passes a dinner plate and asks if you want extra *chile*.

Samuel has been at Juan Bosco for close to ten months, following a deportation from Phoenix after being caught driving without a license or insurance. He has been trying to save money to cross the border with fake paperwork, some-

Lining up for the restroom at Juan Bosco shelter, 2009. Photo by author.

thing that would cost him at least a few thousand dollars. He tells me, "I don't want to walk very far in the desert like Memo and Lucho are planning to do. It's too risky. I don't want to risk my life." Originally from Puebla, Samuel has spent months supervising the day-to-day operations at the shelter and taking orders from the owners, Doña Hilda and Don Paco Loureiro,[36] who are on the premises only a few hours each day. After three decades of assisting almost 2 million migrants, they have relegated much of the on-the-ground management and manual labor to Samuel and a few others who, following their deportations, settled into permanent low-paid or volunteer work at the shelter. As recent deportees waiting to attempt another crossing, Memo and Lucho somehow charmed Hilda into letting them stay beyond the three-day limit. Memo's goofy smile and gentle manner are endearing and seem to work small miracles for him. He and Lucho promised to behave and help maintain order and cleanliness.

The deported men line up in front of Samuel's desk. They are a wild-looking bunch with scraped-up faces, dirty shirts, and frayed sneakers. Some are carrying dusty backpacks that still have the DHS tag on them from detention. A nineteen-year-old kid in a hospital gown and flip-flops is sporting a broken nose and fourteen stitches across his forehead. "Our *coyote* tried to outrun Border Patrol and our truck flipped over," he tells me. A one-armed man from Chiapas asks someone to help him operate the spigot on a nearby water cooler so that he can fill a small plastic cup. He was lost in the desert for six days after trying to cross by himself. His one good arm has a faded black stain on it that once depicted the face of Christ complete with a crown of thorns and praying hands. He says that God protected him in the desert and saved his life.

A somber-faced *chilango* named Lalo says he was just deported from Phoenix after living there for many years. Lalo was arrested for trespassing while he and his buddies were standing in a vacant lot soliciting day labor from people leaving the local Home Depot. Two middle-aged men from Oaxaca whisper to each other in Mixtec. In broken Spanish they ask Memo if there will be any food because they haven't eaten in two days. Memo tells them about the imaginary seven-course meal complete with cold beers that is waiting for them in the kitchen. Despite their grumbling stomachs everyone laughs at the *chiste*. It's all you can do to keep from crying.

This scene plays out in slight variations 365 days a year at Juan Bosco. Women, men, and children line up for intake. Husbands and wives, cousins, siblings, and strangers who met en route tell stories of exhaustion, dehydration, heartbreak, and hard luck to anyone who will listen. After a while the tired faces and traumatic tales all blend together.

> "We are going to do one person at a time," Samuel says. "Please take out your *comprobante* [deportation slip]."
>
> "Have your paperwork out in your hands," orders Memo.
>
> "Name."
>
> "Miguel López Peña."
>
> "How old are you?"
>
> "Twenty-seven."
>
> "Where are you from?"
>
> "Tapachula, Chiapas."
>
> "Name."
>
> "Raul Paz Ornelas."
>
> "How old are you?"
>
> "Thirty-seven."
>
> "Where are you from?"
>
> "Oaxaca, Oaxaca."

"Name."

"Guillermo Wilson Torres."

"How old are you?"

"Nineteen."

"Where are you from?"

"Apizaco, Tlaxcala."

Roll call goes on for twenty minutes. Oaxaca, Chiapas, Veracruz, Guerrero, Jalisco. It's a lesson in Mexican geography with certain spatial patterns emerging after only a few intakes. Oaxaca, Oaxaca, Chiapas, Oaxaca, Veracruz, Chiapas, Oaxaca. The poorest states with the highest indigenous populations are overrepresented. Most deportees are from Mexico, but a few people arrive each day from Guatemala, Honduras, and El Salvador. An estimated 15 percent of all annual apprehensions and removals are people from these countries.[37] Seventeen years old, forty-one years old, sixty-three years old. Occasionally you even see an infant or a person in their seventies. There is no age restriction here. These same geographic and age patterns will be repeated later when the women line up for their intake.

A man gets caught lying about his nationality.

"Where are you from?"

"Yucatán."

"The Yucatán? Really? We don't get a lot of people from the Yucatán here. Where are you from in the Yucatán?"

"OK, I'm from Honduras."

"That's what I thought. You don't have a *comprobante,* so you can only stay tonight. You have to be gone tomorrow."

Without a deportation slip, people are given only a one-night pass, especially Central Americans still making their way north. Although the discrimination against non–Mexican nationals is rampant, this rule is more about trying to keep drug addicts and petty thieves who pretend to be migrants out of the shelter.

The intake process is eventually completed and everyone's name and information are recorded in the books. This will have to be repeated at midnight and then again at 3 A.M., when Grupo Beta drops off additional truckloads of recently deported people. The shelter workers won't get much sleep until the following morning.

After every round of intakes, the exhausted group of migrants is told the rules and regulations. Rafael (or Rafa) steps forward and barks, "Everyone come over here and pay attention!" Thirty-one-year-old Rafa is pudgy and light skinned with a boyish round face and green eyes. You wouldn't guess by looking at him that he previously served in the Mexican military in his home state of Chiapas. He looks more like someone who specializes in playing Xbox and smoking weed. He had been living in Raleigh-Durham for several years when he decided to return home to visit his sick mother. A few months later he attempted to return to Carolina Norte by crossing the desert. Rafa injured his leg while crossing and ended up deported and hobbling around Juan Bosco on crutches. He was allowed an extended stay in the shelter to recuperate and soon became a staff member. Despite telling me on an almost daily basis that he is going to cross the desert soon, he seems quite comfortable in his supervisory role and has been here for almost a year. It is obvious that he likes bossing recent arrivals around.

> *Rafa*: OK, gentlemen, we are not the government. This place is privately owned. We have nothing to do with the government or immigration or Grupo Beta. They bring you all here so that you aren't hanging out in the street. We want to maintain a peaceful atmoshpere here, keep it respectful, and maintain order. The first thing we want to do is to keep this place clean. There is a blue trash can in the bathroom for you to throw away anything you want to get rid of: dirty clothes, socks. Don't leave it on the floor or throw it out the bathroom window. Understood?
>
> *Migrants in unison*: Yes.
>
> *Rafa*: OK. We don't want to hear any swear words or see you walking around here without a shirt on. There are women and children who come here. This is not just a place for men. I don't want to hear people swearing around here. Agreed?
>
> *Migrants in unison*: Yes.
>
> *Rafa*: The bathroom is in the back on the left. It is there for you to use the restroom, wash your feet, or take a bath. There should be water in the hose at the moment, but you need to always check. If there is no water, you will take a bucket or wait your turn until a bucket is not in use and go down the stairs to fill it. There are two black tanks down there with faucets to fill the buckets so that you can take a bath, wash your feet, or use the toilet. Now many people use the bathroom, and when they are done, they get lazy and don't go down to refill the bucket. Then the next person doesn't have water and can't wash their hands. Here no one pays for anything. No one pays for a bed. Everything is shared and for this reason we need to always keep the

bathroom clean. After you wash your feet, collect your shoes and put them in these black trash bags. Keep them in here because of the bad smell. All the shoes go in here. If your shoes will fit in your backpack or bag, keep them with you. If not, put them in the black bags. Once one bag fills up, close it and open another one. Questions?

Migrants in unison: No.

Rafa: It is prohibited to smoke. If you have cigarettes, matches, lighters, leave them on the table and we will return them first thing in the morning. If you have something sharp, something that can cut or stab someone, also leave it on the table and we will return it in the morning. The police will be here soon and will do body searches and check your bags. If they find something, they will throw you out of here. Cigarettes, matches, lighters, knives, and sharp objects. We will return them to you tomorrow. The police will also be here in the morning. It's the law and for your protection and ours.

Gentlemen, the place where you are going to sleep has a folded blanket. There are, however, some people who won't get a bed or a blanket tonight because we don't have enough. There are mats, though, to sleep on the floor.

Migrant: Is there soap?

Rafa: Soap? Check in the bathroom but I don't think there is any. You will have to check. We can't give out products to every single person. You will have to share among all of you. We have no support from the government. They don't support us, so we don't have a lot of things. We can only offer you what we have. Any questions? Memo, anything else?

Memo: Don't put your socks or underwear in the windows because later when someone goes to take a bath, they gotta smell your fucking dirty underwear. [laughing]

Once the rules have been stated, Rafa and Memo start assigning beds.

Rafa: You get that top bunk. Hey, you, come this way. You take this bed next to your dad. Anyone else traveling in a group? OK, you guys will sleep together on the same bunk.

Memo: Don't leave your shoes on the ground. Put them in the bags.

Rafa: You take that top bunk. You don't want the top bunk? Why not?

Migrant: I can't climb because of my feet. It hurts.

Rafa: OK, you take the bottom bunk. Is there anyone else here that is hurt and can't climb the bunk?

While beds are being assigned, the police show up and start conducting searches. Brown bodies are lined up and frisked. The contents of backpacks are dumped onto the floor. The cops try to keep the mood light: "Gentlemen, we are here looking for your drugs, guns, and condoms!" While waiting to be searched, a few people rattle off text messages to loved ones to let them know where they are. I strike up a conversation with a sad-looking kid named Johnny from Honduras who is standing in the corner. He is filthy; his clothes are stained and threadbare as if he's been living under a bridge. Johnny has had a rough trip: "I left Honduras almost three weeks ago. I'm trying to get to Louisiana where I have cousins. I thought it would be easier once I got closer to the border, but here it is even harder. Entering and leaving Mexico is fatal." He then looks at the cops and at Rafa and whispers to me, "No one here will help you."

After searching everyone except a man with bandaged feet who has trouble standing up, the police leave empty-handed. No drugs, guns, or condoms. Memo announces that dinner will soon be ready and that the first twenty people can be served down the hall once the women have finished eating. As I start walking toward the kitchen, Samuel grabs me by the arm and pulls me aside. "I saw you talking to that kid from Honduras. You need to be careful because he will rob you." I tell him that I think he is in worse shape than most of the Mexicans in the room and probably the most afraid. In his quiet stern manner he coldly says, "Hondurans are all robbers and liars. All of them. They are just really good at putting on sad faces."

———————

Down the hall, the women and three kids are all sitting along rectangular plastic tables devouring bowls of beans and small stacks of warm corn tortillas. Pato is huddled over the stove stirring a giant pot and playfully teasing some of the younger women. He has been at Juan Bosco for years following a deportation from San Diego, where he was a cook in a series of high-end restaurants. "I can cook Italian food, sushi, you name it," he often brags. Rather than return to his home state of Oaxaca or risk a desert crossing, Pato has settled into a semicomfortable life at the shelter. Nowadays, like some kind of culinary magician, he pulls together delicious meals with whatever random or expired goods get donated to the shelter or purchased on its shoestring budget.

Several women compliment him on his cooking. He grins and informs them that he is single. I sit down and strike up a conversation with a young girl named Lety who looks to be about eight months pregnant. She has removed her shoes from her swollen feet and unbuckled her pants to release some pressure on her giant belly. She tells me and Pato that she is fifteen years old and from Chiapas. She and her husband walked for five days in the desert. They made it to their pickup spot, but their ride never showed up. With no options left, they turned themselves into the Border Patrol. From the looks on everyone's face, the entire table feels especially sorry for her. In this sea of misery, there is always someone worse off than you.

Two sisters from Oaxaca in their late twenties start teasing Pato about how hard it is to believe that someone who is such a good cook can still be single. He tries to deflect their attention onto me by telling them that I am in the shelter looking for a "Mexican girlfriend" to keep me company while I'm away from my wife. The sisters get a kick out of this and start telling me their story. The oldest, Barbara, has lived in Pennsylvania for many years and works at a Cheesecake Factory near a giant shopping mall. She went home to visit her children in Oaxaca, and her younger sister decided to travel back with her to find work in the United States. They spent five days in the desert before getting caught by Border Patrol. When I ask who else they are traveling with, Barbara points to a woman in her early forties quietly eating next to them. I am introduced to Ester, who immediately asks me if I have any children. I tell her no, and she responds, "I walked five days in the desert and will walk another five days if I have to. I don't care. *Primero Dios tengo que pasar.* I have to see my kids." In the Obama era of mass deportations, the phrase "I have to see my kids" has become a campaign slogan for determined deportees. She starts sobbing and Barbara puts her arm around her. Ester then asks, "Do you know when I can take a shower?" "As soon as dinner is over you will be able to shower," Pato tells her. "It might be about thirty minutes or more, though. I think there is a line." Ester wipes the tears from her eyes and then turns to me and starts laughing as she says, "I've waited five days to take a bath. What's another hour?"

The women finish their meals and head to their segregated dormitory. Pato and I start bussing the table as Memo brings in the first twenty men to eat. The group is fairly quiet, with the conversation mostly revolving around whether there is any salt or extra tortillas. They eat like people who haven't seen food in days, which is probably not too far from the truth. As I am warming up tortillas on the stove, someone bangs on the metal door of the dining area that leads out to the street. Pato opens it and finds Flaco, a tall, wiry Grupo Beta agent standing outside. "Hey, I got this girl with me who I need to drop off. She's in the truck." I peek out the window to see a woman in her early twenties sitting in the passenger seat of his official vehicle.

"Why didn't you drop her off with the rest of the women two hours ago?" Pato asks. "I had to take her to make a phone call," Flaco says with a toothy grin. He then turns to me, winks, and makes the international sign for fellatio. With a blank expression on my face I nod and try not to let my anger show. Everyone knows that Flaco is an asshole and a predator who routinely tries to get sexual favors from female migrants in exchange for extra assistance such as helping them find lost relatives. He carries an unauthorized handgun in his truck that he likes to show off late at night after he drops off a load of migrants. Once during one of our poker games, he pulled his firearm out and started waving it around the kitchen like a child. I was positive he was going to accidently shoot one of us. None of the shelter workers like or trust him, but no one has the power to say anything about his abuses. Pato tells him to bring the woman in, and he quickly escorts her into the dormitory. "Don't worry," he says, "I'll bring you a plate of food in a minute."

Over the following three hours two more truckloads of people arrive. Pato serves more than eighty bowls of food before finally running out of beans. We start feeding people cucumbers with salt, slices of bread, and anything else we can scrounge from the cupboards. Around midnight Pato tells the new arrivals that there is no more food. Several go to bed exhausted and hungry. By now all of the bunks are full and people are sleeping on the floor in the chapel.

After an hour of bullshitting with Memo and Lucho, I decide to get some sleep. As I walk to the men's dormitory, I step over several late arrivals who have set up beds in the hallway. I find Samuel's bunk and pull out the floor mat he has squirreled away for me. I lay it on the ground and plop myself down next to Lucho's bed. Despite my exhaustion, it is difficult to sleep. The combination of the air temperature, the minimal indoor ventilation, and seventy-five sweating bodies has turned the room into a foul-smelling sauna. A few men are enviously snoring loudly, while others can be heard quietly texting under blankets or just tossing and turning in the stale heat. I finally drift off to sleep only to be awoken half an hour later by rustling sounds and someone swearing. It's dark in the room, but I recognize one of the voices as Lucho's.

"What the fuck do you think you are doing?"

"Nothing."

"What do you mean 'nothing'?"

"I was looking for my shoes."

"Why do you need your shoes right now? You're supposed to be sleeping. Hey, that's my goddamn T-shirt!"

Suddenly Samuel jumps over me and grabs the person Lucho is yelling at. "I thought I recognized you!" he screams. "This is the fucker who stole someone's shoes a few weeks ago." I sit up and hear a few dull punches land. A crack of light breaks into the room as Lucho opens the front door of the shelter. For a brief second I see Samuel dragging someone out by the neck before the door slams shut, returning the room to darkness. A minute later both of them are crawling back into their beds to catch a few fitful minutes of sleep before the next Grupo Beta truck arrives.

LA LINEA

By 7 A.M. most of the men in the shelter have gotten dressed, picked their shoes out of the black trash bags, and collected their belongings. Since no one is allowed to stay there between 7 A.M. and 6 P.M., everyone has to evacuate the premises. If you arrived in Nogales the previous day, you will fortunately be able to return to Juan Bosco for two more nights of rest and hot meals. People who have just spent their third and final night at the shelter will now have to come up with a new game plan that includes finding a place to sleep. As the men walk out the front door, those who had packs of cigarettes dig them out of the giant plastic bag where the shelter workers were "guarding" them overnight. Many will find their packs slightly less full, the result of Rafa's midnight tobacco tariff, collected when no one was looking.

A Grupo Beta truck loaded with women and children drives off. The agents will drop them at their office, a bright-orange cement structure that sits about a half-mile from the Mariposa port of entry and a mile west of the DeConcini gate, through which everyone was previously deported. The men, many of whom have just spent multiple days trudging through the desert, will have to walk several miles to reach the office. This narrow strip of land along the border wall where the Grupo Beta Office is located and where deportees usually end up is often referred to as *la linea* by migrants.

Like a never-ending scene from Steinbeck's *Tortilla Flat*, every day on *la linea* a drama starring a revolving cast of heroines, hustlers, ne'er-do-wells, and saints plays out on the streets. It's a performance both heartbreaking and inspiring. In the same conversation or interaction you can find people weeping and laughing uncontrollably, swearing off the human race and simultaneously being surprised by the kindness of strangers. Standing on *la linea*, I quickly saw that there was no beginning or end to this particular part of the border-crossing story. It is futile to try to place a firm boundary around this field site populated by a dynamic roster of people involved in all types of social relationships, economic exchanges, and political maneuvering.

Similar to the hybrid collectif in the Sonoran Desert, this cultural landscape has too many moving and evolving parts for its totality to ever be seen all at once. As a researcher working with a mobile population, you do your best to engage with the diverse group of people who pass you on all sides on any given day. Their stories come in and out of focus as if viewed through a twisting kaleidoscope. The people who open up their lives to you over a plate of cheap tacos one day will likely be gone the next, only to be replaced by new faces and stories. As the days progress, some narratives show themselves to be variations of well-worn motifs: "I was deported for driving without a license and I need to get back to my children." Other stories appear out of nowhere and are extraordinarily shocking, funny, sad, schizophrenic, or mundane. A thorough ethnography of what happens on *la linea* is an ethnography that by design is incomplete, sometimes chaotic, and always morphing. The following ethnographic glimpses reflect my humble attempts to capture a fraction of what happens on the streets of Nogales every single day between the town's two major ports of entry.

In the remainder of this chapter I walk the reader through various moments on *la linea* that I observed or experienced between 2009 and 2014. I have purposefully folded ethnographic time in these descriptions because, in the end, the migrant experiences I describe are relatively timeless and continue to happen to this day. Border writer Luis Alberto Urrea summed it up perfectly: "Anyone who knows anything about the border can tell you that Mexican border towns change radically every twenty-four hours, yet never—and never will—change."[38]

These migrant narratives have no formal structure. They are Polaroids; stories with no resolution. After one or two conversations with someone I encountered in Nogales and later watched enter the desert, I usually never heard from them again. This border town, like all others, is just one stop along the migration route. All I could often do was take notes as people passed through my line of vision before disappearing over the horizon.

Grupo Beta

Deportees find themselves with limited options. A few may simply give up their hopes of crossing the border and decide to return home to Mexico or Central America. These are typically first-time migrants who had an especially traumatic experience in the desert. Most recent arrivals, though, will try their luck again as soon as they can rest up and scrape together funds to pay for the needed hiking supplies and, if they can afford it, the *coyote* fees. This may take only a few days, especially if a relative can wire them some cash. For the less fortunate, this preparation stage can last a week (or weeks) and may include a great deal of hustling down on the line to make ends meet. One's hustle might include daily calls to any family member or friend who will pick up the phone or washing windows, begging, stealing, and selling various items on the street. Most local businesses don't want to hire migrants, and those that do tend to exploit their labor. This is the moment when the value of mantras such as "I have to see my children" or "There is nothing to go back to in Oaxaca" becomes most evident. You need something to keep you motivated during this difficult preparation period that often bookends crossing attempts. No matter what you decide, though, it all happens in and around the Grupo Beta Office.

It is impossible to miss the Grupo Beta Office. The bright-orange paint on both the official vehicles and the main building sticks out amongst the dusty brown and gray cement houses that make up the bulk of the working-class neighborhood where it is located. Here, kids walk to school, homemakers do their grocery shopping, and migrants wait around for something to happen. The Grupo Beta Office is spitting distance from the American dream, close enough to Arizona that I still get reception from my US cell phone provider. I sit down on a curb in front of the office next to Ricardo, a handsome thirty-six-year-old man who has recently been laterally deported from California. He is tall with green eyes and a kind face. His deep laugh and easy manner are disarming. Ricardo starts telling jokes about trying to keep up with some *campesinos* he met on the trail who were obviously more accustomed to physical strain than he was. He manages to make me laugh out loud as he spins colorful yarns about crossing the border and getting mistreated by Border Patrol on various occasions.

Ricardo has lived in the United States for fifteen years, since arriving at the age of eighteen with a simple plan to work for a year, save some money, and then return to Jalisco, Mexico. He quickly grew accustomed to the comfortable wages he earned working in a hotel and soon married an American citizen. She gave birth to a baby girl a few years later. After multiple failed attempts to become a legal citizen, which included being swindled by an immigration attorney for several thousand dollars, he resigned himself to life in the undocumented shadows. Ricardo tried to stay out of trouble with the law but got deported after being arrested for a DUI. He is now in the unfamiliar town of Nogales, where he has recently hooked up with a local *coyote* he met in front of Grupo Beta. The *pollero* promises to get him through the desert in the next few days. Ricardo is desperate to get back to his family and is busily making plans. I hand him my cell phone and he calls his wife to tell her where he is. "I'll be home soon," he says. "Just make sure if a *coyote* calls you, don't send any money until you talk to me first."

Several migrants sit on benches that run along the fenced-in front patio of Grupo Beta's office. The group today is mostly Mexicans, but two Afro-Belizeans with long dreadlocks are hunched in the corner trying to remain unnoticed. Their skin color, hair, and accents make it clear they are not Mexican nationals and mark them as easy targets for robbery, assault, and kidnapping. Their safest move is to stay at the office and wait for a ride to the shelter at nightfall. As a safety measure, Grupo Beta has lined the courtyard with black tarps so that you can't see how many migrants (or what type) are present unless you enter the office. This is supposed to protect people from smugglers and criminals trolling the area.

Two well-dressed *coyotes* are standing in the parking lot of the office sweet-talking a group of recent deportees. One of the men leans on a Grupo Beta truck and asks people about their experiences in the desert. This *pollero* is soft-spoken and inquisitive, taking a less aggressive approach to *pollo* wrangling compared to some who try to bully bewildered migrants they find walking on the street into getting in their car. The *coyote* tells two dirt farmers from Durango who are clad in busted cowboy boots and sweat-stained pearl-buttoned shirts that traveling with him would be different from their previous experience. The two rubes listen intently as the smuggler promises a short and easy hike through the desert for a low price. "Just a few hours walking," he says.

A few new arrivals pass me and Ricardo and enter the office. They register with the agent sitting at the desk and then take a seat outside. You have to sign in if you want to use the restroom or make a free phone call to let your family know that you are stuck in Nogales. On both sides of the border, migrants find themselves filling out paperwork in one form or another. Undocumented migration produces a surprisingly long paper trail.

Rosa, the heavyset private security guard who works the door, steps onto the porch and yells, "*¡Erik Susunaga! ¡Llamada!*" Erik scrambles through the door to receive his phone call. Many have been here for hours waiting for a

Esperando. Grupo Beta Office, Nogales, Mexico, July 2009. Photo by author.

relative to call back. "*Oye primo,* can you send us seventy-five bucks to get a hotel room so we can rest up a few days before trying again?" Some hard-luck cases have been sitting in front of Grupo Beta for over a week waiting for an aid check from the Mexican government that deportees can qualify for if they are patient enough. The approximately $120 is supposed to help defray the cost of a discounted bus ticket to help someone return to a distant community in Mexico. Unfortunately, spending upward of two weeks on *la linea* waiting for a check is difficult and dangerous when you have little money, no place to stay, and look unmistakably like a shipwrecked migrant.

An older couple pull up to the office, their rusted-out pickup truck dragging a cloud of red Sonoran dust behind them. A woman steps out of the vehicle and approaches me and Ricardo. She tells us she is looking for her twenty-three-year-old son who was just deported from San Ysidro. She cries as she recounts the harrowing twelve hours they drove to get here and the various fines and bribes they had to pay to government officials they encountered on the highway. She clutches a framed photo of her hugging her son. She hands it to anyone who makes eye contact. No one has seen him. Rosa steps out onto the patio and shrieks, "¡Rene Ojeda! ¡Llamada!"

An hour later a shiny silver SUV with government logos on the doors approaches the office. A dark-haired middle-aged man in a crisp white dress shirt and pleated pants steps out. He carries a briefcase and an armful of brightly colored fliers that he immediately starts handing out to everyone in the vicinity. They are documents produced by the Mexican government that warn of the dangers of crossing the desert. Anna and Juan, an older indigenous couple from Oaxaca, take the paperwork and start flipping through the glossy pages decorated with dramatic photos of blazing suns, scorpions, and blistered feet. The two of them were robbed by bandits during their last crossing attempt and then deported after getting abandoned by their smuggler. Juan says that a Border Patrol agent punched him in the head when he asked about his wife's whereabouts while they were in detention. Anna's legs and feet are in bad shape from the trek. Both of them are wearing flip-flops and have no personal effects. They have been hanging out on *la linea* for almost ten days trying to figure out how to get to Kentucky where they have family doing agricultural work. They have recently taken up residence in an abandoned storage container across the street. The giant metal canister is furnished with two stained La-Z-Boys and a poster for the Partido Acción Nacional. PAN is Mexico's economically conservative political party that supported the trade agreements with the United States that pushed people like Juan and Anna to leave the Oaxacan countryside because they could no longer make a living wage from farming. The two of them sleep in the storage container at night, while others use it as a restroom during the day.

The official immediately begins a canned and slightly condescending speech to all those sitting on the benches. He informs everyone how risky it is to cross the desert and why they should not do it. A few audience members yawn and zone out. Everyone present knows how dangerous the desert is, and no one will likely be swayed by this public service announcement. The migrants are then told that they should report any abuses experienced at the hands of American law enforcement: "If the abuse took place in the United States, it is important that you remember all of the details when you tell your stories. Not just the women, but also the men. What kind of uniform was the agent wearing? What color was it? Their last name is normally on the front of the uniform, so you should try to remember it. If the person who abused you was driving a vehicle, try to remember what color it was and what the license plate number was." Someone says he was mistreated by Border Patrol several times. The official tells him he should file a report. No information is given on exactly how one would go about doing this, but the official reiterates the importance of filing a report. More yawning, especially from those who slept on the streets or at the port of entry the night before. A few folks are having their own private conversations, oblivious to these important safety messages. Others are visibly bored and checking their watches to see if it is time to walk to the *comedor* up the street that hands out free breakfast and lunch to migrants. The official knows that most of this information is falling on deaf ears, but he tries to drive home a few last key points:

> If you need medical attention, want to make a phone call, have money sent to you, or want a discount bus ticket, Grupo Beta can help you. All of these services are free. Still, these are not permanent services. You can get these for just a few days until you can return to your point of origin. . . . After this meeting, if you decide to throw away the pamphlet I have given you, make sure to tear out and keep the last page. It has important numbers for you to call in case you need help. For example, there is a number on there that you should use to call us from the United States if you encounter a dead body in the desert or someone hurt and abandoned. Also, the number for the Mexican consulate is in there. Some of you will be taken to court, and you have the right to see the Mexican consulate when you are detained. If you are detained, you have the right to tell Border Patrol that you want to see the consulate.

The fact that there is an official hotline to call if you see a dead *compañera* shocks no one. The official then explains the Alien Transfer and Exit Program to a group half composed of people who have already had firsthand experience with it:

> Mexicans will be deported here to the border. They can return you to any border town. They are not obligated to return you to the place where you crossed. For example, if you get caught in Nogales, don't think that they will have to return you to Nogales. . . . The Americans can leave you wherever they want along the Mexican border. The intention is so that you will not try and return again through the same place. That is their intention. They are trying to "break the chain." There are occasions where you may come with someone, perhaps a family member or a friend. They may send one of you to one town and the other to another. . . . In all border towns there are Grupo Beta offices and human rights officials who can help. . . . As soon as you contact your family, make sure that you give them the phone number of the office where you are located.

Finally, after half an hour of lecturing, the official picks up his briefcase and wishes everyone good luck. He gets into his shiny vehicle and speeds away. It is almost lunchtime, so people stand up and start making their way up the hill. As they walk out the front gate of the Grupo Beta Office, they leave behind a trail of abandoned brochures.

waiting 'round

We are sitting on a cement wall in front of the rundown basketball court a few hundred feet from the Grupo Beta Office when Diego asks me, "Are you gonna put the truth in your book or are you going to change our words around?" He continues: "I want you to put that Chicano Border Patrol agents are the worst sons of bitches there are and the ones who treat their own *paisanos* like dogs. When they give you food in detention, the Chicanos throw your food on the floor so that people have to pick up scraps like dogs. The *gringos* will sometimes say nice things like 'Take care of yourself' or 'Go with God.' The Chicanos will tell you to go fuck your mother." Fifty-eight-year-old Diego has a bitter disposition that has only gotten worse after spending the last week sitting on the basketball court waiting for his check from the Mexican government. He plans to use the money to travel to Tijuana with Salvador, Chino, and several other down-and-out migrant men he recently met. Their plan is to pool all available cash for bus fare to Baja California because Salvador, a twenty-four-year-old gangbanger from Van Nuys, says he knows how to get them across the fence near San Ysidro. "I've been deported like ten times, bro," he proudly states in English. "I can get across in San Diego. I'm too much of a wimp, man, for this desert shit." Diego also realizes that he might not be in the best shape to enter the desert again:

> We [he and a fifty-one-year-old traveling companion] were slow making it up the hills while the young guys and *coyote* were running to the top. By the time we would get there, everyone was rested except for us. We had to keep going without any rest. Our *coyote* also had better equipment than anyone else in the group. He had *suero* and stuff. He brought stuff with him that no one else knew we should have brought. He also ended up eating and drinking our food. They left us behind finally. We got so delirious that at one point we were trying to flag down airplanes.

Salvador and Chino, a middle-aged mechanic originally from Mexico City, have taken Diego under their wing. Their tiny band has been inseparable for several days. In a place where you can get robbed by the police, kidnapped by smugglers, hassled by local gangs, or assaulted by the mescal-chugging hoodlums who live in the municipal cemetery next to the basketball court, everyone recognizes there is strength in numbers on *la linea*, even if it is only temporary. This type of migrant social group is what some refer to as an "accidental community."[39] Despite the short-term benefits, people like Diego understand that theirs is a tenuous relationship of convenience: "Around here this is the brotherhood of the defeated. All of these poor migrants have very little except each other. There is a lot of brotherhood around here because we have nothing. As soon as someone gets a job or something better, though, they forget who you are."

Most of the men sitting around the basketball court have become persona non grata at Grupo Beta. Salvador recently got into a fight with *el panadero*, a taco vendor whose stand sits out in front of the office. In addition to selling food, *el panadero* (the bread man) makes a great deal of cash by acting as a go-between for people getting money wired to them. Without this service those who for various reasons lack identification would not be able to receive payment. Rosa, the security guard, funnels clients to the *panadero*, who then rides his bike to the Western Union Office to pick up money. His service charge can be anywhere from $10 for a small transaction or a percentage of the total amount. It all depends on how savvy your negotiation skills are.

Salvador recently threatened to pummel the bread man after he got wind that he ripped off a young indigenous woman from Guatemala who didn't speak much Spanish. Upon witnessing the verbal altercation, Rosa expelled Salvador from the office. Any harm that comes to the taco vendor could interrupt the lucrative side game she has going on. Everything on *la linea* is about business.

Fifty-one-year-old Claudio has also just been banished to the basketball court after someone in the office heard him complaining about Grupo Beta. He doesn't mince words:

> I've been in some very tough neighborhoods in *el DF* [Distrito Federal, Mexico City]. I'm from Tepito [a notorious Mexico City barrio], but nothing compares to being here in Nogales. Everyone seems to be out to get you here. . . . I don't understand what Grupo Beta does. Before I came here, I heard lots of good things about them: "They give you food, they help you." Then I get here and I see that they don't do anything. They don't feed you; the churches feed you. They don't let you bathe; the shelters do that. You can't stay there; the shelters

do that too. All Grupo Beta does is make you fill out a form and put your name on a list. They tell you that you can't do anything unless you sign their list. I only finished *la primaria* [elementary school] and I can still figure out that Grupo Beta doesn't do anything. They fill out those long lists so that they can show the government, "Look at how many people we help." They have nice new trucks and big salaries. Those lists help them, not us.

Although they have been stuck waiting for their aid checks to arrive, Diego, Salvador, and Chino have fared slightly better than Anna and Juan. The men have found lodging in a tiny one-room cement structure that sits on a small hill just 100 feet from the border wall. The gray windowless building is an ad hoc migrant shelter started by a group of impoverished Christian missionaries. As long as they are willing to pray several times a day and declare their love of Jesus Christ, they can sleep on cardboard mats for free. It is significantly better and safer than crashing in the abandoned storage container, but seems to provide little protection from local police officers who have taken to robbing migrants at gunpoint and threatening to murder those who report abuses.[40]

Estrella Blanca

Everyone knows Chucho. He is a disheveled angel of mercy who tirelessly walks up and down *la linea* handing out water, toothbrushes, razors, and anything else he can acquire that might be of some service to migrants. After three decades of living undocumented in Arizona, he ended up one day deported, homeless, and roaming the streets of Nogales. Since then, he has been living hand to mouth while hustling to find resources that he can then hand off to deportees. I run into him at the Estrella Blanca bus station, uphill from the basketball court. This is where you can purchase discount tickets to get "home" or someplace where a relative or friend will take you in. For some migrants, this may be the first time in their adult lives that they return to their community of birth.

Chucho is in the midst of providing first aid to a kid with a deep gash on the underside of his arm, the result of getting caught on a barbed-wire fence while running from Border Patrol. As he applies iodine to the gaping wound, Chucho tells me that he doesn't like to help migrants receive money transfers anymore. He says most will use it to try to cross the desert again instead of buying a bus ticket. In the same breath he says, "The bus goes through Mexico City, but if there aren't enough people to keep driving to Oaxaca or Córdoba,

Triage in the bus terminal. Photo by author.

people get dropped off at the station and are given 100 pesos." Being a farmer from rural Oaxaca who gets abandoned in Mexico City is as bad or possibly worse than life on *la línea*.

A forty-one-year-old woman named Lucy is waiting for her bus to leave. She has just come from detention and has decided to return to her home state of Guerrero:

> I never never never never thought in my life that they would chain us up like that. What are we, *pinches* criminals? I thought they would grab us and return us to where we came from. I never imagined they would chain us up. . . . I was in there for almost a week. You feel really awful being in a place like that. You never think you will be in a place where they treat you like an animal. . . . Imagine that you come hot from the *pinche* desert and then they put you in a freezing cell. . . . The lawyer told me when I was leaving court that if I try to cross again, they would put me in prison.

She is only one of three people who are taking the bus today. Dozens of others are congregated down the hill at Grupo Beta and the basketball court, passing time in the desert's waiting room. As we leave the bus station, Chucho nods his head toward the few waiting passengers and chuckles, "Today the *polleros* win."

When we see María and her seven-year-old daughter, Lupita, coming up the dusty road toward us, our hearts sink. I met them more than a week before when I walked into the empty chapel at Juan Bosco and saw them both kneeling in deep prayer in front of the Virgen de Guadalupe painting. The image of pious Lupita holding her hands together and squeezing her eyes closed tight could have been the cover of a Sunday school advertisement. María and her husband had traveled with their daughter up from Chiapas and failed on their first crossing. The family had been separated in federal detention in Tucson, and María had not heard from her husband since their arrest. After a week on *la línea* with no word from her spouse, she headed to the town of Altar to try their luck again. Chucho and I had hoped they would succeed this time and wouldn't have to come back to Nogales. Seeing them means that they have once again been arrested and deported.

We stop to greet them and find out what happened. María, wearing all black and carrying her few possessions in a tiny backpack, looks exhausted. It has been only a week since we last saw her, but her face looks as though it has aged ten years. Lupita, however, is still bright eyed in a pink striped shirt, tiny blue jeans, and nylon sneakers with cartoon characters on them. She looks ready for second grade. María tells us that they contracted a new *coyote* in Altar but got caught after only a day of walking. Some of her group managed to escape, but María couldn't run with Lupita in her arms. They spent the last of their money on crossing supplies and are now penniless in Nogales. In the middle of telling her story, tears start falling down her face. She turns away from Lupita to hide her crying. Chucho immediately kneels down to talk to the child about what kind of candy she likes. Everyone who encounters this kid works extra hard to keep her shielded from what is going on around her. Although she has endured two failed desert trips, multiple days in federal detention, and losing contact with her father, I have never seen her cry or complain in the nearly two weeks she has spent on *la linea*.

We walk to the corner market to buy Lupita a snack and then sit down on the curb out front. María asks if we know of any work available in Nogales. She needs to earn enough cash to take a bus to Tijuana, which is where her husband was deported. "There are no jobs around here, *mija*," Chucho says. "Someone offered me a job working in a *cantina*," she tells us, "but I knew it was more than just being a waitress." She comments that it is going to be hard for her to work with Lupita in tow and tells us that several *coyotes* have offered to "watch" the girl while she travels to Tijuana. "What do you think?" she asks. María is obviously at the end of her rope to even consider this offer. Her voice is desperate and she begins crying again. "Can you watch her?" she asks me. "You seem very nice." I tell her that I can't and that it is better if they stick together. Chucho tells her about the discount bus ticket she can buy to get back to Chiapas. María matter-of-factly responds, "I borrowed $3,000 dollars to pay for the trip. I earn 850 pesos a month [$65 dollars]. I am out of money and can't go back empty-handed. . . . Begging for money to get to Tijuana is easier than going home to nothing in Chiapas. . . . I have to keep crossing."

Lupita, who has been giggling and stomping her feet in the dirt lot next to the convenience store, comes running over to hand me some of her candy. Chucho stands up and turns to María: "*Mija*, you can't stay here in Nogales. There is no work here for migrant women and nothing good for you. If you stay, you will probably end up having to sell yourself. It is better for you to go to the bus station to beg for money. People will feel sorry for you because of the girl." He reaches into his pocket and pulls out a tattered fifty-peso bill. He hands it to her and then is suddenly unable to hold back his tears. Chucho has seen many awful things on *la linea*, but some moments just push you over the edge. "Get her something to eat and then go to the bus station."

Ruiz

We are surrounded on all sides by the dead, but their presence is somehow comforting. It's as if this field of black iron crosses, crooked gravestones, and cheap plastic flowers temporarily shields us from the clatter and commotion of the border. It is a quiet moment with thirty-year-old Ruiz, whom I met five minutes ago when I spotted him and his friend Chuy standing near a rusted-out trash can near the basketball court. They were both covered in a thin layer of desert dust and weighed down with overstuffed green camouflage backpacks. I noticed them not because of their migrant uniforms, but because they had their faces buried in a map of Sonora, a rarity in these parts. "A friend of ours let us borrow it," he tells me. "We just wanted to see where we've been and where we are going." I introduce myself, and soon the two of us are sitting in the cemetery talking about his current situation.

Originally from the Mexican state of Puebla, Ruiz is about five foot seven with shiny black hair and sharp facial features. He is soft-spoken and gives off an air of seriousness undermined by how easily and often he cracks a sly smile. Like many recent deportees, Ruiz had been living in the United States since he crossed the desert as a seventeen-year-old in 2000. Sitting on a curb crowded by tombstones, he tells me how he recently ended up in Nogales:

> I was driving in my car and following all the laws. I had my car registered. They pulled me over and said I was driving recklessly. I was driving the speed limit. I told the police officer, "You were the ones driving recklessly because you came chasing after me." I said, "You have no reason to pull me over." The police officer responded, "Show me your identification," and I said, "Truthfully, I don't have any." He said, "Don't give me a false name," so I gave him my real name, and I said, "You want the truth? I'll tell you the truth."
>
> Yeah, they arrested me because I didn't have identification or papers. They grabbed me and took me to Tempe. That's where I saw the judge. He asked me if I was guilty, but he was already saying that I was guilty. They said if I was guilty, they wouldn't lock me up, but if I said I wasn't guilty, they were going to keep me locked up. I said, "Well, I'm guilty, then, because I want to get out of here."
>
> When they first grabbed me, they told me they were going to send me back to Mexico, but in the end they took me to Sheriff Joe Arpaio's jail.[41] I asked them to call ICE [Immigration and Customs Enforcement] and release me on a bond of $500, but they told me no. They said I wasn't going to pay. So they kept me. I was in there a while. They treat you really terribly in there. You have to take all your clothes off in front of everyone. They gave me some clothes but

they were too big for me. They didn't care. . . . They took me to another jail for two days and then turned me over to immigration.

I wanted to fight my case, but they took me out of Arizona. They sent me to detention in El Paso and I was there for six months. No one would help me and I couldn't trust anyone. I lost all contact with my family. They threw away everything that I had. My telephone, everything. Since then I haven't had contact with anyone. Even now I don't know where my family is. . . . I was going to family court at the time because of problems with my wife. I got arrested by the police during this process and I couldn't show up for court. I couldn't do anything. . . . I think the state was going to take away my kids. Right now I'm pretty sure that the state has them. I want to get back there to find out where they are. . . . I lost everything.

Ruiz has crossed the desert on numerous occasions. The first time was in 2000 when it cost him $1,000 and took only four hours. After getting beat up by his neighbor in Arizona in 2009, he was arrested when the cops were called and he couldn't produce any identification. It took him six tries to get across the border that year. In 2013, he says it is more difficult than ever to migrate.

Jason: What is the *camino* like now?

Ruiz: It is even more *peligroso* now. You have to walk farther and in more difficult places. The desert is treacherous. In the day everything can seem fine, tranquil. At night, you see that it is infinite, enormous, dark. The animals that come out at night are dangerous.

Jason: What does it sound like?

Ruiz: You hear coyotes. You hear the coyotes getting close to you. Hiding behind you. You hear everything alone. It is as if there is no one else except you out there. It's just you.

He and his companion Chuy have already been arrested twice trying to cross the desert. They have been living on the streets of Nogales, sleeping under bridges and in the cemetery. These men have been subsisting on what they can find in the trash and on the kindness of strangers. Ruiz tells me he is diabetic and that an old man who gives sandwiches to migrants on Sundays recently bought him two bottles of insulin. As soon as they have enough food and water, they will enter the desert again without a guide. Ruiz has no identification but carries a tiny piece of paper with his cousin's address on it. If he loses it, he still has the number memorized.

Regardless of the current dangers, Ruiz is determined:

Ruiz: I tried to cross in Juárez with no money or nothing. Just like I am now trying to find a way to cross here in Nogales. I am trying to cross so I can find out where my kids are. I want to cross to ask the court where they sent them, to know something. I want to see if I can do something. I ask God to give me a small opportunity, nothing more. Right now we are trying to find food for the trip. It is not that easy. Here and over there in Juárez, it's the same.... I just try to keep moving forward. I haven't lost everything yet. I just keep moving forward. Anything can happen, but with God nothing is impossible.

Jason: Do you think about your family when you are crossing?

Ruiz: Yes. I just want to get there so that I can see them and be with them; to give kisses to my sons; to find out where my children are. Maybe they think I left them behind. If so, I want to tell them that's not what happened. I want them to know that I left because immigration got me because I didn't have any papers. I need to explain to them face to face what happened. I want to tell them not to be afraid and that I am here to help them.

At this point, Ruiz pulls out a small plastic bag from his backpack that contains photos of his three US-born children ages four, six, and seven. The photo of the youngest child shows him smiling and pointing his finger at the camera.

Jason: Do you ever look at these while you are crossing?

Ruiz: No. Sometimes I just look at them right before I leave for the desert. It makes me sad but it also energizes me. It gives me something positive to think about.... I also carry a tiny Virgen de Guadalupe. I pray for her to protect me on the road and guide me.

At the end of our brief conversation, I ask Ruiz if there is anything else he wants to tell me or people who might read this book about his experiences.

Ruiz: Everyone here is trying to get there. We are all over here in Mexico suffering. For me, I want to return and have another chance to see my family. That's what I want. There are times when I didn't do anything. They say there are things that we migrants do illegally but we don't all have the money. That is the difference. The white people [*güeros*] want us to enter your country legally. I know that it is their country, but they should have a little bit of heart and know what is happening on this side of the border. They need to see the differences. We are going there for our dreams. Sometimes the dream is only halfway realized. Sometimes people return. I have seen people return in mourning because they lost a family member. It doesn't matter, though; we all just try to keep moving forward.

We shake hands and Ruiz walks away. After a few feet he turns around and says, "I'm gonna get across."

CYCLES

A dehydrated body with shackled hands and feet begs a judge for mercy. A frightened man steps through a port of entry straight into a den of wolves. A woman breaks down over dinner and is escorted to bed by strangers. A young mother stares over the border wall in preparation for another go at it. For many migrants, the post-deportation world of *la linea* is just one chaotic stop on the way to another crossing attempt. It is where the Sonoran hybrid collectif begins (and sometimes ends). A few may experience the many things described in this chapter in just a matter of hours. Numerous individuals may pass through the bureaucratic deportation machine and the Nogales minefield several times before they succeed or change course. The complexities of the post-deportation world can rival what people experience in the desert or can be far worse. Just like what goes down on the other side of the fence, much of what happens on *la linea* comes down to luck, skill, and persistence. There is no resolution to *la linea's* narrative, because it has no end. It is a space where bodies are in perpetual motion. Some make it through and some don't. Those who finally get across may remain safely hidden in the United States until a broken taillight or an immigration raid at their workplace lands them once again in front of the Grupo Beta Office.

Ricardo left with the *coyote* he met in Nogales. Less than half an hour into his journey he and his group were ambushed by *bajadores* who stuck a pistol to his temple and took everything he had. The last time I saw him, he was crying in front of Grupo Beta, telling me he was headed to Tijuana, where he thought it would be safer to cross. Diego, the bitter old man, finally received his check from the Mexican government that he planned to use to travel to Tijuana with Salvador, Chino, and others who promised to help him. Rosa the security guard talked Diego into letting her safeguard his money until everyone else was ready to leave the state. She told him it was too dangerous to be walking around with that much cash in his pocket. When he went to collect his money from her, she pretended not to know what he was talking about and had him physically removed from the Grupo Beta Office.

Salvador, the gangbanger from Los Angeles, eventually did leave with Diego, Chino, and a few others to try their luck crossing elsewhere. When I visited him at his house in Van Nuys, California, he told me that he separated from the group after Chino stole their money so that he could get drunk. This was around the same time that Chino called my cell phone to ask for money and to say that Salvador was a bastard who had left them stranded in a Tijuana migrant shelter. The last time I spoke to Salvador, he told me that he was planning to go into the human smuggling business in Arizona because he "knew some white people who could pick up migrants in the desert and then drive them through the checkpoints." On the same day that Chucho gave María and Lupita his last 50 pesos to buy some food, they left with a man they met at Grupo Beta who promised to help get them to Tijuana. After a few years of hustling on *la línea*, Chucho was able to build a new life. He went from sleeping under a bench at the bus station to working for a nonprofit organization in Nogales. He now earns a living assisting recently deported migrants. I am sure he is still giving away his money to those who need it more. Six months after I spoke with Ruiz, he sent me a text message that said, "I'm in Arizona."

———————

It is late in the afternoon when I walk up to the Mariposa port of entry. There is a soup kitchen run by Jesuits and an abandoned Red Cross trailer that sits at the top of a hill on the Mexican side. Several migrants and a few homeless locals are already in line for the afternoon meal. A skeleton of a dog lingers by the door, hoping that someone will toss him some scraps on their way out. Two teenagers in polo shirts are standing across the street. Both are holding binoculars and walkie-talkies and closely monitoring Border Patrol vehicle activity along the fence. Their radios periodically chirp and crackle as they update someone on the other end about *la migra's* whereabouts. A few men and women in dark clothes are patiently lying in the shade underneath the trailer. The desert is waiting for them.

CHAPTER 6

Technological Warfare

"LEAVING TOMORROW"

A few days after I meet them, Lucho and Memo tell me one evening that they are going to cross the border very soon. "I should rest up tonight because I think we're leaving tomorrow," Memo nonchalantly states. Admittedly, I get excited about the prospect of watching them prepare and then following them as they go into the desert. As I head out the door that night, I tell Samuel about this development and that I will be back early the next day to document the preparations. He smirks, nods his head, and says, "OK, then, I guess we'll see you tomorrow."

I arrive at 7 A.M. the following day and find Lucho and Memo lounging around on their bunks enjoying the downtime after the shelter clears out. They don't look like people getting ready to do anything, much less cross the desert. "I think we are leaving tomorrow instead. We're not ready yet." I'm disappointed, but don't want to push the subject. What do I know about being ready? Instead I spend the day with them and help clean the shelter. That evening while we prepare dinner, I ask Memo a hundred questions. What will they buy? How will they prepare mentally? When is the right time to go? "Tomorrow you will see," he tells me. "Tomorrow you can see how we do it." Once again, I show up the next morning with my camera and voice recorder. Once again, Memo tells me that they still aren't ready to go. "The weather is not quite right. We want to wait a few more days." I begin to understand Samuel's smirk.

Shopping for the apocalypse. Photo by author.

By the end of the week, I stop asking when they are leaving and start thinking that Memo and Lucho might transition into permanent shelter staff like Pato, Rafa, Samuel, and Patricio—migrants who achieve a minor level of comfort working for room and board and whose dreams of crossing slowly fall by the wayside as the days turn into months (and in Pato's case, years). Samuel and the rest of the guys are always joking that they are "leaving tomorrow." As I continue to work with migrants on *la linea*, Memo and Lucho become permanent fixtures at Juan Bosco. Weeks go by. We become friends and I stop asking when they are going to cross. I don't want to know anymore. Not because I don't care or believe them, but because I selfishly don't want them to abandon me. Hanging out with them at night makes my fieldwork on *la linea* easier. Their friendship fills an important void created by listening to people's difficult crossing stories day in and day out and then watching recent acquaintances—people who have opened up to me about their lives over a few short hours or days—walk off into the sunset. This is probably why I am in utter disbelief when Memo comments one afternoon that they are going to buy supplies the next day and enter the desert that following evening. He tells me to show up early so I can document it. "I promise," he says, "we're leaving tomorrow."

TWENTY-SIX DOLLARS' WORTH OF GROCERIES AND A BIBLE

I get to Juan Bosco early, just as the last group of guests are departing for the day. Memo and Lucho are in good spirits and seem excited about the shopping trip.[1] We walk down the street to the local market and begin working our way down the aisles. This *tienda* does not carry the specialized migrant goods that you often find in the desert archaeological record such as camouflage backpacks and black water bottles. It's your everyday grocery store. This makes Memo and Lucho's mission all the more bizarre. It's a strange sensation watching them push a cart and stop to read labels and price tags on items. Trying to get their money's worth, they spend close to an hour bargain hunting. While other customers are buying meat for a Sunday *carne asada*, these guys are shopping for a trip through Hades. I take a final inventory of the contents of their cart:

    4 gallons of water
    3 bags of instant refried beans
    11 small cans of tuna
    2 large cans of sardines
    0.5 kilo of limes
    2 bags of flour tortillas
    1 loaf of bread
    0.10 gram of raw garlic
    0.22 gram of fresh jalapeños
    1 packet of lemon-flavored Halls cough drops
    1 pouch of beef jerky

Many of the goods they select are obvious necessities. Tuna and sardines have high salt content and will help them retain water longer and slow down the dehydration process. The bread, beans, and tortillas are carbohydrate-heavy foods that they hope will keep them full during the crossing, when they will burn thousands of calories a day. Water is essential, but they can carry only two gallons each in their backpacks. They don't want to hold bottles in their hands, because that would slow them down and make it hard to move quickly across rough terrain. The cost of these supplies comes to $26. By US standards, that is not much money, but it has taken them several weeks to scrape together the funds. I think back to a conversation I had with Lucho and Samuel at the shelter a few weeks before.

> *Lucho:* Hey, how much does a pizza cost here in Mexico?
>
> *Samuel:* 120 or 130 pesos [9–10 US dollars based on August 2009 exchange rates].
>
> *Lucho:* That's what you would make in a day, huh?
>
> *Samuel:* Yeah.
>
> *Lucho:* Imagine that. You work an entire day so that you can buy a fucking pizza. You work eight hours so that you can buy a pizza. How much does a pair of pants cost?
>
> *Samuel:* Good ones?
>
> *Lucho:* Yeah, good ones.
>
> *Samuel:* It depends. Maybe like 600 pesos [$46 US dollars].
>
> *Lucho:* 600 pesos. That's like a week of work! A week! Forty hours of work for a pair of pants.

Buying provisions for each of their crossing attempts has been difficult because Memo and Lucho are not able to find steady employment in Nogales. For the past month they have worked the occasional one-day construction job and have been making less than 120 pesos a day. According to labor statistics published by the Mexican government, the average minimum daily wage in 2009 was 53.3 pesos (4.10 US dollars).[2] Luckily for them, they are making more than double this amount, partly because wages tend to be higher in northern border towns where American dollars and Mexican pesos are used interchangeably. Still, because they are recent deportees and lack the proper paperwork to work legally in Nogales, they have been getting paid under the table and receiving lower daily wages compared to what locals make doing the same work. Even in their "own country," their labor is exploited.

We head back to the shelter, where I watch them start to cram their low-tech supplies into their bags. As they pack, they give me a running commentary about the importance of each item.

> *Memo:* Garlic [shows me the bulb as he places it in his pack].
>
> *Jason:* Why garlic?
>
> *Memo:* It's for the snakes. For rattlesnakes. You rub it on your clothes and shoes.

¡Saca el arma! Photo by author.

Jason: Does it work?

Memo: Yes.

Jason: Who says so?

Memo: I don't know who says it.

Lucho: The animals don't like the smell of garlic. It's like when you eat food with a lot of garlic and the mosquitoes don't bite. They show up and leave.

Jason: But how do you know that it works for rattlesnakes too?

Lucho: That's what they say.

Memo: The *coyotes* tell you that. We only use garlic here in the desert, though. Not in California. It only works in the desert.

I could find no scientific evidence to support the assertion that garlic keeps snakes away. This doesn't stop the Mexican Red Cross from handing out brochures that recommend rubbing your body, clothes, and shoes with this pungent plant before entering the desert. Lucho shows me his extra socks and foot powder, which may come in handy if his feet get wet or he starts to get blisters from his knock-off Adidas sneakers. He also packs two black T-shirts that he says will help him avoid *la migra.* "It makes it harder for them to see us at night," he says. I ask about the discomfort from the extra heat generated by wearing black in the scorching desert, and he replies, "It's better to be hot than caught."

Memo and Lucho are doing their best to answer all of my questions and also maintain an air of humor during the packing process. We are all laughing and cracking jokes. Lucho says to me, "This is the most important thing for the trip," and brandishes a plastic cap gun and points it at Memo. "What the hell are you gonna do with that?" I ask. "It's for the little animals. You scare them off with it. They don't like the sound or the smell of the smoke." I start thinking about what kinds of animals they might run into: Mojave greens,[3] black bears, mountain lions. I picture Lucho firing a child's toy pistol at a charging javelina.

While this is all going on, Rafa and Samuel start writing farewell messages on their backpacks. I grab the marker and write, "Memo, don't forget that you owe me an apple juice." "Apple juice" is the code we used when we would sneak off to get beer for our late-night poker games. Someone would always crack, "Hey, we are almost out of apple juice! Better head to the store." To be inconspicuous, we would wrap the *caguamas* (quart-sized beer bottles) in a towel and sneak out the back door. They ended up looking like bundled-up babies, which only led to more jokes: "*Oye*, Yason, I think the baby needs more milk. Better take him to the store." "Hey, *cabroncito*, you better drink your apple juice so someday you can grow up big and strong!" This last line would almost always be followed up by a vulgar retort that someone in the room would be willing and able to dispense milk to the rest of us should we need sustenance.[4] I start replaying these comical hypermasculine moments in my head. Thinking about the good times is easier than acknowledging that Memo and Lucho are about to do something very dangerous.

After loading their packs with food and clothes, they both attempt to jam their two gallons of water inside. The seams of their bags look as if they are going to burst, but they finally manage to zip them up. Memo jokes that he is going to make some room in his backpack to stick in a few *caguamas* for the road. We are laughing at the ridiculous image of him sucking on a giant bottle of beer while traipsing through the wilderness. *¡Toma tu leche!* In typical Memo fashion, he starts telling a story about actually drinking *cerveza* while crossing the desert.

> Memo: When we crossed with García, we stopped in Río Rico [Arizona] and drank some beers. [laughs] Remember, Lucho? We were drinking and having a good old time!

Jason: Where the hell did you get beer from? [laughing]

Memo: We stopped near Río Rico where there is a little store. We were hiding but could see the store and some guys doing construction work on the road. We were out of food, so I volunteered to walk down to the store. There was a sheriff parked near the construction site, but I just headed down and acted like I was one of the workers. I was dirty from the desert, so I looked like I was one of them. I walked right past the sheriff and went into the store to get some food. Then I thought I might as well grab a six pack too. I grabbed the food and beer and walked out and went to where Lucho and García were hiding. I handed everyone their share of tortillas and tuna and also some Cokes. Then I said, "OK, you only get two of these each!" and pulled out the beers. We sat there and started drinking the *chelas* and having a little party. [laughing] We were partying and telling jokes. We were all a little drunk because we were so dehydrated and tired from walking. We were laughing so hard, it was like we forgot what we were doing! It was like we were having a party out in the woods. [all of us laughing] Then we heard a vehicle drive by and we got scared and started moving.

At this point, everyone is laughing and talking about the mountain of beers they are going to drink once they get across the border. Memo starts clowning around with his backpack on and waving good-bye to all of us.

The joke telling at this point is less about machismo and more about lightening the mood. Our conversation avoids any discussion of the dangers these guys are about to face. Samuel and Rafa are saying positive things like, "Give us a call when you get to Arizona. You have our cell phone numbers." It is the middle of August and the recent temperatures have been in the low 100s. Everyone knows that they are not carrying enough water to survive more than a few days in the desert. They will have to find water along the way and will likely end up drinking the green liquid from the bacteria-laden cattle tanks that dot the southern Arizona desert. It is also obvious that they are underequipped. Memo is wearing clunky construction boots and Lucho's cheap sneakers will no doubt get shredded by the desert terrain. Given the amount of calories they are going to burn, the food they have will probably last no more than four days. They are also going to have to navigate their way through the mountains based on things they have learned from previous trips and Lucho's knowledge of the area. They have no map or compass. If Border Patrol were to catch them with either of these items, they would be labeled smugglers and face real jail time.

They have clothes, food, and water but not much in the way of nonessential items. Lucho has a small notebook, in which he has written his full name

Headed to *la linea*. Photo by author.

and Memo's along with the date of departure. Lucho is also carrying a dog-eared Bible that someone gave him while he was in jail after his DUI arrest. Memo has no personal possessions. Everything he owns at the moment—literally the clothes on his back—was given to him by people at the shelter. I find a Mexican phone card in my wallet that has a picture of the Virgin of Guadalupe on it and I give it to him. He tells me that it will give him luck and protect him. They are entering the desert with $26 in groceries, a Bible, and hope.

We jump on a bus and silently ride to the outskirts of Nogales where the two will enter the desert on foot. Out of nowhere Memo turns to me and says:

> A lot of things are going through my head right now. I'm thinking about my family and I'm scared that I am going to die out there. Each time is different. You never know what is going to happen. . . . The *bajadores* should be out partying tonight because it's Saturday. We should be able to avoid them. We have food and water and, God willing, we will get across. . . . We are going to hang on as long possible, as much as we can.

The three of us get off the bus and head toward a tunnel just west of the Grupo Beta Office. I have walked by this tunnel every day while doing field-

work on *la linea*, but until now never realized what it is used for. It runs underneath the highway. Migrants who enter it pop out on the other side just on the
edge of Nogales where a trail leads into the desert. The two of them have used
it before and have a system:

> *Memo:* It is very dark in the tunnel. When you enter you have to listen to hear
> if there are any rattlesnakes to make sure no one gets bit.... You also have
> to make sure that there are no people in the tunnel. If there are, we stop and
> turn around because they are *bajadores.* You can turn around, but if they see
> you they will come after you. They are waiting to jump you. You can some-
> times smell cigarette smoke if one of them is hiding. Then I would just tell
> Lucho to hold on because there are some people hiding in there. If people
> are just crossing, they have no reason to be waiting in the tunnel. Those
> aren't migrants, they are *bajadores* who are going to rob you.... You have to
> always be careful because a lot of people cross through there. We saw people
> going in there, but much earlier in the day. We calculated that we should go
> in the afternoon because my idea is to get to *la linea* when it is a little dark
> and you can only see a little bit.

We get close to the tunnel and stop. We hug and say our final good-byes.
Memo starts walking away and then yells for me to get the camera out: "Take
a picture to show your students! For the book!" It is the first time I don't want
to take any photos. Observing this process has been difficult, but I try to
remain positive and keep a smile on my face. The last thing these guys need is
to see me blubbering right before they enter the desert. Ruth Behar once wrote
that "anthropology that doesn't break your heart just isn't worth doing."[5] It is a
powerful statement that I have long agreed with, but it is not always easy to
put into practice. Watching Lucho and Memo leave is not exciting, nor is it an
inspiring anthropological field moment. It makes me feel worthless and afraid
for them. There is nothing that I can do to help them now.

A thousand thoughts race through my head. I wonder if I will ever see
them again. If I do, will it be to identify their bodies? Waves of apocalyptic
visions come to me: Memo opens his mouth to scream for help and white sand
pours out in violent pulses. The desert is eating him from the inside. Lucho's
Bible lies in the dirt, page by page it is slowly destroyed by wind and rain. The
brown skin on the back of his hands and on his face dries, cracks, and blows
away in a matter of seconds. His defleshed skull is wide-eyed and grinning. I
start thinking about how I will write about this moment later. The thought
that this event will probably be turned into data for a publication that will
benefit me and do little to help them survive makes me sick to my stomach. I

am nothing now but an academic voyeur. The distance between my world and theirs has never felt so vast.

Reluctantly, I pull my camera out and snap a few blurry pictures to appease Memo as they walk away. He stops right before the tunnel entrance and gives me a toothy grin and a wave. He then yells, "Don't worry, I brought the apple juice!" And just like that they disappear into the darkness. I walk 50 feet and slump down on a curb in front of the cemetery. School has just let out. Kids in crisp white uniforms and shiny patent leather shoes walk past me on the sidewalk.

[handwritten annotation: Juxteposition — innocence & fighting young vs older]

TECHNOLOGICAL WARFARE

Cell phone cameras snap photos and a few students giggle. González and I are grinning at the sight of my visibly pregnant wife, who is wearing a 20-pound army-green tactical vest and night vision goggles. She looks like a character from a Terry Gilliam film. González excitedly tells us, "The goggles are cool, but wait till you guys see the gun room. That's where we keep the fun stuff." Agent Ramiro González[6] is like most of the Border Patrol agents who have given me and my students guided tours of their facilities over the years. He is young, male, Latino, and excited to show off his toys. Everyone takes off her or his goggles and follows him through a series of corridors. Walls are decorated with inspirational government posters, memorial images dedicated to those who died on September 11, and photos of grinning agents crouching next to giant pyramids of confiscated marijuana bricks and car trunks full of methamphetamines. The men in these photos (they are almost always male) look like big-game hunters standing next to their kills. We pass a bulletin board covered in Most Wanted fliers featuring America's top-listed terrorists, drug runners, and *coyotes*. There is a Xeroxed piece of paper depicting a Mexican national wanted for human smuggling. Someone has taken a pencil and poked a hole through this man's forehead and written "Haha."

The gun room is a windowless white cubicle stuffed with enough pump-action shotguns and assault rifles to fight a small civil war. I stare at a matte-black Heckler and Koch HK-33 5.56 mm assault rifle. It can fire 750 rounds a minute and has a muzzle velocity of 950 meters per second. It's familiar because I have occasionally come across agents walking in the desert carrying one. It is the same type of rifle that a masked man was wielding in 2010 when he and ten other Border Patrol agents surrounded our field house in Arivaca and began interrogating the college students standing outside washing and cataloging migrant artifacts recovered in the desert. It is an intimidating weapon to say the least. I have no doubt that it scares the shit out of corn farmers from Morelos and out-of-work schoolteachers from Tegucigalpa who find themselves staring at the business end of it after being tackled to the ground for trying to run away. "¡Parense putos! Don't make me have to shoot!"

The tour moves on, and we see many more gadgets that the Border Patrol relies on to "gain situational awareness to better detect, identify, monitor, and respond to threats to the Nation's borders."[7] It's a dizzying list of mechanical hoodoo: "Biometrics, Thermal Hand-Held Imaging Devices, Mobile Surveillance System[s], Unattended Ground Sensors, Mobile Video Surveillance System[s], . . . Remote Video Surveillance System[s], . . . Vehicle and Cargo Inspection System[s], . . . Night Vision Devices . . . Integrated Fixed Towers."[8] Don't forget assault rifles, drones, four-wheelers, horses, handcuffs, stun guns, and the old-fashioned combat boot to the neck.

Every time I find myself in the middle of the Border Patrol's technological show-and-tell time, I start thinking about Memo's clunky construction boots and Lucho's Bible. I think about their twenty-six dollars' worth of groceries versus the billions of dollars spent annually on boundary enforcement. We keep pouring American tax dollars into the border security industrial complex and migrants keep buying garlic and dark clothes. Both sides are confident in the efficacy of their tools and strategies. It's like a scene from Malinowski's *Argonauts of the Western Pacific*: "It must be realized that the natives firmly believe in the value of magic, and that this conviction, when put to the test of their actions, is quite unwavering, even nowadays when so much of native belief and custom has been undermined."[9]

In 1989, the year after Memo first crossed the border, the annual federal budget for the US Border Patrol totaled $232 million. By fiscal year 2010, that annual budget had increased to $3.8 billion, a growth linked to changes in enforcement practices in the mid-1990s and enhanced security concerns following the events of September 11, 2001. As astonishing as this current annual boundary enforcement budget is, it still does not include the billions of dollars allotted to other agencies such as Immigration Customs and Enforcement that police ports of entry or those responsible for fence construction and maintenance. Based on rough estimates derived from a recent congressional report, $14.8 billion were spent on boundary security in fiscal year 2012.[10]

Ex-governor of Arizona and former head of the Department of Homeland Security Janet Napolitano once told a reporter, "You show me a 50-foot wall and I'll show you a 51-foot ladder at the border. That's the way the border works."[11] There is a wall between the United States and Mexico, but everyone knows that it doesn't stop the flow of people or illegal drugs. Just ask those who routinely find new and inventive ways to get past it. There are the smugglers who build catapults to launch drugs over the fence.[12] There is the masked man caught on video casually talking on his cell phone while using an ordinary car jack to lift the wall up so people could crawl underneath it.[13] There are also those enterprising drug runners who construct ramps so they can drive their cars over the fence[14] and the really ambitious who build multimillion-dollar tunnels to pass directly underneath it.[15] Let's not forget about the run-of-the-mill migrants who just say, "The hell with this *pinche* wall!" and climb over it. Although not as common as it was prior to Prevention Through Deterrence, fence hopping still happens often enough to be a concern for law enforcement. A federal document from 2009 shows that over the course of a year, the Nogales fence was breached an average of eight times a week,[16] an astonishing number given the high density of cameras, agents, and motion sensors in this area. I once watched two men climb the wall in downtown Nogales in broad daylight and crawl past a parked Border Patrol vehicle on their hands and knees. Where there's a will, there's a way.

Despite the evidence that the border wall is no match for catapults, car jacks, and other forms of human ingenuity, the United States can't seem to shake the fixation that building more of it will somehow solve many of our country's economic and social problems. Politicians are well aware of this fixation and routinely use it to their advantage. For example, while on the presidential campaign trail in 2011, Republican candidate Herman Cain received thunderous applause while making the following statement to a crowd in Cookeville, Tennessee, regarding his plans for immigration security: "We'll have a real fence. Twenty feet high with barbed wire. Electrified with a sign on the other side that says, 'It can kill you.' . . . Then I get criticized: 'Mr Cain, that's insensitive.' What do you mean insensitive? What's insensitive is when [people] come to the United States across our border and kill our citizens and kill our Border Patrol people. That's insensitive and I'm not worried being insensitive [when I] tell people to stop sneaking into America!"[17] I always wonder who conservatives like Cain would get to build their superfence. Perhaps he could use the California-based construction firm that was fined in 2006 for hiring undocumented laborers to help build the border wall between Tijuana and San Ysidro.[18]

Playing on the fears that many conservative Americans hold regarding brown-skinned invaders ruining their economy, destroying their neighborhoods,

Border wall, Nogales, Arizona. Photo by Michael Wells.

and killing citizens is a tried-and-true political strategy.[19] Unfortunately for these extremists, no amount of fear or hate can convince the government that walling off the entire border would be effective or feasible. These structures are too expensive to erect and maintain,[20] and they cause a significant amount of environmental damage.[21] This is why only 351 miles (18%) of the 1,954 miles that make up the US-Mexico border have anything resembling a wall.[22] These tall and imposing monuments are intended to make it difficult for people to climb over but are found only in and around urban ports of entry. The behemoths are what the Border Patrol proudly shows off to visiting politicians. These are the fences that you see in publicity photos and political photo ops. What you rarely get to see are the places where the wall abruptly vanishes.

Ask any Border Patrol agent or migrant about the wall, and they will tell you the same thing: it doesn't stop migration. For agents, it funnels people toward more remote areas where Border Patrol has the "tactical advantage."

Walker Canyon border fence. Photo by Bob Kee.

For migrants, it's a road sign that directs you toward the Arizona desert where you stand a fighting chance of making it past *la migra*. At the end of the day, the billions of dollars spent annually on security technology camouflage the dirty little secret that, compared to fences, motion sensors,[23] drones, and infrared cameras, the best and most lethal weapon the Border Patrol has is nature.

————

Many places along the border are marked by a three-strand barbed-wire fence or nothing at all. In Walker Canyon just northwest of Nogales, there is even an unlocked gate you can open and close at will. These are the same areas where Border Patrol are few and far between. In general, the agents have few incentives to heavily police these open areas. Catching someone at the moment of entry and deporting them back to Mexico leaves the person relatively fresh and energized to try again right away. Besides, the agency lacks the personnel to post people across the entire border, though that is changing.[24] The Border

Outdoor market specializing in crossing supplies, Altar, Sonora, Mexico. Photo by Michael Wells.

Patrol recognizes that it is better to let migrants go a few rounds with heat stroke, *bajadores*, and whatever else they might encounter in the wilderness. Only after they have taken some licks does law enforcement become interested in chasing people down and trotting them back to Mexico. Border crossers are easier to apprehend if they are exhausted or dead. Anthropologist Rocío Magaña recorded this strategy in a candid interview with an agent:

> They have a tactic in which they let the migrant walk. They let him walk for two or three days so he would suffer hunger and heat. They have them very well localized, they know where the crossers are. [And they say,] "Well, this [crosser] is going to be there, he is going to walk for two to three days. I am going to go home and sleep; tomorrow, when I come back, I'll get him underneath a tree while he is tired or waiting. I am not going to need to chase him. Why? Because he is not going to run, the migrant is already too tired." I'm telling you . . . two to three days. They have it well studied. They know when they are going to pick them up, they know the area and know where [the crossers] are going to try to get into. They have everything very well monitored.[25]

Customs and Border Protection statistics seem to confirm this strategy. Between 2010 and 2011 only 21 percent (68,813) of all apprehensions in the Tucson Sector happened within one mile or less of the border.[26] Twenty-six percent (83,194) of people caught were apprehended after traveling more than 5 miles, and 27 percent (89,972) had gone more than 20 miles.[27] These data suggest that more than 53 percent (173,166) of the migrants arrested by Border Patrol during this period spent a significant amount of time experiencing the Sonoran hybrid collectif's choke hold (see appendix B).

TECNOLOGÍA

If the estimate that between 92 and 98 percent of all unauthorized border crossers eventually get through is even remotely accurate,[28] it makes you wonder what the billions of dollars spent annually on boundary security actually does. If so many people weren't getting hurt or dying during this costly game of cat and mouse, you could almost laugh at these statistics. Those who do seem to be laughing, though, are the government contractors filling their pockets with cash after selling the United States government overpriced machinery and infrastructure that rarely does what it is supposed to.[29] They are, however, not the only ones turning a huge profit. Besides the thousands of dollars per client that smugglers make, there is an entire underground industry dedicated solely to helping people avoid detection and survive the desert.

Specialized vendors in Mexican towns such as Altar and Sasabe have cornered the market on camouflage backpacks, black clothes, water bottles, high-salt-content food, and first-aid equipment.[30] For inflated prices, border entrepreneurs will sell you things like black bottles of water that they "guarantee" will decrease visibility and sneakers with carpeted soles that they swear will prevent you from leaving footprints. Walking around downtown Altar, you're bound to hear someone say something like, "*Oye, carnal,* these special shoes don't make any sound when you walk. *Te lo juro.*" In addition to tricked-out sneakers and a wardrobe composed almost exclusively of black and camouflage (if you can afford it), you are also going to need foot powder to keep your feet dry, extra socks for the blisters, pain medication for sore legs, electrolyte-infused beverages to keep you hydrated, Red Bull to keep you energized (and dehydrated), glue to fix your shoes (which will inevitably come apart), and bandages to wrap your soon-to-be-sprained ankle. Last but not least, don't forget your crucifix, prayer card, and any other talisman you can think of.

Technología. Juan Bosco shelter. Photo by Michael Wells.

Like the runaway spending of the federal government's border security industrial complex, migrants also shell out an exorbitant amount of cash on technology that promises to get them past *la migra* and their Sonoran Desert henchmen. The problem for border crossers, which is eerily similar to that faced by those trying to keep them out, is that most of what they purchase is marginally effective at best. Granted the food, water, and first-aid kit can relieve some pain and possibly stave off an early death, but beyond helping you endure the desert, they do little to undermine surveillance technology. Other items, such as dark clothes and black bottles, may actually be doing more harm than good. For example, both might make you less visible in some circumstances, but they also absorb more sunlight, causing the former to speed up your body's core temperature and the latter to boil your drinking water. If you're being remotely monitored by a Border Patrol agent sitting in her scope truck checking the infrared camera, this rise in temperature makes it look as though you are wearing a neon sign on your back that says, *¡Aquí estoy!*

When you point these technological conundrums out to people, they remark that you never know when any little thing is going to work in your

A Border Patrol scope truck. Photo by Michael Wells.

favor, so it's better to cover all your bases. Luck aside, migrants recognize that you get smarter about the process each time you try and fail to get across the desert. Every attempt is a crash course in wilderness survival and subterfuge, and people learn their lessons quickly. The trauma induced by extreme dehydration and punishing terrain on a first failed crossing attempt makes for a steep learning curve if you survive. Social scientists call this acquired knowledge *migration-specific capital*,[31] and it has been shown that as you accumulate it, you increase your likelihood of joining that 92nd percentile of border crossers who make it through.[32]

Migrants know they are outgunned—literally and figuratively—when it comes to the border war. But they are also in on a little *secreto* that those standing watch at the gate refuse to believe. That secret is that *la migra's* fancy equipment is no match for the sheer determination that propels hundreds of thousands of economic migrants toward the United States each year. As a deportee laughingly told me once while we ate tacos on *la linea:* "*Para los Mexicanos no hay fronteras* [For Mexicans there are no borders]. We will keep trying until we cross. We have faith in *la Virgen de Guadalupe* to help us. Unfortunately, sometimes your body can't keep up with your faith."

FAILURE

I can hear the kitchen television from the street as I approach Juan Bosco. The Mexican edition of *America's Funniest Home Videos* is playing at a painful volume. Before setting foot inside, I can already tell by the aroma that Pato is making his delicious rice and beans. I am starving and looking forward to sitting down after spending all day walking around Nogales in the blistering summer sun. As I turn the corner and enter the kitchen, I am shocked when Lucho, not Pato, looks up from the stove where he is stirring a giant simmering pot. I stop in my tracks. It's been five days since I watched him and Memo enter the tunnel. I am speechless. Lucho gives me a soft grin and just shakes his head. Memo hears me enter and steps out from inside the kitchen supply closet and quietly says, "They got us." I don't know whether to be happy that they are alive or sad that they have failed for the third time. "What happened?" I stupidly ask. "They got us," Memo repeats. He tries to fake a smile for my benefit and fails miserably. It is the first time I've seen him unable to crack a joke. "Come sit down," he says. The three of us crowd around a plastic table while the television screams in the background.

They both look like shit. They are ghosts of themselves. The level of physical exhaustion they are suffering from has changed both their speech and posture. Lucho is nursing a horrible cold and his gruff voice is barely audible. Memo appears sedated. His physical movements lack their usual spastic energy. They both start telling me what happened, but the narrative is devoid of their characteristic humor.

> *Jason:* How many days were you in the desert on this trip?
>
> *Lucho:* Three days.
>
> *Memo:* We walked really far.
>
> *Lucho:* Yeah, we walked all the way to Agua Linda,[33] near the checkpoint. They caught us there and sent us back. Border Patrol was chasing a group of about seventeen people and we were there too. We made a big mistake. We got caught in the middle of the chase. There was an area where they kept cattle. That is where we were hiding. We were sleeping under a tree, but out in the open. If we had headed for the mountains, they wouldn't have caught us. *Migra* passed by and found us and they were like, "Hey! What are you guys doing here?" We were just sitting there sleeping when they showed up. They started asking us questions. The Border Patrol agent called his friend on the walkie-talkie and asked how many were in that group he had just caught, and he said, "Seventeen." "OK. I got two more for you. Let's go!" he said. So they threw us in with the rest of them. If we had gone more into the mountains, they wouldn't have caught us. They don't go there into the mountains. Instead, we decided to sleep out in the open.

It is obvious that Lucho doesn't feel well or like talking. He stands up and excuses himself. He enters the men's dormitory and crumples onto a bottom bunk bed. I can see him through the long hallway. He is lying there, staring up at the cot above his head in silence. Memo then says:

> It is hard for him. When they deported us back to Tucson, we drove past Lucho's house. We were on the bus and he said, "Check it out! That's where I live." He pointed out his house and then started getting really sad. I felt horrible. I said, "Lucho, don't worry. God is protecting us. We're going to be fine. Nothing is going to happen. This is only a setback. Don't worry. We will be back." He asked me, "Memo, do you really believe that?" I said, "Of course! We'll be back." I tried to cheer him up.

> *Jason:* Is it hard for you to stay positive *en el camino*? You always seem to be so positive.
>
> *Memo:* Always. I have faith in God. When we were on the trail, we got going at 4 A.M. and I was sure that we were going to pass. I said, "We're getting there tomorrow! Don't worry, Lucho, everything is going to be fine."

ESCAPE

After this third failed crossing, it takes them several days to recuperate. Eventually things return to normal. Lucho and Memo even find temporary employment helping with the remodeling of a seafood restaurant near Juan Bosco. During this period I am also able to spend more time with them and the other shelter staff when they're not working. We attend a Sunday baseball game and then end up one afternoon at their favorite bar. It's a local dive called *La Banana*, a sad-looking structure with no windows. They specialize in playing *banda* music at deafening volumes. I am the only one with money, so I buy a few rounds of *caguamas*, and everyone tries to forget his situation. A pack of cigarettes appears, probably confiscated from one of the shelter guests the night before. We all lean back and someone starts making crude jokes about someone else's sexual potency. Everyone laughs. It's a temporary escape.

No one can drink very much because they all have to return to work in the afternoon and can't appear inebriated. After our laughing settles down, we sit and nurse our beers. I can tell that the recent failure has been weighing heavy on Memo, because after a few drinks he turns to me with tears in his eyes and says, "We are like a family right now. Right now we have no problems. Everything is fine right now." I want to believe that everything is fine, but I know it's not. They are stuck in Nogales again, and it is unclear when they are going to be physically and psychologically able to attempt another crossing. I have less than a week left before I have to return home and start teaching fall classes. Memo puts his arm around me and someone takes our picture with my camera. I start to wonder what will happen after I leave and if I will see him again.

I get to the shelter early in the afternoon. It is my last day in Nogales and I want to say good-bye to everyone. Samuel cooks an amazing pot of *caldo de camarón*, and we spend a few hours laughing and making plans for my next visit. Memo and Lucho are working and not able to eat lunch with us, so around 7 P.M. I walk down to their job site to say farewell. I also hand over two disposable cameras that they have promised to take with them on their next attempt. Instead of heading back to the shelter, they offer to accompany me to my hotel in downtown Nogales. We get a ride from their boss, and Lucho shows me a wad of pesos that he received for his recent construction work. "This is my first Mexican paycheck in thirty years. Can you believe that? [laughing] I told my family I finally got a paycheck and they laughed when I told them how little it was!"

We get dropped off at the Hotel Regis, which is less than half a block from the border wall. We can see Nogales, Arizona, from the street. I invite Memo and Lucho to join me for one last beer. One beer turns into several, and Lucho starts spending his meager paycheck on rounds. I keep slipping the waiter cash when drinks are ordered in hopes that I can prevent Lucho from blowing all his money. After several buckets of beer, everyone starts getting emotional. I tell Memo I am afraid he is going to die in the desert. Tears fall onto the table and more drinks are ordered. The room heats up as the evening crowd of local drunks, hustlers, slimy ex-pats, and sex workers starts to shuffle in. The music gets louder. Memo tells me that his father was murdered when he was a child and that to this day his death has gone unavenged. It is the first time I have seen him angry. Tears well up in his eyes and he uses the palm of his hand to wipe them away. I look over at Lucho and realize he is loaded. He begins harassing the waiter and then starts talking shit to Memo during the story about his father's murder. "You need to stay calm and relax," Memo tells him. Lucho screams, "Fuck you, *cabron!*"

The cheap plastic table in front of us is pushed away as Lucho rises in anger. He gets into Memo's face and I squeeze myself between the two of them. I start patting Lucho on the chest telling him to relax. "We are brothers, Lucho! We need to stick together!" Memo pleads. The waiter comes over and I assure him that it is just a little misunderstanding. Lucho apologizes and finally sits down. He then starts sobbing and says, "We have to cross. We have to cross. We have to cross." The three of us keep drinking.

CHAPTER 7

The Crossing

EN TUCSON

When my cell phone rings and registers an unknown Arizona number, a flood of mostly negative thoughts come to mind. Are they dead? Did someone in the morgue find my business card in Lucho's pocket? Are they now looking for next of kin? Did *la migra* catch them and are they now calling from detention? This is a moment when Memo would undoubtedly remind me to be more positive: "*No te preocupes. Todo va a estar bien.*" Perhaps they finally did make it. Two weeks have gone by since I left them in Nogales. Two weeks of radio silence. I've been checking my phone incessantly for a missed call. Nothing. When this one finally comes in, I am so nervous that I almost don't answer it. "*¿Bueno? ¿Bueno?*" The person on the other end of the line yells out, "We are here! We are here!"

Memo excitedly tries to fill me in on all of the details over the phone. He reassures me that the disposable cameras I have given them are safe and full of undeveloped photos. I tell him that I want to hear the stories in person and will come to them. I land in Arizona a week later and call Lucho for directions to his house. "It's really close to where *la migra* are," he says. He's not exaggerating. On my way from the airport I pass almost a dozen Border Patrol *perreras*[1] and two deportation buses.

I pull up to a modest home in a dusty trailer park. A wobbly screen door swings open and Memo pops out to greet me with a giant smile. He is wearing clothes I don't recognize and has a warmth to his face that conveys deep happiness and relief. He looks like a changed man. I climb out of my rental car and we quickly hug. It feels as though we haven't seen each other in years. In a deadpan voice I whisper, "*Oye, mano,* I brought you a present," and reach into the backseat. I pull out a bottle of real apple juice and shove it in his hand. We both start cracking up like little kids. Lucho hangs his head out of the trailer door and grins. "Hurry up and get in here!" he commands.

I step inside and encounter a tiny place with the characteristic patina of a bachelor pad. The living room is clean and tidy, but you can tell that only *hombres* live here. There is a *fútbol* game on the television playing at full volume (of course) and a small mountain of empty Natural Light beer cans on the glass coffee table. The two of them have been prepartying in anticipation of my arrival. I flop down on a well-worn pleather couch and proceed to spend the next ten hours drinking beer and listening to what happened to them *en el camino.*

If you are not a researcher working along the border, getting the opportunity to hear a migrant's story is rare. Many do not like reminiscing about their time in the Sonoran Desert hybrid collectif. Who can blame them? Even when their crossing is successful, the event can be traumatic and have lasting emotional, psychological, and physical effects. The act of remembering can conjure pain, fear, and despair. Among American families with undocumented members, it is not uncommon for the topic of their crossing to be a forbidden subject. A former undocumented woman once told me: "I came here illegally thirty years ago when I was about four years old. We are citizens now. My mom, brothers, and I crossed a river and my aunt came through the desert. It's a taboo subject in our household and never talked about."

In the second half of this chapter I outline Memo and Lucho's final crossing attempt using a combination of interview excerpts and photos they took en route. These data are unique, to say the least. I am privileged to include their stories here along with images shot from their perspective, but it is important to note that millions of others have crossed the desert whose narratives will never be heard. Some died along the way, and many others don't want to recall painful memories, or their tenuous social position as undocumented people robs them of a public voice to tell their stories. Like other immigrant groups before them, these Latino families may have to wait one or more generations before reaching a status in US society that allows them to vocalize their migration experiences without trepidation or shame. The worry, though, is that with the passage of time these histories may become sanitized, edited, or forgotten

United Colors of Benetton (BK-3 site near Lobo Peak, Arizona). Photo by Michael Wells.

altogether. Examining the archaeological fingerprint of this clandestine social process can provide a different and perhaps safer approach to the excavation of these hidden narratives.

RESIDUES OF THE RECENT PAST

Walk out into the wild and uninhabited areas surrounding the town of Arivaca and you are likely to come across objects that border crossers have left behind. It's a breadcrumb trail of ripped clothes and bone-dry water bottles. It is American immigration history in the making. For years these items have been at the center of public discourse regarding the detrimental impact of undocumented migration.[2] Migrant "trash," as it is often referred to, has become the physical evidence used by anti-immigrant activists to demonstrate that Latino border crossers are destroying America. As one reader posted on the comment section of a 2012 article about desert crossings: "Mexico is a DUMP and they [Mexicans] turn anywhere they go into a dump, starting in our deserts, and then the communities they settle."[3] This comment is emblematic of the dominant tone used to discuss the things migrants leave in their wake. It's part of a simplistic discourse which posits that these items are garbage with little cultural, historical, or scientific value. The general public often has difficulty grasping the idea that the things people throw away or leave behind today are the artifacts that archaeologists will study in the future. Although some of these items are refuse, many of the things border crossers drop in the desert are valued objects not meant to be left behind, such as pocket Bibles, family photos, and love letters. For these reasons, I avoid blanket terms such as *trash* when referring to them. Reducing these things to "garbage" is not only a value-judgment; it also compresses a diverse range of materials into a problematic category that hides what these artifacts can tell us about the crossing process.[4]

In recent years, a growing number of archaeologists have argued for the relevancy of the discipline in understanding contemporary social issues. Drawing inspiration from William Rathje's Tucson Garbage Project, which as early as the 1970s showed that archaeology had much to contribute to modern society, this movement known as *archaeology of the contemporary* is demonstrating how this type of approach can provide new insight into recent histories that we often erroneously assume are well understood.[5] Researchers are deploying excavation, site mapping, and other archaeological methods and theories to better comprehend the relationship between artifacts and various sociopolitical

Woman in front of hotel. Weatherworn picture found in Ironwood National Monument, Arizona. Photo by Michael Wells.

contexts and themes.[6] As "the archaeology of us who are alive," this paradigm is deeply entrenched in the unpleasantness of the postmodern world, including the emotional distress and trauma that accompany the global devastation of humans, animals, and the environment that is now part of our planet's everyday life.[7] A focus on the material traces of ongoing contested social phenomena such as political violence, homelessness, and warfare can offer fresh perspectives distinct from the dominant narratives often written by those in power.[8] Alfredo González-Ruibal offers a compelling rationale for this approach: "Much historical archaeology is justified by the belief that we need alternative stories—that oral and written data do not tell us everything about the past, that there are other things to be learned from artifacts and other experiences that have to be accounted for. . . . Archaeology . . . can do more than produce alternative stories: it can also tell stories in an alternative way."[9]

An archaeological approach can foster engagements with the recent past and its material remains in novel and meaningful ways and produce new information that may be lost in narrative translations of history, collective memories, or accounts of individual experiences. Moreover, as British archaeologist John Schofield astutely points out, "We can use archaeology to question the distinctions that exist between what we are told, and what actually happened."[10] This is especially true regarding polemical topics such as undocumented migration in which the stories of participants are often ignored, downplayed, or selectively edited. As I note in chapter 4, journalists writing about immigration often want extraordinary tales and tend to avoid more mundane, ambiguous, or complicated narratives. In the context of migration, archaeology can get at elements of the process that are overshadowed by exceptional incidences of trauma or violence,[11] and can help decenter the story away from the perspective of outside observers, such as journalists who shadow border crossers.

THE CROSSING

In this chapter I highlight the archaeological approach that the Undocumented Migration Project has used over the years, including our typology of migrant sites, analyses of wear patterns on recovered objects, and the absolute and relative dating techniques that have helped illuminate how the social process of clandestine migration has evolved over time. I put these archaeological data into direct conversation with the narratives of Lucho and Memo's final border crossing. My intent is to superimpose an ethnographic scale of analysis, which tends to be individualized and temporally truncated, on an archaeological data set that is both polyvocal and ambiguous, as well as more spatially and temporally expansive. Rather than seeing these data sets as distinct or disparate, I envision the photos and stories that Memo and Lucho provide about their trip as breathing life into the countless number of objects that have been left in the desert and that represent millions of crossing stories.[12]

The following account is constructed from a combination of field notes, interview excerpts, photographs that Memo and Lucho took, and discussions when they provided me captions for their images. To highlight the connections and tensions between the material record and migrant voices, I have juxtaposed their story and photos with data from archaeological surveys conducted in the Sonoran Desert. When relevant, I provide a brief discussion of the archaeological evidence or comment on its absence.

Meet Ángel

Jason: You guys were in pretty bad shape when you got to the shelter after the third trip.

Memo: Yeah, dehydrated.

Jason: How many days did it take you to recover in Nogales?

Memo: Like two weeks. It was a while, huh, Lucho? Like ten days, but we stayed three more because we found a job.

Lucho: That is when that dude Ángel showed up looking for me. He went to Grupo Beta to find me, and they sent him to the shelter. He showed up at the shelter and I recognized him. I'd met him before because he was dating my girlfriend's daughter and she was with him. He said, "Hey, Lucho, I've been looking for you because we're gonna cross. Let's go! I'll take you across for free." He didn't have any money, though, or anything with him.

Jason: Why was he there?

Lucho: He was hanging out with his girlfriend in Nogales. She drove down to Mexico to see him and they were getting drunk in a hotel for four days. She told him that I was stuck in Nogales. He came looking for us and wanted to leave that night, but we needed to wait until we got paid for the construction work we had been doing.

Memo: We stayed that night in the shelter and left the following morning when Ángel showed up for us.

Lucho: They wouldn't let him stay at Juan Bosco. Everyone could tell he was a *malandro* [punk]. He showed up the next day really early, but was hung over. He didn't have anything with him. We had to give him some clothes.

Memo: Yeah, we found him a backpack in the shelter. Samuel gave us some clothes for him.

Lucho: We bought food and stuff and got ready. We went to the same store that we took you to before when we crossed the third time.

Memo: We went to the main bus station, and from there we hitchiked to Santa Cruz [a small town about 45 kilometers east of Nogales, Mexico]. From there we got a ride in the back of a pickup truck to the line.

Waiting Game

Jason: Did you run into any military?

Lucho: Yes, we ran into soldiers while we were walking.

Memo: Yeah, two times!

Lucho: The first time their lietunatent searched us. He asked what we were doing and if we were carrying drugs. Then he started searching Memo's bag. We said we weren't carrying anything, that we were just trying to cross the border. He said, "That's dangerous to not be carrying anything because the *bajadores* will kill you if you don't have anything." Then they left.

Jason: What did Ángel say?

Lucho: He didn't say nothing, but they stole his cigarettes. [laughs] They walked away smoking his cigarettes.

Memo: That was one time. The other time happened right before we crossed the line. Another group of soldiers showed up. Like ten or twelve guys and they talked to us.

Lucho: We waited in Mexico to cross the line. We waited for four hours until it got dark and then we crossed. We walked until about 3 A.M. and then rested for a little while.

This was not the first time that Memo and Lucho had stopped at the border for a time before crossing. They described how during their previous crossing attempt, they had spent an entire night waiting:

Lucho: Memo walked down to *la linea* [referring to the border fence] to check on stuff. A *pollero* came out of nowhere and started yelling, "Hey, what are you doing? I hope you're not a *bajador* because if you are, we are gonna fuck you up!"

Memo: Yeah, he got superaggressive with me.

Lucho: Memo was like, "No, I'm just checking to see if we can cross." The *pollero* was yelling, "You're not checking nothing! Let's go! Get the fuck over there." He had like fifteen or twenty migrants with him who were waiting. We went and sat with them.

Jason: You sat with them?

Lucho: Yeah, we ate some food and waited with them for a while. Later, this old lady came by with a bunch of bags of food and he said, "Get over here!" The *pollero* had an assistant, and he was like, "Go grab that old lady!" and the guy said, "No way, you do it." She just kept walking. She was carrying food for another group that was farther down the line. She walked from Nogales to bring food to the *polleros.*

Memo: This old lady might have been bringing food for the mafia.

Lucho: Later, this group of three *vatos* ran by us. The pollero who yelled at Memo started shouting at them saying, "Hey! Where are you going? Stop!" They yelled back, "Don't worry, we are drivers [for the mafia]. We work for—" They mentioned somebody's name who was a mafia guy.

Jason: So you spent the day with a group of migrants? What did you guys talk about?

Lucho: We just all chatted and hung out. We stayed the night there. Finally, groups started leaving in the morning. First, the guy who yelled at Memo left with a group. Then another group went and then another. Finally, we left. We were the last ones to cross the line.

TYPOLOGIES

The Border Patrol uses the generic phrase *layup* to describe the many places where migrants eat, rest, seek shade, and hide from law enforcement. The Undocumented Migration Project (UMP) has conducted detailed analyses of different sites created and repeatedly used by people while en route. Our results indicate that border crossers are doing more than simply "laying up" in the brush and hiding from immigration officials. These site types are archaeologically distinct and signal different types of behavior and engagement with the environment. Sometimes these behaviors can easily be gleaned from artifacts, and other times the perspectives of migrants are needed to correct archaeological interpretations or fill in the details for processes that leave no material trace. Rather than labeling all locations "layups," we have developed a typology to distinguish between sites where people camp for long periods, briefly rest, get picked up, practice religion, get arrested, and die.[13]

During four archaeological field seasons between 2009 and 2013, the UMP collected material and spatial data from 341 locales associated with undocumented migration and border enforcement in the Nogales-Sasabe corridor.

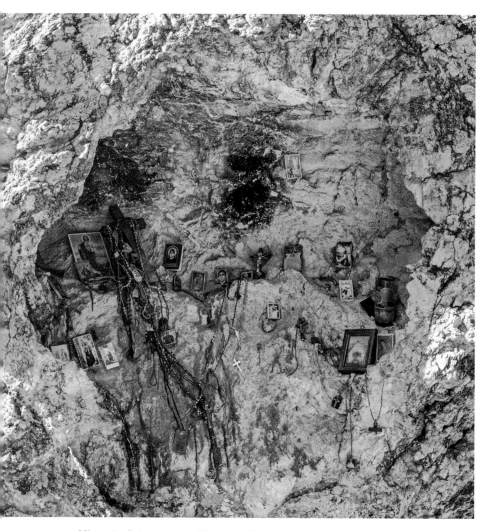

Migrant religious shrine. Photo by Michael Wells.

Based on location, site features, artifact inventories, and interviews with migrants, we were able to divide sites into various categories including (but not limited to) *campsites* where people congregate and rest for a period ranging from few hours to an entire night; *rest sites* where people stop briefly and consume food and beverages; *pickup sites* where migrants dump all of their desert supplies and get picked up by smugglers in vehicles; and *religious shrines* where offerings are left to ensure a safe journey. We have designated the locations just

¡Puro monte! Photo by Memo and Lucho.

beyond the boundary line on the Mexican side where crossers wait *border staging areas.* These locales can be relatively simple (containing just a few empty food cans and bottles) or more complex, with fire pits, sheltered sleeping areas, substantial religious shrines, and large amounts of clothes and consumables. Migrants, smugglers, and drug mules can spend anywhere from a few hours to several days waiting in these locations for the right time to cross.[14] One woman interviewed in 2013 reported that her group slept for nine days at a border staging area.

En Route

> *Lucho:* Here are the mountains that we walked over. Remember, Memo? At this point we are standing just over *la linea.* We have just crossed the border and are looking at what we have to do. We have to go between those two peaks in the distance.
>
> *Jason:* What are you thinking about when you look at something like this?
>
> *Lucho:* We are thinking just how far we actually have to walk. I mean look at all of that! We gotta cross all of that to get to Tucson. All of that.
>
> *Jason:* It's hard to imagine. That's a lot of mountains.
>
> *Memo:* Too much!

Lucho: It's all mountains! [*¡Puro monte!*] We crossed all of that. But look at the difference between here and Sasabe.[15] Here there is grass; you can see life, trees, and all that. Places where you can hide. On that other side, near Sasabe, there is nothing. Just cholla cactus. Here there is more chance for success than over there through Sasabe. There it is just pure desert and rocks.

Jason: How did you know this route?

Lucho: Ángel knew the route. He was a guide for *polleros* and for *burreros* [drug mules]. But we still got lost. Instead of crossing through this pass, we ended up on the wrong side and had to double back. For that dude Ángel it was nothing. He had crossed a lot, like four or five times.

Memo: This was the first and only time we crossed through there.

Lucho: From Santa Cruz to Tucson there are lots of trees, plants, and stuff. From Sasabe it is different. Through Arivaca it is all bald, naked land with small rivers. The way we went, there are big trees, arroyos full of water. Ángel knew all of the cattle tanks, and he would say, "OK, this gallon of water will last you until the next cattle tank." At the next tank he would say, "OK, with this gallon of water you just have to drink a little bit at a time because we are going to walk a long way to get to the next cattle tank." That is how it was. He knew more or less where to go.

Jason: How did he learn this?

Lucho: He was a guide for drug mules. The guide has to know all of this to lead a group.

Memo: I imagine that he was a *burrero* first to learn all this stuff, and later he became a guide.

Lucho: He would say stuff like "Look, this is where *burreros* rested. They just crossed through here a little while ago."

On multiple occasions, Memo and Lucho remarked that Ángel had work experience as a *pollero* and a *burrero,* which is why he knew the route. However, on a few occasions they described him in much scarier terms. The following is an excerpt from my 2009 field notes just a few months after they successfully got to Arizona:

> After beginning their trip, Memo and Lucho learn that Ángel is actually a *bajador* who makes a living robbing drug mules in the desert at gunpoint. They seem to be genuinely scared of the guy. He told them stories of almost killing drug mules in the desert, coming up behind them to hide his face, and putting a gun to their heads. Memo is convinced that this guy has done some really bad things to people.

Migrant architecture. Photo by Michael Wells.

Most of the sites used by migrants are also opportunistically utilized by drug mules. This includes humanitarian water drops, religious shrines, and resting areas. Still, compared to migrants, drug smugglers leave a light archaeological footprint, some of which is ambiguous. Distinguishing between these two groups is complicated by the fact that some work as *burreros* to pay for their crossing fees and people involved in both activities may be wearing the same types of clothes and carrying the same basic equipment.[16] The clearest archaeological signature of contraband smuggling that the UMP has identified is the homemade backpacks constructed of burlap sacks used to haul bales of marijuana.[17] More ambiguous evidence of drug smuggling is the informal architectural features that people construct in the desert out of tree branches and rocks. Empty burlap sacks, along with food and camping supplies, have occasionally been found inside these structures. During interviews with migrants who were shown photos of these locales, they commented that *burreros* or lookouts who had more time and necessity for long-term shelter were primarily responsible for building these hideouts. These people, however, also reported sometimes using these shelters to get out of the sun or avoid detection when they came across them in the desert.

"This *cabron* is taking pictures of me sleeping! Maybe he's in love with me?"
Photo by Lucho.

Lucho: Look, I took that photo! That *pinche güey* [referring to Memo] is
passed out! [laughing]

Memo: This *cabron* is taking pictures of me sleeping! Maybe he's in love with
me? [laughs] We had walked pretty far already. This is where I started
getting cramps. I had to rest because of the fucking canyon that was full of
black rocks.

Lucho: Yeah, that was where we stopped to drink water quickly, and Ángel was
like, "Let's go! Let's go! No stopping!" We were rushing through this canyon.

Memo: That is where my blood pressure started dropping.

Lucho: It's because we went down into a really steep canyon and started climbing
and climbing to get out of there fast. Memo couldn't breathe. It was rough. It
was like midday and very hot. Memo was dehydrated and vomiting up foam.

USE WEAR

Identifying evidence of the physical suffering, such as dehydration and bleeding blisters, experienced by crossers in the archaeological record has proved
difficult. This is partly because injuries often produce traces that either are
biodegradable, such as blood or vomit, or leave no footprint at all (e.g., exhaustion). To identify pain and bodily trauma materially, I have employed the

Migrant shoes recovered in the Tumacácori Mountains. They have been repaired with a bra strap and cord to reattach the soles to the uppers. Photo by Michael Wells.

dusty archaeological concept known as *use wear,* which refers to modifications to objects that occur when people use them in various ways. I have subdivided this concept into two categories: *wear patterns,* resulting from an item's use in intended tasks, and *modifications,* changes made to improve an object's function or to repair damage. For example, a shoe found in the desert that has holes worn through the sole suggests that a person's feet experienced intense trauma from walking, while a shoe whose sole has separated from the upper and that has been subsequently repaired with a bra strap indicates that the owner was desperate to keep her footwear functioning so that she could continue moving (see photo above).[18] Those who can't keep up with a group because of blisters or worn-out shoes are often left behind, which can be a death sentence. Knowing about this phenomenon of abandonment and then recovering destroyed or haphazardly repaired shoes in the middle of the desert can often be an emotionally challenging moment of archaeological interpretation.

General physical pain and desperation can be inferred from these use-wear patterns, but it is only when paired with ethnographic data that these objects come to tell more nuanced stories. On multiple occasions I encountered individuals at Juan Bosco limping around with heavily bandaged feet in hospital-issued sandals. These women and men reported that their shoes were stolen by bandits or that they broke down in transit. Some even reported trying to walk barefoot or in socks across the spiky desert floor. Although items such as distressed-looking shoes don't provide names or specific details about a particular crossing experience, they do hint at a generic phenomenology of suffering shared by many.

RANCHEROS

Jason: You guys took a lot of photos of cows. Why?

Memo: [laughing] That was when we were cracking ourselves up chasing cows around. People who read this book are gonna think we are cowboys or own a *pinche rancho!*

Lucho: We were chasing cows around and Memo was trying to grab their tails. Ángel grabbed one by the tail and it was dragging him around on the ground!

Memo: We were entertaining ourselves and making all kinds of noise laughing. Those are the moments that you forget what you are actually doing.

Lucho: We only had a little bit of food at this point.

Memo: This was when the three of us shared a *tuna* [prickly pear].

Jason: *Tunas* you found in the desert?

Memo: Yeah, *nopales* [cacti]. It was full of spines and dried out. It was all bone [*puro hueso*], but we ate it! We ate some plants we found as well. We were starving and it was so good!

Lucho: We found some plants that were OK to eat. They were plants that my grandmother used to eat in Mexico. We put a little bit of salt on them. It was from what they feed to cattle.

Jason: Really?

Memo: Yeah. [laughs] There are these blocks of *sal* in the desert. We cut little corners off of it. Man! Or remember when we ate that piece of maguey [plant]? That hurt so bad. It gave me these fucking awful cramps. I was in pain. Lucho was like, "No worries, have another piece. There is plenty!" [laughing]

Lucho: We didn't really have any food left at this point.

Rancheros. Photos by Memo, Lucho, and Ángel.

CHRONOLOGY

Memo: We had walked for several days when we took these photos [see p. 184].

Lucho: We were exhausted. I remember that we dropped down into an arroyo and lay in the sand exhausted until it got dark. We just tried to rest for like half an hour.

Memo: Here I am exhausted. It feels really incredible to lie down for a little while using my backpack as a pillow.

Lucho: It looks like Memo is dead there.

Memo: This was a day before the rock climbing.

6/25/2010: *Green Valley, Arizona*

The smell of grilling meat hangs thick in the air. It makes everyone's stomach grumble and resent the soggy ham sandwiches awaiting us in the back of the truck parked down the street. Whoever fired up the Coleman is also jamming out to a Tucson classic rock station and probably sipping an icy

Memo and Lucho rest during the crossing. The bottom photos are of migrant campsites documented south of Green Valley, Arizona. Photos by Memo, Lucho, and Michael Wells.

beverage on this oppressively hot afternoon. Steely Dan's "Reelin' in the Years" plays loudly from their patio and provides a soundtrack to our clandestine archaeological fieldwork. The person cooking lunch is completely unaware that six of us are digging through the thick brush that lies less than 1,000 feet from her backyard wall, which demarcates the southern boundary line of this Green Valley, Arizona, retirement community. We are documenting a site we have designated Snake Pit, its name based on the abundance of reptiles we encountered on the initial survey of the area. I counted four in the first twenty minutes of being on-site. We are here because I met a female Border Patrol agent in Arivaca who joked, "Just walk out into the trees south of that retirement community in Green Valley. You'll see that the illegals have made little condominiums out of brush." The features we record at Snake Pit include clothes and other items neatly laid out on the ground. These *in situ* objects give the impression that the owners left just prior to our arrival. I wonder if their stomachs growled while they waited for nightfall and for their ride to show up.

Collecting archaeological data on clandestine human behavior that may have occurred just minutes or hours before you arrive on the scene generates a strange sensation. Sometimes you feel as if you're studying wild animals who have just been scared away; this feeling makes you question whether you are only further contributing to the dehumanization of undocumented migrants. "Scientifically" recording footprints and the remnants of someone's recent meal may bring you physically close to them but can also contribute to a strong sense of estrangement. You find yourself constantly asking the question, "Should I be doing this?"

As with all archaeological research endeavors, chronology has proven crucial for the Undocumented Migration Project (UMP). Dating sites is important for understanding how technology, material culture, and people's physical encounters with the desert have evolved over time, and we have relied on both absolute and relative dating techniques. Absolute (calendric) dates, are inferred through time-stamped documents, such as bus tickets, deportation slips, or food expiration dates. Relative dating usually relies on the degree of rust, if any, on metal goods, the structural integrity of items such as plastic bottles, and the preservation of biodegradable materials such as meat, fruit, and other foods. Some artifacts are unique or reflect styles whose initial appearance have a fixed date. These *horizon markers* provide a chronological baseline. For example, the black water bottles mentioned in chapter 6 were first manufactured in late 2009 and indicate a date no earlier than that year. Given the fragility of the migrant archaeological record and the rapid decomposition of paper items such as bus or airplane tickets, it is crucial to document these sites while they are relatively "fresh" (again conjuring unfortunate analogies with wildlife biology). This means literally following in the immediate footsteps of people who are doing everything in their power to leave no trail behind.

When you do discover a recently occupied camp, the feeling is unsettling. Compare the photos of Memo and Lucho lying on the ground with those of features from the Snake Pit site, where people constructed beds out of clothes and backpacks (previous page). The newness of these deposits and the configuration of material culture give the feeling of stumbling upon a crime scene where the body has only recently been removed. While some critics are uncomfortable with the political implications of an archaeology of undocumented migration, I am personally more troubled by the issue of timing, given that UMP researchers have likely walked into sites and made enough noise to cause

"You see how much he is drinking in this photo? That's why he ran out of water!"
Photo by Ángel.

occupants to quickly flee before being seen. This means that the anthropologist is partly responsible for the construction of these archaeological freeze frames and is also occasionally the source of distress for people already in a precarious position. Unlike ancient sites buried under stratigraphic layers of dirt and gravel, these migrant archaeological contexts are alive and dynamic. What is recorded today may drastically change tomorrow as a locale is destroyed by environmental conditions or modified by other people passing through.

"DON'T STOP! KEEP GOING!"

Lucho: I think it's better to walk during the day because Border Patrol can see you at night with those cameras. During the day there is more heat and it is harder to see people with the [infrared] cameras.

Memo: But it's harder and you walk much slower during the day. You end up drinking more water.

Lucho: Like, Memo, man, he drank all his *agua.* I tried to sell him some of mine. [laughs]

Memo: Yeah, he had a lot left. I was like, "Lucho, give me some water!" He replied, "Why'd you drink all of yours?" I was out because I had been sharing my gallon with all three of us. Pretty soon I realized that it was all gone. The only person who had water left was Lucho. I walked like more than three miles with no water. I asked again, "Hey, Lucho, give me some water, man; I'm thirsty." He grabbed the *galón* and said, "I'll sell you some." I said, "*Cabron,* I don't have any money!" Then he told me, "OK, I'll loan you some so you can buy it from me." [laughs] I grabbed the bottle and took some little sips.

Lucho: You see how much he is drinking in this photo? That's why he ran out of water! [laughs] I remember that around this time we crossed an arroyo and then one of the roads used by Border Patrol. It was like midnight when I heard a Vicente Fernández song playing at high volume all through the canyons. It was coming from a truck, but it was hard to see what kind.

Memo: Border Patrol plays music like that to trick people into asking for a ride because migrants think it's a *paisano* [Mexican]. Fuckers! [laughing]

Lucho: Yeah, also *polleros* doing pickups will whistle in the dark and call out to people, "*Vámonos!*" *La migra* will do the same thing to trick people into thinking they are smugglers so that migrants will come out of the woods and walk toward them.

Memo: Border Patrol also makes animal noises like birds or coyotes. These are signals that smugglers sometimes use.

Mountain climbing. Photo by Memo.

Lucho: We were just about out of water. Pretty soon we had to start drinking from cattle tanks.

Memo: At this point I started thinking that we needed to keep moving forward with as much energy as possible. We had just climbed this giant hill, and below us we could see *la migra* was passing by. That was right after the javelinas came out. We ran into javelinas with their babies. We didn't know whether to run or climb up a giant mesquite tree because they came back and tried to attack us. There were some branches and we used them to fend them off. We were picking up rocks and throwing them. They finally left . . .

Lucho: Our feet were bad and hurt a lot.

Memo: Lots of blisters.

Lucho: And giant rocks. We found a mine near Patagonia Lake. There was dark soil there and a little bit of water. We were so thirsty and wanted to drink it, but Ángel said it would make us sick. It was full of chemicals.

Memo: That was when we saw the bear, right?

Lucho: Oh yeah.

Jason: You ran into a bear?

Memo: Yeah, a big black bear. We saw his giant footprints.

Lucho: Ángel said that if we start getting chased by a bear, we should throw our packs down because all he wants is the food.

Jason: [incredulous] But you really saw a bear?

Lucho: Yes, we saw one bear and then later saw footprints of another one near a lagoon.

Memo: He was probably there drinking water like us.

Jason: What did you do when you actually saw the bear?

Lucho: We ran. [laughing] We ran down an arroyo and up the other side. Everyone was yelling, "Don't stop! Don't stop! Keep going!"

Memo: We got to the other side of the arroyo, and the bear was standing on the other side looking at us.

Lucho: He was just staring at us but couldn't do anything.

Memo: I think he might have been more afraid of us. We were yelling, "Keep running! He will get tired!"

Jason: When you are climbing stuff like this, what are you thinking about?

Lucho: We are thinking about how they are not going to catch us up here. It's like we were climbing a mountain there.

Memo: And the drop was crazy! Man, so crazy!

Jason: How is it for *la migra*?

Lucho: *La migra* doesn't go up there! They're afraid. [laughs] The road is really far from there. They have to walk like two miles to get where we are in this photo and leave their car on the road. Their car won't make it in that far. That's why they hardly ever go into that area.

Memo: Man, that is farther than two miles!

Jason: Do you think you learned some stuff on that third crossing before this one?

Lucho: Yeah, we learned a lot.

Memo: Walk off the trails as far as you possibly can.

Lucho: You need to put yourself into the most difficult places that you can where people can't get to. You understand? Where there are lots of trees, mountains, rocks . . . off the trail. That's where you need to go. If you walk in the easiest places, they will catch you quick.

Jason: But that's gotta be harder for you guys.

Lucho: More difficult, but more difficult for them too. At this point we've been out like four days in the desert by the time we got to those rocks. When we climbed that, we were almost to Elephant Head [Mountain]. This is about the time that I called my family on my cell phone. We walked another three hours from this point, and as it was getting dark, we could see Tucson in the distance. We could see all the lights.

Memo: We climbed up higher and saw Tucson. We said, "That is where we need to walk to."

A migrant's personal effects left in the desert. Photo by Michael Wells.

Lucho: Ángel started getting excited and yelling, "Yeah! We are almost there!"

Memo: We kept walking and walking. Then we stopped and just threw every-thing away. We made a giant pile out of the jackets, clothes, and socks we brought. We kept just an extra pair socks for each of us and one backpack. We tossed everything else. We couldn't carry it anymore.

Lucho: We couldn't carry anything anymore.

Memo: All we ended up with was one backpack and Lucho's Bible.

DEPOSITION

A common racist assertion by anti-immigrant activists is that border crossers, and Latinos in general, have little regard for the natural environment and are prone to litter.[19] This point was undermined on numerous occasions when I showed migrants photos of piles of backpacks and clothes only to hear people lament about how sorry they felt for throwing stuff on the ground or in many cases losing their personal possessions in the desert. There are generally three reasons people leave objects on the trail. First, some things (empty water bottles, food wrappers, worn-out socks, broken backpacks) are discarded because they are no longer of any use.[20] Second, as Memo and Lucho mention above, after many days of walking, people may be too tired to continue carrying a heavy pack. UMP researchers have often found full backpacks on or just off trails that still contained food, beverages, and clothes. It is not uncommon to come across bleary-eyed migrants in the desert with nothing but a water bottle.

In addition to exhaustion, people can be startled by Border Patrol or animals and, in the confusion of fleeing, leave objects behind. Law enforcement officers may also force a person to abandon all her belongings before being loaded into one of their vehicles. We frequently recovered backpacks with food, medication, clothes, and identification documents in areas where border crossers had recently been arrested. These areas, designated *apprehension sites*, are also usually littered with disposable handcuffs and other items associated with the Border Patrol, including chewing tobacco tins, expended alkaline batteries for GPS units and walkie-talkies, bullet casings, and fast food wrappers. In 2013 I watched a Border Patrol agent arrest three men on a dirt road in Arivaca. When I drove by the area twenty minutes later, three full backpacks of clothes, food, and personal effects had been left lying in the dirt.

The most common reason, however, for leaving things behind has to do with the final stage of movement out of the desert. Although *layup* is a generic term used by law enforcement to describe any and all places where migrants hide and where artifacts associated with crossing are deposited, usually when people use this term, they are referring to the areas where large amounts of clothes, backpacks, and other items have accumulated. These locales, which we call *pickup sites*,[21] represent the end of a multiday trip and are near rendezvous points where *coyotes* have arranged for vehicle transportation. Between 2009 and 2013 we documented forty-eight of these sites, which yielded hundreds of thousands of objects. These areas contained high proportions of backpacks and clothes, as well as

Monsoon. Photo by Lucho.

diverse assemblages of hygiene, cosmetic, electronic, and personal items.[22] Typically when people arrive at pickup sites, their smugglers tell them to clean up their appearance (e.g., brush their teeth, put on deodorant, and change into clean clothes) so it is not apparent that they just wandered through the desert. This shedding of clothes and backpacks is an attempt to discard all incriminating evidence that would signal someone as an undocumented migrant. Unfortunately, during the often rapid and chaotic process of changing clothes and climbing into vehicles, people may unintentionally lose personal items they were carrying with them. This can include identification cards, photos, and other valuables.

EMPTY BOTTLE

> *Lucho:* We stayed in a cave that [second-to-last] night. Memo and Ángel went inside and I stayed in the front. Those *pinches* vampires [referring to bats] wouldn't let me sleep. [laughing] They kept flying all around my head. We got up at 6 A.M. and started walking. We were out of water at this point, but as soon as I saw Elephant Head, I knew where we were because I had worked out there before. We passed a golf course, but we couldn't drink from the sprinklers because the water has chemicals in it. There was a house that was under construction. We got to the house at like 3 P.M. We soaked

ourselves under that hose! We were dying of thirst. I was hallucinating at that point. We were surrounded by dirt but I kept seeing water everywhere in the desert.

Memo: Lucho kept saying he could see water, but there was no water.

Lucho: It was just dirt. There was nothing.

Jason: This was after four or five days?

Memo: Yeah, we had no food, no water, nothing. Just an empty bottle. Three miles after we stopped at the house that was under construction, it started to rain.

Lucho: This is when we got to an arroyo. The water was running really hard and we got stuck. It was running quick, and if you fell in, it was up to here [points to chest]. It was raining really hard in Sahuarita [Arizona]. At this point we were almost there. We were really happy and finally energized. It was also easier because we had water at this point.

Memo: Yeah, we were making so much noise laughing and yelling. We were screwing around acting like we were on a picnic. Man, that was right when it started raining. We only had one raincoat left, because we had thrown away our things.

Lucho: It was like 9 P.M. We sat down and it started to rain.

Memo: Poor Lucho, he didn't have a raincoat. I said, "Put mine on and we can share it." I found a plastic bag and put that on. We were sitting in the rain while Border Patrol was looking for us. We could see them driving by.

Lucho: We were energized at this point because we were so close. We were walking in the dark and ran into a lot of trees. Lots of giant mesquites. It was dark and hard to see.

Memo: We got into a field of mesquite trees and struggled to get through it.

Lucho: It was like 8 or 9 P.M. at night when we finally got picked up.

Lucho: We walked the whole day, something like fifteen or eighteen hours walking. We walked from Elephant Head to Sahuarita [a distance of more than twenty miles]. It was a long time. That's far, huh? My family was waiting for us. I had called them and told them we were coming and that we were starving. They took us to the house and they had made us food. There was *carne asada,* rice, sodas. We got there soaking wet. Everyone was so happy that we made it safely.

Memo: We were so happy to finally be in a house and out of danger. Man! It was so nice. I remember, though, that I was starving and my throat was burning. It was so hard to swallow, but I had a hunger you can't imagine.

Lucho: [softly whispers] Yeah. Very hungry.

Memo: I remember when we first sat down and were eating dinner. I looked over and said, "Hey, Lucho! Look at this soda!" All I wanted was a really

Home. Photo by Memo.

cold Coke. It wasn't a Coke. I remember that it was Fanta. I still remember how good that cold soda was.

Lucho: We probably walked like fifty miles, all at night. The rest of it we walked during the day.[23] We crossed in only the most difficult areas. There were no roads or trails. That is why I think we didn't get caught. *Puro monte.* Giant rocks and mountains. Places where Border Patrol doesn't really go.

MEMORIES

Jason: You guys tell a lot of jokes when you talk about the desert, and you laugh a lot when you are crossing. It gets serious sometimes, though.

Memo and Lucho: [in unison] Yeah.

Lucho: [in a low voice] Those javelinas . . .

Memo: It's because you need to find ways to keep yourself motivated. You can talk about stuff like it's a joke, but it's something dangerous. It's dangerous, but you can't let it slow you down. You're tired. [snickers] It's like that cow stuff. When we got to that point we were exhausted. Totally exhausted. But it calmed us down because that crazy Ángel . . . Those jokes, man! He was cracking us up.

Lucho: Yeah, we forgot how tired we were. He got us motivated with those *pendejadas.*

Jason: After these experiences, how do you guys feel about the desert?

Lucho: Well, some are traumatized, and later you have dreams about it at night. Yeah, you have dreams about walking in the desert or dreams that you are being chased.

Memo: Yeah, those first days back.

Lucho: *Sueños* about the police and *la migra* and all that. It's like you're traumatized.

Memo: In the middle of the day it will sometimes feel like you are still living the crossing.

Jason: Do you still feel like that?

Lucho: Yes.

Memo: Right now, no, but in the beginning, in those first few days, yeah. Like the first eight days.

Lucho: For me it sometimes still feels like it. Still . . .

Jason: Like nightmares?

Lucho: Right on, like nightmares. When I am sleeping, I see them. Like I'm being persecuted and chased and I'm hiding. All the things that happened to me in the desert.

Memo: Later, we'd be sleeping, and Lucho would wake up and say, "Hey, I had another dream about the crossing." I'd say, "Shut up! I don't want to think about that stuff for a while." [laughs]

Lucho: Forget it, man! Those memories!

Jason: There is always the possibility that you would have to cross again right?

Lucho: Yeah, for whatever little thing they can grab you. You never know when. They can grab you and be like, "Let's go!" Then you gotta cross again.

Memo: Yes, but now you have more experience.

Lucho: No, no, no, no, no, no. I don't want to have more experiences out there.

"BACK TO LIFE"

It is 2015 and more than five years since Memo and Lucho last crossed the border. Since that time, their lives have remained relatively steady. They, along with thousands of other undocumented Latinos in Arizona, continue to live and work under the radar of immigration authorities while they eke out a living doing odd jobs and temporary contract work. After two decades of toiling in the agricultural fields, Memo is proud that he has learned new construction skills, including how to put up drywall, lay flagstone, and pour cement. Still, the transition back has not been easy. For the first year or so, Memo and Lucho lived together in a small trailer park, taking any available work while hitting the bottle hard. On numerous occasions, I watched them get drunk and argue for seemingly no reason and often found myself trying to break up fights. Lucho eventually separated from his wife. She gained possession of the trailer, which forced the two of them to move out. Memo moved in with friends, while Lucho stayed with relatives. Both men continued to drink heavily and on New Year's Eve 2010, Memo got drunk and fell down a steep drainage canal behind his house. He lay at the bottom of a ditch with a broken ankle until daybreak because none of his neighbors could hear his screams over their loud music.

For months afterward, Memo was confined to crutches and unable to work. It was at this point that he and Lucho decided to temporarily give up drinking, which dramatically improved their friendship. Soon after the accident, they moved into a one-bedroom apartment in the greater Phoenix area where they currently reside. They managed to weather the economic downturn of the past few years and are enjoying semipermanent employment that keeps a roof over their heads and food on the table. They are both currently single but have active social lives. Their apartment is located in a neighborhood where they are surrounded by friends. Despite their constant struggle to find work, Memo and Lucho are seemingly content. Memo even saved up enough money to buy a car. The only hints of unhappiness I have ever noticed have occurred when I was driving with Memo and we passed a police officer or a Border Patrol vehicle. He will immediately stiffen up and look forward. Once when this happened, he told me to "act normal and not show any fear."

It is clear that five years after the crossing Memo's and Lucho's memories of the event and the months spent in Nogales have been affected by the passage of time. Some of the more painful parts of the story have been edited to seem less dire, while other moments have evolved to accentuate humorous or positive elements of the journey. Memo's telling of the story continues to get funnier, while Lucho often gets serious and morose upon reflection. My sense is that they reminisce now about their crossing only for my benefit. Over the years, I have had to remind them of certain details, and in other instances new information has arisen. Given their many experiences in the desert, the stories have started to blur together and some parts have been forgotten. Like all memories, theirs are evolving.

Using Memo and Lucho's final crossing as a backdrop, I have shown that an archaeology of undocumented migration can provide new insights into border crossings and can improve our understanding of both the different types of engagements people have with the desert hybrid collectif and the material traces of these interactions.

There is compelling evidence that archaeology can help preserve fragments of these historical events that are for various reasons either fading from people's memories or partially locked away in America's undocumented society. Archaeology may also help correct erroneous characterizations of the crossing process that are written by those in power or by those invested in demonizing Latino migrants and distinguishing them from previous generations of "noble" immigrants.[24]

Still, persuading the American public to recognize the importance of the material traces of clandestine migration is no easy task for a host of reasons. In 2011 the popular magazine *Archaeology* published one of the first international articles about the Undocumented Migration Project, in a piece called "The Journey to El Norte." Several angry readers subsequently wrote letters to the editor complaining about the story, including the following:

Decay. Photo by Michael Wells.

I am appalled that you could even consider publishing an article like The Journey to El Norte. It casts a romantic light on illegal immigration. To compare
these criminals to the millions of Europeans who immigrated in the late 19th
and early 20th centuries is an insult to their memories and efforts to give their
children better lives. My grandparents came to this country legally. They
wanted no handouts, learned English, and eventually owned their own company. To document the trash heaps of these current illegal immigrants as artifacts, as if they are sacred, is beyond credibility.[25]

This comment exemplifies the historical amnesia many have regarding the
experiences of early European immigrants in America. It also illustrates the
typical, race-based value judgments many make about modern immigration
history and contemporary archaeological heritage. The hypocrisy of this reader's letter is easily illuminated by taking a quick historical glance back at how
new European arrivals to the United States were viewed in the late nineteenth
and early twentieth century. One hundred and fifty years ago, Matthew Hale
Smith published a book about the children of Five Points, New York, then an
infamously poor neighborhood heavily populated by new arrivals from Europe.
Hale lamented the societal impact of the children of first-generation immigrants: "Their parents are foreigners. They are too dirty, too ragged, and carry

too much vermin about them to be admitted to public schools. Their homes are in the dens and stews of the city, where the thieves, vagabonds, gamblers and murderers dwell. With the early light of morning they are driven from their vile homes to pick rags and cinders, collect bones, and steal. . . . They are familiar with every form of wickedness and crime. As they grow up they swell the ranks of the dangerous classes. Our thieves, burglars, robbers, rioters, who are the most notorious, are young persons of foreign parentage."[26]

Another issue undermining the conservation of this immigration history is the fact that we live in an era when undocumented people increasingly exist in a "state of exception."[27] Immigrants are tolerated when they do the jobs that citizens won't, but the American public has little interest in hearing their voices, preserving their history, or affording them any rights. This "exceptionalism" pervades all aspects of undocumented life and calls into question our country's notion of democracy. As Doty writes:

> The less extreme manifestations of exceptionalism should not be dismissed as unimportant. They can and do have devastating effects on the individuals and communities subjected to them. They raise important questions about the depth and breadth of our professed democratic values and about how we attribute worth to human beings with or without documents and citizenship. . . . This exceptionalism works its way into people's daily lives, affecting their most basic elements of existence and relationships. It creates a group of people set off from the rest of society, considered "others" and at least potential enemies of the rest of the population.[28]

This exceptionalism is even working toward erasing the archaeological record of migration.

Border crossings leave physical traces, but there is no guarantee that future generations of scholars will be able to access this archaeological record. Since the early 2000s, there has been a concerted effort by federal, state, and private organizations to "clean up" the desert. Over more than a decade now, hundreds of tons of material associated with migration have been removed annually.[29] A 2011 report from the Bureau of Land Management (BLM) highlights the logic of these efforts: "The cleanup and remediation projects were focused in the area within 100 miles of the United States border with Mexico. . . . Major impacts of smuggling and undocumented immigration include the accumulation of trash along smuggling corridors, the creation of illegal roads and trails and look out points throughout the border landscape. Disturbances to the natural and cultural landscape fragment wildlife habitat, damage archaeological

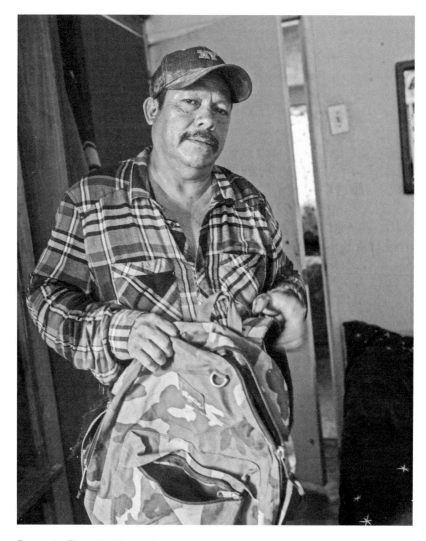

Recuerdo. Photo by Michael Wells.

and sacred sites, cause erosion, and increase the presence of invasive plant species. . . . [T]he effects of this have begun to be reversed as trash is removed."[30]

Federal guidelines generally do not recognize anything less than fifty years old as "historically important," which means no law is in place to protect the artifacts that migrants leave behind. Ironically, the above statement from the BLM highlights how the bureau's efforts to "clean up" migrant sites are directly linked to its attempts to protect other "archaeological sites." In this instance, the government perspective that migrant material culture is trash means that it can be justifiably erased. If we could fast-forward fifty years, these materials would be classified as "historic" and be protected. There is currently little interest, however, in preserving this ongoing historical record because of its political volatility and what it represents in terms of human suffering and government culpability.

Viewing the traces of undocumented migration as an environmental blight that needs to be sanitized shapes the formation of the archaeological record for future generations, much of which has already been destroyed before it could be recorded.[31] Site formation processes, like taphonomy, are political.[32] Historian Ewa Domanska might be on to something when she writes that those interested in understanding the manipulation of the past and its associated relics in contemporary political discourse might be able to *"forthell* the future."[33]

As memories of border crossings fade with time, physical evidence is being systematically removed by the political system that created this phenomenon. This erasure, much like the destruction of dead bodies, is the tail end of the violence produced by the hybrid collectif. This process seems to confirm Paul Farmer's remark that "erasing history is perhaps the most common explanatory sleight-of-hand relied upon by the architects of structural violence. Erasure or distortion of history is part of the process of desocialization necessary for the emergence of hegemonic accounts of what happened and why."[34]

Sitting with Memo and Lucho in their cramped living room, I hold out hope that some of the narratives of border crossers and the things they leave behind can be salvaged before all is forgotten or lost. I ask Memo how he feels after so many crossings:

> It's something that I really value. I truly value the experience. I always feel horrible for the people who come walking through the desert, who arrive beat up just to get ahead, to make progress. It's so horrible when they get detained, or assaulted, or killed. It's something so ugly. People get left behind and no one knows where. When you finally arrive here, it's like, "Thank God!" You are reborn. That's the point for me where you come back to life. For this reason we always go to church to thank God that we are OK and to keep moving forward with the people who come here to struggle. For me, my goal is to be here for a little bit and then go back to Mexico. But only when I have something that can help me survive. Right now it is very dangerous to cross . . . I keep this backpack as a memento of that last trip.

PART THREE

Perilous Terrain

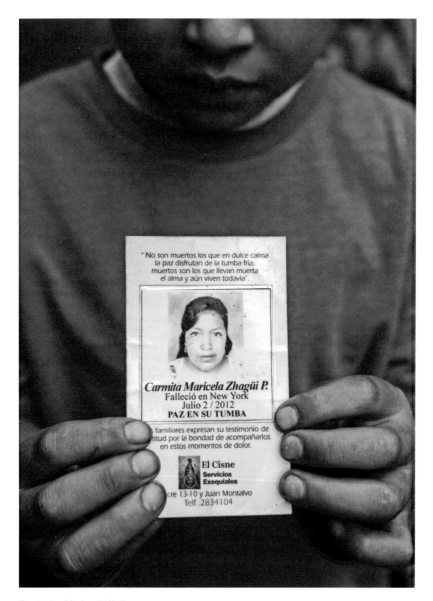

Photo by Michael Wells.

CHAPTER 8

Exposure

CARLOS FROM EL SALVADOR

On June 28, 2012, three students associated with the Undocumented Migration Project summer field school spent the day with volunteers from the Tucson Samaritans.[1] The research goal was to observe the organization's humanitarian efforts and collect ethnographic and archaeological data on the various water and food drops that it maintains in the desert.[2] The following are excerpts from an interview with UMP student Justine Drummond,[3] who was with the Samaritans that day:

> We were with Roberto [a Samaritan] when he got a phone call from two other volunteers. . . . They were asking if we could come out to Batamote Road and bring food and medical supplies to a migrant they had encountered. . . . We parked close to the GPS coordinates that were given to us by the volunteers and walked back to that location. One of them came out to meet us and brought us to the little wash where they were sitting with a young migrant named Carlos. Roberto, Linda, and Monica [the latter two also Samaritans] went to talk with him. Me and two other students sat away from Carlos and spoke to the volunteers who had been sitting with him. . . . They told us that he had been waiting by the side of the road when they drove past, so they stopped. He basically told them that he had been walking with a large group and the *coyote* had said that . . . Well, basically the smuggler was upset that there were people who were sick and weren't able to go as fast as he wanted to go. So he had called out that the Border Patrol was near and everyone scattered.
>
> In the chaos, Carlos found a woman from the group. I believe he also said that there was a man. He was traveling with two people. I am not entirely sure.

He had been walking with them, and four hours before the volunteers had found him, he separated from the woman because she was sick and he wanted to get help. He'd been walking out of the hills and later pointed towards them to show us where he was coming from. . . . We sat down and had lunch with him and introduced ourselves. Every so often Border Patrol would drive by on Batamote Road. We couldn't see the road but we could hear vehicles going by.

Carlos was nineteen years old and from El Salvador. He was wearing a blue shirt with a guitar printed on the front and had gray suede shoes and jeans on. On one wrist he had a pink nylon string that had his sister's name on it. . . . He was glassy eyed and very quiet. He was smiling, though. He just seemed sorta physically exhausted and really dehydrated.

The decision was made to call the sheriff to take him to the hospital. . . . We started chatting with him as we walked back to the vehicles. At that point we were asking him how many people were in his group and where he was hiking from. That was when he started pointing at the Lobo Peak area.

I didn't hear him say her name. He just said he was with two people, although the two initial volunteers who found him didn't speak Spanish. He may have known their names but I'm not sure if anyone got them.

LEFT BEHIND

The trail had been cold for years. I first walked it in 2009 when I made my initial fieldwork trip to Arizona. During that visit, the area was a debris field of Red Bull cans, potato chip bags, dusty blue jeans, and various other items that people fleeing Border Patrol had either intentionally discarded or accidently lost along the way. It was an active landscape then. The fresh footprints of agents and the people they were chasing were clearly visible in the dirt and sand. A mosaic of heavy and imposing military-style boot prints mixed with the light impressions left by sneakers. Sometimes you would see fragments of shirts caught in the trees or freshly broken branches signaling where someone had recently tried to bushwhack. Walking through that part of the desert, you knew you were in the middle of something but couldn't quite see it. Movement was happening, but it was in your blind spot.

One of the first migrant sites that I visited on that trail, later designated BK-3,[4] felt fresh and overwhelming. There were mountains of backpacks, arroyos swollen with tangled clothes. The items left behind were shiny and new. Food containers were still sealed or their contents only half eaten. Animals and insects had not had time to finish off the perishables. Bottles still had water in them. It was like entering into some strange village where the sound of the anthropologist's footsteps had sent everyone running mid-meal. During the initial summer we worked on that trail, I was constantly worried that we would accidentally walk up on some unsuspecting group of people resting in the shadows. Although we didn't see anyone out there that year, it was clear we weren't alone.

When I returned in 2010, many of the things left by migrants had been removed by some unknown person or organization. The desert had been decontaminated, its ghosts cleansed. Most of the evidence of hidden human occupation had been picked up and no doubt sent straight to the trash dump. What remained was largely sun bleached, worn, and breaking apart. After only a year, objects that had once seemed alive and vibrant were slowly dying, victims of solar radiation and rain. People assume that plastic water bottles and nylon backpacks will lie intact on the desert surface forever. It's not true. Things out here fall apart. Clothes are reduced to shreds, leaving only the stitching behind. Backpacks evaporate leaving only metal zippers and polyurethane buckles. Water bottles turn brittle, crack into pieces, and blow away. When I visited again in 2011, barely anything was left to signal that people had once existed here. Nothing on the landscape suggested this route was used anymore.

The trail had become well known to law enforcement after a few years of heavy use. Some of the migrant sites in the area that we documented in 2009 were so large that we could see them using Google Earth. If we could do that, Border Patrol could no doubt spot them from the air-conditioned seats in the helicopters that border crossers refer to as *el mosco* (the fly). After many chases and arrests, the spot had become burned. *La migra* was smart about it. They started placing underground motion sensors along the trail to alert them anytime someone passed through. Migrants and smugglers are smarter. They simply stopped using the route altogether and moved someplace else. There is always a canyon or mountain trail that *la migra* doesn't know about or that is too difficult for them to access on foot. Over five years of hiking, we rarely encountered Border Patrol agents on foot. They often lack the fortitude or motivation to head deep into the brush. Better to sit in your vehicle with a can of Skoal Long Cut Wintergreen and listen for ground sensor alerts. Migrants just keep heading deeper and deeper into the wild. Many get so deep that they eventually just disappear.

By 2011 I liked hiking this particular trail because it was familiar, like an old friend. I had cut my teeth out here, and many of the archaeological techniques that we now use to document and analyze migrant materials were first tested on this ground. I could also use the terrain to talk to students about the previous seasons' archaeological work and joke with them when we inevitably would set off a motion sensor and soon have *el mosco* swooping down on us. We had a running bet as to how much money it cost the federal government each time their agents went up into the sky to spy on anthropologists, hikers, and cows. From the archaeological evidence, it was obvious that they weren't catching many migrants out here anymore.

On the morning of July 2, 2012, I decide on a whim to revisit this old trail to check out a cleaned-up site that we have been studying as part of an ongoing project on desert conservation and its impacts on migrant material culture.[5] We expect to find very little in the way of artifacts and certainly no people. I want to show a group of students what it looks like when the evidence of migration disappears. We park our rented SUV and begin the three-mile hike toward a high clearing near Lobo Peak that once had hundreds of backpacks strewn across its surface. Our caravan starts the long and arduous climb up and down several large rolling hills. We intermittently snake down into washes where the soft sand makes each step more difficult than the last. All we encounter are a few scattered remnants of backpacks and clothes. A weather-stressed shoe. An empty, rusted can of tuna.

Our group drops into a steep ravine after noticing a torn black tarp and a water bottle buried under a large mesquite tree. At one point someone hid here but the material looks old. Olivia Waterhouse, an undergraduate at Barnard College and one of the more precocious students in the group, decides to take a closer look. She wedges herself deep into the underbrush and pulls out a twisted wreckage of muddy clothes and plastic sheeting. The stuff has been there for a while, and it is difficult to determine what the items originally looked like. She keeps digging and, to our surprise, finds a vibrantly colored *serape* (Mexican blanket) buried deep beneath the pile of soiled clothes. The plastic sheeting has somehow protected it from several seasons of rain and mud flow. The blanket's lines of deep blue and red cut a sharp contrast with the brown backdrop of the desert. It could have just come off a loom and is an unexpected find on a day when our goal is to find nothing. We deem the site too deteriorated to warrant filling out a field form. Still, we can't leave the blanket behind. It is so rare to find something that beautiful and out of place in this context. "Take a GPS reading and bag it," I say. Olivia puts it into her pack and we move on.

We come out of the ravine and begin the ascent up a hill toward a site known as BK-5. It's a long, slow climb, the type you feel in your upper thighs and chest. The grade is deceiving and it's not usually until you're midway that you realize how tough the hike is. We have documented BK-5 on multiple occasions. Having eaten lunch under the shade of various trees there, I feel as familiar and comfortable with the place as one could possibly be with a landscape lately known more for being anonymous and unforgiving. The student leading our group hurriedly makes his way up the trail while the rest of us try to keep up with his overactive legs. He is far enough ahead that it is difficult to hear him when he starts yelling back at us, "Hey! Hey! There is someone up here! There is someone up here!" I can't see what he is yelling about, but I figure it's a migrant who has been left behind and needs water or first aid. I throw my pack down and begin to run up the trail. By the time I reach him, I can tell from his wide eyes that it is something more than a person with a sprained ankle. When I am finally close enough to see her, there is no mistaking that she is dead.

N31° 44′ 55″, W111° 12′ 24″

The eight of us stand around her in a semicircle. It is obvious that not everyone has seen a corpse before, because someone asks if she is really dead. Most of the students go and sit under a nearby tree while I figure out what to do next. I walk to the top of the hill to try to get cell phone reception. After fifteen minutes I finally get a 911 operator on the line. I tell her that we have found a dead body while hiking. I give her general directions to our location but it is a fairly useless endeavor: "About three miles northeast of Batamote Road near Lobo Peak." She is not familiar with the area, so I give her the GPS coordinates of our location. She is not sure what they mean, so I tell her that we will send someone back to the road to get law enforcement. There is no way they are going to find us with verbal directions. Haeden Stewart, a graduate student from the University of Chicago, agrees to run back to the vehicle to get help. I tell the rest of the group that we will wait for the sheriff to arrive but in the meantime we need to document and photograph the scene. No one seems particularly enthusiastic about this prospect, me included.

At this point there is the realization that unpleasant work has to be done. I remind myself that directing a research project focused on human suffering and death in the desert means we can't ignore certain parts of the social process just because it sickens us or breaks our hearts. This means looking at the body of this unknown woman up close and recording as much information as possible. This means taking photos. The decision to do this will later lead me to being questioned and criticized by some colleagues who don't think we should have taken pictures of the body or used them in any publication. It makes readers and viewers uncomfortable, which is fine because it made (and continues to make) us as researchers uncomfortable. When this type of death starts to feel normal, that's when we should worry. I start taking photos of her because it feels imperative to record what this type of death looks like up close. The objective is to document this moment for those who are not here.

I am well aware, though, that despite our best intentions, dangers and ethical issues can arise from circulating images such as these. As Susan Sontag warns, "The photographer's intentions do not determine the meaning of the photograph, which will have its own career; blown by the whims and loyalties of the diverse communities that have use for it."[6] I cannot control the life of these pictures or the meanings that viewers will attach to them. My only hope is that these images can stand as undeniable material evidence that a woman died at N31° 44′55″, W111° 12′ 24″ and that witnesses saw her corpse in "flesh and blood."[7]

––––––––––

She is lying face down in the dirt and it appears that she died while attempting to get up the hill. To get to this point, she easily walked more than 40 miles and likely crossed the Tumacácori Mountains. She is wearing generic brown and white running shoes, black stretch pants, and a long-sleeve camouflage shirt. The shirt is something you expect a deer hunter to wear, but over the last several years migrants and drug mules have adopted the fashion. The brown and green design blends in perfectly with the Sonoran backdrop this time of year. Her position lying face down, exposed on the side of a steep hill, suggests that her last moments were a painful crawl. She collapsed mid-hike. To be left on the trail like this likely means that she died alone out here.

Rigor mortis has set in and her fingers have started to curl. Her ankles are swollen to the point that her sneakers seem ready to pop off at any moment. The back of her pants are stained with excrement and are bubbling with copper-colored fluids that were expelled from her body upon death. It is surprisingly hard to look away. Dead only a few days, the body is in what forensic anthropologists term *early decomposition:* "Gray to green discoloration, some

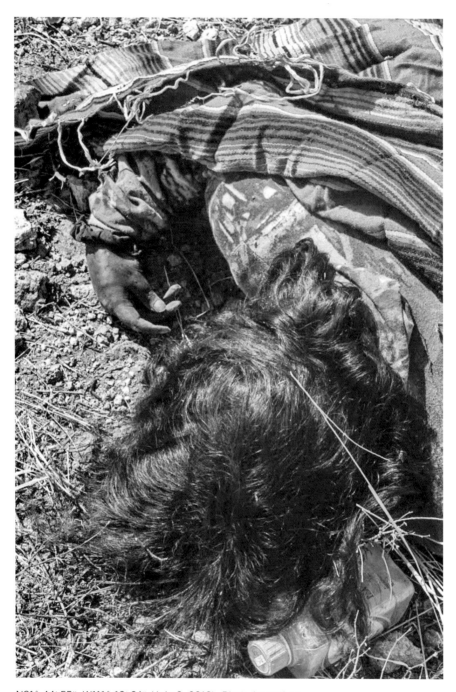

N31° 44′ 55″, W111° 12′ 24″ (July 2, 2012). Photo by author.

flesh relatively fresh . . . Bloating . . . Brown to black discoloration of arms and legs."[8] These descriptions don't do justice to what bodies left out in the desert actually look like, smell like, or sound like. Nothing does. Against the quiet backdrop of the desert you can hear the buzzing of flies busily laying eggs on her, in her. There is a steady hissing of intestinal gases escaping from her bloated and distended stomach. It sounds like a slow-leaking tire.

High above, stiff-winged turkey vultures circle her corpse like black paper airplanes effortlessly surveying the scene. I count at least four of them and marvel at how quickly they have arrived. At this point in 2012, we are two weeks into our first round of forensic experiments, and I have recently been watching video footage of birds scavenging pig carcasses. The site of them now flying overhead is disturbing and I do my best to ignore them. I get close to the body and awkwardly scribble down more field notes: "No backpack or obvious personal possessions . . . a bottle of electrolyte fluids tucked under shoulder and face." As I lean in to look at her, the wind whips across her body sending the sweet smell and taste of rotting flesh directly into my nostrils and mouth. It is the taste of *la muerte*.

After several days in the boiling summer heat her body has begun to change. Her skin has started to blacken and mummify and the bloating is beginning to obscure some of her physical features. While parts of her are transforming into unfamiliar shapes and colors, her striking jet-black hair and the ponytail holder wrapped around her right wrist hint at the person she once was. I focus on her hair. It is smooth; the color of smoky obsidian. It's possibly the darkest hair I have ever seen, and its texture gives the impression that she is still alive. I think about reaching down to touch her, but I can't. She has been out here too long and I know that her skin will not feel human. I want to see her face but don't dare roll the body over. This is a "crime scene" and I don't want to destroy any evidence. I start thinking about who she might have been in life. Was she a kind person? What did her laugh sound like? What compelled her to enter this desert? Would she be angry that I am taking her picture? Finally I ask Olivia to get out the blanket that we found, and we use it to cover her. It makes those of us still alive feel better.

I go over and sit with the remaining group of students under a tree a short distance from the body. The silence among us is tense and only occasionally broken when a breeze comes through and rustles the branches of nearby mesquite trees. Out of the blue someone starts crying uncontrollably and is immediately consoled by a neighbor's kind embrace. Others sigh deeply and someone

Esperando. Photo by author.

angrily walks off into the distance to be alone. We sit quietly for what seems an eternity. Vultures continue to patiently circle overhead. They are simultaneously implicated in and oblivious to the complex human drama playing out below them. All they know is that we have disrupted their lunch plans.

I want to say something to our group that will comfort us or make this death seem peaceful or dignified. It's a ridiculous thought. There is nothing you can say in this scenario that doesn't sound contrived. Months later someone will corner me after a talk and complain that the photos I showed of this woman's body robbed her of her dignity. I will point out that the deaths that migrants experience in the Sonoran Desert are anything but dignified. That is the point. This is what "Prevention Through Deterrence" looks like. These photographs should disturb us, because the disturbing reality is that right now corpses lie rotting on the desert floor and there aren't enough witnesses. This invisibility is a crucial part of both the suffering and the necroviolence that emerge from the hybrid collectif. As Timothy Pachirat notes, we live in a world where "power operates through the creation of distance and concealment and [where] our understandings of 'progress' and 'civilization' are inseparable from, and perhaps even synonymous with, the concealment (but not elimination) of what is increasingly rendered physically and morally repugnant."[9] These photos thus make visible the human impact of a United States border enforcement policy intended to kill people, and they provide compelling evidence that we don't need to go to "exotic" places to get "full frontal views of the dead and dying."[10] The dead live in our backyard; they are the human grist for the sovereignty machine. You need only "luck" to catch a glimpse of the dead before they are erased by the hybrid collectif.

Desert border crossings are cruel, brutal affairs in which people often die slowly and painfully from hyperthermia, dehydration, heatstroke, and a variety of other related ailments. To paint these deaths in any other way is both a denial of the harsh desert reality and a disservice to those who have experienced it. Judith Butler reminds us that the American public rarely gets to see these types of photos for fear of causing internal dissent or undermining nationalistic projects: "Certain images do not appear in the media, certain names of the dead are not utterable, certain losses are not avowed as losses, and violence is derealized and diffused. . . . The violence that we inflict on others is only—and always—selectively brought into public view." It is unclear, though, what impact the photos of this woman's body will have on those who flip through the pages of this book. Will the images evoke sadness or disgust? Does looking behind the curtain at the inner workings of US border enforcement elicit responses that get us closer to political action? Can these images effectively and affectively pierce the American public's consciousness? Or, as poet Sean Thomas Dougherty writes in reference to Kevin Carter's (in)famous photo of a "starving Sudanese child being stalked by a vulture," will the violence depicted here become nothing more than an "aesthetic" capable only of evoking appreciation?[11]

Sitting there on that dusty afternoon, I finally blurt out, "At least we got to her before the vultures did."

"BODIES"

It takes Haeden and another student close to five hours to find a sheriff and then bring him back to where the body is. When a migrant dies, he or she stops being the federal government's problem and subsequently the case is handed over to the county. However, in rural areas the Border Patrol often provides local law enforcement with logistical support. In our case, a lone sheriff shows up with three Border Patrol agents in tow. Two of the agents are young and are accompanied by a senior officer. They have hiked the three miles in from the road, pulling a wheeled stretcher specially equipped with off-road tires.

The sheriff is polite and cognizant of the fact that six of us have been sitting with her body for hours. He knows that we are going to scrutinize his every move to make sure she is treated respectfully. It is obvious the sheriff has done this numerous times before. He quickly dons light-blue medical gloves, pulls out his point-and-shoot camera, and snaps a few photos of the corpse. He then takes a GPS reading.

"Was that blanket on top of her like that?"

"No, we covered her up."

"Did she have anything with her?"

"She had no obvious possessions outside of that bottle of *electrolit*."

"All right, time to move her."

This is the extent of the investigation of this death. No survey is done near the body to look for additional personal effects. The trail is not checked for other people or corpses. Some photos are taken and geographic coordinates are recorded. It takes a total of five minutes.

The sheriff looks at the two young Border Patrol agents, one Mexican American, the other white, and says they need to help him move the body. The senior agent starts fiddling with the equipment on his tactical vest and then walks up the hill. He is clearly not going to be involved in this next stage. The young agents are visibly uncomfortable with the whole scene. Olivia asks the white agent, who seems to be the more nervous of the two, how old he is. "Twenty-two," he says. Four of the students in our group are older than him. The agents are handed medical gloves, and the sheriff starts planning how he will move her. "Hopefully, she doesn't burst when we pick her up," he says. The white agent nervously laughs and seems to be unsure if that was a joke.

They wheel the stretcher close to her and lay a white body bag on the ground. "We gotta roll her over and put her in the bag because she is gonna leak," he tells the men. The sheriff grabs her arm and shoulder while the agents reach down to take hold of her feet. As the white agent gets close to her, he catches a whiff of her rotting flesh. He drops her feet, steps back, and starts dry heaving. His eyes are watering and he is holding himself to prevent from vomiting. As he starts to crack a joke about how "gross" it is, he notices that eight of us are coldly staring at him. The irony of this scene is undeniable: Border Patrol routinely refer to living migrants as "bodies" in everyday discourse,[12] but many of them seem totally unprepared for dealing with the actual dead ones. The sheriff gives the agent a stern look, which forces him to regain composure. "All right, we're gonna flip her on three." They reach down and stiffly roll her over.

As her body turns, I see what is left of her face. It is frightening and unrecognizable as human. The mouth is a gnarled purple and black hole that obscures the rest of her features. I can't see her eyes because the mouth is too hard to look away from. The skin around the lips is stretched out of shape as though it has been melted. Her nose is smashed in and pushed up. She died face down, and the flesh on the front side of her skull has softened and contorted to fit around the dirt and rocks beneath her. The scene is a pastiche of metallic gray and pea green. Whatever beauty and humanity that once existed in her face has been replaced by a stone-colored ghoul stuck in mid-scream. It's a look you can never get away from.

They get her leaking body into the bag and zip it up. She still needs to be lifted onto the stretcher. Even though she is now hidden behind a shroud of white plastic, the two agents are still uncomfortable with touching her. As they struggle to get a grip, I step in to help. I grab one ankle; it is rock hard like the leg of a coffee table. There is a collective heave. By this time another agent has arrived on an ATV. She is loaded onto the back of the four-wheeler and driven away. We pick up our things and silently begin the three-mile march back to our vehicle.

MEDICAL EXAMINER

All migrant bodies recovered in the southern part of the Tucson Sector are delivered to the Pima County Office of the Medical Examiner (PCOME) for processing. Since 2000, the office has received an annual average of 184 deceased migrants. As of January 2013, approximately 900 of these human remains were unidentified and unclaimed.[13] Attaching names to these recovered bodies is not an easy task. The environmental conditions can quickly decompose human tissue, animals can rapidly disarticulate and scatter skeletons, and people are often found without documents that could aid in their identification. The PCOME employs a small team of anthropologists who

Unidentified human remains from the Pima County Office of the Medical
Examiner. Photo by Michael Wells.

have been tirelessly working for years both to identify bodies and to help the
families of the missing file reports. One member of this team is Robin Reineke,
a cultural anthropologist who has been working with the families of the missing and dead since 2006. In 2013 she founded the Colibrí Center for Human
Rights, a nonprofit organization dedicated to helping people reunite with
loved ones who lose their lives while migrating. Robin is a good friend who,
just a few weeks before we found the body, had given my students a tour of her
office.

Visiting the medical examiner's office is a somber affair that brings you face
to face with both migrant death and the lonely existence of the unclaimed. It
can be emotionally difficult and physically nauseating to see the areas where
the county stores animal-gnawed human bone fragments and pungent body
bags that are leaking fluids. For some visitors, however, the most difficult part
of the tour is a tiny windowless room where the personal possessions of those
yet to be identified are kept. If the sour smell of rotting corpses doesn't get you,

Personal effects of the unidentified, Pima County Office of the Medical Examiner.
Photo by Michael Wells.

looking at the friendship bracelets, wallet-sized photos of babies, or prayer cards sometimes found with unidentified bodies often will. Although these items may elicit emotions, they can't necessarily tell you who these dead people were in life. As the staff at the PCOME can attest, migrants often travel with forged identification documents, documents belonging to someone else, or no ID at all.[14] The body that we found was taken directly to the medical examiner's office and placed in one of its large storage freezers. She had no identification and no personal effects.

That evening I call Robin and tell her what happened. She promises to keep us up-to-date on any developments with the case. Two weeks later I receive an email:

> Hi Jason,
>
> Just a quick update regarding the woman that your group found—
>
> The case number is 12–01567, and as of yet, she has not been identified. I just spoke with [one] of the Samaritans. . . . She relayed some useful information regarding the people left behind by the Salvadoran man. Here is what I got from her on the phone. Let me know if you have any corrections or more information:
>
> 7/17/12: I received a call from [someone] from the Samaritans group, who has been communicating with those who found the body of 12–1567. She said that the day before the body was located,[15] several Samaritan volunteers in the same area (4.5 miles from Arivaca Road) encountered a young man by the name of Carlos who was from El Salvador.
>
> He said that he had recently left behind two fellow travelers who were in serious medical distress. The names of the two people he left behind were:
>
> 38 y/o Marsela Haguipolla (or Maricela Ahguipolla) of either Guatemala or Ecuador, and an older man by the name of Tony Gonzales of Ecuador. The older man was 70 years old. . . . It isn't certain that this group is related to ML 12–1567, but it is highly likely.
>
> I will contact Guatemalan and Ecuadoran consulates regarding new missing person cases.

Apparently, Carlos knew their names after all.

CHAPTER 9

You Can't Leave Them Behind

QUEENS

Roosevelt Avenue in the heart of Jackson Heights, Queens, is loud and eclectic. It carries the street urchin aroma that only New York City can unapologetically cultivate. It is also one of the most ethnically diverse neighborhoods in the United States and the epicenter of America's Ecuadoran immigrant community. I told Christian that I would wait for him on the corner of 82nd and Roosevelt, just underneath the subway platform. I pace nervously and look for him in a sea of brown faces. We've never met and I don't know what he looks like. I scan the passing pedestrians and try to envision him. Based on our phone calls, I imagine him as tall, in his late forties, and dressed like a construction worker. He should be wearing cement-stained coveralls and brown steel-toed boots. Ten minutes later a short raven-haired man in his early thirties approaches me. As he walks up, I can tell he is a bit apprehensive. I can't say I blame him. I'm nervous too. Christian is younger than I expected, and I am a bit surprised to see that he is wearing a tight-fitting Abercrombie & Fitch T-shirt and flashy tennis shoes and is wielding an iPhone. His aesthetic is not working-class day laborer, but rather urban Latino fabulousness.

I would soon learn that Christian was one of the hundreds of thousands of people who emigrated from Ecuador following the economic meltdown the country experienced in the late 1990s. A costly border war with Peru, combined with a decline in export revenue, increased debt, painful austerity measures, and political instability, led to the worst economic crisis Ecuador had seen in more than a hundred years.[1] The poverty rate during this decade rose to 40 percent. An estimated 900,000 Ecuadorans permanently left the country between 1993 and 2006 to find employment in the United States, Spain, and other countries in Western Europe.[2] As Jokisch and Pribilsky note, "In just two years (1999 and 2000) more than 267,000 Ecuadorians emigrated (net) and remittances increased to more than $1.41 billion in 2001 from an estimated $643 million in 1997."[3]

Christian left in 2001 as part of the wave of approximately 137,000 Ecuadoran migrants who arrived in the United States between 1999 and 2005.[4] He is one of the estimated 425,700 *cuatorianos* who live in the northeastern United States. Like many of his generation, he left his country to find work abroad when he was a teenager, leaving behind a pregnant girlfriend and a household living hand to mouth. For over a decade he has been sending money home to support an extended family, to build a house he has never set foot in, and to clothe, feed, and educate a son whose hand he has never held.[5]

These are details about his life that I will learn over the course of many phone calls and visits to New York. At this moment, though, we are still strangers.

Christian introduces himself. The combination of the rattling subway train passing overhead and the cacophony of daytime traffic force us to almost scream at each other to be heard. When I ask if there is someplace quiet where we can talk, he recommends a nearby Ecuadoran restaurant. Next thing I know I am staring across the table at him, struggling to properly explain myself. In an unsure voice I tell him, "Thank you for agreeing to meet with me. This whole thing is a little strange. As I said on the phone, I got your number from the Ecuadoran consulate, and I wanted to meet you because I am the person who found Maricela's body."

Awkward pause.

I continue. "I guess I wanted to know who she was and how her family is. I wanted to tell you what happened when we found her and maybe answer any questions that you might have. I'm writing a book about what happens to migrants in the desert, and I wanted to ask your permission to write about her life and your family's experiences when she went missing."

Although he already knows everything that I have just told him based on our numerous prior phone calls, I am still unsure how he will respond in person. After just a few seconds, he looks me in the eyes and says: "I told them many times that it was difficult. I told them that I didn't want Maricela to come. They thought that I didn't want my sister-in-law to come here to work, but it was really because of what happened to me. I knew about the things that occur during the crossing when you are in the desert. It is horrible ... You would never believe the things that happened to me. I didn't want her to go through it."

As bad as things can be in the Sonoran Desert for many non-Mexican nationals like Christian who travel to the United States undocumented (*"por el camino"* or *"por la pampa,"* as Ecuadorans say), that stage of the migration process is usually the end of an arduous journey that can last weeks and sometimes months.[6] *Cuatorianos* and others may end up paying more than $10,000 to the *pasador* who arranges their clandestine travel across multiple countries.[7] These Central and South American migrants, who accounted for 31 percent of all people deported by the US federal government in 2013 (a percentage that seems to be steadily increasing),[8] pass through multiple borders using a variety of transportation methods. This includes walking or running for their lives, crossing rivers on rafts, and riding on the tops of freight trains,[9] all before arriving at the US-Mexico boundary for the chance to try their luck in the desert. As he recalled the details of his crossing during our first meeting and my subsequent visits to New York, it became clear why Christian was adamant about not wanting his sister-in-law Maricela to migrate.

In what follows, I have chosen to present Christian's migration story largely in his own words with minimal interference or interruption. My rationale for this discursive shift is twofold. First, his telling of the story is more realistic than any ethnographic translation or summation I could come up with. As I stress throughout this book, there is no appropriate substitution for an emic account of a border crossing. Second, by pushing his words to the forefront, I seek to rectify the paucity of first-person published accounts of undocumented migration, especially those of South Americans. In his recent book on the life experiences of migrants from Uganda, Burkina Faso, and Mexico, anthropologist Michael Jackson writes: "If we are to avoid the trap of becoming infatuated with our own intellectual-cum-magical capacity to render the world intelligible, then the vocabulary 'we' all too glibly project onto 'them' must be tested continually against the various and changing experiences of actual lives."[10] Although I have included some brief analyses and connective tissue in the text, sometimes embedded as footnotes, I largely use this chapter to let Christian's words breathe and to provide him the opportunity to render his world intelligible to us.[11]

"YOU CAN'T LEAVE THEM BEHIND"

Christian: The day that Maricela left my country, I don't know . . . I think she had the hope, the dream to get here with so many goals. She had a lot of dreams that she wanted to achieve. She was thinking about getting here and nothing else. But also, she was coming with a broken heart. It's like when I left in 2001, it was really painful that first day. I never thought about coming to New York. My aunt was the one who wanted to go. Things were good with my girlfriend, the mother of my child. She was pregnant at that time and we were going to have a son. I was very excited. I wanted to get married, get a job, and work to support him. I wanted to be there and live with him. I was dreaming about all of this. When we decided to come here, my aunt was saying things like, "It is going to be better for your son and for all your family. For your dad and mom." My mom was sick and my dad made very little money.

I was sleeping in a tiny house made of adobe. Supposedly the government was going to build a big road through our neighborhood and they were going to take away what little we had. I was thinking about this. If this happens one day, what are we are going to do? Where will my parents go? Where do me and my siblings go? That is why I came here. To be able to build a house. My little sister, Vanessa, she is grown now. I loved her very much. I wanted her to study. None of us had ever gone to school because there was never any money. I was thinking about her. I wanted to have her *quince años* party. There were so many things that were never going to happen. I would never be able to do those things there. I was thinking about all of this, and then I said, "I'm going." I asked my father to help me find the money. He asked my grandparents if they would let us use their land for collateral. And, yeah, I decided to leave.

Jason: What did you think when you were preparing to go?

Christian: I just had a lot of faith in God. I asked God for help. I told him that if I go, I am going for my parents and my son. After two or three years maximum, I would return to Ecuador.

I was sleeping. It was like 7 or 8 A.M. when the first plane hit. My grandmother came in and told me to turn on the TV. She said, "Something is happening in New York." She was crying because she had two sons there. This was an enormous event for us there in Ecuador and for the whole world. This happened and my family didn't want me to leave. I thought about it, but I also thought that there was going to be a lot of work. I thought that if I got there to New York, I could help clean up all the destroyed buildings because the only thing that *illegales* really do here are construction and cleaning and stuff. I figured that I would start working in construction. After September 11 happened, we departed a few days later on like the 16th or 17th.

It really affected Vanessa when I left because we were always together. I worked when I was there and I always took her out shopping. I bought her clothing, dresses. She was a little girl then. She was like the little princess in our house and I treated her like she was my daughter. I tried to give her everything I could. . . . The day that I left was horrible. I didn't want to wake her. I left at dawn while she was asleep in her bed. I just gave her a kiss and left. I always thought about her while I was crossing. Once *en el camino* we got in a truck and I had to ride alone in the back because there was no room up front. We were going down the road and I saw her sitting right next to me. I imagined her. It was terrible and it made me cry. My son wasn't born yet and she was the person that I loved the most at that time. These are things that leave a mark on you. You can't leave them behind . . . I was seventeen when I left. I turned eighteen while crossing through Mexico.

POR LA PAMPA

Christian: We went to Guayaquil [Ecuador]. From Guayaquil we flew to Peru. From Peru we flew to Panama. From Panama we went to Costa Rica by bus. Then we went to Nicaragua, then El Salvador and then Guatemala. In Peru and Panama, they treated us well. We were in hotels. We were supposed to be tourists so we had luggage and were dressed nice so that no one would say anything. We had money in our pockets to look like we were on vacation. But in Costa Rica, man . . . I don't know . . . We crossed a river in Costa Rica and then it got bad. I actually thought we were really close to [New York]. I was like, "We're almost there!" We crossed a river and I thought we were in New York! [laughing]

When we got into Costa Rica, we ran through a field where they were growing sugarcane. Man, the snakes! Wow! We were running to a little house where we had to change clothes because we were dressed nice and stuff. They gave us new clothes and then put us into the trunk of a car. Six people in the trunk. This was how we got into Nicaragua. We were in the trunk for six hours. I would never do it again . . . Man, it was so scary how fast they were driving. If we had gotten into an accident, we would have all died. . . . My aunt and I almost never talk about this stuff now. Everytime I think back it affects me, makes me feel horrible.

I think we were in Honduras. They took us to a house in the jungle. We were there for a month and couldn't leave. From there they took us to Guatemala. They started to treat us bad as soon as we got close to the border with Mexico.

They dropped us off at this woman's house that was really nice looking. We thought we were going to stay in the house, but no. They stuck us in a chicken coop in the backyard. We slept in there with the rats. Everything was muddy. There were giant rats fighting under our bed and the toads were making all kinds of sounds at night. It was unbelievably hot. We couldn't leave the chicken coop. We could see outside through the cracks in the wood where the lady was cooking our meals. We had to pay her for our food, for tortillas and beans. We slept there for two nights.

Then they dressed us like *guatemaltecos* [Guatemalans]. They put clothes on us like we were from there. The women put on blouses and long skirts and we walked down to the [Suchiate] river because it was really close. They said, "If someone asks, you are just out shopping." We got in a canoe made of tires and they crossed us with paddles into Mexico, into Chiapas.

We ended up on the outskirts of a town where they put us in a building on the top floor. Wow, the heat was incredible. We spent the night and left the next day. Again they put us into a taxi; three and three in two taxis. They said, "If we stop and say, 'Hide,' you need to hide. We will pull the seat down and the three of you need to climb into the trunk." When we crossed through a checkpoint, we had to do this. They also told us what to say. We had to know what the president's name was, what the currency was, the national anthem. We learned Mexican phrases like *chingada* [fucked], *odelay* [right on], and *chinga su madre* [fuck your mother]. [laughs] Then they dropped us off in a place that was near the coast, but I don't know where.

¡VIVA MÉXICO, CABRONES!

As the crow flies, it is more than 1,600 miles from Mexico's border with Guatemala to Nogales, Sonora. Many of the non-Mexican migrants who make this cross-country trek will tell you that this expansive obstacle course is far more dangerous than what awaits them in the desert. Those, such as Christian and his aunt, who are fortunate enough to be traveling with a guide will find themselves handed off from one smuggler to another in a never-ending exchange of currency for bodies.[12] These hypervulnerable undocumented migrants simultaneously embody illegality and the transformation of human beings into cargo to be smuggled by any means necessary.[13] This clandestine passage typically involves weeks of checkerboard movements through an archipelago of "safe houses," chicken coops, and dusty attics via a mixture of creative transportation methods and disguises. Along the way, people do their best to avoid falling in the shark-infested waters where kidnappings, robbery, physical assault, rape, and murder by locals, organized crime, and law enforcement are the norm. For Central and South Americans, Mexico is its own hybrid collectif of immigration enforcement.

Christian: In Mexico there was a woman who we stayed with who treated us really well in the beginning. I don't know what happened later. Like a week and a half later she started treating us really badly. I guess our families or the *coyotes* didn't give her any money. She had this enormous dog that wouldn't let us leave the room we were in. We couldn't go outside. Finally, it was like three weeks later when the day to leave came. The lady said, "They paid your passage. We are going to take you to the edge of the water where you can catch a boat. Then you will catch the train."

Around this time they told us, "Look, you are all going to go on a boat, and we will give you life jackets that will save you if you fall in the water." We were like, "OK, at least they are gonna give us life jackets." Well, when we finally got to the edge of the water they gave us plastic trash bags. We asked, "What do we do with this?" and they said, "Those are your life jackets."

At first, being on the boat was a really smooth ride. We were out in the middle of the ocean and we were content. I was only seventeen. I was at the front of the boat and putting my arms out like the film *Titanic* because the wind was blowing and stuff. [laughing] There was fresh air and everything.

But after about 6 in the evening another boat got close to us, like a patrol boat. They told us that they were thieves who wanted to rob us. The guy who was driving our boat was using drugs. He had some powder. He took a sniff. Made another line. Took another sniff. Made another line. The third time he took a sniff he just said [using Mexican accent], "*¡Agarrense, cabrones!*" and gave it everything he had. He yelled, "Those who fall overboard, fall overboard!" Boom! When he hit the gas, everyone fell on the floor. We were flying. Now we realized why we had the bags. The bags were to cover us because of all the water that was coming in. We were taking a bath in there. We were soaked. Everyone was screaming and crying and saying that we were going to die. We were yelling for him to stop, but he didn't. It was horrible, horrible. We could see we were in the middle of the ocean. It was dark and suddenly the driver stopped the boat and said, "Get in the water. We are close to the shore." We jumped in. When my aunt jumped in the water, she disappeared. She was nowhere to be seen. I was splashing around looking for her.

I finally found her and we made our way to the shore. But when we got there, it was really muddy and there were thorns all over the place. We didn't have shoes on and had to come out running onto the beach. Our feet were hurt. The guide then told us, "There is a road that you will need to follow. You will come to a hut but don't stop before that because there are many people who live around there who may rob or shoot you." We ran until we got to that little hut, and there was an old man who they called "*abuelo*" who said we could hide there. We went in there to sleep. We were covered in mud. He told us that we would have to wait a little bit and that the train[14] would come by at daybreak.

The old man took us to a place that was a five-minute walk from the hut where the train was going to pass by. "As soon as it stops," he told us, "get on." The area was full of mango trees. Abuelo told us to climb up into the trees to act as lookouts to see if people from other ranches were coming, or if immigration or the police were on their way. If we saw that the train was coming, we were supposed to jump down and try to get on it in any way possible.

My aunt was up in the tree crying. She cried on the whole trip. She was always nervous. She thought about going back, but was thinking about her kids in Ecuador and how she wanted to send them to school. This wasn't going to happen until she got across. There were times when we did think about going back, but we also thought about the *plata* that we paid. It was $12,000 for each person. We didn't have any money, so we had to borrow it against my grandfather's land. If I went back, my grandfather would have lost his land.

A little while later the train showed up and we got on and hid. We got between the cars and sat there. Once we were hidden, the train started again. Everytime we came to a city or small town, we would duck down. They told us if the conductor stops the train and blows the whistle, we need to jump off and hide because there is a checkpoint where the police will search the train. The conductor stopped and blew the whistle, but he didn't stop completely. He just slowed down but we were still going very fast. We had to jump off while it was moving.

In each place we were given to a new person. There was a kid that was with us on the train who was our guide. He told us where to go after we jumped off. We walked and walked and found a chicken coop and went in there all wet and dirty and covered in mud. Our guide said that we were going to wash up and then go to a *pueblo* at nightfall where they would give us new clothes and food. We walked to this town when it got dark. We were scared because there were a lot of people around that we thought were going to rob us.[15] We got to a house and took baths and they gave us new clothes. The guide then said, "Eat and then at midnight we will take you to a bus station. You're all going to Mexico, *al DF* [Distrito Federal, Mexico City]."

They took us to the bus terminal and said, "If someone gets on the bus to check, like the police, you should pretend that you are all asleep. If they ask, you are headed to *el DF* for vacation." The guide told us that when we got to Mexico City, a taxi driver would be waiting for us. He said, "You will see a driver with a certain color hat. That is how you will know him. You will then get into his taxi." This is exactly what happened. We got to Mexico City at dawn and got off the bus and the driver was there. We got into the taxi and he took us to his house. We ate breakfast and then he said, "You aren't going to be here for very long. Someone else is coming for you."

In the afternoon another man came and took us to a different house. We were locked up again for like three or four days. Finally, the man said to us, "You guys are going to a *rancho*." The money had just run out, and we needed to give them more to keep going [north]. The man let us make phone calls to do this. I called my dad and said, "Please, the money is gone and I want to get out of here." Then they took us to an enormous abandoned ranch. I thought we were the only people there, but when we arrived, they turned on the lights. Wow! There were more than three hundred people lying on the ground. They told us to grab a floor mat and find a place to sleep. This was where they kept all of their migrants.

An abandoned Mexican ranch where men in tight white jeans and alligator-skin boots wield *cuernos de chivo*[16] while guarding three hundred kidnap victims from around the globe sounds like a lost scene from one of Robert Rodriguez's *Machete* films. But for migrants crossing Mexico, this is a horrifying reality that has only gotten worse in the fourteen years since Christian's crossing. In the wake of the Mexican Narco Wars, drug cartels have become more involved in human smuggling, and 70,000 to 150,000 Central American migrants have gone missing while crossing the country.[17] These people have met any number of different fates, ranging from being held for ransom to being trafficked for sex and forced into working for the cartels.[18] The bodies of seventy-two migrants who had been blindfolded and shot were found in 2010 in the northern border state of Tamaulipas, representing only a small fraction of the people who have been murdered while en route.[19] The American public, including those who consume the drugs that fuel this violence, hears about these bloodbaths only when they are too brutal to be folded in with news of the other, everyday narcoviolence in Mexico that the United States has become accustomed to hearing about and generally ignoring.

For Central and South Americans who must pass through the literal and figurative Tierra Caliente on their way north, this country-turned-battleground is a vast, heterogeneous labyrinth where a wrong turn can get you hurled into a black void. The murkiness of the human-smuggling process across Mexico means that many will never know if their loved ones disappeared in the desert or had something far worse happen to them along the way.[20] The mothers of missing Central American migrants who have spent years traversing the country looking for any sign of their children can attest that the Mexican hybrid collectif is capable of producing its own unique forms of necroviolence.[21]

As Christian's story continues to unfold, we see that getting through the smuggler's spider web often requires ingenuity and sheer luck.

> *Christian:* There were a lot of people there from all kinds of countries. There were Chinese people, Brazilians, Salvadorans, Nicaraguans. Almost every

country was represented. They had a kitchen and they made groups of us take turns cooking for all of the people. There were so many people . . .

I made some friends with migrants who had been there a month, a month and a half, two months. No one had come for them. We couldn't leave because we were in a giant enclosure that was always being watched. They would see you trying to walk around and they would say, "Hey, what are you doing?" Outside all we could see were mountains surrounding us. There was nothing else. Supposedly I was going to get out of there soon. I was there a week and the *guía* still hadn't come for me. They wouldn't let me use the phone. After two weeks I was like, "This isn't right." It was around this time that I came up with a plan. I had become friends with some women who I asked to help me. I said to them, "I am going to do something and I need you to cover for me." I was walking around on the patio with my aunt and another woman when I pretended to faint and fell on the floor. The people who were guarding us came to see what happened. They called their boss to tell them that I had fainted. Then they called someone who had a car, and they took me to the hospital because I told them I was dying.

They had a doctor who helped them. He was like their private doctor. He checked me out and said that I had bad nerves and that I was anemic because I had already been *en el camino* for weeks. After the doctor left, a nurse came into the room. I told myself, "It is now or never" and I asked her to help me. I told her the whole story. I was crying. I said, "I have been away from my family for like two months. They have us locked up. My aunt is sick on a ranch and they won't let us call anyone." I asked her to help me communicate with my family so that I could tell them what was happening to me. She said, "I can't. I don't want to get mixed up in any trouble. Here everything is controlled by *la mafia*."

I begged her. I cried and cried. I think she felt sorry for me. She said, "Don't tell anyone I did this," and then she brought me a telephone and I called my dad. He answered the phone and I said, "Papi, I don't have a lot of time. Look, please go see Señora Alvarez." That was the name of the *pasador* who arranged for me to leave Ecuador. She had all the contacts to get here. "Go see her and ask her where we are. Go with as many family members as possible when you talk to her. Ask her where we are, *Papi*. I don't have much time." Then I hung up. That was the only thing I said, and two days later they came and got the six of us out of there. From there they brought us to the desert, to the border. They took us to a place where we would cross into Arizona.

SONORA

The Border Patrol apprehended 449,675 people in the Tucson Sector the year that Christian migrated. In comparison, in 2009, when Memo and Lucho entered the desert, 241,667 people were caught and deported in the same area. This decrease in apprehensions is likely the result of the US economic downturn of 2008, which both lowered the number of jobs available for undocumented workers and ignited a wave of anti-immigrant sentiment that seemingly discouraged many potential crossers. Although there are some parallels between the two crossing narratives, it is important to note that Christian's took place during an earlier era (before the post-9/11 escalation in security). During this period, distances walked through the desert were relatively short, and people traveled in large groups that ensured that at least some of them got through. There were also no measures such as the Alien Transfer and Exit Program or Operation Streamline in place to deter people from trying again immediately after an apprehension.

> *Christian:* We got to the border and they took us to a house. It was the first week of December and it was freezing. The *guía* said, "We are really close to the United States but we can't cross near here. We have to take a trip through the desert so that we can enter clandestinely." They came for us in a car at like ten o'clock at night and dropped us off at the edge of a mountain. They said, "Everyone grab your two bottles of water. Grab whatever you think is necessary."
>
> Man, it was freezing. In Ecuador everyone was always saying that you will die from thirst in the desert so you need to take a lot of water. This is what we were all imagining. Each of us had two gallons of water when they dropped us off and we started walking. I swear, I'm not lying to you. After like fifteen or twenty minutes, we looked down and our water bottles were frozen! Frozen! It turned into a rock! Everyone was so scared. None of us from Ecuador had ever seen water freeze like that! [laughs]
>
> The guide climbed a hill to check the area, and then he said, "We can't cross here. There is a lot of surveillance. We are going to have to sleep here." I said, "How are we going to sleep in the middle of the mountain when it is freezing?" There were like twenty-five people in our group. In less than five minutes we were all shivering from the cold. Someone finally said, "We're going to make a group of women and a group of men so that we can sleep. We will put everyone together so that we don't freeze." We started to group people one on top of another on top of another so that we could warm up. That is how we spent the night.
>
> At daybreak, the guide said, "We are going to keep going but we are only going to walk at the base of mountains, under cliffs, and in ravines." So we walked and walked. Finally, we got to a dry wash and our guide said that we were going to cross in separate groups in case someone showed up like a plane or a patrol car. If that happened, they wouldn't be able to see everyone

because the rest of us could duck down and lie on the ground. The guide said we would cross tomorrow, so we all went to sleep again.

The next night we started walking, and after a while we passed some fences and got to a highway. The *coyote* said, "This is Mexico and on that side is the United States. If we cross that road, we have gotten through. This highway is hard to cross, though, because there are a lot of Border Patrol." He made us line up, and I have no idea why, but I ended up the last person in line. I lost track of my aunt at this point. She was one of the first people in line. When we started crossing, it was totally dark. I don't know who said "Run," but I guess Border Patrol was there. We ran and I ended up alone with just one of my friends.[22]

We didn't know where everyone else went, so we hid behind a tree. We could see the lights from Border Patrol. Our guide had told us to hide if *la migra* showed up. He said they would come look for us later. We could see that Border Patrol was using their lights to look for people hiding on the side of road. We hid and tried to figure out what to do. Right around this time a Border Patrol agent shined his light on us. He had caught us. Right then all the things that had happened to me *en el camino* came flooding back. I started thinking about terrible things. I started to cry. This was the first time that we got arrested.

We were always told that if we got caught, we needed to say that we were from Mexico, so this is what we told them. They gave us some papers and we signed them. They fingerprinted us and everything. We were detained for like an hour. They gave us a hamburger and we were content! A delicious hamburger! It was hot and everything! [laughs] After we ate, they put us on a bus, and I thought it was going to be a long ride. It was like five minutes on the bus, and then we were back at the border. I said, "So many days walking and five minutes later we are at the border?" We went back into Mexico and they took us to the same house as before.

The following night we tried again. We crossed exactly the same as before but in less time. This time it was only one day. It was all much faster. This time we weren't twenty-five people, either. There were now like seventy people and four *coyotes*. They told us, "When we say 'Run,' you'll run across the highway." We started running, and right about when half of the people had crossed, Border Patrol showed up. Those who got to the other side of the highway kept going. Half of the people stayed back. I was one of those who stayed back. I grabbed my aunt's hand and we started to run away. We escaped back to Mexico. Three hours later we tried again.

This time the *guía* said that the women would go first and then the men. They separated us and I couldn't do anything. The same thing happened again. They caught the first group and I couldn't do anything for my aunt. Once again I had to run back to Mexico. I saw my aunt get caught by immigration with the other women. I was sure she would tell them that she is

Mexican and they would send her back to the border. I was 100 percent sure of this. I figured at least my aunt would get something to eat! [laughs]

We ran back and hid. At daybreak our guide said, "Border Patrol is positive that we're going to try again on a different day, but instead we are going to try again right now." And this time we got across. The guide took us to a safe house and said, "It is daybreak and we are going to wait a couple of hours for our ride to come for us." I had to go to the bathroom, so I went outside, and when I did, I saw lights everywhere. People were on their knees. Border Patrol had us surrounded. The *coyote* yelled for us to run but there was no place to go. That's how they captured us. I thought they would just send us back quickly like the last time. I told one of my friends, "Hey, let's hurry! Let's get on the bus and get something to eat!" They give you food in detention and we were starving. So we lined up and tried to give them our names ahead of everyone! [laughs]

They took us to detention and then things started to fall apart. They were looking for our fingerprints and asking us a lot of questions about Mexico like, "Who was the previous president? Where did you go to school? What was the name of your school? What is the name of the street where you live?" Man, it was hard. They asked if I had been to *el DF* and what the name of the street where the Basílica de Guadalupe was located. I didn't know. [laughs] They asked us questions that we couldn't answer. They were asking us this stuff, and then they said that we weren't Mexican. They said, "Look, if you tell me where you are from, tomorrow you can go back to your country."

I started thinking about it. It was mid-December, and I was thinking about how I would prefer to spend Christmas with my family and be able to go to mass. I figured I could try crossing again later. I don't know. It had just ended like that, after all that time. After everything that had happened like being sick and missing my family and then it had just ended. I was thinking about Christmas and I decided it was better to go and be with them. So I decided to tell them I was from Ecuador and gave them all my information. They said they were going to deport me the following day and started taking more fingerprints and more photos. They stripped us naked. Then they bathed me and gave me an orange uniform. I started asking about my aunt. I was asking people who were detained if they had seen her, but they hadn't. I was really worried about her. The next day they called me and I thought they were sending me back. They gave me a little bag to put all of my possessions in, and then they put me in a cell.

After all that I had been through, I felt so helpless. I was like, "Look at what has happened to me." I never imagined that I would end up in jail. You go through all that stuff and end up like that. When I got on the bus, I thought they were going to take me to the airport and send me back to my country, but no. They took me to another prison. I asked them when I was getting out, and they said they didn't know.

Christian: The other prison that they took me to was enormous. There was a giant room with a lot of beds. When I walked in and saw all of the people detained that I had been thrown in there alone with, . . . well, I just dropped my bag on the floor and started to cry in front of everyone. I was crying inconsolably thinking about my mom and dad and how much they were suffering thinking about me. It was horrible. Horrible. Horrible. Horrible. Everything that I had gone through. I had almost died. The starvation and everything and then in the end this happens to me. Sometimes it makes you lose faith in God. Like, there is no way God would do this to you. God is so angry at us, and all we wanted was to come here to work and nothing else. We had gone through too much. It was almost three and a half months of trying to cross to just end up in jail. All the money we had spent. Almost losing our lives. This made me cry that day and no one could console me.

I knew the phone number of my house in Ecuador and my uncle's in New York. I called my mom and dad first. I started to cry on the phone with them. My dad was crying for me. He was going crazy not knowing what he could do. Then I called my uncle and he calmed me down. He said he was going to get me a lawyer to get me out of there.

I was only eighteen years old and was all alone. There was no one from my group there with me. I had never been separated from my family for so long. I spent three days in jail, where I wouldn't eat. I wasn't hungry. I didn't want anything. The only thing I was thinking about was seeing my family. I made friends with a man from Guatemala who told me that nothing was going to happen to me and that I just had to wait until the judge decided when I could leave. Little by little, the days passed. A week went by, and I didn't really talk to anyone. I just ate and slept. I was there for twenty days and still hadn't left.

I spent Christmas in prison. December 24 was horrible. I called my parents and cried on the phone. My mom and dad were inconsolable. They said, "You are so far away and in jail and we can't go to see you." It was the worst Christmas my family has ever had. The judge still hadn't called me. On December 31 I thought to myself, "This is going to be the first year that I don't get to see the moon or the stars at sunrise on the New Year. I can't let this happen." So I decided to fake being sick. It was around 12:30 in the morning and everyone was saying, "Happy New Year!" I told the guards that I had stomach pains, and they put me on a gurney and took me to the infirmary. I knew that the infirmary was really far from our cell and that they would have to take me outside to get there. I just needed to see the moon and the stars of the New Year. [laughs] I went outside and saw the stars and it made me happy. It calmed me down while I thought about my family and my mom and dad crying. They took me to the infirmary and they said that

I was fine. They said that I might just have an infection or something, and then they took me back to my cell.

A few days later they called and told me that I had a court appearance and needed to be ready. It was now January. My uncle had gotten a lawyer to represent me. They took me to court and told me stuff, none of which I understood. Everything was in English. I only spoke with my lawyer, who was on the phone. She said things were going to be OK and that my family had given her money to pay my bond. A few days later they told me to get my stuff and that I could leave.

They gave me some papers and then dropped me off at a bus station. There was an official who spoke Spanish and I asked him, "Where am I supposed to go?" He said, "I don't know. That's your problem. You can go to New York where you family is." I didn't really have any money. I had twenty dollars. I called my aunt who had gotten out on bail before me and told her that they let me out. She asked me to find a Western Union, and luckily there was one in the terminal. She said, "I'm going to send you money so you can buy a bus ticket to New York."

When I left Arizona, I was still wearing the same clothes that I went to jail in. My clothes were filthy when they arrested me. They smelled bad and that is how they stored them in plastic bags. I was wearing these dirty clothes and my hair was long. I met nice people on the bus at every stop, though. I met a Mexican lady who asked me what was wrong. I told her everything that had happened to me. It was freezing, and she bought me some clothes, sneakers, and a blanket. Then she gave me twenty dollars for the trip because it was three days to get from Arizona to New York. I met other people who bought me food. There were really good people who helped me.

I went through all of that and arrived here! I thought New York was going to be different. I was thinking about big beautiful buildings in Manhattan and people living the good life. I got to the bus station in Times Square. It was really incredible, all of the buildings and the lights. But then I took a car to Queens. [laughs] I was like, "This is it?" There was trash all over the ground. It was really noisy because of the train.

I always thought that my uncle lived in a nice apartment. When we got to the building, it was really great. I was like, "Wow!" Then he took me around the back and I said, "Why don't we go through the front door?" It was because he lived in the basement [laughs] in a tiny room where you could barely turn around. He lived there with seven other people. I went through all of that for this? It was like someone threw a bucket of cold water on me. When you see New York on the Internet and in movies, it is incredible. All the people are fair skinned and there is no trash. That is what you think New York is like. Also, the photos that my family members sent me from here were when they were out having fun, not when they were working! They send photos of nice places. When I got here to Queens, everything

Christian. Photo by Michael Wells.

was dirty! All of that happened. And from the day that I got here, I started working. I started paying off my debt. I owed $21,000 for the trip including interest.

Despite the high drama, Christian's incredible narrative should not be considered atypical. Hundreds of thousands of women, men, and children from various Latin American countries who work their way north every year to reach the United States have similar or worse experiences. Rape, murder, beatings, robbery, kidnapping: these are the leitmotifs of the argonauts who cross Mexico. For many like Christian, the US-Mexico border may be a relatively minor component of their violent journey; the desert hybrid collectif is just the last in a series of hurdles to survive and overcome. It is easy to see why he tried to discourage Maricela from coming to New York.

"THEY SAY THAT EVERYONE HAS THEIR OWN LUCK"

Six months after my first meeting with Christian, I find myself back in Queens. It is close to midnight on a Saturday, and Christian, Mike Wells, and I are sipping on beers in a neon-lit bar. Electronic dance music blares on the house speakers while scantily clad men and woman gyrate on the overhead television screens. Christian is busy thumbing text messages to friends whom we are going to meet up with later that night when we head to a Latino club that he likes to frequent. Cuenca at this moment feels a world away. After more than a decade since he left home, it is obvious that Christian has done his best to make a new life for himself in New York. He shares a modest apartment with extended family members and a long-term partner and gets by on various construction jobs. When his schedule permits, he takes English classes and works on getting his High School Equivalency Diploma. He and his aunt spend their weekends at a nearby park playing with his nephews and nieces. Still, despite the many liberties, experiences, and economic opportunities he has enjoyed during his time in the United States, Christian is always cognizant of the high personal cost he has had to pay in order to support his family back in Ecuador. The tension of being caught between two disparate worlds is the source of much pain.

> *Jason:* How do you feel about the crossing after more than a decade?
>
> *Christian:* Well, I feel like now it was worth it, because thankfully I got through. It really helped me to go through all of that. It makes you value life more. You feel like you were born for a reason and with a purpose. After going through all of that, my perspective changed. I wanted to live my life for me. I guess perhaps it all happened to me for a reason. I don't know, though. Sometimes it is not worth it, because you leave your family behind. Supposedly, I was only going to be here for two or three years maximum. In two or three years, I was going to work to get some money together and then go back. But after you have been in this country awhile, you start to get accustomed to making *dinero*, and later your family over there gets used to living a better life. We were really poor when I left. I mean, we are still poor, but at least now my family can eat every single day. They have food. They live in a place that is much safer and more comfortable.
>
> My son is about to turn twelve, and his mom [who is also currently in New York] wants to bring him here *por el camino*. I told her that I don't want that. He is a kid and I don't know what would happen to him. It is better to help him there in Ecuador so that he can study. I am not against people who try to bring their kids here; I just don't want to bring my family

here. I got through, but my family could die *en el camino,* get raped, get assaulted. I know that the most important things are the love and affection of your parents, but this is our situation. At least my son has people to take care of him there, to give him food. He can get an education in Cuenca.

Thank God, things are going well. I have worked so much. Right now things are better. At least for my family in Ecuador. Here, it is more or less. I mean, here, without documents, you can't really do much. You do what you can do. With documents it is much better. There are better jobs and you can do what you want. But whatever, thank God it has gone OK. I am not bad off. My only fear is that one day I might get caught by immigration and they will deport me. I don't know what is going to happen. But I want to go back so that I can finally know my son. That is where I am at now. I want to go back. To finally meet my son. To see him grow up. [sighs]

Jason: Did you tell Maricela about all of this?

Christian: Yes, but no one believes. They think they will make it. They say that everyone has their own luck. There are a lot of stories about so and so who got through . . . or those who made it after two or three days. Or those who made it here in two weeks and nothing happened to them like what happened to us. But other people have it worse than we did. In reality, I never want to go through that again. For example, my fear is that if I go back, everyone says that when you return to Ecuador or whatever country you are from, you are no longer accustomed to life there. You are not used to the economic crisis you have to return to. My fear is that I will go back to Ecuador and then want to come back here and have to go through all that stuff again. I was thinking about all this before Maricela left. Before this thing happened to Mari, I thought about going to Ecuador. I wanted to go there and tell her how it was in person. I always thought that when I got there, I would tell my sister-in-law just what it was like, all the things that we went through. And now look—it never happened. People risk everything, sometimes for nothing. Many come here for their family, but only encounter death. My aunt always tells me that we are alive because of a miracle. Maricela came with the same idea that I had. She came here because of her kids. She wanted to give them what they needed. They couldn't get ahead in Ecuador.

CHAPTER 10

Maricela

I don't want this life and I don't know what to do.
—Marisela Esqueda, "Sin El"

CHRISTIAN'S HOUSE

Through a barred window you can see the lush green mountains that completely surround the city of Cuenca. Peaks crowned with soft halos of low-lying clouds float above picturesque lakes of blue-steel water. If you look closely, sometimes you can spot grazing llamas stopping for a cold drink, or light snow falling from the sky in the distance. This is a land where a cool mist covers everything like a thin wet film. It is difficult to imagine the Sonoran Desert from here.

Although they have lived in this house for almost two years, many rooms are empty, unfinished, and unheated. January in the Andes at 2,500 meters above sea level means that we are all wearing sweatshirts and jackets indoors and can occasionally see our breath inside the house. Mike Wells; Vanessa, Christian's twenty-four-year-old sister; and I are standing in the expansive, empty living room, populated with just a few metal chairs, a tiny blinking Christmas tree, and a handmade nativity scene in the corner. The seasonal decorations, subsidized by remittances from New York, are melancholy reminders that Christian's family has just celebrated their thirteenth Navidad without him. Although he is not physically present and has never set foot in this three-story block-and-concrete structure, the members of his extended family who live here—including his young son, Christian Jr., his sister, his parents, doña Dolores and don Ernesto, his brother Theo, and Theo's three children—all refer to this place as "Christian's house."

Maricela and her family, Cuenca, Ecuador. Photo by Vanessa.

Christian's house, Cuenca, Ecuador. Photo by Michael Wells.

In spite of the physical distance, their benefactor's presence is always felt via phone calls, Skype conversations, and the money and gifts he diligently sends home. Like many others in this working-class *barrio* situated in one of the largest international migrant-sending areas in South America,[1] this is a transnational family occupying a house being built piece by piece, room by room, with the money that has been sent from New York every month for over a decade. When Maricela left Cuenca in June 2012, she was carrying with her the dream to someday build her own family a house just like Christian's. It would be a place where her husband, Theo, and their three children, Jaime (thirteen), Laura (ten), and Edgar (six), could celebrate their own migration-sponsored Christmas in "*la casa de Mari.*"

The Vicente Fernandez song "*La ley del monte*" starts playing on a tiny boom box. The sounds of shiny trumpets and cascading violins bounce off the bare cement walls and cold gray floor, adding natural reverb to this song of heartbreak. Jaime is standing in the middle of the floor with one hand on his heart and a lanky teenage arm raised high into the air. He looks like someone about to testify in church. Although only Mike, Vanessa, and I are in the room, Jaime pretends that thousands of his adoring fans are cheering for him. He closes his eyes tight and lip-synch's the song's first line, "I wrote your name on the leaf of a maguey next to mine, intertwined. This was proof to all that we were in love there." Jaime then spins, wildly gesticulates, and starts dancing like the whole world is watching. The three of us are hollering and cheering. As the song finishes, we scream for an encore. Jaime's younger siblings, Laura and Edgar, and his cousin Christian Jr., who have all been giggling at this spectacle through an open window, join us in our clapping. Vanessa turns to me and says, "This is how Mari used to act. The kids put on music and sing because it reminds them of their mom."

––––––––

When Mike Wells and I, along with our spouses and two small children, first pull up to this house in a taxi, three days before this impromptu concert, I don't know what to expect. In preparation for the trip, I had tried to put myself in this family's shoes. How would I feel if the person who found the body of my dead mother, sister, or wife decided to come visit me because he was writing a book? This mental exercise was not reassuring. Christian has explained to them who I am and has vouched for me and Mike. I have been communicating intensively with Vanessa via Facebook, and she has been the one preparing the kids and the rest of the family for our visit. We are scheduled to stay with them for a week, but I am not sure how we are even going to get through what I envision to be an awkward first meeting. I start preparing my introduction as I step out of the taxi and approach the family waiting outside for us. Before I can mutter anything, a tiny dark-haired woman with long onyx braids shuffles forward and hugs me as if she knows me. With wet eyes and a shaky voice, doña Dolores softly says, "Thank you for coming."

The week that we spend with Maricela's family in Cuenca is an emotional roller coaster for all parties involved. Within five minutes of our arrival, we are all sitting in a tiny bedroom crying with doña Dolores and Vanessa as they tell us about Maricela's life and her death. While their grandmother and aunt speak, Mari's three children listen quietly. They are the only ones not crying. They are too busy doting over my eight-month-old son. This scene will repeat over and over again in different settings as the family opens up to me about Maricela and the trauma they experienced following her disappearance, death, and return to Cuenca in a wooden box. The adults will cry and the children will giggle and pass the baby around. For doña Dolores, who breaks down with just the mention of her daughter-in-law's name, it is as though her own child perished in the desert. Vanessa, on the other hand, has been traumatized not only by the loss of her best friend and confidant but also by the fact that she suddenly finds herself at twenty-four years old being surrogate mother to three kids. It was through the narratives of these two women that I learned the most about who Maricela was in life and the heartbreak caused by her death.

Although most of the dialogue in this chapter comes from various interactions I had with Christian in New York and with doña Dolores and Vanessa in Cuenca, I also had multiple conversations about Maricela with every adult member of her immediate family in Ecuador, including don Ernesto and Mari's husband, Theo. The week of our visit I spent time with Theo in the late evenings after he got off work and on his one day off, but he and I rarely spoke directly about his wife. It was obvious that his wounds were still raw. Out of respect, I never spoke about Maricela unless he brought her up, which only happened a few times. His pain seemed exacerbated by the unfortunate coincidence that our visit overlapped with their wedding anniversary. Instead of talking about his wife, we focused our conversations on either small talk or the lives of his children and the economic difficulties that he and other members of the Cuenca working class face daily. Although he was hesitant to talk about Maricela, Theo opened up his home and his family life to me and went out of his way to make sure that we were treated like honored guests during our stay.

In addition to the above-mentioned people, I also spoke with some of Mari's former neighbors and other relatives when we visited the tiny room that she and her family shared before she left for the United States. Their previous residence was a one-room shack constructed out of sheets of paper-thin plywood, a tin roof, and a stamped dirt floor. It was located in an urban shanty where semiwild dogs and chickens had free range into households. It is no wonder she was dreaming of building a new home.

Despite the painful memories that our visit triggered, I think that talking about Mari's death to one of the people who had found her body was therapeutic for the family, especially Vanessa and doña Dolores. While her relatives gained some modicum of comfort in learning more about Mari's death in the desert, I am the one who should be grateful for the way they welcomed me, Mike, and our families into their home and for the many small moments of joy we shared. Much of our time that week was spent with Vanessa and Maricela's children walking around Cuenca, visiting parks, eating pizza and ice cream, preparing Jaime and Laura for their participation in a parade, and generally entertaining my son. Although the children liked talking about their mom and were eager to show us her grave, I never saw them cry. They seemed to be the

Maricela's grave, Cuenca, Ecuador. Photo by Michael Wells.

most resilient members of this family that has been utterly devastated by death.

Carmita Maricela Zhagüi Puyas was thirty-one years old when she decided to leave her husband and three children in Cuenca in early June 2012 to try to make it to the United States. What follows is her story told through the eyes of the relatives who watched her leave, desperately searched for her when she went missing, and dealt with the aftermath of her death.

"IT'S BEEN DECIDED"

> *Doña Dolores:* She was crazy for music! My God, it was amazing! She loved to dance all the time. She went out dancing a lot and loved throwing parties for the kids. [laughs] . . . That is why her husband still has so many CDs in his room, because she loved music so much. Every time they went to the *centro*, she had to get *discos*. She was always trying to get new music. She would say to me, "*Mamita*, music is so beautiful to dance to." She really was the happiest when she was dancing. . . . She and my son were married on the 12th of

January. They were married thirteen years ago in a civil ceremony and are going to complete fourteen years this week. Christian helped us pay to have a church wedding. They got married in the church seven years ago.

One of Maricela's cousins: She was so happy. Everyone around here used to call her Mariposa [butterfly].

Christian: Well, in the begining when I first came here to New York, she had only been married to my brother for a couple of years, so I didn't have a lot of time to get to know her. But when I got here, he would tell me all about her. She was a really happy person. Very content. She liked to joke around and play. She liked to dress up and go out a lot. Maricela was also really outspoken. She spoke her mind and told you how she felt about things. When I was there in Cuenca, she gave birth to my first nephew. That was when my mom really started to warm up to her. The two of them started to spend time together. My mom started treating her like a daughter. They spent a lot of years together. They lived together for more than ten years.

She left in June 2012 from Ecuador. She had never been to New York. When my family called me to see if I would help her to come here, I said no. I said no because I had crossed and I was afraid. She has three kids, and I said it would be awful to leave them. They are going to suffer so much. I told her not to come. But I don't know. Her brother was really insisting. He kept saying to her, "Come. Come here to New York." He finally convinced her. I guess it was the need to . . . I don't know. She couldn't give her kids all the things they wanted. I think that's what made her want to do this. She had borrowed money from a bank six years ago. It was $2,000. Now it is like $5,000 that we owe with interest. I don't know, maybe she was hoping to come here to New York with the idea to pay off those debts. To get a job here and pay all that off.

Theo: Life here is fucked. That is why everyone wants to leave.

Doña Dolores: I told her, "Don't leave. Go and live in Christian's house. He wants you to live there with us." Her husband also told her this. But she just said, "No, *mamita,* my brother-in-law will take me across. I need to do my own work." My daughter Mari was so beautiful. In the morning I would be alone after she took the kids to school and she would come back to stay with me. She lived next door and would make me coffee. I know that you might not understand how she was like my own daughter, but she was. I will never forget her. I will never forget her.

Vanessa: She came by on like a Tuesday around 7:30 A.M. and said, "I'm going." I was at the point where I said I couldn't prevent her from leaving. It was her and my brother's decision more than anything. They needed to decide themselves. I couldn't make her do anything she didn't want to do. She talked to Theo, and he said he didn't want her to leave. He had a lot of doubts in his head. He was thinking about the positive and the negative. I couldn't say anything. A little later she told me, "It's been decided. I am going. I am going. I am going. Even if he doesn't want me to go, I am going. He told me not to go but . . ." She wanted to go so that she could get ahead and pay off her debts. She has a lot of debt, and who was going to help her pay them? No one. She had to pay, so it was her decision to go. She needed to do things for her kids.

God has a destiny for everyone, and her decision to go was her own. What were we going to do? We had to let her go. . . . She thought she would go for a year and then come back. She said to me, "The only favor that I ask is that you take care of my kids. I'm doing everything for my kids." I said, "Mari, don't go," but she just said, "It's my time to go. I am leaving." She thought she would get there and then help us here monetarily. We were going to take care of the kids and she was going to send money. We cried so much when she left. We gave her lots of phone numbers to take with her to call if something happened. We said, "Mari, please call us if you get sick so that the family can help you." The last thing we said was, "Don't leave." She said to me, "Whatever my destiny is, I must go."

Doña Dolores: When Mari left she told me, "*Mamita*, take care of *mis wawas* [Kichwa word for children]." I pleaded, "My daughter, why don't you just stay here?" She said, "No, *mamita*, I can't. My kids are dying of hunger here. My kids are suffering. They will stay with you. I know God will protect you. Please don't let them go hungry, *mamita*. Please give them food." When she left, she left her kids with me . . . My daughter . . . Oh, my daughter, you are never coming back! [crying]

Vanessa: It was around June 1 when she asked me to dye her hair. She wanted to get on the airplane looking really elegant. She wanted to look really good when she got to the United States, so I dyed her hair black. . . . My brother dropped her off at the bus terminal and she left for Guayaquil. To this day seeing those buses makes my brother cry. . . . She called eight days later from Panama, or maybe it was Guatemala. She said she didn't like the food. We told her to come home, but she said she couldn't. She told me, "Tell your parents and my kids that I love them and I am leaving for a good reason." She was crying, and I couldn't bear to hear it. I spoke to her again the third week of June. She sent us a Facebook message that said she wanted to talk. She wanted to speak to her kids because they were getting ready to take her into the desert. She told me, "I don't know how I am going to get there but I am going for my family. God willing I will get there."

PERDIDA

Compared to those for men, there are significantly fewer journalistic accounts and ethnographic data focused on the experiences of female border crossers.

Vanessa and Theo. Photo by Michael Wells.

This paucity of research is linked to both a male subject research bias and the fact that women typically make up less than 15 percent of the undocumented migration stream in any given year. Although the details of Maricela's journey across the desert are sketchy, a few sobering statistics are appropriate here. A study conducted by the Binational Migration Institute (BMI) in 2006 found that women were 2.67 times more likely to die of exposure than were men.[2] Some researchers have linked this imbalance to the tendency of smugglers to perceive women as liabilities while en route, which may increase the likelihood of their being abandoned.[3] A more recent analysis by the BMI found that women made up 18 percent of the 2,238 bodies examined by the Pima County Office of the Medical Examiner between 1990 and 2012.[4] During certain periods, such as between 2000 and 2005, women accounted for as much as 23 percent of all border crosser deaths. Females have thus long been over-represented in the morgue when compared to the overall number of women apprehended and deported by Border Patrol. Whatever the reason or the person's gender, being left behind in the Sonoran Desert is practically a death sentence for anyone.

> *Christian:* She was traveling with her brother-in-law. By the third week she was in Mexico. I thought that it was a really quick trip and was thinking

that, God willing, she would get here soon. At the end of June my mom called and told me that Mari was lost, that she hadn't shown up. She didn't call and they knew nothing about where she was. I said that she would show up soon and not to worry. My brother called me that same day and was desperate. He asked if I could help look for her, and I said that I would.

Vanessa: I don't know the exact date, but we started to look for her the same week she left for the desert. It was a weekend. A Saturday. Her brother-in-law had called us because he was the one who took her into the desert. He called to say that Mari was lost and he didn't know where she was. We got very worried about her. We started looking for her everywhere.... We called our family in *los Estados Unidos* to see if they could help us. We asked her brother to help us look because he was the one who paid for her to go. We asked him to tell us who the *pasador* was to see if we could talk to them. We wanted to see if they would help us. To this day her brother hasn't told us anything. He won't tell us who the *pasadores* were. He won't tell us what routes they took. It is all still a mystery.

Christian: She was traveling with her brother-in-law, and on the day that my family called me, he had just arrived here in the US. This was like the 27th of June when she stayed behind in the desert. He arrived here in the US on like the 29th. He called up the family in Ecuador to say that Maricela had been abandoned in the desert. I have no idea how he could have left her there. This is when I started to get really worried because I went through the desert and was familiar with it. This was also during the summer. We still haven't heard the whole story about what happened to my sister-in-law.

Vanessa: Someone told us that she was kidnapped and being kept on a ranch. I sent her Facebook messages every day to see if she was there. I was saying, "Mari, we are so worried about you. Please come back." Theo called her brother to ask where she was. He told them that our family would pay whatever we needed in order to get her back. Her brother just started insulting him and telling us that Mari was fine. It was traumatizing.... We left comments on websites. I was looking at videos on the Internet of migrants crossing. My hope was ... I don't know, maybe I would see her in one of these videos.

Christian: Mari was left in the desert, and I told my family that if she stayed there, immigration would show up and take her to jail. Her brother-in-law said that they were near some bushes or some trees. They had to find shade or were hiding. She had hurt her foot or something. I guess she had been crying on the trail and saying stuff like, "I want to get there," but at the same time she couldn't go on. She was exhausted from the heat and everything. Around the time when Mari and the group were hiding, they heard some noises close by. I imagine that it was Border Patrol. When everyone started to run, she said she couldn't. She was going to stay behind. She couldn't go on. I don't know how this man had the capacity to . . . I don't know how he could have abandoned her.

Vanessa: Her brother-in-law said Mari was feeling sick and wanted to sit down on a rock. Afterward, they got scared by something and they all ran off. Later, she didn't show up. He didn't know where she was after that. He wasn't sure if she was farther ahead on the trail, sitting down somewhere, or if she passed out.

Looking for someone who has gone missing during a crossing is a difficult task, especially for people like Christian, who are undocumented, speak little English, and have no familiarity with the ins and outs of US federal bureaucracy. Even if one could, it makes little sense to call the Border Patrol for help. The agency has no interest in searching for missing migrants, and the only information most would be able to provide is that their friend or family member is "in the desert near Arizona." By design, locating someone in the depths of the hybrid collectif is nearly impossible. As Christian states below, he was under the misconception that Maricela had gone missing near Phoenix, 130 miles north of where she was abandoned.

Christian: Without a doubt I imagine that she was hiding because immigration didn't see her. I think that when immigration really has to look for you, they don't do it. If she had turned herself in, she would have gone to jail but she would still be alive. When my brother called me on the 29th and told me this whole story, I started to call jails, immigration detention centers, hospitals, everywhere in Arizona. I started putting comments on Facebook that said she had gone missing and could people please help us find her. . . . I had photos up on Facebook and was asking people to help look for her because I couldn't travel there to Arizona. It was too dangerous there because of immigration. I was communicating with radio and television programs. . . . I started checking the hospital there in Phoenix, but they said they didn't have a person with her name. The worry was that maybe she gave a false name, so we started to ask things like if they had a person who looked like her. We didn't have any luck.

Days went by and we were still waiting for her to contact us. She never called. She hadn't appeared, but everyone was hopeful that she would show up. This happens in a lot of cases. Two or three weeks go by with no communication from someone. Sometimes people just can't make a call. The smugglers don't let them. We hoped to God that this was what was happening. Other people had said that many migrants were getting kidnapped and then forced into prostitution. I was worried. On top of that, when I would call Ecuador, I would end up talking to Maricela's kids, who were saying,

"Please help us look for our mom!" The oldest is thirteen. The other two kids are ten and six. They would be crying to me, "Please help me, *Tío*. Where is my *mami?*" It was horrible. I didn't know what to say to them, so I would just say, "OK, I am going to help you, but please don't cry." My mom, dad, and my sister were all trying to communicate with the smugglers. They were calling the numbers that they had, but people weren't telling them anything. I just kept saying, "Be calm. She is fine." I told them not to worry, that she hasn't been able to call but she will.

After days and days went by, someone told me that we should look for help in a place called SENAMI [La Secretaría Nacional del Migrante] in Ecuador. The family went there, and then they called the Ecuadoran consulate to help me look for her. I gave them all the information, like the day she went missing, all of that. They started looking for her. I was calling them every day to see if they had any new information, but they kept saying no. They are the ones who eventually found her, but she was in the morgue.

CONFIRMATION

In 1994, while drafting the initial Prevention Through Deterrence memorandum, someone at the US Border Patrol typed the line "violence will increase as effects of strategy are felt." The gravity of these nine words is hard to overstate. Violence has indeed increased over the past twenty years as this policy has been implemented, expanded, and fine-tuned, but in ways than can never be measured or realized in migrant death statistics. The federal government perpetuates the myopic view that the US-Mexico border is a bounded ethereal space where the violence of immigration enforcement tactics can be contained, hidden, or erased. Under this existing logic of sovereignty, those who feel the brutal effects of federal policy are "unreal"; their lives can't be injured because they are already negated.[5] Strategists, Border Patrol sector chiefs, and politicians calling for more boundary security should spend some time staring at the gore inside a rubber body bag or listening to a child scream for his or her mother in a distant Latin American living room. To do so would perhaps force the acknowledgement that the suffering, death, and destruction produced by the hybrid collectif in the desert have not only increased since the start of Prevention Through Deterrence but have extended their traumatizing reach across the globe.

> *Christian:* They told me on July 27 that they had found her. The forensic people asked me if we had her fingerprints, her identification, and stuff like that ... I didn't want to believe that she was dead, but I thought that it

might be true. They were like 90 percent sure that it was her and that she was dead, but they really wanted to confirm it. When I had to call home to ask for paperwork, Vanessa was the person who answered the phone. I told her that they had found Mari, but they wanted to confirm that it was her. I said, "They found her. They found Mari." She said, "Where is she? When is she coming back? When are you going to see her?" Everyone there was holding out hope that she was alive. I said, "I need her fingerprints and the other stuff to confirm it is her." Vanessa said, "What do you mean 'confirm it is her'? Why do you need this stuff?"

Vanessa: We learned about her death around 11 A.M. on a Friday. Christian called the house and asked what I was doing. I told him I was changing to go to work, and he said he wanted to talk to our dad. I told him that he wasn't home and asked why he needed to speak to him. He said that he needed some of Mari's paperwork like her identification, birth certificate, and that type of stuff. I asked him why and he said that they wanted to get her fingerprints because they were like 95 percent sure that they had found her but they wanted the paperwork to confirm. I didn't believe him that it was her. I thought she was still going to appear. I was crying on the phone. Christian told me to ask God for help to be strong. I said, "I have asked God for a lot of help and look what little he does."

I told him that he was crazy and that it couldn't be her but that I would talk to my dad. I walked outside and my eyes were red from crying. I ran into my aunt on the street, and she asked what was wrong. I told her that Mari was dead. My God, the scream she let out. It was the loudest scream that you have ever heard. My entire *barrio* came running over to see what was wrong. My aunt threw herself on the ground screaming, "No! No!" I didn't know what to say, so I ran inside to the kitchen to hide. I wanted to wait for my mom, who was on her way home. People were trying to ask me questions, and I said, "Don't talk to me! Don't ask me nothing!" My aunt kept trying to ask me questions, and I kept saying, "I don't know! I don't want to talk about it!" I told my aunt that Christian had given me this news but that I didn't believe it. I said, "She is not dead. She is still alive. I have hope that she will appear. Without her body, I am not going to believe it. I won't believe it. Never."

I pleaded with my aunt to leave me alone, but she came back with more family. I told them that they wanted to see paperwork to confirm it was her. I also told them not to cry because my kids, I mean my *sobrinos* [nephews and nieces], would be home soon and we don't want them to see this. They left and then came back with more people. By this time there was a crowd outside. It scared my mom when she came home, because there were so many people outside our house. My cousin told me to come running because my mom was outside asking what had happened. My aunt then told her, "Mari is dead." My God. My mom at this point . . .

Maricela and her family, Cuenca, Ecuador. Photo by Vanessa.

Christian's house, Cuenca, Ecuador. Photo by Michael Wells.

In spite of the physical distance, their benefactor's presence is always felt via phone calls, Skype conversations, and the money and gifts he diligently sends home. Like many others in this working-class *barrio* situated in one of the largest international migrant-sending areas in South America,[1] this is a transnational family occupying a house being built piece by piece, room by room, with the money that has been sent from New York every month for over a decade. When Maricela left Cuenca in June 2012, she was carrying with her the dream to someday build her own family a house just like Christian's. It would be a place where her husband, Theo, and their three children, Jaime (thirteen), Laura (ten), and Edgar (six), could celebrate their own migration-sponsored Christmas in *"la casa de Mari."*

The Vicente Fernandez song *"La ley del monte"* starts playing on a tiny boom box. The sounds of shiny trumpets and cascading violins bounce off the bare cement walls and cold gray floor, adding natural reverb to this song of heartbreak. Jaime is standing in the middle of the floor with one hand on his heart and a lanky teenage arm raised high into the air. He looks like someone about to testify in church. Although only Mike, Vanessa, and I are in the room, Jaime pretends that thousands of his adoring fans are cheering for him. He closes his eyes tight and lip-synchs the song's first line, "I wrote your name on

Christian: I called around noon and they went to look for the papers. My family emailed me the stuff, and then I sent it to the forensic people. By the afternoon they had confirmed it. Now it was my turn to tell the family back in Ecuador. There was no consoling them there. Their whole world was turned upside down. My mom, my siblings, my nephews and nieces. There was no one to console them because they were all hurting. One couldn't console another because they were all in pain.

Doña Dolores: Christian called and told me, "*Mamita,* I have some news about Maricela." I was crying, and he said, "Don't cry, Mom. Calm down. Don't cry." I said, "But Son, how am I going to calm down? My daughter is dead."

Vanessa: They say that she died on July 2. That is the date that she was found but she probably died on like the 31st of June . . . We were told that she was dead twenty-five days later and that she had been there in the medical office for a while.

One of Maricela's cousins: She had kidney problems because sometime before she left she got really sick. She was in the room that she rented. It was a little room made of plywood where they lived. Well, one time when she was really sick, my aunt and I went to see her and she was in bed and couldn't get up. We asked her what hurt, and she said it was her kidneys. She said her kidneys were bad. She took some medicine and then got better. Some say that she died because of her kidney problems. They say that a person who has kidney problems is always thirsty.

Christian: My dad was crying. It was horrible. It was so ugly. I felt so helpless. I couldn't do anything. I couldn't help my family. At that point I really wanted to go home, because it was horrible to see them cry so much, to listen to them. This is why I decided to do things really fast. The faster we could do it, the faster they would calm down there in Ecuador.

HOMECOMING

As her decomposing body was loaded onto a plane in New York City, Maricela, like many dead border crossers, transformed from being an anonymous subject unrecognized by the state to a documented Ecuadoran citizen accorded rights and privileges by both her native country and the one that sought to exclude her. She entered the desert hybrid collectif as just another "body" to be deterred and apprehended by Border Patrol. Upon death and discovery she was reanimated as a person and a citizen to be repatriated swiftly. For those on the economic margins of Latin America, it is often only in death that they are claimed by governments.[6]

After weeks of traveling through the shadows of safe houses, crawling across desolate mountains, and lying unidentified in the morgue, Maricela joined the transnational migration stream that moves thousands of corpses a year from the United States back to Latin America.[7]

> Christian: I think they buried her on August 7 in Ecuador. They had waited a month. Imagine it, their desperation. A whole month of suffering as the kids desperately counted the days until their mom came home. She was dead there [in the US] and the family was waiting. My father, my mother, my brother, and more than anything, my *sobrinos*. They weren't going to have any peace until Maricela returned home. Her kids needed to see her. I couldn't take it. They kept calling me saying, "When is she coming? When is she coming?" I said, "It doesn't matter what it costs, I'll pay." I just wanted to get through it . . . I wanted to try to forget this. I didn't want my *sobrinos* in Ecuador to still be waiting for her, so we tried to do it fast so they could get peace quicker.
>
> We went to a funeral home here in Queens and they took care of everything, all the paperwork and arrangements. It cost about $9,500. I, my two uncles, and some cousins got the *plata* together to pay for it. They told us that we could send the body directly from Arizona to Ecuador or we could bring her here for one day to hold a candlelight service. We decided to bring the body here to New York. The coffin was sealed tight when it arrived, and they wouldn't let us see her. They said the body was in bad shape and that they had to identify her by fingerprints. . . . The vigil was one day and one night. It was mostly our friends and family who were there. Only her brother and her cousins came. The next day she left for Ecuador. The family went to get the body at the airport in Guayaquil. There were a lot of people waiting there to accompany the body as they drove it back that night. They came in a big procession to bring her back. The day of the wake there were so many people, like five hundred or six hundred. It was because everyone was so shocked that this had happened and she was so friendly and knew a lot of people. There were *mucha gente* there when they buried her.
>
> Vanessa: There was an enormous caravan from the airport in Guayaquil. There were like fifteen cars. They came from our neighborhood and from her neighborhood. A lot of people were waiting when we got back. The streets here were full.
>
> Christian: At her funeral and at her wake there were hundreds of people. The church was full. She had a lot of friends. At her mass there was a lot of music. There were DJs and mariachis at the burial. She was really well known.
>
> Vanessa: She always said that she had to get there. . . . Her dream was to arrive in the United States. She realized her dream, but she died doing it.

that, God willing, she would get here soon. At the end of June my mom called and told me that Mari was lost, that she hadn't shown up. She didn't call and they knew nothing about where she was. I said that she would show up soon and not to worry. My brother called me that same day and was desperate. He asked if I could help look for her, and I said that I would.

Vanessa: I don't know the exact date, but we started to look for her the same week she left for the desert. It was a weekend. A Saturday. Her brother-in-law had called us because he was the one who took her into the desert. He called to say that Mari was lost and he didn't know where she was. We got very worried about her. We started looking for her everywhere.... We called our family in *los Estados Unidos* to see if they could help us. We asked her brother to help us look because he was the one who paid for her to go. We asked him to tell us who the *pasador* was to see if we could talk to them. We wanted to see if they would help us. To this day her brother hasn't told us anything. He won't tell us who the *pasadores* were. He won't tell us what routes they took. It is all still a mystery.

Christian: She was traveling with her brother-in-law, and on the day that my family called me, he had just arrived here in the US. This was like the 27th of June when she stayed behind in the desert. He arrived here in the US on like the 29th. He called up the family in Ecuador to say that Maricela had been abandoned in the desert. I have no idea how he could have left her there. This is when I started to get really worried because I went through the desert and was familiar with it. This was also during the summer. We still haven't heard the whole story about what happened to my sister-in-law.

Vanessa: Someone told us that she was kidnapped and being kept on a ranch. I sent her Facebook messages every day to see if she was there. I was saying, "Mari, we are so worried about you. Please come back." Theo called her brother to ask where she was. He told them that our family would pay whatever we needed in order to get her back. Her brother just started insulting him and telling us that Mari was fine. It was traumatizing.... We left comments on websites. I was looking at videos on the Internet of migrants crossing. My hope was ... I don't know, maybe I would see her in one of these videos.

Christian: Mari was left in the desert, and I told my family that if she stayed there, immigration would show up and take her to jail. Her brother-in-law said that they were near some bushes or some trees. They had to find shade or were hiding. She had hurt her foot or something. I guess she had been crying on the trail and saying stuff like, "I want to get there," but at the same time she couldn't go on. She was exhausted from the heat and everything. Around the time when Mari and the group were hiding, they heard some noises close by. I imagine that it was Border Patrol. When everyone started to run, she said she couldn't. She was going to stay behind. She couldn't go

on. I don't know how this man had the capacity to . . . I don't know how he
could have abandoned her.

Vanessa: Her brother-in-law said Mari was feeling sick and wanted to sit down
on a rock. Afterward, they got scared by something and they all ran off.
Later, she didn't show up. He didn't know where she was after that. He
wasn't sure if she was farther ahead on the trail, sitting down somewhere, or
if she passed out.

Looking for someone who has gone missing during a crossing is a difficult
task, especially for people like Christian, who are undocumented, speak little
English, and have no familiarity with the ins and outs of US federal bureaucracy.
Even if one could, it makes little sense to call the Border Patrol for help. The
agency has no interest in searching for missing migrants, and the only information most would be able to provide is that their friend or family member is "in the
desert near Arizona." By design, locating someone in the depths of the hybrid
collectif is nearly impossible. As Christian states below, he was under the misconception that Maricela had gone missing near Phoenix, 130 miles north of
where she was abandoned.

Christian: Without a doubt I imagine that she was hiding because immigration didn't see her. I think that when immigration really has to look for you,
they don't do it. If she had turned herself in, she would have gone to jail but
she would still be alive. When my brother called me on the 29th and told me
this whole story, I started to call jails, immigration detention centers, hospitals, everywhere in Arizona. I started putting comments on Facebook that
said she had gone missing and could people please help us find her. . . . I had
photos up on Facebook and was asking people to help look for her because
I couldn't travel there to Arizona. It was too dangerous there because of
immigration. I was communicating with radio and television programs. . . .
I started checking the hospital there in Phoenix, but they said they didn't
have a person with her name. The worry was that maybe she gave a false
name, so we started to ask things like if they had a person who looked like
her. We didn't have any luck.

Days went by and we were still waiting for her to contact us. She never
called. She hadn't appeared, but everyone was hopeful that she would show
up. This happens in a lot of cases. Two or three weeks go by with no communication from someone. Sometimes people just can't make a call. The
smugglers don't let them. We hoped to God that this was what was happening. Other people had said that many migrants were getting kidnapped and
then forced into prostitution. I was worried. On top of that, when I would
call Ecuador, I would end up talking to Maricela's kids, who were saying,

UNRECOGNIZABLE

The annihilation of bodies in the desert is never meant to be seen. When the system functions perfectly, corpses are drained of blood and viscera by unseen monsters; bones dry, splinter, and blow away. When deterrence and erasure are fully achieved, the disappeared can be known or remembered only in stories, unsettling dreams, and outdated photos. Sometimes, though, the hybrid collectif is interrupted before it can finish. Sometimes scraps of the dead are rescued from oblivion: a pack of drunken hunters trip over a grinning mandible with a patchwork of dark metal fillings; the reflection off a cheap gold watch still attached to a mummified wrist catches the eyes of a group of hikers; two dehydrated migrants lead *la migra* back to the spot where they left their dying *compañera*. These recovered bodies show the marks of the everyday, yet hidden political violence used to secure the southern border of the United States. Opening the coffins that hold these repatriated corpses allows people to bear witness to the Sonoran Desert necroviolence that is engineered to be invisible. It opens a door for the living to new forms of postmortem trauma.

For Catholics, who are the religious majority in Latin America, viewing the body is a key element of mourning;[8] it is what makes the death real.[9] However, the corpses put on display during funeral ceremonies are typically embalmed and cosmetically disinfected to give the impression that the dead are at peace and free of distress.[10] The poor condition in which the remains of border crossers are returned to sending communities is why people are often told not to open the casket. These are deaths that cannot be pacified by the mortician's gloved hand. Peering into the coffin at the rotted face or twisted skeleton of someone you once knew and loved is violently unsettling. The brutality evinced by these corporeal conditions can become permanently etched into people's minds, to the point that mourning may never run its course.[11]

> *Christian:* My *sobrinos* were in so much pain. One of them was screaming and he couldn't be consoled. The kids all knew that their mom was dead and the only thing they asked was to see her. When we talked to people in Arizona, we asked them how the body was. They said it was bad and that we couldn't see it. I couldn't tell my mom, my brother, or my nephews this. Imagine, Mari is dead and we can't recognize her anymore. We can't talk to her or say our final goodbyes. It was terrible. Horrible. In the end, I wanted to see her, but I couldn't.

> *Vanessa:* They told us not to open the coffin, but I wanted to see her. My plan had been for her to get to Ecuador and then we would change her clothes. They said she was really messed up, so I wanted to put new clothes on her

for the burial. Christian told me, "*Mija*, you can't open the coffin." I asked him why, and he said, "She is really decomposed and her body is giving off toxic fluids. You guys can get sick from opening the coffin." I said, "No, I'm going to open it. I don't care if I get sick. It doesn't matter." He kept saying that the box was sealed and that I shouldn't open it. I insisted. But then I decided that I didn't want to see her like that.

When the coffin finally got here, one of her children's godparents yelled, "Open it!" I said, "No," and then someone else said, "Get some gloves to open it." It was two o'clock in the morning in the funeral home. Someone found gloves and put them on and then we opened it. At first, we just saw the side of the head. Her face was covered with a cotton sheet. It surprised us to see that sheet there. We moved it and saw that the face was gone. It was pure . . . Her face was destroyed. We put the cloth back quickly and then closed the box as fast as possible. The funeral director said, "I've seen a lot of cadavers of people who died elsewhere and were brought here from Guayaquil or Quito, but I have never ever ever seen a body in this condition. Never." It was just pieces. Her body was dripping. The box was soaking wet.

Christian: You really surpised me, Jason, when you called and said, "I found Carmita." It made me really curious. I wanted to know how you found her. Maybe you had photos. We never really knew what happened. They told us only that they found her there and nothing else.

One of the first things that Christian asked during our initial phone call was whether I had any photographs of Maricela's body. From my perspective, it was an awkward question that I didn't know how to process. I conceded that I had taken a few pictures, but tried to downplay their importance during our first phone conversation and the ones that followed. "Yes," I said, "but I'm not sure you want to see her like that." He kept asking about them. He wanted me to email them to him. I couldn't bring myself to turn Maricela's corpse into an email attachment. That somehow felt more of a violation than publishing her picture in a book or showing it during one of my public lectures. Foolishly, I thought I knew what was best for the photos.

I naively asked myself at the time, "Why would anyone want to see their loved one lying dead in the desert?" At that point, I had no understanding of what the family had gone through with her body. I had no idea how important these images were to them. I told Christian I wouldn't email them, but I promised to bring copies when we met in person.

I've learned over the years that as an ethnographer, I have little control over the settings where important fieldwork moments happen. If I did somehow have a say in these matters, I would choose to be anywhere except a Dunkin'

Donuts in Queens, New York. Christian and I are sitting by the window sipping coffee as Saturday traffic passes by outside. I thought this place would be quieter than the restaurant we just ate lunch in. Instead of being drowned out by clanking plates and salsa music, we are now awash in orange and fluorescent pink, the corporate colors of this doughnut chain, and teenage pop music screaming out of the ceiling speakers. This hardly feels like an appropriate place to reveal the dead.

"Did you really bring photos of her body?" Christian asks me for the third time. Reluctantly I reach into my bag and pull out a small envelope that bears the logo of the pharmacy where I had the pictures printed. I didn't want her to be an email attachment, so I had to stand at a Kodak Film kiosk for twenty minutes while five-by-seven glossies of her bloated body shot out of the machine. None of this seems appropriate.

I hand him the first picture, which shows the back of her head and her right hand. He looks at it in silence for almost a minute.

> *Christian:* I don't understand. How come in this photo the body has hands? Why did she arrive there without hands?
>
> *Jason:* What?
>
> *Christian:* She arrived over there without hands. They cut her hands off. When they saw the body there, in Ecuador, it had no hands.
>
> *Jason:* [stumbling] I think that in order to get the fingerprints . . . Uh . . . They often have to remove the hands. I think that many times it is hard to get fingerprints because the fingers curl and the skin dries out. They have to cut them off so that they can soak them in water to get the fingerprints.[12]
>
> *Christian:* [Stares at the image of her lying on the hillside] It looks like she was still trying to keep going . . . Wow, it can't be. To end up like that. [cries] She was still trying to keep going. Trying to advance . . . She fell on her face. They said that her face didn't have any skin on it when it got to Ecuador. This is why. Because she fell on her face. The worms probably ate her face quickly. The temperature too . . . She had so many dreams. I don't know. She was so close to finishing her journey. Is she in the US here in this photo?
>
> *Jason:* Yes, she had walked over thirty miles from the border.
>
> *Christian:* It was traumatizing to see the body so destroyed. They didn't tell us they cut off the hands. When the body arrived there without hands, we thought maybe an animal ate her. A lot of things go through your mind. We thought some animals got to her or maybe she was raped or beaten. Thank God none of this happened. That day she died over there, God willed it and there was nothing we could do. That was her destiny. We didn't think it

Doña Dolores's kitchen, Cuenca, Ecuador. Photo by Michael Wells.

would happen, but it happened. You know, some still have the hope that it wasn't her. When they saw the body there in Ecuador, they thought, "We hope to God she is still out there." Many hope that she will return one day. For me, at least she is resting in peace. We are thankful she was found, because there are many who are never found. They end up in some hole.

———————

Mike Wells and I are sitting in the backyard kitchen helping Vanessa and doña Dolores prepare dinner. The dirt-floor room has a wood fire burning in the corner. Dozens of scrawny white chickens cluck in a nearby wooden pen. Vanessa has been asking me all day when I am going to show her the photos. Every time I reach for them, one of Maricela's children walks up on us to see what we are doing. Finally, the kids are gone, and she starts talking about the condition of the body the day it arrived.

> *Vanessa:* When she got here, there was no face, no hands. Imagine how difficult it was to see her body like that . . . When she got here, she was destroyed. The coffin was a mess. The wood was dripping wet. It didn't look like her. . . . There was a tag that identified her, but it's really hard for us to believe that she is dead and that they can identify her only from the hand. There are

doubts that it was really her. Maybe she is still out there hiding in the desert. She could still be alive out there, or perhaps she is dead and they haven't found her yet. What we want to know is what condition she was in when you found her. How did they identify her? How did they know it was her? Because when she got here, she was destroyed. No, no. It wasn't like her. I don't know. I need to see the photos of the body.

Jason: I am going to show you some photographs to confirm that her hands were not eaten by animals. I need to warn you that some of them are hard to look at.

I pass a small picture album to Vanessa. She places it in her lap and starts flipping through the pages. The first few images are of a shrine that my students and I built for Maricela, complete with a colorful glass mosaic, votive candles, a Virgin of Guadalupe painting, and various other offerings. I figured I should break the ice with some safer images before getting to the difficult stuff. I warn Vanessa that the next one is of the body. She turns the page and then immediately cries, "It's her! It's her!" Mike and I watch as she grips the photo that shows the back of Mari's head. Tears run down her face in quick succession. With her hand she wipes them off of the album and then looks at me for a moment with watery, heartbroken eyes. Her focus quickly returns to the image. Doña Dolores is leaning against an old wooden table and gazing out the window. She can't bring herself to get close and look. The air is a clouded mixture of Vanessa's staggered breathing, kindling cracking and exploding, and the puttering sounds of chickens.

Mike's camera shutter snaps as he tries to respectfully document this encounter with death. No one is talking. The lid on a boiling pot of meat starts to rattle. Vanessa turns the page and sees the photo of Maricela's body completely covered in a blanket. She passes it to her mother. This seems to be an easier image for the old lady to take in. Doña Dolores touches it softly with her small wrinkled hand and whimpers, "The blanket is so beautiful, so beautiful ... *Mi hija. Mi hijita* ... What were you thinking? [crying] What were you thinking?" Their combined grief overwhelms the small space. I want this moment to be over, but time seems to have ground to a halt. Mike and I are stuck in the midst of this grief as voyeurs who can only look on in quiet incomprehension.

Just when I think it can't get any worse, Vanessa points to the vultures flying above Maricela's body in one of the photos:

Vanessa: What are these birds? Do they eat people?

Jason: We got there before the animals could do anything. I swear. I swear to you. I swear to you. She was complete when we found her. No animals had hurt her. I promise.

I blubber on for a few minutes about the completeness of the body when we found it. I awkwardly search for words in Spanish to try and reassure them that Maricela had her hands intact and that we treated her with dignity and so did the police and the medical examiner. I listen to my own voice stumble out of my mouth. It sounds hollow and empty. It's like the moment when I watched Lucho and Memo enter the tunnel. I was with them as much as I could be, but I wasn't really there. I saw them leave from behind the safety of some invisible glass window. That same feeling returns. I was with Maricela in the Arizona desert for a dark moment on a blinding day in July 2012, but I got to go home that night and cry in my beer. I am alive and she is not. She wasn't my mother. She wasn't my wife. I can never truly grasp what this family lost that day, and sitting in this swirl of wood smoke and tears on a muddy street in Cuenca, Ecuador, there is nothing I can say that means anything. I finally stop rambling on about how we got there before the vultures did. Vanessa then quietly tells me:

In case this is her buried here, thank God we have the body. It is a miracle of God that she came back to us. She is only half complete but she came back. She came back. If it is her, it helps us to move forward. But I am telling you it is very difficult to believe that this is how she is. It was very hard to see her in this form.

After witnessing Christian and Vanessa's reactions to the photos of Maricela's body, I finally began to understand the importance of these images to the family. They needed to see her in the moment of death. They needed a visual of her to replace the one burned into their minds after they opened the coffin. They needed a way to make the desert violence visible, which might somehow make it more intelligible.

AFTERMATH

A few years later, the extent of the devastation caused by Maricela's death is still hard to gauge. It is clear, though, that life for the family in Ecuador has been forever changed as everyone struggles to make sense of the situation they now find themselves in. Maricela migrated for her children, and it is they who are now at the center of trauma and social reconfiguration. Recent anthropological work on the transnational migration of mothers has demonstrated this phenomenon's troubling impact on the "social, relational, and affective worlds" of the kids left behind.[13] Significantly less is known about how the deaths and disappearances of migrant women impact the children and their caregivers who must create new worlds in the wake of their absence.

During my first Skype interview with Vanessa, I got a glimpse of this family's restructuring. She and I had been talking about Maricela's life and how my students and I happened to come upon her in the desert, when we were interrupted by little Edgar walking into the room. He poked his head into the camera frame and looked directly at me. He then cried out, "Why, Mom? When are you coming back?" Vanessa gently hugged him and said, "It's OK. That's why I call you my son now. Did you eat all of your soup?"

Over a year after she returned home, both the adults and kids were still trying to make sense of the disruption and trauma caused by Mari's death.

> Don Ernesto [doña Dolores's husband]: She was young. Really young. She left us really . . . Well, our lives have been screwed up forever after we lost her. We ended up with the kids. My wife and I had a very tranquil life before. We didn't really have any worries, and now we have started all over again with the kids. Everything is new. It is like they are our children. Well, they *are* our children. We have to fight to do everything we can for them now. More so for my wife. She has to wash their clothes, cook for them. I work really far away [kids are laughing and yelling in the background]. I make $100 a week and my small salary does very little to cover our family's expenses. We still don't have enough to buy food with that.

> Christian: I will never understand the sorrow that the kids feel. They miss Maricela so much. Her daughter misses her the most. Right now my parents are watching them, but they are old. They can't give them the same attention that their mom would have given. . . . When I was standing over her coffin, I promised my sister-in-law that I would take care of her kids. She came here for them, to give them a better life and give them all the things that she never had. I promised Mari that her kids would never be deprived of anything. I would give them everything I could. I am working and to this day I am taking care of them. I buy what they need, give them food, send them to school. My brother makes very little money in Ecuador. He makes $240 a month. That doesn't do anything when things there cost the same that they do here.
>
> My brother is a little better now, though. He was destroyed. He didn't care about anything. He was there for the kids but he was a mess, like nothing mattered. Sometimes he felt partly responsible. Like, why couldn't it have been him? He never thought that something like this would happen.

Close to home (cemetery, Cuenca, Ecuador). Photo by Michael Wells.

No one thought this would happen. He feels responsible. I talk to him to try to calm him down. I tell him that he needs to find peace and be good to himself. He needs to fight right now for the kids. He needs to be strong for them because if they leave the children alone they are going to get into trouble. He needs to be strong, but it is hard to get ahead. It is difficult. He was married for twelve years. He loved her. They went through everything together. They were starving together with the kids. . . . The five of them were together and now they are alone.

Vanessa: I wanted to die for a long time after her death. My brother would say, "At least you can be thankful that you have two nephews and a niece. Mari is there in each one of them, so please don't cry. Please don't suffer." It's easy to say, but not easy to do. I know that Mari is in each one of them, but it is very difficult, very difficult. My littlest one suffers so much because of this. He loved his mom very much. He puts music on to remind him of her, and it breaks my heart. He always says, "I miss my mom" and "God, please take me to her." He cries and cries. The oldest one gets mad and says to him, "I don't want you to cry. Our mom is not here. My mom is far away and I don't want you to cry for her." After her death, Jaime went crazy. He was in another world.

Christian: The whole world has dreams, but sometimes those same dreams can destroy a life. We leave home with hope, but we never know when we are going to encounter death there in the desert. It is such an ugly way to die, all alone, so far from your family, so desperate . . . It's like Mari felt that this was going to happen. She had the first communion for her youngest before she left. On Facebook she was putting up farewell songs like she had the feeling that she was going to die.

Edgar, the youngest, is about to turn seven. He is probably doing the best because . . . I don't know, I guess he didn't live that long with his mom. He misses her, but he still plays and goes to school and can get distracted. He is living. But the older ones, Laura, who is eleven, and Jaime, who is thirteen, they are the ones that remember their mom more. They cry. They are always thinking about her. Now the hardest thing is Mother's Day. Jaime is starting to rebel. He doesn't have a mom anymore and no one can tell him what to do. He wants his mom. It was really difficult for my family to live with him. He is starting to calm down now and understand these things. It can't be easy to lose your mother. It really affected us, but imagine what it did to them.

SUEÑOS

I am holding Edgar's tiny hand as we walk down the dirt road leading away from their house. He looks up at me and asks in a delicate voice, "Are we going to see my *mami?*" "Yes," I tell him. "Would that be OK?" He nods his head in youthful approval and then pulls me down the street. The entire group is going to visit the grave: Mike Wells and I, our wives and two children, Vanessa, and all three of Maricela's kids. Mike and I tried to do the visit alone, but Vanessa insisted that everyone accompany us. I am worried about how the children are going to react to this visit, because right before I left for Ecuador, Christian had told me: "The worst part is that the street you take to get to my house is where the cemetery is located. Every single day when the kids go to school they have to pass the cemetery. I wanted to bury Maricela someplace else, but there really was no other option. I think about that a lot. Every single day, no matter whether they want to or not, they are going to see their mommy."

We get to the front of the graveyard, and Jaime runs off to grab the key to the gate from the local caretaker. As we wait in the road, it starts to drizzle, which only adds to the ominous feeling of this whole affair. Jaime returns and quickly pops open the lock. He unravels the oily chain holding the cast-iron doors shut and wraps them around a fence post. The sky is the color of cold slate. It perfectly mirrors the gray cement blocks that compose most of the aboveground tombs here. Everywhere, the dead are stacked like bony cord-wood, shoved into elongated crypts whose facades are decorated with chipped blue and white porcelain tiles. Some have their names scratched into the marble or painted in black scrawls. The more affluent wear brass name plates and rest behind locked metal and glass doors.

Our group passes through brick-and-mortar canyons surrounded on all sides by crucifixes, tipped-over flower vases, and faded pictographs of the dead. It is a labyrinth of cold architecture carpeted in wet grass. Vanessa and Jaime begin to describe the day of the funeral. "There were two thousand people here to see her," she proudly tells me. "This entire place was full," Jaime says as he stretches out his lithe arms for effect. His little sister, Laura, confirms all of this with a quiet nod of her head. We come upon Maricela's grave from the back, and Vanessa shyly states, "I did that" while pointing at the crypt wall where "I ♥ Mari" has been brushed in dull white house paint.

The kids and Vanessa approach first. They say quick hellos to her and then step away so that Mike and the rest of us can have a look. Jaime stands at the edge of the scene staring off into the surrounding mountains. His jet-black hair is lightly blowing in the wind. Laura is next to Vanessa kicking at the grass with her pink sneakers. She has become unusually quiet. Little Edgar climbs up the wall on the back side of his mother's grave like it is a jungle gym. He giggles and asks if we are going to the park afterward.

I stand directly in front of Maricela's tomb. It is modest, but well maintained. The family regularly cleans it and often brings flowers. Her full name and the date that her body was found are spelled out in gold-colored letters. The names of her husband and children are engraved on tiny metal plaques. They keep her company in this cold place. In the center of the headstone is a photo of Maricela. Her head is turned and she is looking right at the camera. She is young and confident, almost smirking. This is how everyone wants to remember her. I reach out and touch the glass. Little Edgar runs up and pulls on my sleeve. "Are you going to take some pictures?" he asks.

————————

It is late in the evening. Mike and I are in the backyard of Christian's house hovering around a fire with Vanessa. Coils of gray smoke reach up to touch the black sky overhead. The air is thin and invigorating. I look through the fire at Vanessa's almond-shaped face and dark eyes. She is illuminated by dancing orange flames; it's some quiet moment caught in a rusted daguerreotype. For hours she cries and whispers stories about Maricela's life and her own, the two forever now intertwined. Her fears and pain are revealed in secretive hushes. These are things sleeping children should not hear. She speaks of wanting to believe that everything is going to be OK and that her sister-in-law is finally at peace. Her words, though, are full of doubt and rumor. What happened to Maricela in the desert now haunts Vanessa here in Cuenca. She too knows the hybrid collectif because it has opened a door to grief that seems impossible to close, even with bones in the ground.

> *Vanessa:* Maricela comes to me in my dreams at night. She has come to me in dreams that were so vivid and told me that she was kidnapped. She says to me, "Who did you all bury there in Cuenca? Who did you bury? I am alive!" In another dream she says, "I am leaving. I am leaving because I have to. I am going because I have to get there. I am going to arrive." Then she says, "Please take care of my kids." She always asks me to take care of them. These are the dreams that I have. In another dream she tells me about being abandoned in the desert. They left her behind and she needed help, so she kept walking and finally found a *rancho* and that is where they are keeping her. She is just waiting. Eventually she will be able to communicate with us and come back. They will finally send her back here. So maybe that is what happened.

The last dream I had, she came to me and said, "Don't worry. Don't cry for me, I am fine." I saw her for a moment and then she disapeared. Maybe she is saying that she is resting in peace and that is why she is telling me not to cry. Maybe it is her there in the cemetery and she is resting and everything is OK. . . . We were surprised to recover her body, because many people say bodies are never found. She came back, but we still aren't sure that it is her that we buried. We are one of the first people to get a loved one back who died in the desert. There is still a lot of doubt that it is her. Maybe she hit her head and has amnesia. I always have hope that she was kidnapped. Maricela's godmother's nephew migrated and then showed up like ten years later married with kids and everything. He was alive but he had left years before and disappeared. They say that she can still be alive.

It is July 24, 2013, and I am sitting at the Tucson Airport, preparing to return home after six weeks of fieldwork in the desert. I get a Facebook message from Vanessa. It is three days shy of the first anniversary marking the date when Maricela's body was identified. Vanessa's brief message reads: "I need to talk to you by phone to ask a favor. We have another family member who is lost in the desert."

CHAPTER 11

We Will Wait Until You Get Here

JOSÉ'S ROOM

José Tacuri's room looks like those of most other fifteen-year-olds. On the cusp of manhood, his windowless cement *cuartito* in a tiny house in a working-class *barrio* of Cuenca is decorated with a combination of items from his fading childhood and his burgeoning adolescence. A couple of white teddy bears are squirreled away in the corner; a comforter decorated with characters from the Disney movie *Cars* blankets his bed. These childish things are juxtaposed to a light-gray suit hanging in the corner next to a pile of hoodies, baggy jeans, and baseball caps stitched with New York Yankees and New York Knicks logos. *Nueva York* is always on his mind. This hip-hop wardrobe, along with a few homemade tattoos and piercings, bite the style of Ñengo Flow, José's favorite reggaeton singer. In practically every recent photo of José, he gives the impression that he is posing for the cover of a mix-tape. "*Real G for life, mami!*" Next to his clothes is an image of Jesus Christ and a retainer case. He may have some ghetto ink and a little swagger in his step, but the kid still wears orthodontics.

On the middle of his bed is a pillow that José's girlfriend, Tamara, gave him for his fifteenth birthday. The airbrushed message on it reads: "Happy Birthday. Today is a special day where God has given you another year of life. I only hope that you can have many more years so that we can be together. With all my heart I want to tell you that I love you." José's room looks like a lot of other teenager's rooms. The only difference is that this place is frozen in time. Nothing here has moved since he left for the United States and disappeared in the Arizona desert just south of Arivaca.

José (age fifteen). Photo by Michael Wells.

A few days after I spoke with Vanessa in July 2013, José Tacuri's family in New York called me and explained what had happened to him. Over the next several weeks, I helped them file a missing person report with the Colibrí Center for Human Rights in Tucson, the same organization that helped identify Maricela. I also acted as a general helpline when questions arose about what the family could be doing to find him. Because of my familiarity with the Sonoran Desert, I thought that getting more details about the route that José took could help us triangulate his last known whereabouts and aid in a search. Two months after he went missing, Mike Wells and I traveled to New York for the first of many meetings with José's parents and the two cousins he had been traveling with. During that initial visit, I interviewed his cousins about the long trip they had taken from Ecuador to Arizona, and began my own journey to learn about José's young life and the reasons for his migration. Four months after meeting his family in New York, Mike and I found ourselves in a house in Cuenca staring at the bedroom of a ghost.

—————

If seeing the ravaged body of a person you love is the physical manifestation of Sonoran Desert necroviolence, then having no corpse at all is its spectral form.

"I only hope that you can have many more years so that we can be together." Photo courtesy of the Tacuri family.

Maybe with time and therapy, if one can even conceptualize the latter as an option, or perhaps enough booze or drugs, you can learn to block out grotesque images: the odd geometries of cross-sectioned radials and ulnas; brittle skin peeling off laughing skulls; seashell-colored long bones heaped in a pile like the remnants of some great carnivore's recent meal. Maybe you are lucky and didn't open the coffin, so you never saw what really happened to your wife's body. You were just happy to have her back. You can always kiss those wrinkled photos of the good times or catch glimpses of her in the faces of your children. The kids remind you of who she was and the beauty and vitality that once lived in her eyes. But how do you grieve when there are no bones to mourn over, no coffin to keep sealed tight? How do you move on when the uncertainty of what happened to someone you love won't let you? How do you find closure when the missing come to you in dreams every night pleading for your help? For José's family, his room serves as both a time capsule of who he once was and a painful reminder that his fate remains unknown. This space is the material representation of the family's perpetual state of grief. As I sit with José's grandmother doña Lorena in her kitchen in Cuenca, she tells me:

> Dear God! We've been praying that he will show up. We've been waiting for a
> long time. We pray and we cry almost every single day, but he still doesn't

appear. There is no peace for us. We are here all alone suffering, crying day and night. We ask God to give us some news. We have gone everywhere we can to get information, but there is nothing. We will never find peace until José comes back. He can return in any form, but we just need him to appear. We need to know something. Whatever it is that has happened to him, we want to know so that we don't suffer anymore and so that we don't think about it anymore. His parents, his aunts and uncles, everyone is suffering. We hope one day to reach God because only he knows where he is. It is hard. [cries] It is so hard to know so little. Is he over there in the United States? Is he alive? We are poor. It was poverty that made his parents leave to support their kids, and they are in New York suffering because he hasn't appeared. They are suffering and waiting for him to show up but nothing happens.

LEFT BEHIND

Scholars have long noted that transnational migration has dramatic effects on family structure and the relationship between those who leave and those who stay.[1] José's experience as the child of parents who migrated without documents to the United States is quite common. Unable to adequately provide for his five children in Cuenca, including a disabled daughter, José's dad, Gustavo, made the difficult decision to leave for New York when his son was just ten years old. Within a year of his arrival his wife, Paulina, decided to join him. Two people could put more food on the table than one. Both newly employed, they were soon able to send money home regularly. This ensured that their children could eat and go to school and that their sick daughter could get the costly medical attention she needed. These remittances also guaranteed that José didn't have to work. Instead, he could be the kid on the block who had a laptop, an iPod, expensive kicks, and an overabundance of clothing emblazoned with the words "New York." He could take his girlfriend out to the movies and treat his cousins to pizza whenever he wanted.

José's aunts and grandmother assumed the role of caregivers for him and his siblings, but he could Skype with *Mami* and *Papi* whenever he wanted because their tiny rented house now had WiFi. This Nueva York to Cuenca virtual parenting was a scene out of Alex Rivera's sci-fi movie *Sleep Dealer*. But, as you can imagine, long-distance parenting isn't the same as being there. It never is. Despite the comfort that his family's newfound economic stability afforded and his own conspicuous consumption, José began to suffer from what some in Ecuador call *el dolor de dólares* (the pain of dollars), a double-edged phrase that refers to both the feelings of abandonment that children of migrants experience and their faraway parents' attempts to assuage this pain with American cash and gifts.[2]

As with many children in his situation, José's feelings of parental neglect and abandonment led to rebellion. He dropped out of school. He stopped going to catechism. He discovered his love of *chelas* (beers) and was soon a regular at the all-night parties down at the neighborhood soccer field. By the time he was a teenager, his *tías* and *abuela* got into the routine of looking for him on the streets at all hours of the night. Rebelling is easy when there is no one around to crack the parental whip.

The stucco and shingle two-story compound in New York occupied by various members of the Tacuri clan and their young offspring is enormous by Cuenca standards. It reflects the relative affluence that some new immigrants are able to achieve after pooling years of cut-rate wages earned by working seventy-hour weeks. Several late-model sports utility vehicles and work trucks fill the expansive gravel driveway. Construction tools and sawhorses function as patio furniture. The palatial backyard is littered with the accoutrements of childhood: soccer balls are everywhere; a sparkling white slide and swing set look as if they just came out of a Pottery Barn Kids catalog; muddy sneakers of all sizes and colors sit in a pile next to the front door. In the living room a flat-screen TV sits next to a cabinet full of gold and porcelain knickknacks. One corner of the room is dedicated to housing teddy bears, strollers for baby dolls, and other important child treasures. A yipping white ball of fur runs wild through the place, snapping at my ankles and growling every time I try to pet him. It is a twenty-first-century Norman Rockwell series on the American immigrant dream. Like many immigrant dreams, though, this one is only half realized. José's dad, Gustavo, sits in this gilded American cage and recounts the detrimental impact that his migration had on his son.

> *Gustavo:* When I was in Cuenca, José was my right hand. He was always with me. We were inseparable. But when I came to this country, he became a really rebellious child. I called him and asked, "José, why have you changed?" He said to me, "No, *Papi*, it's your fault. You left me. We were like brothers. You were my everything and you left me. It's your fault that I'm like this." I told him, "Look, I didn't come here to New York because I wanted to. I came

here to get ahead, because in Ecuador I can't give you the things that you need." I left when he was ten to provide for him and my family. He didn't really understand these things at the time. I kept asking him why he was acting up. I asked him why he had changed from being such a good kid. All he kept saying was that he wanted to come here to New York, but I didn't understand why. He had everything there in Cuenca. He kept saying that my wife and I were to blame. He said he felt empty inside. He said he would go home and we wouldn't be there. He told me that being reunited with us would fill his emptiness inside.

In her analysis of Ecuadoran migration patterns in the 1990s and their impact on family life, Ann Miles noted that some undocumented migrants from Cuenca managed, at great risk and cost, to return home to visit family members every few years.[3] Following the escalation of border security in the wake of 9/11, this pattern of periodic return became too dangerous and prohibitively expensive, especially for non-Mexican migrants like José's parents.[4] Policy analysts have since shown that these increased dangers and economic costs have led to a new, permanently settled undocumented population in the United States, people who, rather than risk a visit home to see family, are more likely to send money for their spouses and children to join them.[5] Those who make it through the Sonoran Desert hybrid collectif rarely want to brave it a second time.

After years of pleading with his parents, José finally convinced them it was time for him to join them in New York.

> *Gustavo:* In 2012 I wanted to bring José, but I wasn't thinking about it seriously. He was still a kid. I told him, "Don't worry, when it's your time, you'll come." A year passed, and this year in March he surprised me by saying, "*Papi*, I want to come and be with you." I said, "No, you're crazy. What are you going to do here? You're too young to come here." He was young but big for his age. He was bigger than me [referring to him in past tense]. He said, "Help me to get there." I told him, "No, son, you shouldn't come." But he said, "I'm alone here." He was saying these things to me. I said, "Look, I'm here in New York for you guys. I left and suffer so that you can be OK." He said, "*Papi*, I want to come and help you. I miss you so much. It's been so long." So he convinced me. I said, "OK, I am going to help you. We are going to contract someone there in Ecuador so that you can leave. We are going to bring you here. We will put our trust in God. *El camino es duro* [The migrant trail is hard]. I know because I have gone through it, but with faith we will get through." A month passed and I paid some money. It was just a few hours' notice to start the trip. José was having second thoughts by this time.

I had only paid like a thousand dollars or something, so I said, "It's time but I don't really want you to come. You should stay there with your brothers and sisters and take care of them." He told me, "No, I decided to leave and I am leaving. I want to be with you. *Papi*, don't worry. I'm going to get there."

"MOUNTAINS AND MOUNTAINS"

On April 3, 2013, José left Cuenca with two cousins, thirteen-year-old Felipe and nineteen-year-old Manny.[6] Much like Christian's trip in 2001, theirs lasted several months but in comparison was relatively uneventful. After leaving Guayaquil by plane, the three of them crossed multiple borders by car and bus. After less than two weeks of travel they arrived in Mexico. Once in Mexico City, the cousins were sent to different safe houses where they then spent forty-five days waiting for transport to Nogales.[7] Unable to leave their houses, they tried to keep themselves busy. They mostly watched TV and paced around a small courtyard. The house where José was kept had Internet, and he was able to periodically log on to Facebook when his smuggler let him (for a fee of course).

Finally, after a month and a half of being cooped up indoors, José's cousins were loaded into the luggage compartment of a passenger bus, given a bucket to urinate in, and told not to make any noise. For two cramped days Manny and Felipe lay quietly under the bus while dozens of unknowing passengers sitting above them snoozed, read magazines, and stared out their windows at the northern Mexican countryside. Although the details of how José got to Nogales are currently vague, it was likely a trip similar to what his cousins experienced. When they finally reached the border, the three boys were reunited and taken to a safe house where they waited, along with dozens of other migrants, for their guide to tell them when it was time to try their luck. Ten days after arriving in the Nogales, a car showed up one night and drove them to the edge of the desert.

> *Felipe:* We left the house in Nogales at night and were dropped off underneath a *puente* [bridge or overpass]. It only took like twenty minutes in the car to get from the house to the *puente*. Everyone was carrying a black backpack and their one bottle of water. A gallon of water. Some bottles were white and some were painted black. . . . José was wearing black Air Jordans with black pants, a black sweatshirt, a black shirt, and black hat with red letters on it. Everyone had black clothes on.

> *Manny:* José had a rosary, a prayer card, and a chain with an owl on it that his girlfriend gave him. He was wearing a belt that had phone numbers written on it. It had his dad's cell phone and house numbers. He had no identification.

Air Jordan, Sonoran Desert, July 2010. Photo by Michael Wells.

Felipe: We crossed a fence and then started walking. We were traveling with two guides. There were around forty people in our group. One of the guides was named Scooby. I don't remember the other one's name. . . . We climbed a hill and at the bottom we crossed another fence. When we climbed the first hill we could see the city of Nogales, and then it disappeared. We walked all night and then rested near a *rancho* around 4 or 5 A.M. We slept in an abandoned house there. In the morning we started walking again.

Manny: We left from the *puente.* We walked a little bit and then climbed a mountain. After the mountain it got flat, and then there was a road with a house on it. After we crossed the road, there was nothing, just mountains and mountains. We walked past a tall mountain that had two blinking antennas on it. They had red blinking lights. The guides called it La Montaña de Cerdo [Pig Mountain].

Felipe: Our group separated that next day. Me, José, and Manny stayed together with Scooby. . . . We would climb a hill and Scooby would be waiting at the top for people. On the second day of walking we got to the start of the hill at about 6 A.M. and rested. José's shoes were starting to fall apart.

The soles were coming unglued. José kept stopping to sit and drink water. We were giving him water so he could keep going. We then climbed a hill and dropped down to a flat area where there wasn't any shade or trees. It was impossible to hide there.

Manny: We had rested at the bottom of a hill for ten minutes when my cousin José started to sleep. He didn't want to get up. Everytime we stopped to rest, he would try to sleep. The guide would say, "We are going to rest and catch your breath and then we are going to start walking again. Don't sleep." Well, José started to sleep. It was the heat. The heat will get you. It robs you of energy. We really didn't have much to drink. José had water in his backpack but he needed more. He started to drink a lot of water. He was just getting thirstier and thirstier. We had brought *sueros* [electrolyte solution] and gave them to him. He finished everything. He couldn't control himself.

Felipe: He stopped walking around 7 A.M. He couldn't go on. José fell down and Scooby started kicking him. Scooby was saying, "Get up or I am going to keep kicking you." José's leg gave out, and he just slumped down on the ground. He said that he'd had enough. Scooby was yelling, "You need to get up or I'm going to beat you." José was sitting on the ground looking dazed [makes woozy head movements], and Scooby just kept kicking him. He tried to get up but fell with all his weight. He was falling on bushes and the branches were breaking. He fell three times and the last time he couldn't get up. He was very sleepy and his eyes were half open. We were all kind of like that but José also had the flu. When we left Nogales he was sick. He said he was going to turn himself in. He told me, "I can't go on, but you should."

Manny: His feet wouldn't let him go anymore. He was on the ground and said, "I am going to turn myself in." Immigration was all around at this point. Where we left him there was Border Patrol everywhere.

Felipe: There were helicopters around because, the day before, they were catching a lot of people in our group. We told José we were going to keep going and we left him sitting at the bottom of the hill. He was in a spot where there was no place to hide, no trees or anything. José had food and a little bottle of water that I gave him. We walked to the next hill where Scooby was waiting. That was the last time we saw him.

A day and half after leaving him behind, the cousins and their guide were spotted by Border Patrol and chased into the mountains. It was at this point that Scooby abandoned them. They were now alone, lost, and out of food and water. To compound issues, thirteen-year-old Felipe was dehydrated to the point that he began coughing up blood. At daybreak they started walking until they stumbled upon a lagoon and were able to fill their bottles with murky liquid. That morning they somehow found their way to Arivaca Road, where they were quickly picked up by Border Patrol. As the crow flies, they had walked almost 30 miles through multiple mountain ranges. Upon mapping the coordinates of where they were apprehended, I realized that Felipe and Manny were caught 8 miles directly south of where Maricela's body was found. It appears that they walked the same route that she did.

When they finally spoke to their families from federal detention days later, Manny and Felipe reported that José had stayed behind. Despite the fact that they left him in an area with heavy Border Patrol presence, José never turned himself in. At the end of our first interview Manny remarked to me, "I don't know why he didn't turn himself in at that moment. Maybe he kept walking. I'm not sure what happened."

AMBIGUOUS LOSS

The uncertainty, pain, and suffering that follow in the wake of a loved one's disappearance are devastating, to say the least. For many, it's like a nightmare you can't wake up from. You never stop wondering what happened to your son, daughter, brother, or wife. You never stop searching for answers even when there is no hope of finding them. Just ask the families of soldiers who go missing in action, the relatives of the passengers on board Malaysian flight 370, or the people still looking for the bodies of those who were swallowed up when the World Trade Center towers collapsed on September 11, 2001. Sufferers of this type of loss can find themselves in an eternal state of grief, confusion, and desperation. Clinical psychologists call this phenomenon *ambiguous loss*,[8] and some argue that it is the pinnacle of human sorrow: "[it] is the most stressful loss because it defies resolution and creates confused perceptions about who is in or out of a particular family. With a clear-cut loss, there is more clarity—a death certificate, mourning rituals, and the opportunity to honor and dispose of remains. With ambiguous loss, none of these markers exists. The clarity needed for boundary maintenance (in the sociological sense) or closure (in the psychological sense) is unattainable."[9]

On June 2, 2013, the Sonoran Desert did what Border Patrol strategists wanted it to do. It deterred José Tacuri from entering into the United States. But instead of just stopping him, the hybrid collectif swallowed him alive, erased all traces of him, and sent shockwaves of grief felt as close as New York City and as far as Ecuador. This erasure was not, however, an "accident" or act of nature. It was part of a clearly laid out federal security plan, whose efficacy

"Esperando por José." Photo by Michael Wells.

is measured by how many people it "deters."[10] Unfortunately, there are no reliable statistics on the number of people who have gone missing and are presumed dead in the desert, a point recognized by those in charge of evaluating Prevention Through Deterrence: "The fact that a number of bodies may remain undiscovered in the desert also raises doubts about the accuracy of counts of migrant deaths. . . . [T]he total number of bodies that have not been found is ultimately unknown."[11]

For families like José's, having no corpse means that they will always maintain hope that he is alive. They will always grieve for him. But the absence of physical evidence of his demise prevents them from publicly mourning. They can't "tear at their clothes and hair, improvising various mourning laments to make the loss that has occurred public and utterable,"[12] because they themselves aren't sure what has been lost. The ambiguity of this situation means they cannot gradually move away from death.[13] Desert necroviolence for them is both ethereal and inescapable.

José's sister sits alone in his room (or is it a cenotaph?), clutching his clothes and praying that he will come back. His grandmother wanders off late at night to look for him down at the dusty soccer field in hopes of catching him drinking beers with his hooligan friends. His aunt avoids eating at his favorite restaurant, because she can't bear to see the empty booth that he once routinely occupied. Like the souls of West African migrants who go missing during their crossing of the Sahara or the Mediterranean,[14] José's troubled spirit hovers above his family and visits them in their sleep. His Aunt Lucia tells me about dreams and visions that family members have of him: "I had a dream that he was near a river and that he was sitting down wearing a white shirt. He is picking up tiny pebbles and throwing them into the water. When I see him I ask, 'What are you doing here?' He says, 'Nothing,' and then just keeps throwing rocks. In another dream he tells me, 'They didn't come for me. I am still here in Nogales.' I don't know why I have these dreams. My dad has dreams where José is scared and asking him for help." Others imagine that he has amnesia, is working for the mafia as a drug mule, or is being held hostage on a ranch. Sitting in her dark, windowless kitchen in Cuenca, his Aunt Paola sums up these frustrations and draws a stark contrast to the suffering experienced by Maricela's family:

> *Paola:* More than anything we just want to get to the bottom of this. To see what happened to him. God give us strength to accept whatever comes. Is he alive or is he dead? We need to finally know something about what has become of him. Imagine not knowing anything. [crying] We ask God to give us strength to keep moving forward. Maybe he is alive. God, send him back or have him turn himself into immigration or the police. We need to know so that we can keep moving forward as before. God willing, José will soon appear. Whether he is alive or dead, we just want to know. We want to no longer have doubts about where he could be or how he is or what happened to him. We don't know anything . . . Maybe the *coyote* did something. Maybe he killed him and buried him so that no one would find him. If he was left behind, they should have found him dead, but they didn't find anything. Sometimes these are the thoughts we have out of the desperation from not knowing. I don't mean to sound ugly, but at least Maricela's family knows that she is dead and they can put her in a tomb and visit her! At least their family can leave her flowers. *¡Aquí no sabemos nada!* We know nothing about what happened to his life.

While his family ponders a million scenarios about where he is and what has become of him, his girlfriend, Tamara, just holds onto hope. As Mike and I sit across from her in a café in Cuenca, we are both struck by her optimism and strength. She is young, but she has the resolve of someone who has known pain beyond her years. For over an hour she tells us the story of how they met and fell in love. She also describes the pain of watching José leave. Despite the heavy sorrow in her words, she refuses to cry. Both of her parents have migrated to New York, and she lives alone with her older sister, with whom she constantly fights. She tells us that José is her best friend and the only one who understands her loneliness and pain. They are two teenagers struggling to make sense of lives forever fractured by transnational migration. They are kindred spirits. In a brightly lit coffee shop in Cuenca she holds back her tears when she tells me, "Right before he left, we told each other that no matter what happens, we would always be together. I have no idea if he is alive or dead, but I am always going to wait for him."

"WE WILL WAIT UNTIL YOU GET HERE"

If you have never watched your own children starve, never struggled to provide medical care for your sick baby or gone years without hugging your son, it might be easy to blame José's parents for what happened to him. After all, they were the ones who abandoned him in Cuenca and the ones who paid a smuggler to take their fifteen-year-old son into the desert. But placing all of the blame on his parents requires turning a blind eye to the global political economic structure that set this entire scenario in motion. How desperate must one be to leave five children behind and accrue thousands of dollars of debt to undertake a dangerous trip with no guarantees one will survive, much less succeed in getting across the border? Success in this case means finding yourself occupying a position in US society where your labor is always exploited and your social position precarious. How desperate must a parent be to see his son that he would entrust him to the hands of smugglers who will run him through a desert gauntlet where, by strategic design, suffering and death are likely outcomes? These are questions that many of the relatively well-off people who read this book will never be able to answer. Rather than blaming or judging José's family, perhaps we can attempt to put ourselves in their position and try to imagine what life must be like when these are the types of decisions one must make.

As I sit in the living room of José's parents' house in New York, it's hard to think about immigration statistics, legalities, the hybrid collectif, or whom to blame for what has come to pass. As Gustavo describes his final conversation with his son, there are no politics, just pain:

Gustavo: It was a Saturday when he called and said, "*Papi,* I'm on my way to be with you. The guides are coming for me and they are going to take me to you." They left on a Saturday at 11 at night. After that day we don't really know what happened to him. A week went by, and then two weeks went by. We still didn't know anything about where he was. I called the *guía,* and he said that there was no way to communicate with José in the desert. I kept asking, "When is he going to arrive?" One Sunday morning we got a call from one of his cousins who got caught. They told me that José had escaped. I said that it seemed unlikely that he would have gotten away. They said, "It's not true; José got away." It's not that easy to get away from immigration. I called the guide again and asked about my son. I said that if he got away, then he should know where he is. The guide started to give me different excuses about where José was. I never heard from my son again.

That Saturday was the last time I spoke to him. Before he left, he said to me, "I am full of hope. You have to have faith that we are going to be together." He wanted me to support him. He said, "Promise me that you are going to help me when I get there." I said to him, "You are my son. I will support you any way that I can. Don't be afraid." "Are you sure that you are going to be there for me?" he asked. I told him, "I promise that I am going to be here for you." He was afraid. He had something he wanted to tell me. He was coming here with something on his mind. The last time I spoke to him, he said, "*Papi,* I really want to talk to you." I said "OK, let's talk." "Not like this," he said. "I want to talk face to face. Like father and son." "OK," I told him, "we will wait until you get here, or if you want to tell me right now, go ahead and tell me." He said, "No, it's not the time to talk about it yet. When I get there, we can talk."

He never said what he wanted to talk about. [Paulina starts crying.] . . . He met a girl in Ecuador and they went out for six months. They were together about two weeks before he left, and this girl got pregnant. He found out while he was in Mexico. I guess this is what he wanted to tell me. He wanted to tell me that this girl was pregnant, and he wanted to know if I would help him. I didn't get to tell him, but to this day I am going to support her and the baby girl she is going to have. I am not going to abandon her. This is the remorse that I have, that I could never tell him face to face that I was really going to support him. It's going to be a girl and it makes me very happy. We have had such sadness since he disapeared. This child that is coming is going to bring happiness into our lives. It gives me hope to keep fighting for José.

His girlfriend calls me every day to see if I have any news about him. To see if we know anything. To see if I have spoken to anyone. I say, "No, there is nothing." It is difficult to say that we have found nothing. She thinks I'm not doing anything here. That we aren't calling anyone and that José is lost and we are just sitting here. That's not true. We are trying to find any person that might know something about José. There is nothing that we can do to get back that joy that we lost until we find him. To know something about what happened to him.

There is nothing we can do. We can't go down to the line and look for him. To lose him like this and not know what happened is going to make us cry for the rest of our lives. He was a very strong young man. [cries] I miss him so much. Sometimes I just want to take everything I own and throw it all away. In these moments I can't let the things I am feeling explode out of me. I have to bottle up all of this pain that I hold inside. It's hard. It's hard because when I leave the house, it's just him that I think about. There is no one else. When I'm at work, I try to concentrate on the things I need to do, but it only lasts for a little while. I am only thinking about him. I say to him, "What happened to you? Where are you? Why don't you call me? You are strong." He was a really strong young man.

Truthfully, I don't really sleep. Normally I'm up until 2 or 3 in the morning. Then I get up at 4 or 5. I can't sleep, because he is always in my dreams. [voice cracks] I can't sleep. I have a photo of him that I always look at. I talk to him in the photo. We talk and I remember when he was a child. It makes me smile, but at the same time the tears come for the many things I haven't been able to do for him.

We decided to bring José here, but we never thought that he would go missing. Never. We never imagined that this would happen like this, but now in reality this is happening to us. It's hard to say that my son is missing and he is never coming back. I have faith that he will return and I will see him again. I don't know how or in what form, but I want to see him. It's OK if somebody says to me, "You know what, we found your son and he is like this or like this."[15] I just don't want to live with doubt about what happened to him. God has given us the gift of a grandchild, but at the same time I am sad that we can't find her dad. That we can't find our son.

Every day that passes we feel more and more out of control. Sometimes it feels as if I am losing the battle. I try to wake up with energy some days and say, "We are going to find him. We are going to find him." It is difficult to live like this. To know nothing, nothing, nothing. [crying] I pray to God that we will somehow be reunited with José in some form or another.

María José came kicking and screaming into the world in November 2013.

CHAPTER 12

Epilogue

PERILOUS TERRAIN

After weeks of planning I am finally able to arrange for José's mom, Paulina, and his two cousins to speak by phone with members of the Border Patrol's Public Information Office and its Search, Trauma, and Rescue team (BORSTAR). The hope is that if Manny and Felipe can remember enough about the crossing and where they left José, we can retrace their steps in the desert and narrow down a survey area to look for him. I am the first person to phone in. I strike up a conversation with several agents who are participating on the conference call:

> *Jason:* Just to give you guys a warning, everyone is holding out that he is still alive. So they are gonna have questions. Some of Paulina's questions are gonna be like, "Is it possible that he is in detention somewhere and he just hasn't been identified with his proper name?" These are things that I have tried to reassure her are highly unlikely after so much time has passed, but she is still going to ask.
>
> *Agent:* We will do our best. Uh, I'm not sure if we would be able to answer a whole lot of questions. We are going to try and gather as much information as we can to be able to assess the situation to see if it's possible to conduct a search for some human remains of this young man.

Paulina, Manny, and Felipe call in. Thirteen-year-old Felipe is the first to be interviewed, and it doesn't go well. He is unable to provide many specific details that would be of use and is also understandably a bit nervous during the process. After less than five minutes one of the BORSTAR agents starts to get audibly frustrated:

Felipe: We crossed under a *puente.* Then we climbed a hill. We climbed up this entire hill and then passed a fenced. From there we started walking north.

BORSTAR Agent: Could you see Nogales?

Felipe: Yes, we could see Nogales from the hill.

BORSTAR Agent: Was it east or west?

Felipe: I don't know. We could see the city, though. From there we kept walking for like an hour, and then we found a small house that was under construction. We went inside for a little bit and then kept walking again. . . . We were in Tucson because we passed a ranch where they had horses. We passed that and got to the road. It was just me and Manny because José stayed behind.

BORSTAR Agent: No, no, no. What I want to know is *when* you crossed because I can't . . . [annoyed]. When you say "this house" or "this *puente,*" you were in Mexico, right? Look, I don't know Mexico. I only know what is in the United States, so I need to know at what point in your trip you crossed from Mexico to the United States. Am I clear? How did you know you crossed the border?

Felipe: There was a fence that we crossed. It was a barbed wire fence. The *coyote* said that we had passed into the United States. . . . We crossed the border between Mexico and the United States during the day. We crossed the border more or less around 5 P.M. in the afternoon.

BORSTAR Agent: How was the terrain near the fence?

Felipe: It was an area full of mountains. There was a hill where the fence was. We climbed it and in the middle of the hill we crossed the fence. Then we kept walking uphill. There were a lot of trees . . .

The interview drags on for over an hour. Manny and Felipe have conflicting accounts regarding how many days they spent in the desert, and their memory of details such as landmarks and the cardinal directions they walked are vague at best. This is not surprising given their age, unfamiliarity with the region, and the fact that they spent a great deal of time walking under the cover of night. They focus on telling the agents about the "large mountains with blinking antennas" and the flat and denuded area where a very sick José was last seen. After an hour of listening to them tell their stories, you can hear the aggravation in the voice of the BORSTAR agent, who isn't getting the details he wants. Finally, Paulina gets on the line, and one of the more sympathetic agents sitting in on the call asks if she has any questions.

Paulina: I don't have any questions. I only ask that you help me find him.

Agent: We are very sorry. I know that this is very difficult for you and your family. All I can tell you is that we are going to analyze the testimonies of these guys and communicate with Mr. De León about possibilities of how we might proceed in this case. I know that this is not something that is going to really help you in this moment, but unfortunately the reality is that this is a big area. Uh, well, it's a very difficult terrain, so we need to talk here and see what we can do.

Paulina: I don't think that José would have gone back to Mexico from the desert, because he spent like a month there. The last day in Nogales he called us to tell us that he was going to leave. He was really happy because he was finally getting out of there and was going to be with us. [cries] There were other calls he made that day. He has a girlfriend in Ecuador. She got a call on her cell phone that was a lot of numbers. She checked the call and it said that it was from a different country.

Agent: Was this before or after he crossed?

Paulina: This was later. At the end of the month there was another phone call. My sister answered it there in Ecuador, and she is sure that it was José because he called out her name and then hung up the phone.

BORSTAR Agent: So you think he might have gone back to Mexico and at one point called Ecuador?

Paulina: Yes.

BORSTAR Agent: [in a condescending voice] Ma'am, let me get this straight. You guys are saying that in the best case, after all of this, after they left him in the desert, you think that he has made some phone calls saying that . . .

Paulina: Yes. Yes, I think . . . [ten seconds of uncomfortable silence]

Before the BORSTAR agent can say anything else, one of his colleagues cuts him off and then hits the mute button. We wait quietly for almost a minute before they come back on the line. One of the agents quickly tells us that they will see what they can do, and then the call ends. Twelve days later I receive the following email:

Dear Mr. De Leon,

I would like to personally thank you for contacting us regarding the disappearance of José Tacuri. We appreciate your patience and the facilitation that you provided with the interviews of Manny and Felipe.

After spending many hours and days analyzing the provided information and conducting interviews of our own, it became apparent that the circumstances in this particular case would not sufficiently provide for any additional Border Patrol searches for José. However, we fully understand his family's wish may be to continue to search for José through a different means. As such, I would like to share with you our perceptions of where José may have crossed and traveled. It is likely that he crossed the international boundary east of Sycamore Canyon, south of the Atascosa Mountain range. The "antennas" referenced in the interviews are most likely to be those on Atascosa Peak. José likely separated from his cousins on the west side of the Atascosa Mountains, probably northwest of Atascosa Peak. His cousins then continued their journey northward, eventually being apprehended somewhere east of Moyza Ranch Road and south of Arivaca Road.

We in the Tucson Sector strongly sympathize with his mother and family during this difficult time. José's story is a tragic and sobering reminder of the dangers faced by so many undocumented migrants who undertake the journey to enter the United States through rough and perilous terrain.

REMAINS

The fate of the poor here in Ecuador is to migrate. My sister migrated. She left for her kids because life here was very hard. There was nothing. She left so that she could send money so that her kids could have chances in life, more possibilities. But she never wanted to leave them.

—Lucia (José's aunt)

I think that this trip we make really changes us. It makes you think more about who you are. It changes how you are. If you were rebellious before, a guy who didn't work hard, you start the crossing and you start thinking about changing those things. Going through something like this changes a person. It makes you into a better person. That's my opinion.

—Christian

In 1891, *Harper's New Monthly Magazine* published an illustration by American artist Frederic Remington titled "Dying of Thirst in the Desert." The image, which accompanied an article on unauthorized Chinese immigration, depicted a coolie with a hat and canteen writhing in pain on the barren Sonoran Desert floor.[1] More than a hundred years later this image is a poignant reminder that as long as there have been desperate people who can't make a living wage in their home country and a need for cheap labor in the United States, migrants have been willing to cross the border regardless of the cost.

The factors that make people leave their homes and families to risk life and limb in the desert for the chance to scrub toilets for minimum wage are relatively obvious: global economic inequality, political instability, war, famine, government corruption, drug cartel violence, unregulated capitalism, consumer demands for cheap goods and services. It is an endless list of political economic issues that defy simple policy solutions. Would a new guest worker program solve America's border problems? Could policing the workforce and penalizing those who employ the undocumented stop the migration flow? What about equalizing the trade relationships between the United States and our neighbors to the south so that people have fewer reasons to leave home? Perhaps more foreign investment in economic development in Latin America and less spending on the Border War? All of these suggestions have been put forth time and again with few results.

In the end, it comes down to the United States' need for cheap labor that can easily be controlled with the threat of deportation and the duplicitous stance that we don't want undocumented laborers in our country. The American public has to first recognize and resolve this fundamental socioeconomic conundrum before any serious immigration policy reform can take place. This book, however, was never about solving our problem of illegal immigration. There is no easy solution. My goal has been to shine a light on the inhumane and hypocritical way that we police our borders and show the devastating impact that our boundary enforcement system has on people's lives. I have tried to demystify the strategy known as Prevention Through Deterrence and show how a strategic network of heterogeneous actors are at work every day to produce complex forms of violence. By looking behind the curtain of this federal policy we can see the marionette strings that connect the hands of Border Patrol strategists to venomous animals, life-threatening temperatures, and "hostile terrain." If this book does anything, I hope that it makes visible the effects of US border enforcement practices designed to be hidden and draws more attention to the violent logic on which the entire immigration security paradigm is based.

In some ways, though, this book is also a testimony given by survivors of the Sonoran Desert hybrid collectif and an obituary for those who succumb to it. The words, stories, and images that the undocumented people in the preceding pages have allowed me to share are their public declarations that their lives are worth noting, valuing, and preserving.[2] They are lives worth grieving for. As Judith Butler notes, rather than viewing grief as private and apolitical, we should conceive of it as public and as facilitating "a sense of political community of a complex order."[3] If we can publicly grieve for Maricela, José, and the thousands of others who suffer and die as the result of a cruel border policy and a globalized economy that continuously pushes and pulls people to seek work in the United States, we might better understand how our worlds are intertwined and the ethical responsibility we have to one another as humans.

————————

When I was kid growing up in McAllen, Texas, in the 1980s, I remember seeing desperate people wade across the Rio Grande from neighboring Reynosa, Mexico, in broad daylight. Prevention Through Deterrence brought this brazen practice to a screeching halt in the early 1990s as migrants were systematically funneled toward Arizona. As security has ramped up in the Sonoran Desert over the past five years, the Rio Grande has once again been breached. Undocumented migrants are now walking for days across the desolate ranchlands of South Texas to evade Border Patrol. This sector has become the busiest crossing corridor in the nation.[4] As this book goes to press, Central Americans, many of them children fleeing a combination of poverty and violence, are joining this mass exodus of people in record numbers. To arrive at the border, these migrants often ride the limb- and life-taking freight trains known as *la bestia* to get across Mexico. The number of adults and kids who have died or gone missing on this new route is unknown, but the discovery of a slew of mass graves of unidentified people in northern Mexico and in various county cemeteries in Texas suggests this is the new killing field.[5]

The US federal government has responded to this unsightly mob of Central American migrants by putting political and economic pressure on the Mexican government to stop people from riding on the tops of trains.[6] Migrants may now have to walk a thousand miles across a Mexican minefield where assault, robbery, murder, rape, and extortion are virtually guaranteed.[7] The United States has extended its southern border to the geopolitical boundary with Guatemala and incorporated Mexico's hostile terrain into the hybrid collectif.

On November 20, 2014, President Obama announced an executive action to temporarily halt the deportation of a large subpopulation of undocumented immigrants who met special conditions. These conditions included people who arrived in the United States before 2010 and have at least one child who is a US citizen or legal resident, or those who came to the country before the age of sixteen. This much needed action has provided temporary relief for an estimated 5 million people currently in the United States. Unfortunately, none of the main actors in this book, nor another 6–7 million undocumented people who don't qualify, will benefit from this stopgap measure. In essence, Obama has provided a federal Band-Aid for some of those already on US soil.

This executive action, however, does nothing to change the way the border is policed. It does not stop the hybrid collectif. It does nothing to slow down the flow of undocumented migration.

Every single day down on *la linea* you can find Lucho, Memo, Christian, Maricela, and José. These are people searching for a better life or looking to repair a family fragmented by transnational migration. For those caught in the complicated and far-reaching web of this social process, there is no "happy ending." Memo and Lucho continue to struggle each day to make ends meet while remaining under the radar of immigration enforcement. Memo keeps telling me that as soon as he has enough money, he is going to go back to Mexico to see his ailing mother. It has been almost twenty years since she kissed his face. These days, though, this family reunion is mostly fantasy. While writing this conclusion, I got a call from Memo, who told me that he had fallen on hard times. Work opportunities had dried up, and he had suddenly taken to soliciting day labor in front of his local Home Depot store. For the first time in our six years of friendship, he asked me for money to buy groceries. Despite these setbacks, he is still an optimist. He keeps promising that after he goes to see his mother, he will take another camera with him when he crosses back through the desert. Lucho, on the other hand, is doing his best to never return to the Arizona wilderness. He spends a great deal of time looking over his shoulder.

Christian has been trying to save money in hopes of getting tourist visas so that he can bring his aging parents to visit him in New York. He hasn't seen them in more than a decade. More importantly, he wants them to bring his thirteen-year-old son, whom he has never held in his arms. Christian has also had a rough go of it recently. In the fall of 2014, he was standing on a fifteen-foot ladder removing asbestos from a building when he slipped and fell through a series of wooden scaffoldings. He lay on the ground unconscious for ten minutes. His coworkers were convinced he was dead. Because many people at the job site lacked papers and were afraid to call 911, Christian was driven to a free clinic where he was given some bandages, painkillers, and an ice pack. When I saw him four months after the fall, he was still limping and suffering from internal pain that had not yet been diagnosed by a doctor. Having gained some mobility in his legs, he was hoping to pick up part-time work doing light cleaning in office buildings at night.

Maricela's three children are slowly adjusting to life without their mom and are now being supported by remittances that Christian sends as often as humanly possible. Every day Vanessa does her best to fill the void left in their hearts by Mari's absence.

José's girlfriend, Tamara, is busy raising their infant daughter, and she maintains her promise to wait for him. She frequently emails me to ask if I have any news about his whereabouts. Tamara wants to one day migrate to New York like her mother so that she can earn American dollars to send back to Cuenca to support her child.

Gustavo and Paulina are still holding out hope that their son is alive. I frequently speak with Paulina by phone about new contacts she has made with *pasadores* who might know the route that José took. I promised her and Gustavo that I would continue to help them search for their son, which means I spend a lot of time on the phone talking to *coyotes* and trying to find people who were traveling in José's group. On sporadic visits to Arizona over the past year, Mike Wells, Bob Kee, and I have stumbled around the Sonoran Desert in the Atascosa Mountains looking for any sign of José. He has not appeared.

During the course of writing this book I discovered a poem by O'odham poet Ofelia Zepeda (1995) titled "The Floods of 1993 and Others." There is one stanza that I now find myself reading over and over again:

> Remains.
> His ashes are now at the bottom of the hill.
> The rain has washed them down,
>   mixing them back into the dirt from where he came.
> He screamed those silent screams.
> You thought you heard them in between his laughter.
> It was a confused message. Like many messages from adolescents.
> A fifteen-year-old can't be expected to understand them all.
> The ashes have found their way to the four directions by now.
> Mixed with clouds that bring rain.
> Or perhaps they have made their way to the Gila River when it flows in
>   Pima country.
> Surely some have made their way to the big rivers, floating on down to
>   Mexico, becoming part of the sandy, warm beach where you smile at the
>   crabs that run sideways.

Wherever José may be, perhaps he is warm and smiling.

ACKNOWLEDGMENTS

MIKE WELLS

I would like to thank Maricela's and José's families in Ecuador and New York; the people of Arivaca; everyone at La Gitana Cantina, including Fern, Penny, and especially Gary; and all the students of the Undocumented Migration Project. Much love to my wife, Grace, and daughters, Poppy and Juniper. Thanks to Jason for including me on this project from the very beginning.

JASON DE LEÓN

This book would not exist without the trust and openness of the people whose lives are documented in these pages. I can never repay their generosity. I only hope that I can be a positive conduit to tell the stories that they are not able to tell themselves. I want to thank Maricela's family, especially the people I call Christian and Vanessa, for opening their homes and lives to me in New York and Ecuador. I want to thank José Tacuri's family for trusting me to tell their painful story even as it continues to lie open like an unhealable wound. Finally, I want to thank Lucho and Memo for all that they have given me over the years. Memo, *eres mi hermano*.

I owe much to the many people and institutions that inspired and supported the Undocumented Migration Project (UMP) over the years and who helped make this book a reality. Victor Baldillo from San José La Laguna, Tlaxcala,

Mexico, shared his harrowing Sonoran Desert border crossing story with me one summer day in 2004 while the two of us sat in an excavation unit. His friendship changed the course of my life and inspired me to become the anthropologist that I am today. *¡Nos vemos en la playa mano!* Lauren Benz, thanks for giving me the crazy idea to travel to Arizona to see what archaeology could tell us about undocumented migration.

The seeds of the UMP were first planted while I taught at the University of Washington (UW). UW's Royalty Research Fund Grant provided me with much needed resources for the first field season in 2009. In addition, I received a RAPID Grant (Award No. 0939554) from the National Science Foundation (NSF) to conduct pilot research in Arizona and Mexico. Thanks to Deborah Winslow at NSF for believing in this project in those early days.

I want to thank Bettina Shell-Duncan, who was the UW Department of Anthropology chair while I was there, for going above and beyond the call of duty to support all of my research efforts. I also want to thank Luis Fraga for all his support during my two years at UW. Danny Hoffman was a great colleague, neighbor, and friend while I was in Seattle. Rick Aguilar was my trusted *compuercñero*. Finally, I owe an incredible debt of gratitude to María Elena García and José Antonio Lucero for their mentorship, friendship, and love over the years.

I am grateful to call the University of Michigan my research home and am consistently humbled by the institution's unwavering financial, logistical, and intellectual support of my work. I want to thank Michigan's College of Letters, Science, and Art for the subvention it provided to assist in the publication of the many photos included in this book.

The Department of Anthropology at Michigan is the most collegial place I've ever worked. Tom Fricke, the department chair, has had my back since day one and I am eternally grateful. My many colleagues in Anthro have been the source of much support and intellectual stimulation, and this book would not have materialized without them. I would especially like to thank Rob Beck, Ruth Behar, Maureen Devlin, Jatin Dua, Gillian Feeley-Harnik, Kriszti Fehervary, Raven Garvey, Matt Hull, Webb Keane, John Kingston, Stuart Kirsch, Alaina Lemon, Bruce Mannheim, John Mitani, Erik Mueggler, John O'Shea, Jeff Parsons, Damani Partridge, Liz Roberts, Andrew Shryock, Carla Sinopoli, John Speth, Brian Stewart, Milford Wolpoff, Henry Wright, and Lisa Young. Chapters and ideas from this book greatly benefited from feedback I received from faculty and students in the Anthropology Department's sociocultural colloquium, the AnthroHistory workshop, and the Museum of Anthropology's brownbag series, and audiences at numerous institutions that invited me to present lectures between 2009 and 2015. I want to thank Amy Rundquist and Julie Winningham for all of their administrative support in the Department of Anthropology, which I needed to do every aspect of this project from fieldwork to time off for writing to procuring funds for elements of book production. I also want to thank our anthropology librarian Jennifer Nason Davis for scouring the archives for possible images to use in this book. A shout-out to my homegirl Amanda Krugliak for being an incredible collaborator in all things exhibition related. Thanks to Richard Barnes for providing new lenses for viewing the migration experience. Thanks to Sid Smith and the Institute for the Humanities for their unwavering support of the UMP and for making the State of Exception exhibition a reality. I want to thank John Doering-White, Amelia Frank-Vitale, and Matan Kaminer for being inspiring students that I am privileged to work with. 谢谢 to Howard "Amigo" Tsai, Jonathan "Uncle Johnny" Devore, and Randall "Kevin" Hicks for letting me into the club. Thanks to Dan Nemser and Loren Dobkin for being awesome friends. I especially want to thank my good buddy and life coach Michael Lempert for helping me at all stages of book writing and for reminding me that there are always good deals to be had on bubble tea.

I wrote the bulk of this book while in residence as a Weatherhead Fellow at the School for Advanced Research (SAR). I want to thank the people associated with SAR for all of their support, especially Lynn Baca, Flannery Davis, Cynthia Geoghegan, Isidro Gutierrez, Laura Holt, Randy Montoya, Lisa Pacheco, Elysia Poon, Carol Sandoval, Ray Sweeney, and Nicole Taylor. Extra gratitude to former SAR president James Brooks for bringing together such a wonderful cohort for the 2013–2014 academic year. I was privileged to spend the year at SAR (mostly in the Billiards Room) with my cohort: Patricia Baudino, Kent Blansett, Debbie Boehm, Jon Daehnke, Islah Jad, George Karandinos, He Li, Amy Lonetree, and Máijá Tailfeathers. Special thanks to Jordan Wilson for all the kitchen tips. I want to thank Laurie Hart for being the special person that she is and Philippe Bourgois for his friendship and mentorship. Also thanks to Chile Torreado for making the best damn breakfast burritos in New Mexico.

Parts of the research included in this book were supported by an Emerging Explorer award that I received from National Geographic in 2013. I want to thank the NatGeo staff for their continuing support, especially Fabio Amador, Anastasia Cronin, Alex Moen, Christopher Thornton, and Cheryl Zook.

Thanks to my many colleagues at other institutions who provided helpful feedback on various chapters and ideas that made it into this book, especially Shannon Dawdy, Randy McGuire, and Lynn Stephen. Thanks to François Richard for being my French partner in crime.

I owe a great debt to Kate Marshall, my amazing editor at UC Press, for her unwavering support, patience, and honest feedback throughout the process of conceptualizing, writing, and editing this book. Kate's editorial spidey sense both pushed this book in the right directions and reined me in when it was necessary. I couldn't have asked for a better writing coach. I want to thank Dore Brown, the production magician at UC Press, for turning my roughly hewn and coffee-stained manuscript into the finished product you hold in your hands. Thanks also to Stacy Eisenstark for wrangling various elements of the book and Ryan Furtkamp and Alex Dahne for all the hard work they have done to promote this project. Thanks to my patient and diligent copyeditor Steven B. Baker for crossing my I's, dotting my T's, and not quitting this project despite my insistence on flooding the pages with untranslated Spanish slang and made-up words. I also want to thank UC Press for believing in this project and allowing me and Mike to include so many photos.

Three reviewers provided honest and productive critiques and comments on an earlier draft of this book. Their insightful feedback greatly improved the manuscript's content. Any errors or omissions are entirely my fault.

Although I don't write too much about the town of Arivaca in this book, it was the heart, soul, and epicenter of the UMP from 2010 to 2014. It has also become my second home. I can never repay the love and support that Arivaca has given me and my students over the years. Thanks to the Arivaca Action Center for letting us run our lab out of its space for several field seasons. I want to give a big hug to my friend Jill Farrell for showing me what community really means. Thanks to Danny McGuire, pool player Gary, Holly, Kenny and Debbie, Octavio, Ronnie, Sean Quintero, Shawn Rojas, Kathy Sheldon, Bradley Staub, Tim and Uncle JoJo. If you the reader are ever in Arivaca, make sure to stop at La Gitana Cantina. It is the best watering hole in North America and possibly the world. I want to thank the cantina owners Maggie and Rich Milinovitch, Penny and Steve Shepard (and Buster and Chico), and Fern Robinson for being amazing folks who were always willing to lend the UMP a hand. Props to my Arivaca cousin Drew C. Do. Love you, brother.

I got to know many incredible people in Tucson over the years. Thanks to Mike Wilson, Norma Price, and all the Tucson Samaritans. Thanks also to my friend Robin Reineke for lending me a hand more times than I can count and for showing me what it means to work daily for change. If you want to learn more about the work that Robin and others are doing to connect families with the remains of loved ones who have died in the desert, check out the Colibrí Center for Human Rights (http://colibricenter.org/). The Tucson filmmaker and author Kathryn Ferguson has long been my desert spirit guide, and I am proud to call her my friend. I owe an unpayable debt to Bob Kee, "Zen Master," for all that he has shown me over the years, including what it really means to be a humanitarian.

In Nogales, Mexico, many people provided me with guidance and support during numerous seasons of fieldwork. Thanks to don Paco and doña Hilda Loureiro for opening the doors of the Juan Bosco shelter to me for research purposes and for helping more than a million migrants get a warm bed and something to eat since the early 1980s. Thanks to the many shelter workers who assisted my research and, more important, showed me how to be positive in the face of the unrelenting pain and misery that they work daily to alleviate. I especially want to thank Fernando, Polo, José, Erik, and Netchy.

Jackson (Jackrabbit) Hathorn was the first student I convinced to accompany me while I trekked through the desert in 2009. I couldn't have asked for a better companion or DJ. Over the years, an army of undergraduate and graduate students worked to make the Undocumented Migration Project a success, and I want to name and thank them here. UMP class of 2009: Briana Ledesma. UMP Class of 2010: Rachel Emadi, Ester García, Morgan Chalmers Hamill, Adrienne Iannone, Ian Ostericher™, Hilary Payne, Graham Pruss, Steven Ritchey, Austin Shipman, Shaylee Stokes, Sasa Vulovic, Sophia Yackshaw. UMP Class of 2012: Johnquil Baker, Reanne Barrett, Mario Castillo, Alarica Dietzen, Sam Grabowksa, Magda Mankel, Lauren Nelson, Rolando Palacio, Ashley (Schewbacca) Schubert, and Parth Singh. UMP Class of 2013: Anna Antoniou, Emily Butt, Andrea Dantus, Marcela Dorfsman-Hopkins, Jordan Edward Davis, Bill De La Rosa, John Lefeber, Hannah Kass, Dan Lee, Erika Loveland, and Leah Mlyn.

Many students at the University of Michigan spent years working to make sense of the thousands of artifacts and hundreds of hours of audio that we brought back each year from the field. The lab would be unpassable were it not for Ariana Dixon, Anna (Bri) Forringer-Beal, Emma DuRoss, Emma Hays, Poli Hristova, Melissa Needham, Michelle Vosters, Joia Sanders, and Greg (2 Dope) Sollish. Thanks to honorary UMP members María Inclán, Eduardo ("Lalo") García, and Alice Wright.

I want to thank the Institute for Field Research (IFR), which sponsored the UMP field schools over the years and enabled me to bring dozens of undergraduates into the desert to learn about migration and anthropology. IFR director Ran Boytner has believed in the UMP since day one, and I am grateful for all his support. The IFR is a world-class organization and I am proud to be affiliated with it.

Thanks to Steve Velasquez at the Smithsonian for believing that the things migrants leave behind are worth preserving.

Thanks to Raúl Pastrana for helping me to raise awareness about the life of José Tacuri.

I want to thank the Drive-By Truckers for providing the southern rock score for the countless hours I spent driving through the Sonoran Desert over the years.

Thanks to Bruce Springsteen for writing Side B of *Born in the USA*. It was the un-ironic soundtrack as I wrote major sections of this book.

During my last season of fieldwork in the Arizona desert and the sixteen months I spent writing this book, I leaned on Jason Isbell's record *Southeastern* both to get me through the bad times and to celebrate the small victories. I want to thank him for consistently demonstrating the power of words and music to create worlds.

My pal (and hero) Will Vlautin provided a ton of moral and editorial support during the course of this project. Thanks, man.

Several people stuck with the UMP over the years and provided me with more inspiration and help than I can ever give back. Kate Hall has become our resident taphonomic expert, and she, Ian Ostericher, and Jess Beck provided much of the data on decomposition in chapter 3. Olivia Waterhouse has consistently reminded the rest of us of what it means to do research with heart. I want to thank Aaron Naumann for showing us how to spirit ride and for keeping me sane the first year we ran a large field project. Maddie Naumann started out as my undergraduate thesis student and quickly became family. I am glad that we are now bonded by the baby lioness that she and Aaron named Leona and superstoked that Josie has decided to join the UMP clan. Thanks to Justine Drummond for being the UMP's moral compass, even when she doesn't want to be. Hugs to Chloe Bergsma-Safar for being one of the kindest souls I know. Thanks to Murphy (Murphette) Van Sparrentak for showing us what it means when someone says, "Let me explain something to you." I'll meet you up on the hill, sister! Haeden Stewart is the one who got away but who still can't seem to get away. I love you, man. Finally, I owe my friend and longtime collaborator Cameron Gokee more than he will ever know. Thanks for everything C$.

I want to thank my family for all of the support and encouragement they gifted me during the research and writing of this book. Lots of love to my in-laws, Barbara and Fred Bigham, and my brother-in-law, Frits Bigham. Special thanks to my Uncle Dave Shields for always reminding me that I could finish this thing.

Thanks to Kirk French for still talking to me after all we've been through.

Much love to Geoff (Jefe) Vasile for being my brother from another mother. Fick-a-dee-dee-dee.

Big ups to Mike Wells for coming with me on all these journeys, starting with that Bad Religion concert at the Santa Monica Civic Center in 1993.

Thanks, Santi, Willie, and Holmes.

I want to thank my mom for encouraging me to dream.

Thanks, Iggy, for teaching me about the important things in life.

Finally, there is no person in the world who I owe more to than my wife, Abigail Bigham. She was there for all of the triumphs, pain, sorrow, and aggravation that went into the last five years of research. Her patience with me throughout the writing process is a testament to her strong character, innate kindness, and sense of humor. Pooch, you are my night and day.

Border Patrol Apprehensions, Southern Border Sectors, 2000–2014

Sector	2000	2001	2002	2003	2004	2005	2006
San Diego, CA	151,681	110,075	100,681	111,515	138,608	126,909	142,122
El Centro, CA	238,126	172,852	108,273	92,099	74,467	55,726	61,469
Yuma, AZ	108,747	78,385	42,654	56,638	98,060	138,438	118,537
Tucson, AZ	**616,346**	**449,675**	**333,648**	**347,263**	**491,771**	**439,090**	**392,104**
El Paso, TX	115,696	112,857	94,154	88,816	104,399	122,689	122,261
Big Bend (formerly Marfa), TX	13,689	12,087	11,392	10,319	10,530	10,536	7,517
Del Rio, TX	157,178	104,875	66,985	50,145	53,794	68,510	42,634
Laredo, TX	108,973	87,068	82,095	70,521	74,706	75,342	74,843
Rio Grande Valley, TX	133,243	107,844	89,927	77,749	92,947	134,188	110,531
Yearly totals	1,643,679	1,235,718	929,809	905,065	1,139,282	1,171,428	1,072,018
Annual percentage of apprehensions by sector							
San Diego, CA	9	9	11	12	12	11	13
El Centro, CA	14	14	12	10	7	5	6
Yuma, AZ	7	6	5	6	9	12	11
Tucson, AZ	**37**	**36**	**36**	**38**	**43**	37	37
El Paso, TX	7	9	10	10	9	10	11
Big Bend (formerly Marfa), TX	1	1	1	1	1	1	1
Del Rio, TX	10	8	7	6	5	6	4
Laredo, TX	7	7	9	8	7	6	7
Rio Grande Valley, TX	8	9	10	9	8	11	10
Total percentage*	100	99	100	100	101	99	100

SOURCE: "Total Illegal Alien Apprehensions by Month," fiscal years 2000–2014, U.S. Customs and Border Patrol, www.cbp.gov.

NOTE: **Boldfacing** indicates the sector with the highest number of apprehensions in a given year.

*Because of rounding, some totals do not equal 100 percent.

2007	2008	2009	2010	2011	2012	2013	2014	Total by location
152,459	162,392	118,712	68,565	42,447	28,461	27,496	29,911	1,512,034
55,881	40,962	33,520	32,562	30,191	23,916	16,306	14,511	1,050,861
37,994	8,363	6,952	7,116	5,833	6,500	6,106	5,902	726,225
378,323	**317,709**	**241,667**	**212,202**	**123,285**	**120,000**	120,939	87,915	4,671,937
75,464	30,310	14,998	12,251	10,345	9,678	11,154	12,339	937,411
5,537	5,390	6,357	5,288	4,036	3,964	3,684	4,096	114,422
22,919	20,761	17,082	14,694	16,144	21,720	23,510	24,255	705,206
56,715	43,659	40,571	35,287	36,053	44,872	50,749	44,049	925,503
73,430	75,476	60,992	59,766	59,243	97,762	**154,453**	**256,393**	1,583,944
858,722	705,022	540,851	447,731	327,577	356,873	414,397	481,385	12,229,557
18	23	22	15	13	8	7	6	
7	6	6	7	9	7	4	3	
4	1	1	2	2	2	1	1	
44	**45**	**45**	**47**	**38**	**34**	29	18	
9	4	3	3	3	3	3	3	
1	1	1	1	1	1	1	1	
3	3	3	3	5	6	6	5	
7	6	8	8	11	13	12	9	
9	11	11	13	18	27	37	**53**	
102	100	100	100	100	101	100	99	

Border Patrol Apprehensions, Tucson Sector, by Distance from the Border, Fiscal Years 2010 and 2011

	Number of apprehensions (percentage)	
	2010	2011
0–1 mile	43,188 (20%)	25,625 (22%)
1–5 miles	56,995 (27%)	29,835 (25%)
5–20 miles	49,405 (24%)	33,789 (28%)
20+ miles	60,091 (29%)	29,881 (25%)
Total	209,679 (100%)	119,130 (100%)

SOURCE: GAO 2012: figures 33 and 34.

NOTES

1. DHS is a cabinet department of the United States federal government created following the events of September 11, 2001. It absorbed twenty-two agencies including the Immigration and Naturalization Service, which had previously housed the Border Patrol. Three new agencies were created to deal with immigration issues: U.S. Customs and Border Protection (CBP), which includes the Border Patrol; Immigration and Customs Enforcement (ICE), which typically handles things like deportations and trade regulations; and United States Citizenship and Immigration Services (USCIS), which processes administrative issues related to citizenship.

2. Falcón 2001; Hsieh 2014; Ortiz et al. 2014.

3. *La linea* (the line) is the name that migrants often use to describe the 1.3-mile physical space between the two major ports of entry in Nogales, Mexico (see chapter 5 for detailed discussion).

4. Grupo Beta is a Mexican federal agency primarily responsible for protecting migrants who are en route to the United States or have been recently deported. This organization is discussed in more detail in chapter 5.

5. All names are pseudonyms unless otherwise noted.

6. *Pinche* may be loosely translated as "damn" in milder contexts and "fucking" in more spirited ones.

7. For example, see Reeves and Caldwell 2011.

8. Vicens 2014.

9. See the excellent historical analysis of this event in Dunn 2009.

10. Roughly translated as a "fucking pile."

11. Durand and Massey 2004; Guerin-Gonzales 1994.

12. *Campesino* means "peasant" or "dirt farmer." *La migra* is slang for Border Patrol.

13. U.S. Customs and Border Protection, "United States Border Patrol: Southwest Border Sectors; Total Illegal Alien Apprehensions by Fiscal Year (Oct. 1st through Sept. 30th)," www.cbp.gov/sites/default/files/documents/BP%20Southwest%20Border%20Sector%20Apps%20FY1960%20-%20FY2014_0.pdf.

14. Anti-Defamation League 2012.

15. Bazzell 2007.

16. Prior to 1986, the O'odham people were officially known as the Papago.

17. See Cadava 2011; Ettinger 2009.

18. It is beyond the scope of this book to address the impact of undocumented migration on the Tohono O'odham Nation, and none of the archaeological work I conducted occurred on the reservation. No community along the southern border, however, has been as negatively affected by border crossings, migrant fatalities, or Border Patrol presence as the Tohono O'odham.

19. Nabhan 1982:26.

20. Zepeda 1982:17.

21. Ettinger 2009; St. John 2011.

22. Hernández 2010; Nevins 2002; Andreas 2009.

23. Dunn 1996, 2009.

24. *Coyote* is a Spanish euphemism for a human smuggler.

25. Clark 2012.

26. Sullivan 2010.

27. De León 2008.

28. Urrea 2004.

29. Those looking for more sensitive popular accounts of border-crossing stories are encouraged to check out Luis Alberto Urrea's novel *The Devil's Highway* (2004) and Ferguson et al.'s book *Crossing with the Virgin* (2010). For an exceptional journalistic take on Central American migrants crossing Mexico, see *The Beast* by Oscar Martínez (2010).

30. L. Chavez does, however, offer some observational data from Tijuana's soccer field (1998:45–52). Also see Sergio Chavez's fascinating ethnography (2011) of undocumented workers crossing through official ports of entry.

31. Spener 2009:169.

32. Holmes 2013. The Triqui people are from the mountainous Mixteca region of Oaxaca, Mexico.

33. Holmes 2013:9.

34. A story that ran on Fox News about the Undocumented Migration Project in 2012 included a stock photo of two masked Border Patrol agents on ATVs with bales of marijuana strapped to the front of their vehicles. The caption to this image read, "Shoes, backpacks and other objects discarded in the desert by undocumented immigrants have been collected by a team of anthropologists to document the difficult journey they make to get into the United States" (see EFE 2012).

35. See Annerino 2009; Connover 1987.

36. Holmes 2013:14–17.

37. I use *gringo* here not in a racialized way, though race often seems to be the elephant in the room during these types of endeavors. *Gringo* is intended to mark Holmes as an American. Mexicans will commonly call all U.S. citizens, including Latinos, *gringos*.

38. Annerino 2009:54–58.

39. Holmes 2013:25.

40. Oscar Martinez's (2013) excellent journalistic account of Central American migrants crossing Mexico is an exception.

41. Holmes 2013:19.

42. Singer and Massey 1998:562.

43. Anzaldúa 2007; Limón 1994; J. D. Saldívar 1997; R. Saldívar 1990, 2006; Paredes 1958.

44. J. D. Saldívar 1997:xiii, quoting Foucault.

45. Marcus 1998:3–132.

46. This jurisdiction includes 262 miles of border, encompasses approximately 90,500 square miles, and contains a wide range of environments (e.g., mountain ranges and valleys). Parts of the Tucson Sector include protected federal lands (e.g., Buenos Aires National Wild Life Refuge [BANWR] and the Coronado National Forest), as well as public state lands. Internally it is subdivided into eight "stations" (see the map on page 15), and our survey work focused primarily on two stations, Nogales and Tucson. The Nogales station, which the Border Patrol describes as "high desert terrain with rugged mountains to rolling hills with numerous deep canyons," includes 30 miles of border and approximately 1,800 square miles. The Tucson station has "terrain that varies from open valleys to rugged mountains and . . . [is] covered with various desert shrubs" and includes 24 miles of border and 3,790 square miles (GAO 2012:54). Our survey area focused on the western part of the Tucson Sector, in the corridor between the Nogales and Sasabe ports of entry. The survey's western edge extended to the foothills of the Baboquivari Mountains, which is the boundary line of the Tohono O'odham reservation, and extended north to the town of Three Points. The survey area's eastern edge was demarcated by US Interstate 19 and extended north to the southern edge of the town of Green Valley. This corridor is approximately 1,081 square miles (2,800 sq. km). The area that we surveyed encompassed approximately 33.5 square miles (86.78 sq. km) and cut across the Santa Cruz and Pima County lines.

Because of the size of this corridor and the difficulty involved in accessing some of the terrain, we were unable to conduct a survey of any large area. Instead we opted to sample parts of this corridor systematically, based on differences in topography, distance from the border, and information obtained from interviews with migrants about where they had previously crossed. Although our survey area is relatively small in comparison to the corridor's overall size, our sampling strategy enabled us to document the different stages of the crossing process and their associated sites and artifacts (see Gokee and De León 2014). Our base camp was the small unincorporated town of Arivaca, Arizona. We focused on this particular corridor because it was a primary crossing point for people leaving from Altar, Sasabe, and Nogales and therefore it was relatively easy to correlate the ethnographic data collected in those Mexican towns with the archaeological data collected on the Arizona side.

47. In subsequent chapters, I describe some of the geographic and environmental features of the UMP survey area that act as natural deterrents to the movement of people. However, much of what is described can be generalized for the entire Sonoran Desert region.

48. Forty-five interviews were conducted by other UMP researchers in the summer of 2013 in Nogales and Altar.

49. Forty-five interviews conducted in 2013 were semistructured.

50. See De León and Cohen (2005) for discussion of this method.

51. The archaeological work was conducted as part of a multiyear field school supported by the Institute for Field Research that involved dozens of students and postdoctoral researchers.

52. This editing sometimes included combining separate interviews with the same person into one narrative. Occasionally, missing words were added to complete sentence fragments and extraneous sections of interviews were deleted to preserve flow (see the comment on editing in Bourgois 1995:341n20).

53. In general, everyone (documented and undocumented) wanted his or her real name used. People were disappointed when I told them that I needed to change names to protect their identity. However, most of the main characters in the book chose their own pseudonyms.

54. Galtung 1969 and Farmer 2004. For specific discussions of structural violence and immigration enforcement, see Nevins 2005 and Spener 2009.

55. See De León, Gokee, and Schubert 2015.

56. Žižek 2008.

57. Ruiz Marrujo 2009.

58. Men do get sexually assaulted during the migration process, but none of my interlocutors described this happening to them. Given the stigma surrounding male rape, it is no surprise that the subject was taboo. On the few occasions that men described male rape, it was in the form of stories they had heard about bandits who assaulted men who tried to stop attacks on women.

59. Ruiz Marrujo 2009:31.

60. The sexual assault that border crossers experience continues to be poorly documented in the migration literature.

61. Mulvey 1975.

62. Simaski and Sapp 2013: table 10.

63. Snow 1989:31.

64. See, e.g., Biehl 2005; Wright 2013.

65. Bourgois and Schonberg 2009; Hoffman 2011.

66. For example, Pulitzer Prize–winning author Jose Antonio Vargas and various student activists have recently "outted themselves" by declaring their undocumented status publicly.

67. Schonberg and Bourgois 2002:389.

1. PREVENTION THROUGH DETERRENCE

1. Lumholtz 1990:337.

2. Not a pseudonym.

3. Moreno 2012.

4. Moreno 2012.

5. Oscar329, 8/18/2012, in Moreno 2012.

6. Agamben 1998, 2005. For border studies drawing on Agamben, see, for example, Doty 2011; Jones 2009; and Salter 2008.

7. Jones 2009.

8. Also see De León, Gokee, and Schubert 2015.

9. Doty 2011.

10. Cornelius 2001; Nevins 2005.

11. Mbembe 2003:24.

12. Doty 2011:607.

13. Salter 2008:369.

14. Data from "Deaths on the Border and the Recovered Remains Project," Coalición de Derechos Humanos, http://derechoshumanosaz.net/projects/arizona-recovered-bodies-project/.

15. Reineke 2013.

16. The flier also refers to the risk migrants face of "ending up victims of organized crime." This phrasing is similar to many other instances mentioned in this book in which the federal government attempts to shift blame to others (e.g., the desert, smugglers, migrants themselves) for injuries sustained during the migration process.

17. See note 1 of the Introduction for a discussion of the relationship between the INS and the Department of Homeland Security.

18. Dunn 2009:21–22.

19. Dunn 2009:59–60.

20. Dunn 2009:61.

21. Dunn 2009:61.

22. Nevins 2002:90–92.

23. Dunn 2009:61.

24. This has also been referred to as the Southwest Border Strategy (GAO 1997). While the official title has changed over the past two decades, the general strategy that uses the natural environment (along with various deportation practices [De León 2013a] and legal proceedings) to impede undocumented migration is often simply known as Prevention Through Deterrence.

25. USBP 1994:6.

26. Ettinger 2009:156–157.

27. In the late nineteenth and early twentieth century, many undocumented Chinese and eastern European migrants who could not pass inspection at Ellis Island or who were banned based on ethnic exclusion laws attempted to cross the Sonoran Desert on foot and died as a result of dehydration, exposure, and murder by bandits.

(Ettinger 2009: fig. 2; St. John 2011:106). Federal agent's 1926 testimony quoted in Ettinger 2009:157.

28. USBP 1994:2.

29. GAO 1997, 2006, 2012.

30. USBP 1994:7.

31. Heyman 1995:266.

32. Heyman 1995; Singer and Massey 1998.

33. USBP 1994:1.

34. Dunn 1996.

35. García 2006.

36. GAO 2001:24 ("harsh"); Haddal 2010:19 ("inhospitable").

37. See, e.g., GAO 2001.

38. USBP 1994:4.

39. GAO 1997:50.

40. Cornelius 2001; Nevins 2002; Doty 2011; Magaña 2012.

41. Haddal 2010:19.

42. GAO 1997: appendix V, table.

43. Comment by "TYRANNASAURUS, 8/19/2012" in Moreno 2012.

44. See Rubio-Goldsmith et al. 2006.

45. GAO 1997: appendix V.

46. Shifts in enforcement strategies have recently made South Texas the most common crossing corridor on the southern border. See appendix B and discussion in the conclusion.

47. GAO 2001:3.

48. Rubio Goldsmith et al. 2006; D. Martínez et al. 2013.

49. Haddal 2012:32.

50. See Haddal 2010: fig. 10.

51. Anderson 2013: table 1.

52. "Deaths on the Border and the Recovered Remains Project."

53. Trevizo 2013b.

54. Nevins 2002:7.

2. DANGEROUS GROUND

1. Cohn 1987.

2. Cohn 1987:690.

3. Callon and Law 1995.

4. Latour 2005.

5. Bennett 2010:21.

6. For example, Harraway 2003; Latour 2004; Keane 2006.

7. See Gell 1988; Basso 1996; Fuentes 2006:129.

8. See Kirksey and Helmreich 2010.

9. Callon and Law 1995:485.

10. Stanescu 2013:143–144.

11. See, e.g., Nading's discussion (2012) of the complex historical relationship between dengue-carrying mosquitoes and health care workers.

12. See, e.g., Smart 2014:4–5.

13. For discussion of beef-processing plants and the invisibility of workers and animals, see Pachirat 2013.

14. Callon and Law 1995:490.

15. Callon and Law 1995:503.

16. See the discussion of human exceptionalism and species hierarchy in Stanescu 2013.

17. Callon and Law 1997:168.

18. Latour (2005:10) refers to this type of agency attribution as reductionistic forms of "symbolic projection" or a "naturalist type of causality," both of which underestimate the actual agency generated by nonhumans.

19. Callon and Law 1995:503.

20. Duarte 2013.

21. Doty 2011.

22. Whatmore 2002. On animals as political subjects, see Hobson 2007.

23. Callon and Law 1995:504.

24. Callon and Law 1995:504.

25. Much of what I describe here can be generalized for the entire Sonoran Desert region.

26. The Border Patrol data come from numerous official visits (including ride-alongs) and dozens of encounters with agents in the field.

27. Humphreys and Watson 2009: table 2.1. Also see discussion of ethnography and fiction in Clifford 1986, Narayan 1999, and Fassin 2014.

28. Although it has not been publicly acknowledged, there is a high likelihood that Customs and Border Protection has been using small hand-held drones, some of which look like birds, to monitor the border in a manner similar to that used in the Middle East. Government contractors have been shopping hand-held drones at the annual Border Security Expo in Phoenix (see Todd Miller, "Tomgram: Todd Miller, Surveillance Surge on the Border," posted July 11, 2013, www.tomdispatch.com /blog/175723/ [accessed February 26, 2015]).

29. Migrants are often referred to as *pollos*, or "chickens." Conversely, smugglers are often called *coyotes* or *polleros* (chicken wranglers).

30. McGuire 2013:475.

31. Trevizo 2013b.

32. See chapter 5 for more detailed discussion of Grupo Beta, the Mexican government's immigration enforcement and search-and-rescue division.

33. For discussions of Sonoran Desert temperatures and rainfall, see Ffolliott and Gottfried 2008:72 and West 1993:9.

34. For discussion of migrant fatalities in the winter, see Trevizo 2013a.

35. West 1993:9; Hadley 1972; Ffolliott and Gottfried 2008:75.

36. See Sanchez 2010 and Lentz 2012.

37. Much of the dialogue is directly quoted from recorded interviews.

38. Magana 2008:x; see also chapter 6.

39. Bennett 2010:xiv.

40. Bennett 2010:xv.

41. Sundberg 2011.

42. Hobson (2007) makes this point when she pushes for the recognition of animals as nontraditional political actors: "I in no way argue for animals as possessing political agency in the rational, liberal sense—they cannot take part in institutional decision-making processes or verbally express a preference that we can interpret as such. Instead, the aim is to argue that animals are already part of the heterogeneous networks that constitute political life, which some have argued ultimately challenges how we conceive of politics in totality" (263).

43. Callon and Law 1997:172.

44. USBP 1994:4.

3. NECROVIOLENCE

1. As Fuentes (2006) notes: "[The] stress response we call 'fear' is a common pattern in all mammals. . . . The same basic physiological reaction occurs in a zebra when being attacked by a lion, a baboon when surprised by a leopard, and a human when involved in a car accident" (126).

2. All university and federal protocols were followed during this event. See the University of Michigan Committee on Use and Care of Animals protocol number PRO00003934.

3. National Pork Board 2008.

4. Shean et al. 1993:939; Reeves 2009:523.

5. Udey et al. 2011; Schultz et al. 2006; Tonkin et al. 2013.

6. Beck et al. 2014.

7. Much of what is presented here is an ethnographic expansion of data presented in Beck et al. 2014. Readers interested in more detailed information (e.g., distances that specific skeletal elements traveled from original death sites) should refer to this work.

8. At the time of this writing, no forensic research lab or "body farm" in southern Arizona exists that could supervise an experiment on human decomposition.

9. Nevins 2005; Magaña 2011; Doty 2011; De León, Gokee, and Schubert 2015.

10. In this case I am using the concept of *bare life* to include animals, which is beyond Agamben's definition (see Stanescu 2012:574).

11. Kirksey and Helmreich 2010:545. See also Malone, et al. 2014.

12. For example, Stanescu 2013; Nading 2012, 2014.

13. The number five includes the one control animal used in the 2012 experiment. See Beck et al. 2014.

14. Pachirat 2013.

15. On the importance of ethnography in multispecies anthropological work, see Smart 2014.

16. Stanescu 2012:568.

17. Haddal 2010:19 (emphasis added).

18. Trevizo 2013b.

19. Foucault (2007) defined biopower as "the set of mechanisms through which the basic biological features of the human species became the object of a political strategy, of a general strategy of power, or, in other words, how, starting from the 18th century, modern Western societies took on board the fundamental biological fact that human beings are a species" (1).

20. Mbembe 2003:12, 18.

21. Mbembe 2003:12, 13.

22. Londras 2008.

23. Human Rights Watch 2014.

24. Carcamo 2014.

25. Mbembe 2003:11.

26. "Deaths on the Border and the Recovered Remains Project," http://derechoshumanosaz.net/projects/arizona-recovered-bodies-project/.

27. "Border Wars," National Geographic, http://channel.nationalgeographic.com/channel/border-wars/.

28. Ortega and O'Dell 2013.

29. Other causes of death include car accidents, heart attacks, homicide, and suicide.

30. Martínez et al. 2013:12–17.

31. Doty 2011.

32. See, for example, Hernández 2010; Heyman 2009; ACLU 2014; De León, Gokee, and Schubert 2015.

33. See, for example, Scheper-Hughes 1992; Rév 1995; Verdery 1999; Klass and Goss 2003; Nudelman 2004; Williams 2004; Crossland 2009; O'Neil 2012.

34. See, for example, McFarland 2008; Krmpotich et al. 2010; Fontein 2010; C. Young and Light 2012.

35. Posel and Gupta 2009:306. See also O'Neil's discussion (2012) of bare death in Guatemala.

36. Díaz del Castillo 1956:352.

37. Ford 1998:103–104.

38. Foucault 1995:34.

39. Foucault 1995. For examples of body desecration in U.S. combat, see, for example, Nudelman 2004; and S. Harrison 2006, 2010.

40. Transcribed from Nina Golgowski, "Marine Filmed Urinating on Bodies of Dead Taliban Has No Regrets and Would Do It Again," *New York Daily News,* July 16, 2013, www.nydailynews.com/news/national/marine-no-regrets-urinating-taliban-article-1.1399764 (accessed February 28, 2015).

41. Coleman 1990:47.

42. Harrison 2006.

43. Quoted in Bassett 1933:48.

44. Johanasson 2012:78, 259; Lomnitz 2005:16.

45. I focus here exclusively on violent messages, but other scholars have highlighted more complex (and often ambiguous) forms of communication achieved through body manipulation (e.g., Verdery 1999; Guyer 2009; Fontein 2010).

46. Taussig 1984.

47. H. Young 2005:652–657.

48. Magaña 2011:164. Recent New World archaeological examples are offered in Townsend 1992:100; Nelson et al. 1992; Spencer and Redmond 2001:187; Sugiyama 2005; Valdez 2009.

49. For example, Holocaust deniers often point out that the corpses of millions of Jews are unaccounted for.

50. Robben 2005.

51. Crossland 2000:153; Robben 2005:131, 399–400.

52. Crossland 2000.

53. Boss 2007.

54. Boss 2007:105. For a discussion of this phenomenon in Argentina, see Robben 2005.

55. See the discussion of political bodies in Domanska 2005:403.

56. See, for example, Solecki 1975; O'Shea 1984; Nelson et al. 1992; Graeber 1995; Dennie 2009.

57. Stiner 2008:2113.

58. In his groundbreaking paper (1940), Efremov defined taphonomy as "the study of the transition (in all its details) of animal remains from the biosphere into the lithosphere" (85).

59. Sorg et al. 2012:477.

60. Nawrocki 2009:284.

61. Schiffer 1975:840–841.

62. Lyman 2010:3.

63. Shipman 1986.

64. Lyman 2010:12–13.

65. A. Darling 1998:735 (wooden mallet); "See the Silent Screams of 100 Mexican Mummies," *Atlas Obscura* (blog), *Slate*, August 26, 2013, www.slate.com/blogs /atlas_obscura/2013/08/26/see_the_silent_screams_of_a_hundred_mexican_ mummies_at_museo_de_las_momias.html (accessed March 2, 2015).

66. Dawdy 2006:719, 728.

67. Galloway et al. 1989; Galloway 1997.

68. Galloway 1997:142. Neither the cause of death nor the citizenship profile is explicitly listed in either publication. The implication is that these are primarily U.S. citizens who were murdered and dumped in the desert or who died of natural causes in this environment.

69. For example, between 1990 and 1999 the Pima County Office of the Medical Examiner handled an annual average of 12 border crosser deaths per year. Between

1999 and 2012, the average number of border crosser deaths was close to 163 per fiscal year (Martínez et al. 2013:12).

70. "Carnivores can also accelerate decomposition by disarticulating remains, consuming soft tissue, and gnawing skeletal material.... In the Southwest, carnivore activity, however, appears to occur during advanced decomposition, initial mummification, and skeletonization. Coyotes are the most abundant free-ranging scavengers in the Southwest, and both coyotes and dogs are known to transport desiccated body segments for consumption elsewhere. Bear and javelina also may be responsible for the consumption and transportation of bone" (Galloway 1997:146).

71. Kirk and Mossman 1998.

72. The focus here is largely on conditions in the summer, the season when these experiments were carried out. Keep in mind that people cross during all times of the year and may freeze to death in the winter, drown during the monsoon season, or die from other causes at any time of the year (e.g., snakebite). Although scavenging and decomposition are more rapid during hot months, carrion eaters likely consume migrants year-round.

73. For example, see the description in Urrea 2004:163–168.

74. Cattle were present on the property where this experiment was carried out, and they periodically sniffed the animal's body and ran into our motion sensor cameras.

75. Galloway 1997: table 1.

76. Unless otherwise noted, this description of the turkey vulture is based on Kirk and Mossman's thorough study (1998) of this bird.

77. Margalida et al. 2011.

78. Turkey vultures commonly feed on mammals ranging from rodents to large ungulates, as well as birds, reptiles, amphibians, and invertebrates (Kirk and Mossman 1998:8).

79. Quoted in Kohn 2007:7.

80. Kirk and Mossman 1998:14.

81. Some of the following information is from Beck et al. 2014.

82. Arizona OpenGIS Initiative for Deceased Migrants, www.humaneborders .info/app/map.asp (accessed February 28, 2015).

83. See De León 2013b.

84. See reviews of sky burial practices around the world in Martin 1996; see also Goss and Klass 1997. For an experiment with raptors, see Spradley et al. 2012.

85. Bloch and Parry 1996.

86. See, for example, Brandes 2001.

87. Posel and Gupta 2009:301.

88. Posel and Gupta (2009) note that even nonreligious people have a "strong resistance to the idea of a dead body as merely rotting flesh" (305).

In her study of political violence in South Africa in the 1980s, Rousseau (2009) describes how some murder victims were covered in explosives and blown up in an attempt to hide evidence. Although these victims were falsely labeled as "terrorists" by the state, what was left of their bodies was collected and buried by the police. The families of victims expressed shock that despite the extreme violence inflicted on their bodies by the police, they were not "thrown away," suggesting that even the state had a limit on how far they would wage war on a body (363).

89. Singer and Massey 1998.

90. In 2013 we observed ants chipping off pieces of pig bone and carrying them into their subterranean dwellings (Hall et al. 2014).

91. GAO 2006.

92. Stephen 2007:xv.

93. Magaña 2011.

94. Maddrell and Sidaway 2010 (deathscape). For a discussion of perimortem and postmortem osteological patterns of violence, see Walker 2001.

95. O'Donnabhain 2011:132.

96. I acted as Spanish translator for parts of this conversation.

4. MEMO AND LUCHO

1. *Habitus* refers to the set of learned perspectives, tastes, and dispositions people use to orient themselves in their relations with people and objects (Bourdieu 1977).

2. Limón 1994:123–140; also see Peña 2006.

3. Spanish speakers often pronounce "Jason" with a *y* instead of a hard *j*.

4. Memo and Lucho were previously referred to as Victor and Miguel in De León (2012). "I don't want to be called 'Victor,'" Memo told me one night. "The only 'Victor' I know looks like a fucking penguin! 'Memo' sounds much better!"

5. All dialogue is translated from Spanish unless otherwise noted.

6. Limón 1994:133.

7. The verb *chingar* means "to fuck" or "to screw," but it has a whole host of other meanings. *Chingaderas* are a form of language play that in this context amounts to "fucking around" with someone in a playful way (see Limón 1994).

8. Rosaldo 1989:150.

9. Scott 1985.

10. Peña 2006:160.

11. Although I interviewed dozens of women during the course of this research, I typically had more access to male migrants along *la linea*. This differential access was partly due to my gender, but women migrants also tended to have more social and economic capital and thus had funds to immediately try another crossing. This meant that they spent less time than men did "hanging out" on *la linea*. In addition, women make up less than 15 percent of all apprehended migrants (Simanski and Sapp 2013: table 10).

12. Limón 1994:135.

13. See the critique in Limón 1994:123–40.

14. Limón 1994:129; Paz 1961:73–82.

15. See Peña 2006:144.

16. To protect their identities, I have modified some of the details of Memo's and Lucho's lives.

17. Mexico experienced an oil boom between 1976 and 1982, the result of the 1973 Arab oil embargo and the discovery of new coastal petroleum sources. Following the end of the oil embargo and an increase in global supplies of petroleum, the Mexican economy crashed. This period of severe peso devaluation and hyperinflation is often referred to as the "lost decade" (Cerrutti and Massey 2004:21). When Memo left Mexico in 1988, undocumented migration flows were the highest they had been in three decades (Cerrutti and Massey 2004: figure 2.1).

18. He is referring to the American economic crisis that began in 2008.

19. Donato et al. 1992.

20. Colonia La Libertad is a neighborhood in Tijuana that sits on the Mexico-U.S. border. Prior to PTD, hundreds of people crossed the border there illegally every night in the 1980s (McDonnell 1986).

21. At one point while living in the United States, both Lucho and Memo were arrested for driving while intoxicated, which is a fairly common problem for working-class undocumented men (and many Americans). Both of them, along with dozens of male migrants I subsequently interviewed, often complained about missing certain cultural freedoms they had in Mexico, including being able to drink on the street and drive while drinking (also see Boehm 2012:77).

22. Keeping track of Memo's crossing stories was challenging, and on numerous occasions during our interviews and conversations, new crossing details emerged ranging from comedic to horrific. I have simplified the narrative here to focus on the last few attempts leading up to his presence in Nogales.

23. See chapter 5 for discussion of lateral deportation.

24. See, for example, Parks et al. 2009.

25. Office of the Press Secretary, White House, "Remarks by the President in the State of the Union Address," WhiteHouse.gov, February 12, 2013, http://www.whitehouse.gov /the-press-office/2013/02/12/remarks-president-state-union-address (accessed March 4, 2015).

26. Cornelius et al. 2008:3.

27. Cornelius et al. 2008:3.

28. Andreas 2009.

29. Boehm 2012:71–80.

30. Methodologically, one of the biggest problems I faced during ethnographic fieldwork was the transitory nature of my study population. Some people may spend only one or two days in Nogales before attempting another crossing, which made getting to know migrants quite difficult. The length of my relationship with interviewees often ranged from just a few hours to a couple of days maximum. In general, throughout the five years of fieldwork I struggled to develop methods that would give me deeper insight into the border-crossing process, which is often rapid, chaotic, and (no pun intended) difficult to document. Although I draw on several excellent previous studies of border crossings in this book, I find that the bulk of them suffer from a series of methodological constraints that limit the amount of ethnographic knowledge that can be produced. First, the majority of research projects focused on border

crossings rely almost exclusively on interviews with migrants conducted either in shelters or long after the crossing event is over (Slack and Whiteford 2011; O'Leary 2009). Admittedly, it is difficult to study a population that is constantly in motion, and researchers have had to develop different strategies to deal with this issue. In talking about her work with female migrants in the Juan Bosco shelter between September 2006 and June 2007, O'Leary (2009) comments on this issue and highlights the difficulty of working in this type of setting:

> On account of this fast-paced population turnover, a Rapid Appraisal (RA) method was chosen for this research.... Consistent with RA methods, a topic guide was used to interview migrant women who arrived at the shelter and to get to the heart of the migrant woman's experiences.... I began to visit the shelter every two weeks, with the goal of systematically collecting data. Each visit consisted of three consecutive nights from 7:00 PM to 10:00 PM in which I interviewed women who had been repatriated by U.S. immigration officials. In the ten months of the study ... I interviewed one hundred women. The number of women who showed up at the shelter each night was unpredictable. (92)

While O'Leary's work has produced important insights about the experiences of female migrants in the Sonoran Desert, the reliance on interviewing people in the shelter has several limitations. First, working inside the shelter often doesn't allow the interviewees to speak freely for fear of saying something that might upset their hosts (e.g., bad-mouthing Grupo Beta or complaining about their treatment by shelter workers). On numerous occasions, I spoke to the same people inside and outside Juan Bosco, and the details and tone of their stories were often dramatically different. For some respondents, the shelter was a setting where they themselves thought they should tell the most "fucked-up story" possible in order to elicit sympathy or please the researcher. Second, working exclusively in the shelter often means privileging the narratives of respondents whom the researcher knows only for a few hours. This limited interaction means that it becomes difficult to paint a nuanced picture of who these individuals are or what happens to them after this particular research encounter. Third, an interview-centered approach provides little ethnographic insight into other parts of the crossing process, including how people prepare to enter the desert and how they navigate the city of Nogales while not in the shelter. Still, I did find on occasion that formally interviewing people (in a way similar to O'Leary's strategy) could be useful for answering specific questions about the migration process and for producing information that complemented the other types of data that I was collecting. For this reason, Undocumented Migration Project researchers interviewed forty-five men and women using a semi-structured survey instrument in the spring and summer of 2013. A few of these 2013 interviews (particularly those with women) were conducted inside Juan Bosco.

31. Cornelius et al. 2008:3.

32. Border Patrol apprehended 4,463,083 people in the Tucson Sector between 2000 and 2013 (see appendix A). This number does not include those who succeeded in crossing without ever being apprehended, which means that the total number of crossing attempts in the region is likely much higher. (For a discussion of the interpretation issues surrounding apprehension statistics, see Andreas 2009:85–112).

5. DEPORTED

1. Dunn 1996; Lucht 2012; Andreas 2009; Andersson 2014.

2. Alvarez 1995:451.

3. That is, forcible removal of "aliens."

4. Peutz and De Genova 2010:6.

5. Peutz and De Genova 2010:1.

6. For a recent exception, see Boehm 2012.

7. I focus here on the decades leading up to PTD. For more in-depth historical analyses of deportation, see Hernández 2010.

8. Heyman 1995:266.

9. Ettinger 2009:132.

10. Heyman 1995; Hernández 2010; Rosenblum 2012:8.

11. Singer and Massey 1998:574.

12. Heyman 1995:270.

13. For example, see the 1987 film *Born in East LA*.

14. Rosenblum 2012:8.

15. Lydgate 2010:481; ACLU 2009.

16. Lydgate 2010:500. See also Trevizo 2014.

17. All statistics for the Tucson Operation Streamline come from Lydgate 2010 unless otherwise noted.

18. All of these case numbers, dates, names, and personal details have been slightly modified to protect identities.

19. Many recent migrants are indigenous-language speakers from the southern Mexican states of Oaxaca and Chiapas.

20. Lydgate 2010:484.

21. Lydgate 2010:528.

22. Agamben 1998:174.

23. Lydgate 2010:515–516.

24. See, for example, Robertson et al. 2012

25. Lydgate 2010:528.

26. National Immigration Forum 2013.

27. No More Deaths 2011; Silva 2013.

28. No More Deaths 2011:29.

29. GAO 2010:11–12.

30. CBP 2008.

31. De León 2013a.

32. Spener 2009.

33. Hernández 2010:134–136.

34. A type of *coyote*, *guías* are the individuals who physically lead groups through the desert.

35. Officially they are known as Grupos Beta, but most refer to them as Grupo Beta.

36. These are their real names.

37. Simanski and Sapp 2012.

38. Urrea 1996:9.

39. Malkki 1997:99.

40. *Arizona Daily Star* 2014.

41. Joe Arpaio is the sheriff of Maricopa County well known for being an outspoken critic of undocumented migrants. His department has been investigated numerous times following accusations of racial profiling of Latinos, especially during traffic stops.

6. TECHNOLOGICAL WARFARE

1. Parts of this event are described in De León 2012.

2. Calculations based on information found at Servicio de Administración Tributaria, Comisión Nacional de los Salarios Mínimos, http://www.sat.gob.mx/informacion_fiscal/tablas_indicadores/Paginas/salarios_minimos.aspx.

3. The Mojave green (*Crotalus scutlatus*) is one of the deadliest snakes in North America.

4. For a discussion of machismo, joking, and homosociality, see Peña 2006.

5. Behar 1996:177.

6. A pseudonym.

7. USBP 2012:15.

8. USBP 2012:15.

9. Malinowski 1984:115.

10. For discussion of these expenditures, see Rosenblum 2012:12–14.

11. Lacey 2011.

12. Associated Press 2011.

13. "Car Jack Used to Breach Border Fence," YouTube, uploaded by NumbersUSA, February 17, 2012, https://www.youtube.com/watch?v=Qdc-kv7nzaU&feature=youtu.be (accessed March 7, 2015).

14. CNN Wire Staff, "Jeep Gets Stuck Trying to Drive over U.S.-Mexico Border Fence," CNN.com, updated November 1, 2012, http://www.cnn.com/2012/10/31/us/mexico-border-jeep/ (accessed March 7, 2015).

15. González 2014.

16. US Customs and Border Protection, http://www.cbp.gov/sites/default/files/documents/fence_breach_3.pdf (accessed March 7, 2015).

17. "Herman Cain's Electric Fence 'Joke,'" YouTube, uploaded October 17, 2011, by talkingpointsmemo.com (originally appeared on *The Daily Rundown*, MSNBC), https://www.youtube.com/watch?v=jO-q5lI7618&feature=youtu.be (accessed March 7, 2015).

18. Horsley 2006.

19. Nevins 2002; Andreas 2009.

20. Annual funding allotted to the fence has widely fluctuated over the past two decades. For example, $25 million was appropriated for fence construction in 1996, and

the amount increased to $298 million in 2006. By 2007, $1.5 billion had been allotted for fencing. By 2012, these funds had dropped to $400 million (Rosenblum 2012:16–17).

21. McGuire 2013.

22. Rosenblum 2012:16.

23. Since 1998, billions of dollars have been spent on remote-sensing technology, and various military contractors have periodically offered new and improved systems for catching migrants, drug smugglers, and terrorists. This security project has gone through a series of names and iterations, including the Integrated Surveillance Intelligence System (ISIS), America's Shield Initiative (ASI), and most recently the Secure Border Initiative (SBI or SBInet). Despite the large sums of money spent on these systems, all three have failed to "meet deployment timelines and to provide USBP with the promised level of 'situational awareness' with respect to illegal entries" (Rosenblum 2012:18). The success of the remote surveillance technology used by the Border Patrol has been spotty at best. In his ethnography of Border Patrol agents in South Texas, Maril (2004) notes that remote sensors were often made of outdated technology, were poorly maintained, and were often unable to distinguish between border crossers and cattle (x). Moreover, the delay between when a sensor is activated and when a dispatcher notifies agents on the ground can be five minutes or longer, making it difficult to predict which direction people have headed in (76). Once a sensor is activated, agents on the ground must then track people using other methods (e.g., sign cutting [i.e., tracking people based on footprints and other traces their movement leaves in the wilderness] or infrared cameras). Still, deploying agents in a timely fashion to an area where a sensor has been activated means that they must predict where people who have a head start have gone. As migrants and *coyotes* use trails over time and as the Border Patrol begins to place sensors in those areas, people change routes and look for areas with less surveillance. Given the vastness of the desert, it is impossible to place and maintain motion sensors everywhere at all times, suggesting that certain technologies have limited use.

24. Since 9/11, the US Border Patrol has had the distinction of being the fastest-growing federal law enforcement agency in the country. Over the past decade it has doubled its staff, and it has seen a ninefold increase in personnel since 1998 (Rosenblum 2012:14). When Lucho first attempted to cross the border in 1980, there were 1,975 agents assigned to the southern border. As of September 2012, the Border Patrol employed 21,444 agents, 18,506 of whom were stationed along the US-Mexico boundary (Rosenblum 2012:14). This steady increase in the number of agents on the ground in specific areas is linked to PTD, which, as discussed in chapters 1 and 2, uses strategically placed personnel to create funnels that direct migrant traffic toward specific parts of the border. As a 1997 government report notes:

> Border Patrol needed to be flexible to respond to changing patterns in illegal alien traffic. According to INS officials, [following the implementation of PTD] the Border Patrol began to notice "almost immediately" an increase in apprehensions in other sectors, particularly Tucson and those in south Texas (Del Rio, McAllen, and Laredo). INS officials attributed

this increase in apprehensions in other sectors to a "shift" in the flow of illegal alien traffic as it became more difficult to cross illegally in San Diego and El Paso. Consequently, in fiscal year 1995, the Border Patrol deployed some of the additional agents funded that year and originally planned for San Diego and El Paso to the Tucson and south Texas sectors, the sectors with the next highest priority after San Diego and El Paso. According to Border Patrol officials, deploying additional agents in a phased manner was a new approach. Prior to the strategy, as additional positions became available, the Border Patrol tried to allocate at least a few additional positions to as many of the 21 sectors as possible. However, under the strategy, 98 percent (or 2,792) of the 2,850 new Border Patrol agent positions nationwide authorized from fiscal year 1994 through fiscal year 1997 have gone to 6 of the 21 Border Patrol sectors. INS allocated 1,235 (about 43 percent) of these positions to the San Diego sector and 351 (about 12 percent) to the El Paso sector, sectors with the highest priority. Nearly all of the remaining 1,264 went to the Tucson and the south Texas sectors, the sectors with the next highest priority. (GAO 1997)

In essence, this show of force of agents in El Paso (and later San Diego) soon made it necessary to hire more personnel in sectors where migration flows were being directed. This included such places as Tucson that historically had low rates of undocumented migration. As traffic was pushed elsewhere, the need to create a "virtual wall" of people near other major ports of entry necessitated more spending on additional agents. PTD thus started a cycle of increased spending that has not slowed since the 1990s. For example, in 1993 there were 281 agents in the Tucson Sector (GAO 1997:16). As of May 2013, there were 4,200 agents in that sector (CBP, "Tucson Sector Arizona," www.cbp.gov/border-security/along-us-borders/border-patrol-sectors/tucson-sector-arizona). In June 2013, an amendment was attached to a larger bipartisan "comprehensive" immigration bill (Senate Bill 744) that proposed to increase the number of Border Patrol agents on the southern border to 38,405 by 2021. Despite the increase in the number of agents in the Tucson Sector between 1993 and 2013, migrants still outnumber Border Patrol on the ground by several orders of magnitude. For example, in 2009, when Memo and Lucho walked into the desert, the number of apprehended migrants outnumbered agents fifty-eight to one. Still, the deployment of agents on the ground as a "virtual wall" happens only in and around ports of entry such as Nogales. Because of the high numbers of agents and the presence of substantial fencing infrastructure, it is virtually impossible to cross undetected within the city limits of Nogales, though people still try. However, migrants need only to walk east or west of town to enter unpopulated areas where agents are rarely present and fencing is minimal. In essence, agents stationed within sight of the border function more as omnipresent deterrents to would-be crossers and signal to people that they should try their luck in more remote parts of the desert.

25. Magaña 2008:37–38.

26. GAO 2012: figure 4.

27. These published data do not distinguish between people who were caught at a vehicle checkpoint as opposed to on foot in the desert. Some may have been smuggled across the border in a vehicle and then caught later at a checkpoint, effectively avoiding having to walk in the desert.

28. Cornelius et al. 2008:3.

29. See note 23 for this chapter.

30. See De León 2012.

31. Singer and Massey 1998:569.

32. Parks et al. 2009; De León 2012; Spener 2009.

33. Agua Linda is about 25 miles as the crow flies from Nogales.

7. THE CROSSING

1. Migrants refer to these trucks as *perreras*, or "dog catchers," because they have built-in holding cells similar to what Animal Control uses for dogs.

2. See, for example, Sundberg 2008; Meirotto 2012.

3. *Huffington Post* online comment, January 17, 2012.

4. Those who cling to the term *garbage* as a way to avoid paying close attention to this material record should take heed of the words of Rathje and Murphy (2001): "Garbage is among humanity's most prodigious physical legacies to those who have yet to be born; if we can come to understand our discards, . . . then we will better understand the world in which we live" (4).

5. Rathje and Murphy 2001. See also Schofield 2005:98.

6. Buchli and Lucas 2001; R. Harrison and Schofield 2010.

7. González-Ruibal 2008:247.

8. Schofield 2005:101. For an archaeological approach to studies of political violence, see Ludlow Collective 2001; on homelessness, see Zimmerman et al. 2010 and Zimmerman and Welch 2011; on warfare, see Schofield 2005 and González-Ruibal 2007.

9. González-Ruibal 2008:248–249.

10. Schofield 2005:104.

11. See De León 2013b.

12. This is a direct challenge to those who think that objects alone can (or should) speak for migrants. For a discussion of the problematic use of border crosser artifacts as "testimonial objects," see De León and Gokee (under review).

13. Gokee and De León 2014.

14. See Gokee and De León 2014.

15. Here Lucho is referring to the flat and barren Altar Valley, which historically was the route taken from the border town of Sasabe. Increased surveillance over the past ten years has caused people to walk through the mountain ranges on both sides of the valley.

16. Slack and Whiteford 2011.

17. For legal and safety reasons, I have avoided both working in areas with high drug trafficking and asking migrants specific questions about their interactions with drug smugglers. Regardless of my aversion to this subject, it routinely came up in interviews with people, some of whom admitted to working as *burreros*. In addition, we would sometimes spot drug mule trains in the desert and give them a wide berth. On one

occasion, a group of UMP researchers encountered *burreros* returning to Mexico after dropping off a load. These individuals were wearing full camouflage gear and asked for directions back to the border.

18. For a detailed discussion of use wear and migrant suffering, see De León 2013b.

19. Meirotto 2012; Hill 2006; Romo 2005.

20. Border Patrol, humanitarian groups, hunters, and hikers are also responsible for the accumulation of material culture in the Sonoran Desert (Meirotto 2012; Drummond and De León 2015; De León, Gokee, and Schubert 2015).

21. Some migrants refer to these sites as *levantons*, which in Spanish may also connote abduction by a smuggler.

22. Based on rough calculations, they probably walked more than seventy miles. This total does account for the impact of terrain and slope on the total distance traveled.

23. For quantitative data on migrant site inventories, see Gokee and De León 2014.

24. For example, Leo Banks (2009) has alleged that evidence of Islamic terrorist activity is visible in the objects that border crossers leave behind.

25. *Archaeology* 2011.

26. Smith 1869:208.

27. Agamben 2005.

28. Doty 2009:84.

29. See the Bureau of Land Management's annual reports for the Southern Arizona Project to Mitigate Environmental Damages Resulting from Illegal Immigration at www.blm.gov/az/st/en/info/newsroom/undocumented_aliens.html.

30. ABLM 2011:1.

31. For a discussion of "micro-facts" and "Minimum Number of Individual" (MNI) analyses and attempts to extract data from "cleaned up" migrant sites, see De León, Gokee, and Forringer-Beal 2015.

32. Domanska 2005:395.

33. De León and Gokee (under review).

34. Farmer 2004:308.

8. EXPOSURE

1. A major component of the Undocumented Migration Project is a summer anthropological field school for undergraduate students that I have directed for numerous years with the generous support of the Institute for Field Research. See www.ifrglobal.org/ for additional information.

2. See Drummond and De León 2015.

3. All students mentioned in this chapter are referred to by their real names.

4. BK stands for "Bob Kee" and represents sites he showed me in the winter and summer of 2009.

5. See Forringer-Beal and De León 2012; De León, Gokee, and Forringer-Beal 2015.

6. Sontag 2003.

7. See discussion of the photos of corpses in Barthes 1981:78–79. The coordinates have been modified to protect a memorial shrine that currently marks this death site. Despite its remote location, the shrine has been vandalized numerous times, likely by hikers or hunters. This vandalism included smashing a picture frame that held a photo of Maricela and her family and then ripping the image to pieces.

8. Galloway 1997: table 1.

9. Pachirat 2013:14.

10. Sontag 2003:70.

11. Dougherty 2006:609.

12. Maril 2004:262.

13. Reineke 2013.

14. De León, Gokee, and Schubert 2015.

15. This date is off by four days. Carlos was actually encountered on June 28 and the body was found on July 2, 2012.

9. YOU CAN'T LEAVE THEM BEHIND

1. Jokisch and Pribilsky 2002:76.

2. Pribilsky 2012:327.

3. Jokisch and Pribilsky 2002:76.

4. Bertoli et al. 2011:59.

5. See, for example, Pribilsky 2001:255.

6. See Pribilsky 2007:161–171.

7. Pribilsky (2007) notes that the highest smuggling fee for Ecuadorans he recorded in 2001 was $13,500 (164). Anecdotal data from interviews with Ecuadoran migrants suggest that the average cost of travel in 2014 was around $12,000 per person. Mexican migrants on average were paying smugglers between $2,000 and $3,500 in the mid-2000s (Cornelius et al. 2008:6), and based on my informal survey of prices in 2014, people were paying anywhere between $3,000 and $5,000, depending on the route and method of crossing.

8. Trevizo 2014. The 31 percent statistic includes people caught crossing the border illegally, as well as repeat immigration violators and fugitives from the immigration courts (ICE 2013). Of the 357,422 people whom ICE removed from the United States in fiscal year 2013, 31 percent were from Central and South American countries. Ecuadorans made up about 0.05% (1,616) of these removals (ICE 2013).

9. Martínez 2013.

10. Jackson 2013:4–5.

11. All of Christian's dialogue has been translated from Spanish.

12. Those without a guide find themselves in much greater danger because they lack the semiprotection that comes with having an escort, as evidenced in Christian's story where periodically one of his smugglers prevents him from being robbed or assaulted.

13. Coutin 2005.

14. The Mexican freight train that migrants ride is referred to as *la bestia* (the beast). Although it helps people get across the country at a relatively quick pace, it is a treacherous form of transportation. People are often injured or killed when getting on or off the train or when it derails. In addition, the police and bandits frequently assault migrants, both while the train is running and when it periodically stops.

15. For a discussion of migrants robbed in Oaxaca and Chiapas by locals, see Martínez 2013.

16. "Cuernos de chivo" (goat's horns) is Spanish slang for an AK-47 assault rifle. The nickname refers to the curved shape of the magazine clip, which resembles a goat's horn.

17. Tele Sur 2014.

18. Slack and Whiteford 2011.

19. Tuckman 2010.

20. This phenomenon is similar to the many risks that Hans Lucht (2012) describes for Ghanaian migrants who risk life and limb crossing the Sahara before attempting to navigate the Mediterranean to reach Italy.

21. Wilkinson 2012.

22. This part of the story illustrates just how easy it is to get lost or separated from a group during the chaos of a crossing.

10. MARICELA

Epigraph: This song is by the Mexican American singer Marisela Esqueda. Maricela posted this track on her Facebook account a few weeks before she left Ecuador. She included the message "With much love for all of my family."

1. Jokisch 2002:528.

2. Rubio-Goldsmith et al. 2006:44.

3. O'Leary 2009.

4. Martínez et al. 2013:23.

5. Butler 2004:33.

6. Coutin 2005:199; Magaña 2011.

7. Félix 2011.

8. See, for example, Brandes 2001; Félix 2011:169.

9. Sandell 2010:196.

10. Cannell 2000.

11. See Guyer 2009:159.

12. For a discussion of this technique, see Shaheed 2014.

13. Yarris 2014:286.

11. WE WILL WAIT UNTIL YOU GET HERE

1. See, for example, Boehm 2012; Stephen 2007:xv. For Ecuador, see, for example, Miles 1997, 2004; Pribilsky 2007, 2012.

2. Pribilsky 2001:268.

3. Miles 1997:68.

4. See, for example, Reyes 2004.

5. Massey et al. 2002.

6. Felipe and Manny are pseudonyms.

7. These details come from multiple interviews with José's cousins, his girlfriend, parents, and other family and friends who were in sporadic communication with him during the trip. Details of this journey have been condensed to focus on the last few moments in the desert.

8. For an overview of this theory, see Boss 1999, 2004.

9. Boss 2004:553.

10. GAO 1997: appendix V.

11. GAO 2006.

12. Das 2007:49.

13. For a discussion of the difficulty people have with "reengaging" with life following the death of loved one, see Das 2007:192–193.

14. Lucht 2012:220–221.

15. Here Gustavo implies that he would have some modicum of relief even if José's body was returned in a fragmented state.

EPILOGUE

1. Ettinger 2009:60.

2. Butler 2004:34.

3. Butler 2004:22.

4. See appendix A.

5. Tuckman 2010; Hennessy-Fiske 2014.

6. Associated Press 2014.

7. Martínez 2013.

REFERENCES

ABLM (Arizona Bureau of Land Management)

2011 "Southern Arizona Project to Mitigate Environmental Damages Resulting from Illegal Immigration." Fiscal Year 2011 Report.

ACLU (American Civil Liberties Union)

2009 "Operation Streamline Factsheet." www.immigrationforum.org/images /uploads/OperationStreamlineFactsheet.pdf. Accessed March 2014.

2014 "Customs and Border Protection's (CBP's) 100-Mile Rule." www.aclu.org /sites/default/files/assets/14_9_15_cbp_100-mile_rule_final.pdf. Accessed February 28, 2015.

Agamben, Giorgio

1998 *Homo Sacer: Sovereign Power and Bare Life.* Palo Alto, CA: Stanford University Press.

2005 *State of Exception.* Translated by Kevin Attell. Chicago: University of Chicago Press.

Alvarez, Robert R., Jr.

1995 "The Mexican-US Border: The Making of an Anthropology of Borderlands." *Annual Review of Anthropology* 24: 447–470.

Anderson, Stuart

2013 "How Many More Deaths? The Moral Case for a Temporary Worker Program." National Foundation for American Policy Policy Brief. March.

Andersson, Ruben

2014 "Hunter and Prey: Patrolling Clandestine Migration in the Euro-African Borderlands." *Anthropological Quarterly* 87(1): 118–149.

Andreas, Peter

2009 *Border Games: Policing the U.S.-Mexico Divide.* Ithaca, NY: Cornell University Press.

Annerino, John

2009　*Dead in Their Tracks: Crossing America's Desert Borderlands in the New Era.* Tucson: University of Arizona Press.

Anti-Defamation League

2012　"Arizona: The Key Players in the Anti-immigrant Movement." www.adl.org /assets/pdf/civil-rights/immigration/Arizona-anti-immigrant-movement-temp-9−7-12.pdf.

Anzaldúa, Gloria

2007　*Borderlands/La Frontera: The New Mestiza.* 3rd ed. San Francisco: Aunt Lute Books.

Archaeology Magazine

2011　Letter to the Editor. *Archaeology* 64(2).

Arizona Daily Star

2014　"Police Raid Immigrant Group Shelter in Nogales, Group Says." *Arizona Daily Star,* July 12.

Associated Press

2011　"Drug Smugglers Use Catapult to Fling Pot to Arizona." azcentral.com, January 27. www.azcentral.com/news/articles/2011/01/26/20110126arizona-border-marijuana-catapult.html#ixzz3BnrtfkNp. Accessed March 7, 2015.

2014　"Mexico Cracking Down on Central Americans Riding 'The Beast,' Sending Them to Deportation Centers." CBS Houston, August 29. http://houston .cbslocal.com/2014/08/29/mexico-cracking-down-on-central-americans-riding-the-beast-sending-them-to-deportation-centers/. Accessed March 30, 2015.

Banks, Leo

2009　"Trashing Arizona: Illegal Immigrants Dump Tons of Waste in the Wilderness Every Day—and It's Devastating the Environment." *Tucson Weekly,* April 2. www.tucsonweekly.com/tucson/trashing-arizona/Content?oid= 1168857. Accessed March 7, 2015.

Barthes, Roland

1981　*Camera Lucida: Reflections on Photography.* 1st American ed. New York: Hill and Wang.

Bassett, Samuel Elliot

1933　"Achilles' Treatment of Hector's Body." *Transactions and Proceedings of the American Philological Association* 64: 41−65.

Basso, Keith H.

1996　*Wisdom Sits in Places: Landscape and Language among the Western Apache.* Albuquerque: University of New Mexico Press.

Bazzell, Robert

2007　"Border Town Hospitals Straddle Care and Costs." NBC News. March 27. www.nbcnews.com/id/17760618/ns/health-second_opinion/t/border-town-hospitals-straddle-care-costs/#.VBHeqcKp18E.

Beck, Jess, Ian Ostereicher, Greg Sollish, and Jason De León
    2014   "Animal Scavenging and Scattering and the Implications for Documenting the Deaths of Undocumented Border Crossers in the Sonoran Desert." *Journal of Forensic Sciences* 60: S11–S20. doi: 10.1111/1556–4029.12597.

Behar, Ruth
    1996   *The Vulnerable Observer: Anthropology That Breaks Your Heart.* Boston: Beacon Press.

Bennett, Jane
    2010   *Vibrant Matter: A Political Ecology of Things.* Durham, NC: Duke University Press.

Bertoli, S., J. Fernandez-Huertas, and F. Ortega
    2011   "Immigration Policies and the Ecuadorian Exodus." *World Bank Economic Review* 25(1): 57–76.

Biehl, João G.
    2005   *Vita: Life in a Zone of Social Abandonment.* Berkeley: University of California Press.

Bloch, Maurice, and Jonathan Parry
    1996   "Introduction." In *Death and the Regeneration of Life.* Ed. M. Bloch and J. Parry. Pp. 1–44. Cambridge: Cambridge University Press.

Boehm, Deborah A
    2012   *Intimate Migrations: Gender, Family, and Illegality among Transnational Mexicans.* New York: New York University Press.

Boss, Pauline
    1999   *Ambiguous Loss: Learning to Live with Unresolved Grief.* Cambridge, MA: Harvard University Press.
    2004   "Ambiguous Loss Research, Theory, and Practice: Reflections after 9/11." *Journal of Marriage and Family* 66(3): 551–566.
    2007   "Ambiguous Loss Theory: Challenges for Scholars and Practitioners." *Family Relations* 56: 105–111.

Bourdieu, Pierre
    1977   *Outline of a Theory of Practice.* Cambridge: Cambridge University Press.

Bourgois, Philippe
    1995   *In Search of Respect: Selling Crack in El Barrio.* Cambridge: Cambridge University Press.

Bourgois, Philippe, and Jeff Schonberg
    2009   *Righteous Dopefiend.* Berkeley: University of California Press.

Brandes, Stanley
    2001   "The Cremated Catholic: The Ends of a Deceased Guatemalan." *Body & Society* 7(2–3): 111–120.

Brighton, Stephen A.
    2009   *Historical Archaeology of the Irish Diaspora: A Transnational Approach.* Knoxville: University of Tennessee Press.

Buchli, Victor, and Gavin Lucas, G. (eds.)

2001   *Archaeologies of the Contemporary Past.* London: Routledge.

Butler, Judith

2004   *Precarious Life: The Powers of Mourning and Violence.* London: Verso.

Cadava, Gerardo L.

2011   "Borderlands of Modernity and Abandonment: The Lines within Ambos Nogales and the Tohono O'odham Nation." *Journal of American History* 98(2): 362–383.

Callon, Michel, and John Law

1995   "Agency and the Hybrid Collectif." *South Atlantic Quarterly* 94(2): 481–507.

1997   "After the Individual in Society: Lessons on Collectivity from Science, Technology and Society." *Canadian Journal of Sociology* 22(2): 165–182.

Cannell, Fenella

1999   *Power and Intimacy in the Christian Philippines.* Cambridge: Cambridge University Press.

Carcamo, Cindy

2014   "ACLU Seeks Name of Border Patrol Agent Who Killed Mexican Teenager." *Los Angeles Times,* September 11. www.latimes.com/nation/nationnow /la-na-ff-border-patrol-shooting-20140910-story.html. Accessed February 28, 2015.

CBP (US Customs and Border Protection)

2008   "Tucson Sector Makes Significant Gains in 2008: Border Patrol Agents Continue to Make Progress with New Technology, Tactical Infrastructure, and Increased Manpower." News release, October 22.

Cerrutti, Marcella, and Douglas S. Massey

2004   "Trends in Mexican Migration to the United States, 1965 to 1995." In *Crossing the Border: Research from the Mexican Migration Project.* Ed. J. Durand and D.S. Massey. Pp. 17–44. New York: Russell Sage.

Chavez, Leo R.

1998   *Shadowed Lives: Undocumented Immigrants in American Society.* Fort Worth, TX: Harcourt College Publishers.

Chavez, Sergio

2011   "Navigating the US-Mexico Border: The Crossing Strategies of Undocumented Workers in Tijuana, Mexico." *Ethnic and Racial Studies* 34(8): 1320–1337.

Clark, Jonathan

2012   "One Year Later, Deadly Shooting Still under Federal Investigation." *Nogales International,* January 6. www.nogalesinternational.com/news/one-year-later-deadly-shooting-still-under-federal-investigation/article_83539752–387e-11e1-ab62–001871e3ce6c.html.

Clifford, James

1986   "Introduction: Partial Truths." In *Writing Culture.* Ed. J. Clifford and G. Marcus. Pp. 1–26. Berkeley: University of California Press.

Coleman, Kathleen M.

1990 "Fatal Charades: Roman Executions Staged as Mythological Enactments." *Journal of Roman Studies* 80: 44–73.

Cornelius, Wayne A.

2001 "Death at the Border: Efficacy and Unintended Consequences of US Immigration Control Policy." *Population and Development Review* 27(4): 661–685.

Cornelius, Wayne A., and Idean Salehyan

2007 "Does Border Enforcement Deter Unauthorized Immigration? The Case of Mexican Migration to the U.S. of America." *Regulation and Governance* 1(2): 139–153.

Cornelius, Wayne, Scott Borger, Adam Sawyer, David Keyes, Clare Appleby, Kristen Parks, Gabriel Lozada, and Jonathan Hicken

2008 "Controlling Unauthorized Immigration from Mexico: The Failure of 'Prevention through Deterrence' and the Need for Comprehensive Reform." Technical Report. La Jolla, CA: Immigration Policy Center.

Coutin, Susan

2005 "Being En Route." *American Anthropologist* 107(2): 195–206.

Crossland, Zoë

2000 "Buried Lives: Forensic Archaeology and the Disappeared in Argentina." *Archaeological Dialogues* 72: 146–159.

2009 "Of Clues and Signs: The Dead Body and Its Evidential Traces." *American Anthropologist* 111(1): 69–80.

Darling, Andrew J.

1998 "Mass Inhumation and the Execution of Witches in the American Southwest." *American Anthropologist* 100(3): 732–752.

Darling, Jonathan

2009 "Becoming Bare Life: Asylum, Hospitality, and the Politics of Encampment." *Environment and Planning D: Society and Space* 27(4): 649–665.

Das, Veena

2007 *Life and Words: Violence and the Descent into the Ordinary.* Berkeley: University of California Press.

Dawdy, Shannon

2006 "The Taphonomy of Disaster and the (Re)formation of New Orleans." *American Anthropologist* 108(4): 719–730.

De Genova, Nicholas, and Natalie Peutz

2010 *The Deportation Regime: Sovereignty, Space, and the Freedom of Movement.* Durham, NC: Duke University Press.

De León, Jason

2008 "The Lithic Industries of San Lorenzo–Tenochtitlán: An Economic and Technological Study of Olmec Obsidian." Doctoral dissertation. Department of Anthropology, Pennsylvania State University.

2012   "'Better to Be Hot Than Caught': Excavating the Conflicting Roles of Migrant Material Culture." *American Anthropologist* 114(3): 477–495.

2013a   "Undocumented Use-Wear and the Materiality of Habitual Suffering in the Sonoran Desert." *Journal of Material Culture* 18(4): 1–32.

2013b   "The Efficacy and Impact of the Alien Transfer Exit Program: Migrant Perspectives from Nogales, Sonora, Mexico." *International Migration* 51(2): 10–23.

De León, Jason, and Jeffery C. Cohen

2005   "The Material Probe in Ethnographic Interviewing." *Field Methods* 17(2): 200–204.

De León, Jason, and Cameron Gokee

Under review   "Lasting Value? Engaging with the Material Traces of America's Undocumented Migration 'Problem.'" In *Cultural Heritage, Ethics, and Contemporary Migrations*. Ed. Cornelius Holtorf, Andreas Pantazatos, and Geoffrey Scarre. New York: Routledge.

De León, Jason, Cameron Gokee, and Anna Forringer-Beal

2015   "Use Wear, Disruption, and the Materiality of Undocumented Migration in the Southern Arizona Desert." In *Migrations and Disruptions: Unifying Themes in Studies of Ancient and Contemporary Migrations*. Ed. T. Tsuda and B. Baker. Gainesville: University Press of Florida.

De León, Jason, Cameron Gokee, and Ashley Schubert

2015   "'By the Time I Get to Arizona': Citizenship, Materiality, and Contested Identities along the U.S.-Mexico Border." *Anthropological Quarterly* 88(2): 445–480.

Dennie, Garrey

2009   "The Standard of Dying: Race, Indigence, and the Disposal of the Dead Body in Johannesburg, 1886–1960." *African Studies* 68(3): 310–330.

Díaz del Castillo, Bernal

1956   *The Discovery and Conquest of Mexico*. Kingsport, TN: Farrar, Straus, and Cudahy.

Domanska, Ewa

2005   "Toward the Archaeontology of the Dead Body." *Rethinking History: The Journal of Theory and Practice* 9(4): 389–413.

Donato, Katharine M., Jorge Durand, and Douglas S. Massey

1992   "Stemming the Tide? Assessing the Deterrent Effects of the Immigration Reform and Control Act." *Demography* 29(2): 139–157.

Donato, Katharine M., Brandon Wagner, and Evelyn Patterson

2008   "The Cat and Mouse Game at the Mexico-U.S. Border: Gendered Patterns and Recent Shifts." *International Migration Review* 42(2): 330–359.

Doty, Roxanne

2009   *The Law into Their Own Hands: Immigration and the Politics of Exceptionalism*. Tucson: University of Arizona Press.

2011   "Bare Life: Border-Crossing Deaths and Spaces of Moral Alibi." *Environment and Planning D: Society and Space* 29: 599–612.

Dougherty, Sean Thomas

2006   "Killing the Messenger." *Massachusetts Review* 47(4): 608–616.

Drummond, Justine, and Jason De León

2015   "Humanitarian Sites: A Contemporary Archaeological and Ethnographic Study of Clandestine Culture Contact among Undocumented Migrants, Humanitarian Aid Groups, and the U.S. Border Patrol." Paper presented at the Society for Historical Archaeology 48th annual meeting, Seattle.

Duarte, Carmen

2013   "3 Decomposing Bodies Found in Desert over Weekend." *Tucson Daily Star*, June 24, 2013. http://tucson.com/news/local/border/decomposing-bodies-found-in-desert-over-weekend/article_338d3b8c-dd2e-11e2-918f-0019bb2963f4.html. Accessed April 18, 2015.

Dunn, Timothy J.

1996   *The Militarization of the U.S.-Mexico Border, 1978–1992: Low-Intensity Conflict Doctrine Comes Home*. Austin: CMAS Books, University of Texas.

2009   *Blockading the Border and Human Rights: The El Paso Operation That Remade Immigration Enforcement*. Austin: University of Texas Press.

Durand, Jorge, and Douglas S. Massey (eds.)

2004   *Crossing the Border: Research from the Mexican Migration Project*. New York: Russell Sage.

EFE

2012   "Border Crossing Trash Worthy of Study, Say Anthropologists." Fox News, January 17, 2012. http://latino.foxnews.com/latino/lifestyle/2012/01/17/border-crossing-trash-worthy-study-say-anthropologists/.

Efremov, Ivan A.

1940   "Taphonomy: A New Branch of Paleontology." *Pan American Geologist* 74: 81–93.

Ettinger, Patrick W.

2009   *Imaginary Lines: Border Enforcement and the Origins of Undocumented Immigration, 1882–1930*. Austin: University of Texas Press.

Falcón, Sylvanna

2001   "Rape as a Weapon of War: Advancing Human Rights for Women at the U.S.-Mexico Border." *Social Justice* 28(2): 31–51.

Farmer, Paul

2004   "An Anthropology of Structural Violence." *Current Anthropology* 45(3): 305–325.

Fassin, Didier

2014   "Revisiting the Boundaries between Ethnography and Fiction." *American Ethnologist* 41(1): 40–55.

Félix, Adrián

    2011   "Posthumous Transnationalism: Postmortem Repatriation from the United States to Mexico." *Latin American Research Review* 46(3): 157–179.

Ferguson, Kathryn, Norma A. Price, and Ted Parks

    2010   *Crossing with the Virgin: Stories from the Migrant Trail.* Tucson: University of Arizona Press.

Ffolliott, Peter F., and Gerald J. Gottfried

    2008   "Plant Communities and Associations." In *Natural Environments of Arizona: From Deserts to Mountains.* Ed. P. T. Ffolliott and O. K. Davis. Pp. 70–119. Tucson: University of Arizona Press.

Fontein, Joost

    2010   "Between Tortured Bodies and Resurfacing Bones: The Politics of the Dead in Zimbabwe." *Journal of Material Culture* 15(4): 423–448.

Ford, Caroline

    1998   "Violence and the Sacred in Nineteenth-Century France." *Historical Studies* 21(1): 101–112.

Forringer-Beal, Anna, and Jason De León

    2012   "Fragments and Females: Using Micro-debitage to Understand the Border Crossing Experiences of Women Migrants in Southern Arizona." Paper presented at the Society for American Archaeology 77th annual meeting, Memphis, TN.

Foucault, Michel

    1995   *Discipline and Punish: The Birth of the Prison.* 2nd ed. New York: Vintage Books.

    2007   *Security, Territory, Population: Lectures at the College de France: 1977–1978.* New York: Picador.

Fuentes, Agustín

    2006   "The Humanity of Animals and the Animality of Humans: A View from Biological Anthropology Inspired by J. M. Coetzee's *Elizabeth Costello.*" *American Anthropologist* 108(1):124–132.

Galloway, Allison

    1997   "The Process of Decomposition: A Model from the Arizona-Sonoran Desert." In *Forensic Taphonomy: The Postmortem Fate of Human Remains.* Ed. W. D. Haglund and M. H. Sorg. Pp. 139–150. Boca Raton, FL: CRC Press.

Galloway, Allison, Walter H. Birkby, Allen M. Jones, Thomas E. Henry, and Bruce O. Parks

    1989   "Decay Rates of Human Remains in an Arid Environment." *Journal of Forensic Sciences* 34(3): 607–616.

Galtung, Johan

    1969   "Violence, Peace, and Peace Research." *Journal of Peace Research* 6(3): 167–191.

GAO (Government Accountability Office)

    1997   "Report to the Committee on the Judiciary, U.S. Senate, and the Committee on the Judiciary, House of Representatives; Illegal Immigration: Southwest

Border Strategy Results Inconclusive; More Evaluation Needed." www.gao
.gov/archive/1998/gg98021.pdf.

2001 "INS's Southwest Border Strategy: Resource and Impact Issues Remain after Seven Years." Report to Congressional Requesters. www.gao.gov/new .items/d01842.pdf.

2006 "Illegal Immigration: Border Crossing Deaths Have Doubled since 1995; Border Patrol's Efforts Have Not Been Fully Evaluated." Report to U.S. Senate.

2010 "Alien Smuggling: DHS Needs to Better Leverage Investigative Resources and Measure Program Performance along the Southwest Border." Report to Congressional Requesters. www.gao.gov/new.items/d10328.pdf. Accessed April 18, 2015.

2012 "Border Patrol: Key Elements of New Strategic Plan Not Yet in Place to Inform Border Security Status and Resource Needs." Report to Congressional Requesters. www.gao.gov/assets/660/650730.pdf. Accessed March 26, 2015.

García, María Cristina
2006 *Seeking Refuge: Central American Migration to Mexico, the United States, and Canada.* Berkeley: University of California Press.

Gell, Alfred
1998 *Art and Agency: An Anthropological Theory.* Oxford: Clarendon Press.

Gokee, Cameron, and Jason De León
2014 "Sites of Contention: Archaeology and Political Discourse in the US-Mexico Borderlands." *Journal of Contemporary Archaeology* 1(1): 133–163.

González, Daniel
2014 "Largest-Ever Drug Tunnel Found in Nogales." *Arizona Republic*, February 13. www.azcentral.com/news/arizona/articles/20140213largest-ever-drug-tunnel-nogales-arizona-found.html. Accessed March 7, 2015.

González-Ruibal, Alfredo
2007 "'Making Things Public': Archaeologies of the Spanish Civil War." *Public Archaeology* 6: 203–226.

2008 "'Time to Destroy': An Archaeology of Supermodernity." *Current Anthropology* 49(2): 247–279.

Goss, Robert E., and Dennis Klass
1997 "Tibetan Buddhism and the Resolution of Grief: The *Bardo-Thodol* for the Dying and the Grieving." *Death Studies* 21: 377–395.

Graeber, David
1995 "Dancing with Corpses Reconsidered: An Interpretation of 'Famadihana' (in Arivonimamo, Madagascar)." *American Ethnologist* 22(2): 258–278.

Guerin-Gonzales, Camille
1994 *Mexican Workers and American Dreams: Immigration, Repatriation, and California Farm Labor, 1900–1939.* New Brunswick, N.J.: Rutgers University Press.

Guyer, Sara
    2009   "Rwanda's Bones." *boundary 2* 36(2): 155–175.

Haddal, Chad C.
    2010   *Border Security: The Role of the U.S. Border Patrol.* Congressional Research Service Report for Congress. August 11. www.fas.org/sgp/crs/homesec/RL32562.pdf. Accessed February 28, 2015.

Hadley, N. F.
    1972   "Desert Species and Adaption." *American Scientist* 60: 338–347.

Hall, Katherine, Anna Antoniou, Haeden Stewart, Jess Beck, and Jason De León
    2014   "Exploring the Taphonomic Processes that Impact the Remains of Undocumented Border Crossers in the Sonoran Desert of Arizona." Poster presented at the Society for American Archaeology, 79th Annual Meeting, Austin, TX.

Harrison, Rodney, and John Schofield
    2010   *After Modernity: Archaeological Approaches to the Contemporary Past.* Oxford: Oxford University Press.

Harrison, Simon
    2006   "Skull Trophies of the Pacific War: Transgressive Objects of Remembrance." *Journal of the Royal Anthropological Institute* 12(4): 817–836.
    2010   "Bones in the Rebel Lady's Boudoir: Ethnology, Race, and Trophy-Hunting in the American Civil War." *Journal of Material Culture* 15(4): 385–401.

Hennessy-Fiske, Molly
    2014   "Migrant Crisis Expands North from Border, into Arid Texas Wilderness." *Los Angeles Times,* July 19. www.latimes.com/nation/la-na-immigration-brooks-county-20140720-story.html#page=1. Accessed March 30, 2015.

Hernández, Kelly Lytle
    2010   *Migra! A History of the U.S. Border Patrol.* Berkeley: University of California Press.

Heyman, Josiah McC.
    1995   "Putting Power into the Anthropology of Bureaucracy: The Immigration and Naturalization Service at the Mexico–United States Border," with "Commentary" and "Reply by the Author." *Current Anthropology* 36(2): 261–287.
    2002   "U.S. Immigration Officers of Mexican Ancestry as Mexican Americans, Citizens, and Immigration Police." *Current Anthropology* 43(3): 479–507.
    2009   "Trust, Privilege, and Discretion in the Governance of the US Borderlands." *Canadian Journal of Law and Society* 24(3): 367–390.

Hill, Sarah
    2006   "Purity and Danger on the U.S.-Mexico Border, 1990–1994." *South Atlantic Quarterly* 105(4): 777–800.

Hobson, Kersty
    2007   "Political Animals? On Animals as Subjects in an Enlarged Political Geography." *Political Geography* 26(3): 250–267.

Hoffman, Danny

2011   *The War Machines: Young Men and Violence in Sierra Leone and Liberia*. Durham, NC: Duke University Press.

Holmes, Seth M.

2013   *Fresh Fruit, Broken Bodies: Migrant Farmworkers in the United States*. Berkeley: University of California Press.

Horsely, Scott

2006   "Border Fence Firm Snared for Hiring Illegal Workers." National Public Radio, December 14. www.npr.org/templates/story/story.php?storyId=6626823. Accessed April 19, 2015.

Hsieh, Steven

2014   "Migrant Children Accuse Border Patrol Agents of Physical and Sexual Assault." *The Nation*, June 12. www.thenation.com/blog/180207/migrant-children-accuse-border-patrol-agents-physical-and-sexual-assault.

Human Rights Watch

2013   "'Between a Drone and Al-Qaeda: The Civilian Cost of US Targeted Killings in Yemen." www.hrw.org/sites/default/files/reports/yemen1013_ForUpload.pdf. Accessed April 19, 2015.

Humphreys, Michael, and Tony Watson

2009   "Ethnographic Practices: From 'Writing Up Ethnographic Research' to 'Writing Ethnography.'" In *Organizational Ethnography: Studying the Complexity of Everyday Life*. Ed. Sierk Ybema, Dvora Yanow, Harry Wels, and Frans H Kamsteeg. Pp. 40–55. Thousand Oaks, CA: SAGE.

ICE (US Immigration and Customs Enforcement)

2013   "ERO Annual Report: FY 2013 ICE Immigration Removals." www.ice.gov/doclib/about/offices/ero/pdf/2013-ice-immigration-removals.pdf. Accessed April 19, 2015.

Jackson, Michael

2013   *The Wherewithal of Life: Ethics, Migration, and the Question of Well-Being*. Berkeley: University of California Press.

Johansson, Karin

2012   "The Birds in the Ilia. Identities, Interactions, and Functions." Ph.D. dissertation. University of Gothenburg, Department of Historical Studies.

Jokisch, Brad D.

2002   "Migration and Agricultural Change: The Case of Smallholder Agriculture in the Highlands of South-Central Ecuador." *Human Ecology* 30(4): 523–550.

Jokisch, Brad D., and Jason Pribilsky

2002   "The Panic to Leave: Economic Crisis and the 'New Emigration' from Ecuador." *International Migration* 40(4): 75–101.

Jones, Reece

2009   "Agents of Exception: Border Security and the Marginalization of Muslims in India." *Environment and Planning D: Society and Space* 27(5): 879–897.

Keane, Webb

2006 "Subjects and Objects." In *Handbook of Material Culture*. Ed. C. Tilley, W. Keane, S. Küchler, M. Rowlands, and P. Spyer. Pp. 197–202. London: Sage.

Kirk, David A., and Michael J. Mossman

1998 "Turkey Vulture (*Cathartes aura*)." In *The Birds of North America*, No. 339. Ed. A. Poole and F. Gill. Ithaca, NY: Birds of North America Online.

Kirksey, S. Eben, and Stefan Helmreich

2010 "The Emergence of Multispecies Ethnography." In "Multispecies Ethnography." Special issue, *Cultural Anthropology* 25(4): 545–576.

Klass, Dennis, and Robert Goss

2003 "The Politics of Grief and Continuing Bonds with the Dead: The Cases of Maoist China and Wahhabi Islam." *Death Studies* 27: 787–811.

Kohn, Eduardo

2007 "How Dogs Dream: Amazonian Natures and the Politics of Transspecies Engagement." *American Ethnologist* 34(1): 3–24.

Komar, Debra

2008 "Patterns of Mortuary Practice Associated with Genocide: Implications for Archaeological Research." *Current Anthropology* 49(1): 123–133.

Kopytoff, Igor

1986 "The Cultural Biography of Things: Commoditization as Process." In *The Social Life of Things*. Ed. A. Appadurai, 64–91. Cambridge: Cambridge University Press.

Krmpotich, Cara, Joost Fontein, and John Harries

2010 "The Substance of Bones: The Emotive Materiality and Affective Presence of Human Remains." *Journal of Material Culture* 15(4): 371–384.

Lacey, Marc

2011 "Arizona Officials, Fed Up with U.S. Efforts, Seek Donations to Build Border Fence." *New York Times*, July 19. www.nytimes.com/2011/07/20/us/20border .html?_r=0. Accessed March 7, 2015.

Latour, Bruno

1992 "Where Are the Missing Masses? The Sociology of a Few Mundane Artifacts." In *Shaping Technology/Building Society: Studies in Sociotechnical Change*. Ed. W. Bijker and J. Law. Pp. 225–258. Cambridge, MA: MIT Press.

2005 *Reassembling the Social: An Introduction to Actor-Network-Theory*. Oxford: Oxford University Press.

Lentz, Ryan

2012 "Investigating Deaths of Undocumented Immigrants on the Border." *Intelligence Report* (Southern Poverty Law Center), no. 147 (Fall). www.splcenter .org/get-informed/intelligence-report/browse-all-issues/2012/fall/death-in-the-desert. Accessed March 30, 2015.

Limón, José E.

1994 *Dancing with the Devil: Society and Cultural Poetics in Mexican-American South Texas*. Madison: University of Wisconsin Press.

Lomnitz, Claudio

2005   *Death and the Idea of Mexico*. New York: Zone Books.

Londras, Fiona de

2008   "Guantanamo Bay: Towards Legality?" *Modern Law Review* 71(1): 36–58.

Lucht, Hans

2012   *Darkness before Daybreak: African Migrants Living on the Margins in Southern Italy Today*. Berkeley: University of California Press.

Ludlow Collective, The

2001   "Archaeology of the Colorado Coal Field War, 1913–1914." In *Archaeologies of the Contemporary Past*. Ed. V. Buchli and G. Lucas. Pp. 94–107. London: Routledge.

Lumholtz, Carl

1990   *New Trails in Mexico: An Account of One Year's Exploration in North-western Sonora, Mexico, and South-western Arizona, 1909–1910*. Tucson: University of Arizona Press.

Lydgate, Joanna Jacobbi

2010   "Assembly-Line Justice: A Review of Operation Streamline." *California Law Review* 98(2): 481–544.

Lyman, R. Lee

2010   "What Taphonomy Is, What It Isn't, and Why Taphonomists Should Care about the Difference." *Journal of Taphonomy* 8(1): 1–16.

Maddrell, Avril, and James D. Sidaway

2010   *Deathscapes: Spaces for Death, Dying, Mourning and Remembrance*. Farnham, Surrey, England: Ashgate.

Magaña, Rocío

2008   "Desolation Bound: Enforcing America's Borders on Migrating Bodies." 2008 Ignacio Martín-Baró Human Rights Essay Prize, University of Chicago Human Rights Program.

2011   "Dead Bodies: The Deadly Display of Mexican Border Politics." In *A Companion to the Anthropology of the Body and Embodiment*. Ed. F. Mascia-Less. Pp. 157–171. Malden, MA: Blackwell.

Makdisi, Saree

2010   "The Architecture of Erasure." *Critical Inquiry* 36(3): 519–559.

Malinowski, Bronislaw

1984   *Argonauts of the Western Pacific*. Prospect Heights, IL: Waveland Press.

Malkki, Liisa

1997   "News and Culture: Transitory Phenomena and the Fieldwork Tradition." In *Anthropological Locations: Boundaries and Grounds of a Field Science*. Ed. A. Gupta and J. Ferguson. Pp. 86–101. Berkeley: University of California Press.

Malone, Nicholas, Alison H. Wade, Agustín Fuentes, Erin P. Riley, Melissa Remis, and Carolyn Jost Robinson

2014   "Ethnoprimatology: Critical Interdisciplinarity and Multispecies Approaches in Anthropology." *Critique of Anthropology* 34(8): 8–29.

Marcus, George E.

1998   *Ethnography Through Thick and Thin*. Princeton, N.J.: Princeton University Press.

Margalida, Antoni, David Campión, and José A. Donázar

2011   "Scavenger Turned Predator: European Vultures' Altered Behavior." *Nature* 480: 457.

Maril, Robert Lee

2004   *Patrolling Chaos: The U.S. Border Patrol in Deep South Texas*. Lubbock: Texas Tech University Press.

Martin, Dan

1996   "On the Cultural Ecology of Sky Burial on the Himalayan Plateau." *East and West* 46 (3–4): 353–70.

Martínez, Daniel E., Reineke, Robin C., Raquel Rubio-Goldsmith, Bruce Anderson, Gregory Hess, and Bruce O. Park

2013   "A Continued Humanitarian Crisis at the Border: Deceased and Missing Migrants Recorded by the Pima County Office of the Medical Examiner, 1990–2012." Binational Migration Institute, Department of Mexican American Studies, University of Arizona. http://bmi.arizona.edu/sites/default /files/border_deaths_final_web.pdf. Accessed April 19, 2015.

Martínez, Oscar

2013   *The Beast: Riding the Rails and Dodging Narcos on the Migrant Trail*. Trans. Daniela Maria Ugaz and John Washington. London: Verso.

Massey, Douglas, Jorge Durand, and Nolan Malone

2002   *Beyond Smoke and Mirrors: Mexican Immigration in an Era of Economic Integration*. New York: Russell Sage Foundation.

Mbembe, Achille

2003   "Necropolitics." *Public Culture* 15(1): 11–40.

McDonnell, Patrick

1986   "Tijuana Neighborhood: La Libertad; Aliens' Last Mexico Stop." *Los Angeles Times*, September 7, 1986. http://articles.latimes.com/1986–09–07/news /mn-12171_1_thousands-of-mexican-migrants. Accessed April 18, 2015.

McFarland, Elaine

2008   "Working with Death: An Oral History of Funeral Directing in Late Twentieth-Century Scotland." *Oral History* 36(1): 69–80.

McGuire, Randall H.

2008   *Archaeology as Political Action*. Berkeley: University of California Press.

2013   "Steel Walls and Picket Fences: Rematerializing the U.S.-Mexican Border in Ambos Nogales." *American Anthropologist* 115(3): 466–481.

Meirotto, Lisa M.

2012   "The Blame Game on the Border: Perceptions of Environmental Degradation on the United States–Mexico Border." *Human Organization* 71(1): 11–21.

Miles, Ann

2004   *From Cuenca to Queens: An Anthropological Story of Transnational Migration*. Austin: University of Texas Press.

Miller, Daniel
   2010   *Stuff*. Cambridge: Polity Press.
Moreno, Caroline
   2012   "Border Crossing Deaths More Common as Illegal Immigration Declines." *Huffington Post*, August 17, 2012. www.huffingtonpost.com/2012/08/17 /border-crossing-deaths-illegal-immigration_n_1783912.html. Accessed April 19, 2015.
Morton. Robert J., and Wayne D. Lord
   2006   "Taphonomy of Child-Sized Remains: A Study of Scattering and Scaveng-ing in Virginia, USA." *Journal of Forensic Sciences* 51(3): 475–479.
Mulvey, Laura
   1975   "Visual Pleasure and Narrative Cinema." *Screen* 16(3): 6–18.
Nabhan, Gary Paul
   1982   *The Desert Smells Like Rain: A Naturalist in Papago Indian Country*. San Francisco: North Point Press.
Nading, Alex M.
   2012   "Dengue Mosquitoes Are Single Mothers: Biopolitics Meets Ecological Aes-thetics in Nicaraguan Community Health Work." *Cultural Anthropology* 27(4): 572–596.
   2014   *Mosquito Trails: Ecology, Health, and the Politics of Entanglement*. Berkeley: University of California Press.
Narayan, Kirin
   1999   "Ethnography and Fiction: Where Is the Border?" *Anthropology and Human-ism* 24(2): 134–147.
National Immigration Forum
   2013   "The Math of Immigration Detention: Runaway Costs for Immigration Deten-tion Do Not Add Up to Sensible Policies." August 22. www.immigrationforum .org/images/uploads/mathofimmigrationdetention.pdf. Accessed March 4, 2015.
National Pork Board
   2008   "On-Farm Euthanasia of Swine: Recommendations for the Producer." Amer-ican Association of Swine Veterinarians. Des Moines, IA: National Pork Board. www.aasv.org/aasv/documents/SwineEuthanasia.pdf. Accessed April 18, 2015.
Nawrocki, Stephen P.
   2009   "Forensic Taphonomy." In *Handbook of Forensic Anthropology and Archaeol-ogy*. Ed. S. Blau and D. H. Ubelaker. Pp. 284–294. Walnut Creek, CA: Left Coast Press.
Nelson, Ben A., J. Andrew Darling, and David A. Kice
   1992   "Mortuary Practices and the Social Order at La Quemada, Zacatecas, Mex-ico." *Latin American Antiquity* 3(4): 298–315.
Nevins, Joseph
   2002   *Operation Gatekeeper: The Rise of the "Illegal Alien" and the Making of the U.S.-Mexico Boundary*. New York: Routledge.

2005 "A Beating Worse Than Death: Imagining and Contesting Violence in the U.S.-Mexico Borderlands." *AmeriQuests* 2(1): 1–25.

No More Deaths

2011 *A Culture of Cruelty: Abuse and Impunity in Short-Term U.S. Border Patrol Custody.* http://forms.nomoredeaths.org/wp-content/uploads/2014/10/CultureOfCruelty-full.compressed.pdf. Accessed March 4, 2015.

Nudelman, Franny

2004 *John Brown's Body: Slavery, Violence, and the Culture of War.* Chapel Hill: University of North Carolina Press.

O'Donnabhain, Barra

2011 "The Social Lives of Severed Heads: Skull Collection and Display in Medieval and Early Modern Ireland." In *Bioarchaeology of the Human Head: Decapitation, Decoration, and Deformation.* Ed. M. Bonogofsky. Pp. 122–138. Gainesville: University of Florida Press.

O'Leary, Anna Ochoa

2009 "In the Footsteps of Spirits: Migrant Women's *Testimonios* in a Time of Heightened Border Enforcement." In *Human Rights along the U.S.-Mexico Border: Gendered Violence and Insecurity.* Ed. K. Staudt, T. Payan, and Z. A. Kruszewski. Pp. 85–104. Tucson: University of Arizona Press.

O'Neil, Kevin Lewis

2012 "There Is No More Room: Cemeteries, Personhood, and Bare Death." *Ethnography* 13(4): 510–530.

Ortega, Bob and Rob O'Dell

2013 "Deadly Border Agent Incidents Cloaked in Silence." *Arizona Daily Star,* December 16. www.azcentral.com/news/politics/articles/20131212arizona-border-patrol-deadly-force-investigation.html. Accessed February 28, 2015.

Ortiz, Ildefonso, Karen Antonacci, and Jared Taylor

2014 "Border Patrol Agent Identified after Suicide, Kidnapping, Sexual Assault of Immigrants." *The Monitor,* March 13. www.themonitor.com/breaking/border-patrol-agent-attacks-family-with-knife-kidnaps-girl-kills/article_c92ea728-aac1-11e3-8d91-0017a43b2370.html. Accessed March 30, 2015.

O'Shea, John M.

1984 *Mortuary Variability: An Archaeological Investigation.* Orlando, FL: Academic Press.

Pachirat, Timothy

2013 *Every Twelve Seconds: Industrialized Slaughter and the Politics of Sight.* New Haven: Yale University Press.

Paredes, Américo

1958 *"With His Pistol in His Hand": A Border Ballad and Its Hero.* Austin: University of Texas Press.

Parks, K., G. Lozada, M. Mendoza, and L. García Santos

2009 "Strategies for Success: Border Crossing in an Era of Heightened Security." In *Migration from the Mexican Mixteca: A Transnational Community in*

Oaxaca and California. Ed. W. Cornelius, D. Fitzgerald, J. Hernández-Díaz, and S. Borger. Pp. 31–61. San Diego: Center for Comparative Immigration Studies, University of California.

Paz, Octavio

1961   *The Labyrinth of Solitude: Life and Thought in Mexico.* New York: Grove Press.

Peña, Manuel

2006   "Folklore, Machismo, and Everyday Practice: Writing Mexican Worker Culture." In "Lessons of Work: Contemporary Explorations of Work Culture." Special issue, *Western Folklore* 65(1–2): 137–166.

Peutz, Natalie

2006   "Embarking on an Anthropology of Removal." *Current Anthropology* 47(2): 217–241.

Peutz, Natalie, and Nicholas De Genova

2010   Introduction. In *The Deportation Regime: Sovereignty, Space, and the Freedom of Movement.* Ed. Nicholas De Genova and Natalie Peutz. Pp. 1–19. Durham, NC: Duke University Press.

Posel, Deborah, and Pamila Gupta

2009   "The Life of the Corpse: Framing Reflections and Questions." *African Studies* 68(3): 299–309.

Pribilsky, Jason

2001   "Nervios and 'Modern' Childhood: Migration and Changing Contexts of Child Life in the Ecuadorian Andes." *Childhood: A Global Journal of Child Research* 8(2): 251–273.

2007   *La Chulla Vida: Gender, Migration, and the Family in Andean Ecuador and New York City.* Syracuse, NY: Syracuse University Press.

2012   "Consumption Dilemmas: Tracking Masculinity, Money, and Transnational Fatherhood between the Ecuadoran Andes and New York City." *Journal of Ethnic and Migration Studies* 38(2): 323–343.

Rathje, William, and Cullen Murphy

2001   *Rubbish! The Archaeology of Garbage.* Tucson: University of Arizona Press.

Reeves, Jay, and Alicia A. Caldwell

2011   "After Alabama Immigration Law, Few Americans Taking Immigrants' Work." *Huffington Post.* October 21. www.huffingtonpost.com/2011/10/21/after-alabama-immigration-law-few-americans-taking-immigrants-work_n_1023635.html. Accessed March 30, 2015.

Reeves, Nicole M.

2009   "Taphonomic Effects of Vulture Scavenging." *Journal of Forensic Sciences.* 54(3): 523–528.

Reineke, Robin

2013   "Arizona: Naming the Dead from the Desert." *BBC News Magazine,* January 16. www.bbc.co.uk/news/magazine-21029783. Accessed July 7, 2013.

Rév, István
1995   "Parallel Autopsies." *Representations* 49:15–39.
Reyes, Belinda I.
2004   "U.S. Immigration Policy and the Duration of Undocumented Trips." In *Crossing the Border: Research from the Mexican Migration Project.* Ed. Jorge Durand and Douglas S. Massey. Pp. 299–320. New York: Russell Sage Foundation.
Robben, Antonius C.G.M.
2005   "How Traumatized Societies Remember: The Aftermath of Argentina's Dirty War." *Cultural Critique* 59: 120–164.
Robertson, Alistair Graham, Rachel Beaty, Jane Atkinson, and Bob Libal
2012   *Operation Streamline: Costs and Consequences.* Grassroots Leadership. September. http://grassrootsleadership.org/sites/default/files/uploads/GRL_Sept2012_Report-final.pdf. Accessed March 4, 2015.
Romo, David
2005   *Ringside Seat to a Revolution: An Underground Cultural History of El Paso and Juarez, 1893–1923.* El Paso: Cinco Punto Press.
Rosaldo, Renato
1989   *Culture and Truth: The Remaking of Social Analysis.* Boston: Beacon Press.
Rosenblum, Marc R.
2012   *Border Security: Immigration Enforcement between Ports of Entry.* Congressional Research Service Report for Congress. January 6. http://fpc.state.gov/documents/organization/180681.pdf. Accessed March 4, 2015.
Rousseau, Nicky
2009   "The Farm, the River, and the Picnic Spot: Topographies of Terror." *African Studies* 68(3): 352–369.
Rubio-Goldsmith, Raquel, M. Melissa McCormick, Daniel Martinez, and Inez Magdalena Duarte
2006   *The "Funnel Effect" and Recovered Bodies of Unauthorized Migrants Processed by the Pima County Office of the Medical Examiner, 1990–2005.* Report, October. Tucson: Binational Migration Institute, Mexican American Studies and Research Center, University of Arizona. www.derechoshumanosaz.net/images/pdfs/bmi%20report.pdf. Accessed March 30, 2015.
Ruiz Marrujo, Olivia T.
2009   "Women, Migration, and Sexual Violence: Lessons from Mexico's Border." In *Human Rights along the U.S.-Mexico Border: Gendered Violence and Insecurity.* Ed. K. Staudt, T. Payan and Z.A. Kruszewski. Pp. 31–47. Tucson: University of Arizona Press.
Saldívar, José David
1997   *Border Matters: Remapping American Cultural Studies.* Berkeley: University of California Press.

Saldívar, Ramón

    1990   *Chicano Narrative: The Dialectics of Difference.* Madison: University of Wisconsin Press.

    2006   *The Borderlands of Culture: Américo Paredes and the Transnational Imaginary.* Durham, NC: Duke University Press.

Salter, Mark

    2008   "When the Exception Becomes the Rule: Borders, Sovereignty, and Citizenship." *Citizenship Studies* 12(4): 365–380.

Sanchez, A. N.

    2010   "Undocumented Border Crossers Shot At in Arizona; Attackers May Be U.S. Citizens." *Think Progress,* June 16. http://thinkprogress.org/security/2010/06/16/176128/shooting-arizona-border/. Accessed March 30, 2015.

Sandell, David P.

    2010   "Where Mourning Takes Them: Migrants, Borders, and an Alternative Reality." *Journal of the Society for Psychological Anthropology* 38(2): 179–204.

Scheper-Hughes, Nancy

    1992   *Death without Weeping: The Violence of Everyday Life in Brazil.* Berkeley: University of California Press.

Schiffer, Michael Brian

    1975   "Archaeology as Behavioral Science." *American Anthropologist* 77: 836–848.

Schofield, John

    2005   *Combat Archaeology: Material Culture and Modern Conflict.* London: Duckworth.

Schonberg, Jeffrey, and Philippe Bourgois

    2002   "The Politics of Photographic Aesthetics: Critically Documenting the HIV Epidemic among Heroin Injectors in Russia and the United States." *International Journal of Drug Policy* 13: 387–392.

Schultz, John J., Mary E. Collins, and Anthony B. Falsetti

    2006   "Sequential Monitoring of Burials Containing Large Pig Cadavers Using Ground-Penetrating Radar." *Journal of Forensic Sciences* 51: 607–616.

Scott, James C.

    1985   *Weapons of the Weak: Everyday Forms of Peasant Resistance.* New Haven: Yale University Press.

Shaheed, Aalia

    2014   "New Technique Better Identifies Mummified Mexican Border Crossers in Arizona." *Fox News Latino,* April 7. http://latino.foxnews.com/latino/news/2014/04/07/innovative-technique-better-identifies-mummified-mexican-border-crossers-in/. Accessed March 28, 2015.

Shean, Blair S., Lynn Messinger, and Mark Papworth

    1993   "Observations of Differential Decomposition on Sun Exposed v. Shaded Pig Carrion in Coastal Washington State." *Journal of Forensic Sciences* 38(4): 938–949.

Silva, Cristina

    2013   "Answers Demanded after Suicides of 2 Guatemalans at Eloy Lockup." *Arizona Daily Star*, May 9. http://azstarnet.com/news/local/border/answers-demanded-after-suicides-of-guatemalans-at-eloy-lockup/article_53664eee-c1cd-51e2-a75b-2e43ca814351.html. Accessed March 4, 2015.

Simanski, John F., and Lesley M. Sapp

    2012   "Immigration Enforcement Actions: 2011." Annual Report, 2012. Washington, DC: Office of Immigration Statistics, U.S. Department of Homeland Security. www.dhs.gov/sites/default/files/publications/immigration-statistics/enforcement_ar_2011.pdf. Accessed March 4, 2015.

    2013   "Immigration Enforcement Actions: 2012." Annual Report. Washington, DC: Office of Immigration Statistics, U.S. Department of Homeland Security.

Singer, Audrey, and Douglas S. Massey

    1998   "The Social Process of Undocumented Border Crossing among Mexican Migrants." *International Migration Review* 32(3): 561–592.

Slack, Jeremy, and Scott Whiteford

    2011   "Violence and Migration on the Arizona-Sonora Border." *Human Organization* 70(1): 11–21.

Smart, Alan

    2014   "Critical Perspectives on Multispecies Ethnography." *Critique of Anthropology* 34(1): 3–7.

Smith, Matthew Hale

    1869   *Sunshine and Shadow in New York.* Hartford: J. B. Burr and Company.

Snow, Edward

    1989   "Theorizing the Male Gaze: Some Problems." *Representations* 25: 30–41.

Solecki, Ralph S.

    1975   "Shanidar IV, a Neanderthal Flower Burial in Northern Iraq." *Science* 190(4217): 880–881.

Sontag, Susan

    2003   *Regarding the Pain of Others.* New York: Picador.

Sorg, Marcella H., William D. Haglund, and Jaime A. Wren

    2012   "Current Research in Forensic Taphonomy." In *A Companion to Forensic Anthropology.* Ed. D.C. Dirkmaat. Pp. 477–498. West Sussex, UK: Blackwell.

Spencer, Charles S., and Elsa M. Redmond

    2001   "The Chronology of Conquest: Implications of New Radiocarbon Analyses from the Cañada de Cuicatlán, Oaxaca." *Latin American Antiquity* 12(2): 182–201.

Spener, David

    2009   *Clandestine Crossings: Migrants and Coyotes on the Texas-Mexico Border.* Ithaca: Cornell University Press.

2010 *"Movidas Rascuaches:* Strategies of Migrant Resistance at the U.S.-Mexico Border." *Aztlán: A Journal of Chicano Studies* 35(2): 9–36.

Spradley, Katherine M., Michelle D. Hamilton, and Alberto Giordano

2012 "Spatial Patterning of Vulture Scavenged Human Remains." *Forensic Science International* 219(13): 57–63.

St. John, Rachel

2011 *Line in the Sand: A History of the Western U.S.-Mexico Border.* Princeton: Princeton University Press.

Stanescu, James

2012 "Species Trouble: Judith Butler, Mourning, and the Precarious Lives of Animals." *Hypatia* 27(2): 567–582.

2013 "Beyond Biopolitics: Animal Studies, Factory Farms, and the Advent of Deading Life." *PhaenEX* 8(2): 135–160.

Stephen, Lynn

2007 *Transborder Lives: Indigenous Oaxacans in Mexico, California, and Oregon.* Durham, NC: Duke University Press.

Stiner, Mary C.

2008 "Taphonomy." *Encyclopedia of Archaeology.* Ed. D.M. Pearsall. Volume 3, pp. 2113–2119. New York: Academic Press.

Sugiyama, Saburo

2005 *Human Sacrifice, Militarism, and Rulership: Materialization of State Ideology at the Feathered Serpent Pyramid, Teotihuacan.* Cambridge: Cambridge University Press.

Sullivan, Laura

2010 "Prison Economics Help Drive Ariz. Immigration Law." National Public Radio, October 28. www.npr.org/2010/10/28/130833741/prison-economics-help-drive-ariz-immigration-law. Accessed March 30, 2015.

Sundberg, Juanita

2008 "'Trash-Talk and the Production of Quotidian Geopolitical Boundaries in the USA-Mexico Borderlands." *Social & Cultural Geography* 9(8): 871–890.

2011 "Diabolic Caminos in the Desert and Cat Fights on the Río: A Post-humanist Political Ecology of Boundary Enforcement in the United States–Mexico Borderlands." *Annals of the Association of American Geographers* 101(2): 318–336.

Sundberg, Juanita, and Bonnie Kaserman

2007 "Cactus Carvings and Desert Defecations: Embodying Representations of Border Crossings in Protected Areas on the Mexico-US Border." *Environment and Planning D: Society and Space* 25: 727–744.

Taussig, Michael

1984 "Culture of Terror—Space of Death: Roger Casement's Putumayo Report and the Explanation of Torture." *Comparative Studies in Society and History* 26(3): 467–497.

TeleSUR

2014 "Central American Women Search for Missing Children in Mexico." TeleSUR, November 18. www.telesurtv.net/english/news/Central-American-Women-Search-for-Missing-Children-in-Mexico-20141118-0045.html. Accessed April 19, 2015.

Tonkin, Megan, Li Foong Yeap, Emma K. Bartle, and Anthony Reeder

2013 "The Effect of Environmental Conditions on the Persistence of Common Lubricants on Skin for Cases of Sexual Assault Investigation." *Journal of Forensic Sciences* 58: S26–S33.

Townsend, Richard F.

1992 *The Aztecs*. London: Thames and Hudson.

Trevizo, Perla

2013a "Winter Cold Holds Own Peril for Border Crossers: Freezing Night Temps, Not Just Desert Heat, Pose an Exposure Risk." *Arizona Daily Star*, January 7. http://tucson.com/news/local/border/winter-cold-holds-own-peril-for-border-crossers/article_2eef0965-73de-5217-aa52-42c855795435.html. Accessed April 22, 2015.

2013b "Decade Brings 2,000+ Sets of Remains in Tucson Sector." *Arizona Daily Star*, May 22.

2014 "How Immigration through S. Arizona Has Changed." *Arizona Daily Star*, August 16. http://tucson.com/news/local/border/how-immigration-through-s-arizona-has-changed/article_aabacaac-cf02-55a9-a221-e2d6d5443f6a.html. Accessed March 4, 2015.

Tuckman, Jo

2010 "Survivor Tells of Escape from Mexican Massacre in Which 72 Were Left Dead." *The Guardian*, August 25. www.theguardian.com/world/2010/aug/25/mexico-massacre-central-american-migrants. Accessed March 28, 2015.

Udey, Ruth N., Brian C. Hunter, and Ruth W. Smith

2011 "Differentiation of Bullet Type Based on the Analysis of Gunshot Residue Using Inductively Coupled Plasma Mass Spectrometry." *Journal of Forensic Sciences* 56: 1268–1276.

Urrea, Luis Alberto

1993 *Across the Wire: Life and Hard Times on the Mexican Border*. 1st Anchor Books ed. New York: Anchor Books.

1996 *By the Lake of Sleeping Children: The Secret Life of the Mexican Border*. New York: Anchor Books.

2004 *The Devil's Highway: A True Story*. New York: Little, Brown.

USBP (United States Border Patrol)

1994 *Border Patrol Strategic Plan 1994 and Beyond*. Report.

2012 *2012–2016 Border Patrol Strategic Plan. The Mission: Protect America*. www.cbp.gov/sites/default/files/documents/bp_strategic_plan.pdf. Accessed April 18, 2015.

2013 "Southwest Border Sectors: Total Illegal Alien Apprehensions by Fiscal Year (Oct. 1st through Sept. 30th)." www.cbp.gov/sites/default/files/documents /U.S.%20Border%20Patrol%20Fiscal%20Year%20Apprehension% 20Statistics%201960–2013.pdf. Accessed December 22, 2014.

Valdez, Lidio M.

2009 "Walled Settlements, Buffer Zones, and Human Decapitation in the Acari Valley, Peru." *Journal of Anthropological Research* 65(3): 389–416.

Verdery, Katherine

1999 *The Political Lives of Dead Bodies: Reburial and Postsocialist Change.* New York: Columbia University Press.

Vicens, A. J.

2014 "The Obama Administration's 2 Million Deportations, Explained." *Mother Jones.* April 4. www.motherjones.com/politics/2014/04/obama-administration-record-deportations. Accessed March 30, 2015.

Vogt, Wendy

2013 "Crossing Mexico: Structural Violence and the Commodification of Undocumented Central American Migrants." *American Ethnologist* 40: 764–780.

Walker, Phillip L.

2001 "A Bioarchaeological Perspective on the History of Violence." *Annual Review of Anthropology* 30: 573–596.

West, Robert Cooper

1993 *Sonora: Its Geographical Personality.* Austin: University of Texas Press.

Whatmore, Sarah

1999 "Hybrid Geographies: Rethinking the 'Human' in Human Geography." In *Human Geography Today.* Ed. D. Massey, J. Allen, and P. Sarre. Pp. 23–39. Cambridge: Polity Press.

2002 *Hybrid Geographies: Natures, Cultures, Spaces.* Thousand Oaks, CA: SAGE.

Wilkinson, Tracy

2012 "Mothers from Central America Search for Missing Kin in Mexico." *Los Angeles Times,* November 6.

Williams, Howard

2004 "Death Warmed Up: The Agency of Bodies and Bones in Early Anglo-Saxon Cremation Rites." *Journal of Material Culture* 9(3): 263–291.

Wright, Christopher

2013 *The Echo of Things: The Lives of Photographs in the Solomon Islands.* Durham, NC: Duke University Press.

Yarris, Kristin Elizabeth

2014 "'Quiero Ir y No Quiero Ir' (I Want to Go and I Don't Want to Go): Nicaraguan Children's Ambivalent Experiences of Transnational Family Life." *Journal of Latin American and Caribbean Anthropology* 19(2): 284–389.

Young, Craig, and Duncan Light
    2012   "Corpses, Dead Body Politics and Agency in Human Geography: Following the Corpse of Dr. Petru Groza." *Transactions of the Institute of British Geographers* 38(1): 135–148.

Young, Harvey
    2005   "The Black Body as Souvenir in American Lynching." *Theater Journal* 57(4): 639–657.

Zepeda, Ofelia
    1982   *When It Rains: Papago and Pima Poetry—Mat Hekid O Ju, 'O'odham Nacegitodag.* Tucson: University of Arizona Press.
    1995   *Ocean Power: Poems from the Desert.* Tucson: University of Arizona Press.

Zimmerman, Larry J., Courtney Singleton, and Jessica Welch
    2010   "Activism and Creating a Translational Archaeology of Homelessness." *World Archaeology* 42(3): 443–454.

Zimmerman, Larry J., and Jessica Welch
    2011   "Displaced and Barely Visible: Archaeology and the Material Culture of Homelessness." *Historical Archaeology* 45(1): 67–85.

Žižek, Slavoj
    2008   *Violence: Six Sideways Reflections.* New York: Picador.

INDEX

Page references appearing in *italics* indicate illustrations or material contained in their captions.

CALIFORNIA SERIES IN PUBLIC ANTHROPOLOGY

The California Series in Public Anthropology emphasizes the anthropologist's role as an engaged intellectual. It continues anthropology's commitment to being an ethnographic witness, to describing, in human terms, how life is lived beyond the borders of many readers' experiences. But it also adds a commitment, through ethnography, to reframing the terms of public debate—transforming received, accepted understandings of social issues with new insights, new framings.

Series Editor: Robert Borofsky (Hawaii Pacific University)

Contributing Editors: Philippe Bourgois (University of Pennsylvania), Paul Farmer (Partners In Health), Alex Hinton (Rutgers University), Carolyn Nordstrom (University of Notre Dame), and Nancy Scheper-Hughes (UC Berkeley)

University of California Press Editor: Naomi Schneider

University of California Press gratefully acknowledges the following generous donors to the Authors Imprint Endowment Fund of the University of California Press Foundation.

Wendy Ashmore
Clarence & Jacqueline Avant
Diana & Ehrhard Bahr
Nancy & Roger Boas
Robert Borofsky
Beverly Bouwsma
Prof. Daniel Boyarin
Gene A. Brucker
William K. Coblentz
Joe & Wanda Corn
Liza Dalby
Sam Davis
William Deverell
Frances Dinkelspiel & Gary Wayne
Ross E. Dunn
Carol & John Field
Phyllis Gebauer
Walter S. Gibson
Jennifer A. González
Prof. Mary-Jo DelVecchio Good & Prof. Byron Good
The John Randolph Haynes & Dora Haynes Foundation / Gilbert Garcetti
Daniel Heartz
Leo & Florence Helzel / Helzel Family Foundation
Prof. & Mrs. D. Kern Holoman
Stephen & Gail Humphreys
Mark Juergensmeyer
Lawrence Kramer

Mary Gibbons Landor
Constance Lewallen
Raymond Lifchez
David & Sheila Littlejohn
Dianne Sachko Macleod
Thomas & Barbara Metcalf
Robert & Beverly Middlekauff
Jack & Jacqueline Miles
The Estate of David H. Miller
William & Sheila Nolan
Dale Peterson
Sheldon Pollock
Stephen P. Rice
Robert C. Ritchie
The Rosenthal Family Foundation / Jamie & David Wolf
Rémy & Nicole Saisselin
Carolyn See
Lisa See & Richard Kendall
Ruth A. Solie
Sidney Stern Memorial Trust
Michael Sullivan
Patricia Trenton
Roy Wagner
J. Samuel Walker
John & Priscilla Walton
Kären Wigen & Martin Lewis
Lynne Withey
Stanley & Dorothy Wolpert